The Tibetan Spaniel

A Gift From the Roof of the World

by
Susan W. Miccio

Illustrated by Karen Chamberlain

Susan Waller Miccio
Felton, Delaware

ON THE FRONT COVER: *Tibetan Spaniels* by Maud Earl, 1898. Courtesy of the Karlyn and Norman Volk Collection. *Ellen Fisch photo*

ON THE TITLE PAGE: Finnish Ch. Tashi-Gong Ava Gardner, bred by Katriina Venäläinen and owned by Leena Hiljanen.

ON THE BACK COVER: Beauandel Brandon, bred and owned by Michael Fenwick, of Australia.

ISBN 0-9767282-0-6 (previously published by OTR Publications, ISBN 0-940269-12-0)

© 1995 by Susan W. Miccio

The photo on page 32, "Mounted Infantry Mess at Lhasa," is from *Bayonets to Lhasa* by Peter Fleming, © 1961 by Peter Fleming. Reprinted by permission of HarperCollins Publishers, Inc.

All Rights Reserved. No part of this book may be reproduced or transmitted in any form or by any means, electronic or mechanical, including photocopying, recording or by any information storage or retrieval system—except by a review to be printed in a magazine or newspaper—without permission from the publisher.

Library of Congress Cataloging-in-Publication Data

Miccio, Susan W., 1951–
    The Tibetan spaniel : a gift from the roof of the world / by Susan W. Miccio ; illustrated by Karen Chamberlain.
       p.   cm.
    Includes index.
    ISBN 0-9767282-0-6 (paperback)
    1. Tibetan spaniel.   I. Title
SF429.T5M53   1996
636.7'2--dc20   96-13302
                                                                                                   CIP

Printed in the United States of America

10 9 8 7 6 5 4 3 2 1

Although the author has extensively researched sources to ensure the accuracy and completeness of the information contained in this book, we assume no responsibility for errors, inaccuracies, omissions or any inconsistency herein. Any slights of people or organizations are unintentional.

Susan Waller Miccio
4670 Carpenter Bridge Road
Felton, DE 19943
www.susanwallermiccio.com

DEDICATION

For all the Tibbies
waiting at the Rainbow Bridge

Contents

Acknowledgments 5

About the Author 6

Preface 7

1. Meet the Tibetan Spaniel 9

2. The Tibetan Spaniel in His Homeland 27

3. The Tibetan Spaniel in the United Kingdom 39

4. The Tibetan Spaniel in the United States 51

5. The Tibetan Spaniel Around the World 61

6. The Tibetan Spaniel At Work and Play 83

7. Finding Your Tibetan Spaniel 95

8. Caring for Your Tibetan Spaniel Puppy 105

9. Caring for Your Adult Tibetan Spaniel 113

10. Training Your Tibetan Spaniel 131

11. Your Tibetan Spaniel's Health 155

12. Showing Tibetan Spaniels 177

13. Breeding Tibetan Spaniels 209

For More Information 250

Selected Bibliography 251

Index 253

Acknowledgments

My thanks go out to all the Tibetan Spaniel owners and breeders, around the world, who generously shared their memories and experiences and entrusted me with irreplaceable photos, to the many hard-working honorary secretaries and breed representatives who coordinated contributions from their countries and to Don Roy, archivist of the Tibetan Spaniel Club of America, who has given me his longstanding support.

Determined that no language barrier would stand in my way, I am indebted to John Thielke, Elizabeth Worthington, Hannie Tijman-Logtenberg, Sarina Valenti and Anna Miccio whose translations enabled me to use contributions in seven languages. I am also grateful to Juliettte Cunliffe who has provided an invaluable service to all breed enthusiasts (especially those of us who labor outside the U.K.) by reprinting historical articles about the Tibetan breeds in *Tibetan Breeds International Magazine*.

Nancy K. Bromberg VMD, DACVO, MS kindly reviewed the text on eye problems. Mary Beth Soverns DVM, who loves this breed and has an endless supply of energy, spent untold hours researching and reviewing health topics.

Anyone reading this book soon realizes the immense creative contribution made by my colleague Karen Chamberlain, whose artistry, precision and insight grace many of these pages. Thanks also to photographers Kris Gilmore, who spent hundreds of tedious hours in the darkroom on my behalf, and Scott Chamberlain, who managed to come up with any photo I asked for.

Finally, thanks to my mother Nora Waller who cooked and kept my house running as I whiled away the hours at the PC.

Susan Miccio

About the Author

Susan Miccio brings a solid journalistic background to this, her first book. During an 18-year career with the U.S. government, she rose to managing editor of national systems procedures. During this period, she received many prestigious awards. The new writing technologies that she implemented, to improve communication, earned her the Distinguished Service Medal, one of the government's top civilian awards.

Susan describes herself as a "life-long animal lover." When she resigned her government position, she turned her attention to working with and writing about animals. In addition to her family of five Tibbies, Susan shares her home with a gregarious African Grey parrot. "Between the Tibbies and the parrot," she laughs, "you can imagine how much talking goes on in our house."

Susan is a member of the Tibetan Spaniel Club of America, the Tibetan Spaniel Association (UK), the Tibetan Spaniel Association of Victoria (Australia) and a founding member of the Potomac Valley Tibetan Spaniel Club. She lives in rural Delaware and works for the State of Delaware. Susan says, "I can no longer imagine my life without my joyful little Tibbies."

Preface

My first Tibetan Spaniel swept into my life on the hand of fate—a foundling that, during a raging storm, leapt into my arms and straight into my heart, "Daffodil" utterly captivated me. Soon, I became involved in showing and breeding, and my family of Tibbies (as they are affectionately termed) began to grow. With my background in writing and editing, I became convinced that the most logical and enduring contribution I could make to my breed would be to celebrate the fascinating Tibetan Spaniel in a book.

When I began this project, nearly three years ago to the day that I type these words, my first task was to find out what people who own Tibbies want to read in a new book. I found no shortage of opinions. I hope that the result is an entertaining as well as informative work that appeals to cross-section of readers, ranging from the owner of a single pet Tibbie to the multi-Tibbie breeder-exhibitor.

Given such a diverse readership, I have endeavored to strike a reasonable balance between the needs of newcomers and the interests of long-time owners. As may be expected, the hundreds of owners I have interviewed have met with a wide range of experiences and expressed a wide range of viewpoints. Where possible, I have merged their experiences and opinions into a consensus but, where opinions and experiences diverge, a range of viewpoints is presented. Raising these issues will hopefully stimulate further thought and dialogue.

By seeking candid photos as well as show photos, I was rewarded with hundreds of snapshots sent by proud owners. Selecting the photos that appear here was an enjoyable but unenviable task. Many photos that could not be included nonetheless helped to inspire the original artwork created for this book. Although I was able to feature only a fraction of the hundreds of stories and anecdotes told to me, all were considered and, if possible, the experiences described were blended into the narrative.

I strongly believe that we Tibetan Spaniel owners must view ourselves as a world community whose interests in common far outweigh our differences. While I was understandably somewhat more successful in collecting American material, I solicited contributions from every country in which Tibbies live. The result is an overview of the breed's status worldwide and a summary of the issues that face all of us.

The Tibetan Spaniel always excites enthusiasm in this devotees, and my greatest pleasure in compiling this book has been to "talk Tibbie" with so many of these enthusiasts. Their voices speak from these pages along with my own.

Susan Miccio
August 1995

Nearly a decade has passed since I wrote the Preface above. Over these years, the internet has grown up and now provides us with resources never dreamed of when I was writing this book. Thanks to Jan Allinder, the Tibbie world has a fantastic website at www.tibbies.net. Please visit it for up-to-date Tibbie information and links to websites around the world. Meanwhile, I am gratified that demand for this book has continued to grow, which has lead to my decision to reprint it in paperback. I hope that it will continue to entertain and educate new Tibbie owners for another decade.

Susan Miccio
March 2005

The Tibetan Spaniel

by Karen Chamberlain

Chapter One

Meet the Tibetan Spaniel

It has been just a century since the Tibetan Spaniel left its mysterious homeland on the "roof of the world" to journey to the West. And yet, after a hundred years, the breed is still rare and largely unknown. Among his human enthusiasts, the Tibetan Spaniel is called the "best-kept secret in the dog world."

Soon after I began to interview the hundreds of Tibetan Spaniel owners, who contributed their experiences to this book, I realized I am not alone in my devotion to "Tibbies." Like me, they cherish the Tibbie's affectionate but sometimes inscrutable personality. They excuse his mischievous nature in a rush of admiration for his ingenuity. They know that beneath the pretty coat is the tough, vigorous body of an athlete. In short, they are people who prefer quality to quantity and understated elegance to overblown flamboyance.

The Tibetan Spaniel is nothing if not an enigma—a contradiction in terms that challenges preconceived notions. He defies categorization. He is small but not delicate, devoted but not slavish, sensitive but not temperamental, beautiful but not flashy. He questions our authority, teases our intellect, and tweaks our hearts. As Raymonde Dufourg (France), writing about her Belg. Ch. Coo-Kai de Wand'Ioni, explains:

> *We just call her Cookie,*
> *it's short, it's clear and quickly said.*
> *But more than that, it suits her well:*
> *she is like American cookies—*
> *crispy and crunchy but, at the same time,*
> *creamy and sweet, all rolled into one.*
> *Her immaculate white coat*
> *is enriched by beige markings.*
> *On her face so asiatic,*
> *with an expression enigmatic,*
> *Nature, full of goodwill,*
> *has let fall a black mask*
> *that envelopes her velvety eyes,*
> *so deep, dark, and filled with love.*
>   Translated by Susan Miccio

"I couldn't live without him" is a refrain I heard again and again in speaking with Tibbie owners. Once you meet him, you may find yourself joining the small, but devoted, following who can no longer imagine life without the Tibetan Spaniel.

APPEARANCE

As I walk my Tibbies, I am often greeted with coos of approval from passersby. Children reach to pet. Adults, more restrained, query me about the breed but eventually stoop for a pet, too. Why are people attracted to Tibbies? Their small size is certainly an appealing feature, but there is more to it than that. Often described as monkey-like, their faces remind us of babies. The oval eyes that look straight forward, the shortish muzzle, domed head, and chubby cheeks (cushioning on the muzzle) trigger a protective response in adults and curiosity in children. No matter his age, the Tibbie is perpetually puppy-like, a quality that appeals to deep-seated emotions in most people and makes him irresistible.

What Makes a Tibbie a Tibbie?

The Tibetan Spaniel always breeds "true." That means that Tibbie puppies always grow up to look like Tibetan Spaniels and not some other breed. For example, a puppy born from pure-bred Lhasa Apso parents occasionally grows up to look exactly like a Tibbie, but a Tibbie never grows up to look like a Lhasa Apso. This genetic oddity has been cited as evidence that the Tibetan Spaniel is the ancestral breed of the Lhasa Apso.

Without exception, "Is that a Pekingese?" is the most common question Tibbie owners are asked. To someone who knows the Tibetan Spaniel, the question is incomprehensible. To us, a Tibbie in no way resembles a "Peke." And yet, larger "old-style" Pekes of the late nineteenth and early twentieth centuries, with their longer muzzles and less elaborate coat, sometimes

A typical male Tibetan Spaniel. *Karen Chamberlain ills.*

resembled Tibbies. The appearance of the historical Pekingese makes the idea that they, too, are related to Tibbies very credible. Although critics have sometimes ridiculed the Tibetan Spaniel as a "poor specimen" of the Pekingese, today's Pekingese and Tibetan Spaniel are simply different breeds, each with distinctive traits.

The overall impression given by the Tibetan Spaniel is elegance without exaggeration. Parts of his coat are long and silky, but not so long that it sweeps the floor, and lying flat rather than lifting away from the body. His muzzle is short, but not as short as the Pekingese muzzle. His tail arches gaily over the back, but does not curl into a corkscrew like that of the Pug. He is compact and sturdy but neither coarse nor chunky. While he may lack the long-legged grace of a Greyhound, neither does he clumsily waddle or roll; he covers the ground briskly, smoothly, and efficiently. In summary, the Tibetan Spaniel is a study in moderation. Let's look more closely at the appearance of the Tibetan Spaniel.

Size and Proportion

One of the features of our breed that most attracts people is its "perfect size" for modern life—small enough to fit in your lap but not so small that he is always underfoot, small enough to live comfortably in an apartment but not too small to jog down a country road alongside you, and small enough to "go everywhere" with you without the hassle of a larger dog.

For show and breeding purposes, the ideal weight range for Tibbies is between nine and fifteen pounds. Today, more Tibbies may tip the scales at the upper end of this range than the lower, and pet Tibbies weighing between fifteen and twenty pounds (but not obese) are relatively common.

Larger Tibbies tend to have heavier "bone," but average-size or smaller Tibbies with moderate bone are just as sturdy. In the early years of the century, a famous female Tibbie called Doma of Ladkok was, at five pounds, one of the smallest known. However, as we near the close of the century, fewer Tibbies weighing around ten pounds are seen, perhaps due to breeding, but also to improved canine nutrition.

A Tibbie's height is ten inches, more or less, at the shoulder. Ideally, he is longer than he is tall, so that, when viewed from the side, his outline is rectangular. The perfectly proportioned Tibbie is only slightly longer than tall (an inch or two), but an average Tibbie may be somewhat longer.

Coat

The Tibbie has a double coat. There are two layers: a short layer close to the skin to insulate and a longer overlay of hair to keep water and dirt away from the skin. The texture of the undercoat is fuzzy, while the overcoat is silky. The overall sensation is one of luxurious softness. Of course, coat texture may vary based on inheritance, nutrition and conditioning.

A mature Tibbie's coat is longer than a puppy's coat. The puppy coat lacks the long guard hairs and thus often has a poufed or scissored look. As the puppy matures, longer hair grows from the ear leathers (fringes), around the neck (mane or shawl), on the back of the forelegs, along the back, from the tops of the toes and between the pads (gloves or toe fringes), and from the buttocks (trousers, skirts or culottes). The plume of the tail also fills out and lengthens with age. In fact, his fringes may not be fully grown until the Tibbie is three to four years old. The length of his fringes varies greatly with the Tibbie's age and family. Here are some typical lengths for mature Tibbies:

Mane (male)	4"-6"
Shawl (female)	4"
Trousers	6"
Forelegs	4"
Gloves	1"-2"
Ear fringes	2"-3"
Tail plume	6"-8"

The thickness of the coat varies with the season of the year and with female hormonal cycles. In regions with pronounced summers and winters, Tibbies of both sexes usually shed the bulk of the undercoat in the spring or early summer and gradually replace it in the fall or early winter. In the jargon of the dog world, shedding the undercoat is "blowing the coat" and the resulting sparse coat condition is called "out of coat." Females also "drop" their coats while nursing puppies and after their heat cycles.

Clean, healthy Tibbies do not tend to have a "doggy" smell. With simple grooming, your Tibbie's skin and coat should remain fresh between baths.

Coloring and Marking

A Tibbie's coat comes in all colors: black, white, gold, cream, red, or silver (gray or blue) and all shades of these colors. The variety and unpredictability of colors continually fascinate breeders. In the first decade of this century, Mrs. McLaren Morrison, an early patron of the breed, was amazed when her cream bitch's four puppies, by a black sire, were cream, black, chocolate-brown and orange. Raymonde Dufourg (France) was similarly surprised when her particolor bitch, Cookie, produced four puppies whose coats were gray, gold, reddish-brown and solid black. Mrs. Dufourg remarks, "The mystery of genetics further astonished me because their sire was fawn-colored!"

The most common "color" is sable, which is easier to understand if you think of it as a marking pattern rather than a color. A sable Tibbie has black hair (even if it is only a trace) somewhere in a coat of another color. The black is usually in a mask, among the ear fringes, on the tail, or in the mane or shawl. The

A typical female Tibetan Spaniel. Karen Chamberlain ills.

TERMS FOR TIBBIE FEATURES

Buddha Mark	White spot on the forehead.
Culottes	*See Trousers.*
Cushioning	Padding in the upper lips of the muzzle.
Drop ear	Ear in which the leather falls rather than stands up (as in the prick ear).
Fringes	Long hair that grows from ear leathers, backs of the forelegs, buttocks and thighs.
Gay tail	Tail that lifts and arcs gently over the back.
Gloves	Long hair that grows on the toes and eventually extends beyond the tips of toes.
Harefoot	Paw on which the middle toes are longer than the outside toes.
Mane	A ruff of long hair around the neck and shoulder of a male. *See also Shawl.*
Mask	Facial hair of a contrasting color, whether lighter or darker.
Pants	*See Trousers.*
Particolor	A predominantly white dog with patches of another color.
Plume	Long hair that grows from the tail, sweeping over and falling to one side of the back.
Scowl	Facial marking consisting of a "V" on the forehead that meets an inverted "V" between the eyes.
Shawl	A ruff of long hair around the neck and shoulder of a female. *See also Mane.*
Skirts	*See Trousers.*
Trousers	Long hair that grows from the buttocks and thigh.
Undercoat	Short, fluffy coat of insulating hair that lies next to the skin and is covered by the longer, silkier, flat-lying overcoat.

A pair of winsome Bet'R puppies bred by Herb and Betty Rosen (U.S.). Herb Rosen photo

rest of the coat may be any shade or gold or red. The silver sable, a very rare color, is a gray or bluish coat with black highlights. The gray/blue may be a light or dark shade.

A Tibbie's "sabling" may range from heavy (meaning that black hair is noticeable and often shot through the coat) to light (meaning that the black is almost imperceptible). The extent of a Tibbie's mask, if he has one, also varies; it may cover only the tip of the muzzle or may extend to the eyes and beyond. Similarly, the scowl may be pronounced or muted.

If black is entirely absent, the Tibbie's color is considered to be the predominant shade of his coat—whether it is gold, white, cream or red. The various shades of pale cream through bright gold are the most usual, while all-white and ruby red Tibbies are very rare. A Tibbie's fringes, particularly the trousers and tail, may be a lighter shade of the same color.

Particolor Tibbies, the harlequins of the breed, are predominantly white with patches of another color—usually a shade of beige or gold, but sometimes of red or black. The extent of the patches over the head and body varies considerably. Patches on the body are rarely distributed symmetrically.

Black-and-tan Tibbies are predominantly black with tan "tips." When they have white markings, as they often do, they are called "tricolors." The black Tibbie, much rarer than the black-and-tan, has no tan tips but may have white markings.

White markings include bibs, tail tips and socks. A white blaze on the forehead is called the Buddha Mark. Many Tibbies have a whitish beard on the chin.

Markings often change with age. For example, a three-month-old puppy may have a pronounced black mask but, at two years old, only the vestige of the mask remains on his muzzle. Similarly, by age two a puppy's beautiful Buddha Mark may have diminished to a wisp of white on the forehead. A light-colored mask on a puppy often fades away completely. Naturally, aging may add gray to the coat.

The nose, rims of the eyes, and the lips are usually solid black. The eyes are generally a deep, doe-like brown.

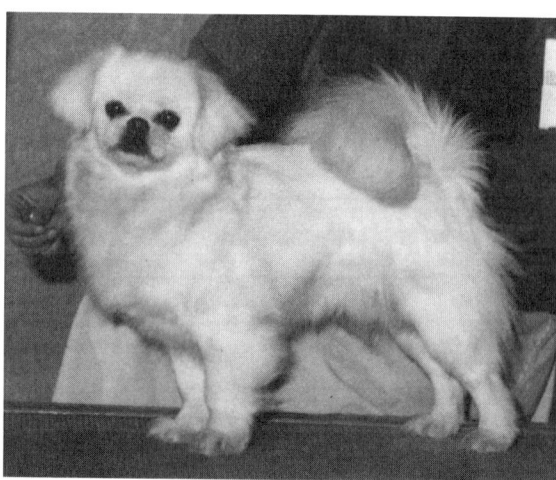

Am. Ch. Aki Shima's Major Moves, bred by Barbara Berg (U.S.), is an all-white Tibbie with excellent pigment, a rare combination. Ken Schwab photo

Toyway Emblem is a particolor puppy bred by Jouko Leiviskä and owned by Heli Immonen (Finland).

Head

Since it gives him his characteristic monkey face, the head is the most distinctive of the Tibbie's features. The skull is slightly rounded and small in proportion to the body. The male's head is noticeably masculine. By contrast, the female's head is smaller and more elegant.

Where the muzzle meets the skull, the junction (stop) is ideally slight so that the muzzle looks firmly attached to the skull but not pushed into it. The best muzzles are medium-length (so that breathing is not impaired) and blunt, rather than tapered or pointed. The upper lips are cushioned (padded) and whiskered.

To make room for the lower incisors, the ideal chin is pronounced, and an undershot mouth enhances the depth-of-chin effect. In the undershot mouth, the upper incisors fit neatly inside the lower incisors when the mouth is closed; this is also called the reverse scissors bite. Some Tibbies have "level mouths," where the tips of the upper and lower incisors meet each other. Ideally, the teeth are neatly aligned within the mouth. In reality, molars and incisors (especially the lower ones) are sometimes crooked or misaligned because the teeth are overcrowded in the shortened muzzle.

The ideal eyes are oval-shaped. The placement of the medium-sized drop ears should be fairly high so that, when he lifts them, the Tibbie looks alert.

When excited or happy, a Tibbie lifts his ears, rounds his eyes, and "smiles." Like us, he shows pleasure by stretching his mouth and upturning the lips. When he looks up at you, a Tibbie's lower teeth may show (mainly because he is undershot), which only enhances the impression of the smile. By the same token, it is apparent when a Tibbie is sad or anxious. His expressive face communicates eloquently.

Body Features

The structure of a Tibbie's body determines how well he moves as well as what he looks like. Three distinctive traits of the body are the bowed forelegs, harefeet and gay tail.

Ideally, the Tibbie's forelegs are slightly bowed. However, his forepaws should naturally point forward, rather than at an outward angle, when he stands and moves.

The perfect Tibbie paw is called a harefoot. Since the middle toes of the harefoot are longer than the outside toes, the Tibbie paw appears to be elongated and flat-footed rather than rounded and arched

Deanford Nogbad's head shows the points of a black-and-tan Tibbie. "Oliver" was owned by Marguerite High (U.K.)

like most dog paws. Unlike breeds that walk up on their toes, the Tibbie's weight falls on the large pad instead of the toe pads. This leaves his toes free to grip, just as ours do. Since the harefoot is more dextrous than the conventional dog paw, Tibbies are sure-footed and often use their forepaws like hands.

The Tibbie's tail arcs over the back, and the plume tends to fall naturally to one side or the other. His tail is the weathervane of his mood. If he drops it while he is standing still, he may be relaxed, inattentive, bored or anxious. If he drops it while he is moving, he is probably very anxious.

Movement

Movement is a reflection of the Tibbie's musculo-skeletal structure—that is, it indicates how well he is put together. Well-structured Tibbies are built for moderate speed and good endurance. They move straight with a lively, confident step that they are able to maintain for long periods of time.

The Ideal vs. the Real

As humans go, few of us can claim to be supermodels. Even if we groom ourselves perfectly, most of us probably possess several imperfect physical

THE SCOWL

A scowl is a marking created by the contours of the face and fine lines of darker hair around the eyes and on the forehead. The resulting shading tends to suggest two "V's," the one on the forehead upright and the one below it inverted, that meet in a point between the eyes. The lines of the upper "V" may extend in an arc over each eye. The scowl is most noticeable on heavily sabled Tibbies. On pale sables, it may be altogether absent or muted to the mere hint of eyebrows.

The term "scowl" has always troubled me because it implies that a Tibbie, marked in this manner, looks perpetually disgruntled. On the contrary, the scowl enhances the monkey-like expression with an impish quality. Although it is not required by the official Breed Standard, the scowl is considered a "breed trait" (that is, a characteristic unique to the breed), and most enthusiasts urge breeders not to allow the scowl to fade away.

This pair shows many of the traits that differentiate the female (L) from the male (R). Note the markings and "scowls" on these sable Tibbies. *Kris Gilmore photo*

traits, any one of which would disqualify us from the ranks of those who are considered truly stunning according to today's standards of beauty. Perhaps we are too short or too chunky, thin-lipped or big-nosed, knock-kneed or bow-legged, etc.; the list is depressingly long!

The same is true of dogs. The supermodels in the world of the dog show are few and far between. Around them clamor the more numerous show quality dogs who attain their championships, but not superstar status among the top-winning dogs. And beyond these are the great mass of "average" dogs that are called "pet quality."

Pet quality Tibbies possess traits which fall short of the ideals of physical perfection as defined by the Breed Standard, an official description of the ideal Tibbie. Perhaps they have grown too large or long, with legs too short or tall. The muzzle may be too short or too long, the bite a little overshot or too undershot or the skull a bit too round or too flat. The eyes may be more round than oval or the nose liver-colored instead of black. Perhaps the paw is a "catfoot" instead of a "harefoot," or the forepaws turn out rather than point forward. The Tibbie may move with what has been described as a "Marilyn Monroe" wiggle, a side-to-side action which, although charming, causes him to expend more energy and move less freely. These are all examples of "faults" in pet quality Tibbies. Frankly, anyone who does not breed or show Tibbies probably would not notice most of the subtle differences between show and pet quality dogs.

You will see many top-winning and show quality Tibbies in the pages of this book, but you will also meet many pet quality Tibbies. Since Tibbies are outstanding companions, my aim is to introduce you to the real as well as the ideal Tibetan Spaniel, the average fellow as well as the supermodel. This is not intended to in any way diminish the importance of striving for the ideal in showing and breeding, merely to put it into perspective. Ultimately, even the supermodels retire from their show and breeding careers to become loving pets and bed dogs, and that is what the Tibetan Spaniel is really all about.

PERSONALITY

While listening to people describe the Tibetan Spaniel's personality, I am struck with how often they juxtapose seemingly contradictory adjectives. In the same breath, Tibbies are characterized as endearing but exasperating, dignified but clownish, affectionate but manipulative, enchanting but stubborn, and smart but mischievous. They are likened to a "big dog in a small body" and then called "cat-like" in their habits. Why the apparent inconsistencies?

From such characterizations, you might deduce that the Tibetan Spaniel is an incomprehensible breed. In fact, it is his very complexity, tinged with inscrutability, that his owners find fascinating and, at the same time, challenging. They may grumble over his transgressions but, moments later, admire the very qualities that spawned them.

Bringing the Tibetan Spaniel to life for you is best achieved through anecdotes told by those who love them. The Tibbies you will meet in these pages are: Penni owned by Barbara Balbort (U.S.), Gianni owned by Pamela Basile (U.S.), Bertha owned by Barbara Berg (U.S.), Oscar owned by Cindy Chrisos (U.S.), Moose owned by Joel and Peter DeCloux (U.S.), Kramer owned by Pam Dunlop (Australia), Lady Jo owned by Julie Hall (U.S.), Vesla owned by Karin Olsen (Norway), Tachy owned by Werner and Natalie Steurbaut (Netherlands) and Joi-Li owned by Lynne Walker (U.S.), as well as my own Tibbies: Ciana, Patches, Bear, Shen, Sassy and Kissie.

Fin., Swed. Ch. Zibbans Tribute for Toyway, bred by L-L Selén-Andersson (Sweden) moves out for owner Jouko Leiviskä (Finland). Note the "reach" of the forelegs and "drive" of the hindlegs.

Inheritance vs. Environment

All dogs descend from wolves, and all dogs possess certain instincts in common with wolves and with one another. After humankind domesticated the dog, we began to mold him into different shapes, sizes and personalities to serve our purposes. The results of these efforts were the various dog breeds.

Some canine personality traits are inherited while others are the result of upbringing. All pure-bred dogs inherit traits that reflect the place where they evolved as a breed and the purpose for which the breed was created. Collies were bred to herd, Beagles to hunt, and the Terriers to "go to ground" for small animals and vermin. The Tibetan Spaniel was bred to be a companion and watchdog. Roaming at will through monasteries and compounds with other household dogs, he climbed to the rooftops where his keen senses enabled him to forewarn of the distant approach of intruders. By day, his clownish charm warmed his owner's heart and, by night, his soft body warmed his master's bed.

Modern-day Tibbies that have never set paw in Tibet still possess inborn personality traits, such as the urge to climb and watch, that originated on the "roof of the world." Knowing what is "built in" and what is not helps you better understand your Tibetan Spaniel's personality. It may be possible to control, but not to eliminate, instinctual behaviors, whereas personality traits that result from upbringing are more easily modified with training.

Male and Female Behaviors

Perhaps the most obvious "built-in" behaviors are those that are gender-related. Owners agree that most Tibbies are sweet, happy-go-lucky, affectionate and undemanding. However, in keeping with his duties as a leader, a "top dog" (that is, a dominant male) may be demanding, possessive and territorial. Like males of other breeds, a mature, intact male Tibbie may be aggressive toward other male dogs. Fights between males in this context are dangerous. As you may expect, pregnant or nursing females or females in season may behave differently than those that are not. A dominant female may be as demanding as her male counterpart.

Although some owners are convinced of strong personality differences between male and female

GB Ch. Amcross Jimbu (L) and GB Ch. Jinda (R), litter brother and sister bred by D. Jenkins and M.C. Hourihane, are male and female versions of the same breeding. *Thomas Fall photo*

THE TIBETAN SPANIEL IN FINE ART

That the Tibetan Spaniel is relatively scarce as a subject in the fine arts is a reflection of the breed's rarity. Tibbie-like dogs first appeared in Eastern art during the Ming Dynasty (1368-1644). The earliest Western rendition of our breed, entitled *Tibetan Spaniel*, was painted by Simon de Vos (1603-1676) of Antwerp. No one knows his owner's name, but the subject has harefeet, a short muzzle and fringes. The bell on his collar suggests that he was a beloved pet. Although no one knows whose dogs were the models, *Tibetan Spaniels* (1898) by Maud Earl (shown on the cover) is the most notable portrait of the breed. William Secord, an authority on dogs in art, has called it the "archetypal pet portrait." *The Tibetan Spaniel Llassa Lying on a Stool* (1915), a portrait by Florence Jay, honors the Tibbie who walked out of Tibet with Col. F.M. Bailey after the Younghusband Expedition of 1904.

Frances Fairman, famous for her exquisite portraits of Japanese Chin, owned a Tibbie called Yatsu in the first decade of this century. Is it conceivable that she was not inspired to paint his portrait? Perhaps other early portraits of Tibbies are moldering in attics!

Inscribed "Léon," this painting purchased at a London auction may be the undiscovered portrait of a Tibetan Spaniel. *Collection of Don Roy. Ellen Fisch photo.*

A sampling of the work of contemporary artists who have rendered portraits of Tibbies appears in this book.

Tibbies, I am not. All evidence indicates that intelligence, independence, affection and other breed traits have been doled out equally to the sexes. We humans, however, may interpret and characterize a trait differently depending on the Tibbie's sex. For example, an intelligent male who makes mischief is "clever," but an intelligent female who makes mischief is "calculating." What is definitely true is that great diversity exists in the personalities of individuals of both sexes—just as it does in the breed as a whole.

Individuality

When Barbara Berg's new vet arrived at her home to give her dogs their vaccinations, Mrs. Berg remembers introducing each Tibbie to him by saying, "Now this is my favorite dog and I'll tell you why." Each of her Tibbie's personalities is unique, and each is her "favorite" in his own way.

"They're all so different!" is a comment often made by people who own several Tibbies. Just as variety in the Tibetan Spaniel's appearance defies a cookie-cutter description, a blend of intelligence, independence, intuitiveness, sensitivity and affection puts an individualistic spin on each Tibbie's personality. No two Tibbies, even closely related ones, have identical temperaments, and a personality trait may be more or less intensely expressed in one Tibbie than in another. This variety enriches the breed and challenges us owners.

Dog-Cat-Monkey

There is a wonderful saying that a Tibetan Spaniel is dog, cat and monkey, all rolled into one. It is a good way to describe the breed's enigmatic personality. He possesses the faithfulness and watchfulness of the dog, the independence and curiosity of the cat, and the cleverness and mischievousness of the monkey.

The Reincarnation

As he watched our puppy Sassy play with a ball, my husband Chris suddenly remarked, "I think that Sassy is the reincarnation of Jackie." Although I had heard Tibbies described as "cat-like," Chris' comparison of Sassy to Jackie, our favorite cat who had died two years earlier, struck me like a thunderbolt. I turned to look at the puppy. As Sassy batted the ball this way and that, manipulating it down the length of the room like a soccer player down the field, she twisted her lean body and, springing, pounced on the ball from the side. Although her creamy coat did not in the least resemble Jackie's tabby-cat fur, my mind's eye could see Jackie's ghost in her movements.

A clever cat, we had always thought of Jackie as "dog-like" because he came when called and loved to retrieve. Now I see clearly that Sassy resembles him in other ways as well: the way that she climbs to the highest possible point and reposes, Sphinx-like, to watch the goings-on around her; the way she curls up for a nap with her head turned upside down; the way she stares at me unblinking, gazing directly into my eyes. Undoubtedly, the most uncanny coincidence is the way she dashes up behind me and leaps to give my well-padded bottom a harmless little nip, just to say, "Pay attention to me!!" All his life, Jackie did exactly the same thing.

Intelligence

Intelligence is usually defined as the ability to solve problems. The Tibetan Spaniel is highly intelligent. In fact, owners sometimes remark that their Tibbies are "too intelligent" and explain using verbs such as "plan," "scheme," "figure out" or "manipulate"—all of which indicate the ability to solve problems.

Tibbie problem-solving was recently witnessed all over Australia when Pam Dunlop's Kramer (Aust. Ch. Buquet Midnight Sun) took part in an intelligence contest on a popular national television program. Pitted against a mixed breed and five other pure-breds (including Border Collie and German Shepherd), Kramer adroitly tipped over a flower pot to reach a piece of chicken, opened a door and hammed for the audience. Incidentally, opening doors is a classic indicator of canine intelligence. When my Shen wants a treat, he opens the cupboard where the treats are kept. When the DeCloux' Moose wanted to nap in the bedroom closet, he pushed open the closet's sliding door.

Other indicators of intelligence are the ability to mimic and the capacity to understand a large vocabulary. Dealer had a favorite stuffed bunny that he carried everywhere. One morning, Mrs. Dahlen asked him, "Where's Bunny?" After pausing to think, he pricked his ears and darted through the dog door into the backyard. He found "Bunny" where he had left her the night before and brought her to Mrs. Dahlen. Joi-Li knows Lynne Walker's neighbors by name. If Mrs. Walker tells her to "Go get" a particular neighbor, Joi-Li knows which neighbor to fetch.

Most intelligent beings are highly curious, and Tibbies are no exception.

How to Capture a Beetle

The Tibetan Spaniel's face is eloquently expressive. His smile reminds us of the Cheshire Cat. *Karen Chamberlain ills.*

The day that Joi-Li arrived, Mrs. Walker remembers their first walk together. Joi-Li spied a beetle, one of those two-inch horned varieties indigenous to East Texas. Although Mrs. Walker restrained her, Joi-Li, in typical Tibbie fashion, insisted on pulling toward the object of her interest. Meanwhile, the beetle turned to face the puppy, poised its pincers and leapt—right on to her nose! Crying out, Joi-Li tried to dislodge the beetle with a paw, but the beetle dug in and the puppy's cries intensified to a squeal. Placing a paw on either side of her muzzle, she finally pushed the beetle off.

Later that day, Joi-Li again went for a walk and again spied a beetle. Rather than avoid it, she wisely pinioned the beetle by resting her chin on it. She then investigated it at leisure. To this day, this is Joi-Li's method of capturing and examining insects

Playfulness

Some breeds are driven by the urge to retrieve, others by the urge to hunt, others by the urge to herd. Although the power of the drive may vary from dog to dog within a breed, inborn breed-related drives are nonetheless irresistible. The Tibetan Spaniel is driven by an urge to play. Although it accounts in part for the breed's clownish reputation, the significance of the play drive to Tibbie owners is that play, often in the form of games, must be a key element in training this breed.

An offshoot of the play drive is the immense pleasure a Tibbie takes in teasing his owner and other dogs.

Ride 'Em, Penni!

The thrill of Penni's life was playing pranks on Muffin, a miniature American Eskimo. While still a tiny pup, Penni constantly plagued poor Muffin either by chewing up or "going" in Muffin's bed. As she grew, Penni conceived more advanced pranks to capitalize on Muffin's anxieties. Having observed that Muffin hid under a table next to the sofa whenever a thunderstorm rolled in, Penni climbed onto the table beneath which Muffin cowered during a storm. She extended her paw and delicately nudged a cow bell lying there off the edge. The resulting clamor flushed Muffin from her hiding place and, the moment she emerged, Penni pounced. Grabbing Muffin's hair, Penni hung on like a bronc rider while Muffin streaked around the house. With each passing thunderstorm thereafter, Penni and Muffin played the rodeo game.

If your Tibbie is an only dog, you should actively participate in playtime. If you are lucky enough to own more than one Tibbie, their inventive play will be a constant source of amusement. Three typical Tibbie games are jinking (running with abrupt directional changes), tussling and muzzle-butting.

Writing in 1910, John C. White described his Tibbies playing: "The tail has long thick hair, and is usually carried curled over the back, except when running, when they use it almost as a rudder, holding it straight out behind. They have extraordinary powers of jinking, and it is a pretty sight to see three or four of them racing over the ground, making the most wonderful twists and turns to avoid each other." As anyone who has seen Tibbies jink will attest, Mr. White's description is as perfect today as it was 85 years ago.

As they chase one another—twisting, turning, rolling—each Tibbie tries to grasp the other(s) by the hair on the neck, by an ear, by the tail or by a leg. They may also stand up and spar. This morning, I watched Bear and Sassy, who are best buddies, rise up on their hindlegs and run toward each other. When their chests made contact, they bounced away from one another and then began to box with their forepaws. This was no serious conflict. It was simply a Tibbie tussle.

In muzzle-butting, each Tibbie opens his mouth as wide as possible and butts it against the opponent's muzzle or cheek. Butting Tibbies often argue volubly. The butting and arguing continue until one contestant pulls away, but the contest is usually rejoined in a matter of seconds. They continue butting, sometimes for several minutes, until one of the contestants withdraws.

A Tibbie loves toys. To wrangle a desired toy from her brothers, my Ciana bickers and whines to egg them into an argument. As soon as the boys are engaged in noisy muzzle-butting, Ciana's strategy becomes evident; while the boys argue over the toy, she deftly steals it and sprints to some neutral location. Meanwhile, the silly boys continue disputing the now-vanished toy.

Although they love chew toys, a fuzzy toy is the Tibbie favorite.

> *To know them is to love them!*
>
> Mrs. McLaren Morrison (U.K.), 1909

The Tibby and the Teddy

Kramer, my one-year-old Tibby, dearly loves his Teddy. He sleeps on it and loves to play endless games of "Fetch" with it. If you have the nerve to ignore him when he wants you to play, he demands your attention by marching up and hitting you on the leg with Teddy.

Kramer also greets all our guests with Teddy. When a guest comes to the gate while Kramer is sitting on the lawn, he cannot say "hello" until he has fetched his Teddy, even if he has to hunt through the house to find it! When Kramer hears me returning from

Karen Chamberlain ills.

work each afternoon, he climbs atop the couch and peers out of the lounge-room window. I can't see his tail but I know it is wagging because the lace curtain is flapping frantically. As I pass by the slightly opened window, he leans over and tries to lick my face through the screen. By the time I open the door, Kramer is there waiting, Teddy in his mouth of course, wagging his tail and talking. After greeting me, he swaggers up to my partner, toting Teddy still firmly clenched in his jaws.

Fortunately, Kramer can cope without the Teddy while in the show ring, but we must always be sure that Teddy is waiting on the sidelines!

Contributed by Pam Dunlop (Australia)

Tibbie Talk

Tibbies are highly communicative dogs. Not only do they speak through facial expression and body language, but they also speak "Tibbie talk." Tibbie talk is yet another facet of their wonderful intelligence.

Tibbies vocalize with a variety of grunts, chirps, squeals, trills and whines. Multiple Tibbies tend to all talk at once, and the resulting crescendo of noise can be overpowering. Although quick to warn of intruders, Tibbies neither "yap" nor bark randomly or endlessly. When a real bark is required, Tibbie barks range from a basso profundo "woof," that my males reserve for serious warnings, to the soprano "arfs," which my females use to greet friends.

While we talk-oriented humans may sometimes misinterpret canine body language, Tibbie talk sends us clear messages.

The Power of Speech

My Vesla was a very quick-learning little lady. She loved sweets, and there was no end to what she would do for one. She would dance on two legs, play dead, play baby, and—strangest of all—say "Mama."

I will never forget a train trip we took when I was a little girl. Vesla always traveled sitting in a handbag on such trips. Into our car came a man. When he discovered the little dog in the bag, he laughed scornfully at the "creature" and began to boast about his fantastic, intelligent Shepherds. None were more intelligent and quicker to learn than they!

After a polite pause, my mother said that our dog was also smart and could say, "Mama." The man began to laugh but became pale and quiet when, without a prompt or a sweet, the Tibbie sat her eyes on him and pronounced loudly and clearly, "Mama." The man disappeared from the car without a word, and Vesla has never said "Mama" so clearly before or since then.

Contributed by Karin Olsen (Norway)
Translated by John Thielke

Energy Level

A dog's energy level is partly the result of breeding and partly of age. Some breeds are highly energetic while others expend little effort. The Tibetan Spaniel is considered a moderately energetic breed but not in the least "hyper." Of course, puppies and young adults are livelier than older adults. How much he plays, how much exercise he needs, and how well he tolerates cuddling is related to your Tibbie's energy level.

Regardless of his natural energy level, all Tibbies crave and need exercise. Kissie, my middle-aged female, is not usually very energetic, but she is occasionally seized by the need for speed. She smiles, bugs out her eyes and streaks through the house, running circles around or bouncing over the furniture. The other Tibbies are drawn into the merry chase, at the end of which everyone happily collapses. I call these episodes "the sillies" and sometimes join in the game myself. The sillier you are, the better Tibbies like you.

> *I never knew dogs could own such a vocabulary intelligible to man. They "roo" and "rumble", "maiow" and "huff". They scold me, croon to me and use a falsetto shriek when they have to demand. They also "purr" and "bumble" - all this and a decent bark as well. What more could any human ask?*
>
> Lyn R. M. Donaldson (U.K.), 1967

Independence

"Gianni," says Pamela Basile, "has a oneness of purpose. She is a tyrant, and she sulks and pouts until she gets what she wants." Mrs. Basile nicknamed Gianni "She Who Must Be Obeyed," and laughs as she adds, "When I die, I want to come back as my dog!" With few exceptions, all Tibbies are more-or-less independent. A highly independent Tibetan Spaniel knows what he wants and how to get it. He does not care what you want and ignores your commands. He behaves as though he does not need you and considers anything you give him as simply his due. An independent Tibbie is "his own dog."

The most dangerous byproduct of the independent personality is the propensity for escape. Given an incentive, an independent dog will elect to run off rather than stay at home. Since Tibbies are notorious for escaping all types of confinement, you must escape-proof your home, spay or neuter pet Tibbies and provide basic obedience training. All of these subjects are discussed later in this book.

If any breed deserves "I Did It My Way" as its theme song, it is the Tibetan Spaniel. Tibbies are noted for persistence, a trait linked both to independence and intelligence. They conceive strategies in pursuit of a goal and, if Plan A fails, they doggedly try Plan B. For example, if Mrs. Walker does not wake up "on time" in the morning, Joi-Li clacks the dresser bails with her paw. If that fails, she bats a bell with her nose. One way or another, Joi-Li's persistence pays off.

A Heat Wave

Summers in East Texas are brutally hot. Mrs. Walker cannot remember the power failure that shut down her air conditioner. All that she remembers is opening her eyes to see Joi-Li panting wildly. Her house had been transformed into a furnace. Overcome by the heat, it was only Joi-Li's furious and incessant scratching at her hand that helped Mrs. Walker fight the urge to faint again. Dizzy and disoriented, she remained conscious long enough to escape, with Joi-Li, from the house.

> *Tibetan Spaniels are a joy to own. I will always be grateful for knowing [our Tibbie] Glen because it was he who opened up a new world for us, that of the Tibetan Spaniel.*
>
> Diane Zammit (U.K.)

Returning home later, Mrs. Walker discovered that the temperature in the house had surpassed 106° F. Only then did she realize that Joi-Li's persistence in awakening her, always such a nuisance on weekend mornings, had probably saved her life.

In humans, independence is an admired trait but, in a dog, independence translates into negative words such as hardheaded, defiant, manipulative and stubborn. If this were all there was to the breed's personality, few people could tolerate the Tibetan Spaniel. Luckily, other traits, such as his sociability and immense affection for us, offset his independence. On balance, it is the interplay of all of these traits that determines the nature of each Tibbie's personality.

Sociability

Dogs are social creatures, both with dogkind and humankind, and the Tibetan Spaniel is no exception. However, a Tibbie's innate sociability is sometimes at odds with his fabled independence. Julie Hall

Tibbies have been "bed dogs" for centuries. *Karen Chamberlain ills.*

ONE OF MOOSE'S NINE LIVES

The DeCloux horse barn was always one of Moose's favorite hangouts. One day, Peter and Joel were busy storing hay in the loft of the barn when, nearby, Moose flushed a pigeon from its roost in the rafters. He joyfully chased and teased it as it flew back and forth. To help the frantic pigeon escape, Peter pushed open the door to the loft. Out flew the pigeon with Moose in pursuit—straight through Peter's legs and out the loft door into the air. Joel called out, but it was too late.

Peter scrambled down from the loft in a panic and ran into the barnyard. Moose lay still where he had landed—in the pile of horse manure that had cushioned his fall. Just as Peter reached him, Moose roused himself unsteadily. He shook each leg, one by one, and then shook his head. He stood quietly, slightly dazed, until Peter swept him up and held him close. After only a moment or two of Peter's reassurances, he wiggled to get down and then trotted on about his business, stinky but otherwise undamaged.

Moose survived this accident, but he did not survive when he walked into the road and was struck by a car. Accidental death is the second leading cause of death in American Tibbies. For information about accidental death and injury, see Chapter 11.

Karen Chamberlain ills.

describes Lady as both sociable and independent: "[Lady was] affectionate and companionable but not fawning. She wanted to be outside during the day, but she was an indoor dog at night." In fact, most Tibbies seem to be torn between these conflicting personality traits; they want to be independent of you and yet they want to be near you.

When first meeting a stranger, a Tibbie may respond with an aloof rebuff—refusing eye contact and turning away slightly or even turning up his nose. The friendlier the stranger is, the more aloof the Tibbie becomes. Aloofness is just another outward sign of independence. Once his owner assures him that the stranger is acceptable, the Tibbie's sociability soon overwhelms his independence.

Since they are so intelligent and sociable, Tibbies do best living in the home. They do not flourish in a kennel, where the isolation and emotional barrenness of the setting deprive them of the stimulation and human contact they crave. Tibbies that must be housed in kennels should be frequently rotated into the home and given as much human contact as possible.

Affection

The Tibetan Spaniel's affection for us is a quality that attracts many people to the breed. Once you are accepted, Tibbies are exuberant in their displays of affection.

Lavishing kisses are one way Tibbies show their affection. Licking is a very natural canine behavior that carries over from puppyhood, when the puppy's licking signals his mother to nurse. A Tibbie tries to lick your face because, behaviorists say, puppies instinctively lick at their parents' mouth to receive food.

Some Tibbies are lap dogs, and others are not. If pressed to generalize, I suspect that more Tibbies prefer being out of your lap than in it. Instead, they remain nearby, watching you with an unflagging scrutiny that can be unnerving. Again, it is a question of which trait, his independence or his affectionate nature, most influences your Tibbie's personality. My Patches is a perfect example of the dichotomy. He prefers resting next to my chair (with his paw touching my foot) to sitting in my lap. Periodically, he rouses and reaches up to demand a hug. He is very insistent and will not be ignored. Once cuddled briefly, he returns to nap contentedly at my feet.

Most Tibbies enjoy their role as bed dogs. In Tibet, where the monasteries and homes were usually unheated despite the bitter cold, Tibbies have been sleeping with people for centuries—on their sides, on their backs, with all four paws in the air, or on their bellies, with hindlegs stretched out behind and chin resting on forelegs. And don't be surprised if your Tibbie takes over your pillow or demands one of his own!

Intuitiveness and Sensitivity

Mrs. Basile calls her Gianni a "psychic little being." Owners universally agree that the Tibetan Spaniel forms a bond (or as one says, a "mind meld") with you. He intuitively knows what you are feeling and thinking. He understands when you are upset or ill, when you are going away or when he has been naughty. Detractors would argue that the dog simply responds to non-verbal signals or to an established pattern or schedule. They contend that we humans paint our own emotions onto the blank canvas of the dog and interpret his random actions in the way that we find most compatible with our own beliefs and wishes.

The truth probably lies somewhere in between. All dogs are hard-wired to respond to non-verbal signals, to one degree or another, because that is the way they communicate with one another. Since Tibbies are so intelligent, they may better "tune in" to non-verbal signals that we send and more easily remember past experiences. There is simply no question that they learn to "read" us.

But does all of this mean that they are intuitive? I cannot answer this question definitively. I can

> *Gabby, a Tibetan Spaniel, rode high in owner Terry Smith's wheelchair in yesterday's dog hero parade of honor through Adelaide streets. Gabby was one of seven dog heroes to receive medallions and certificates of appreciation for "Service to Man" from the Lord Mayor...*
>
> The (Adelaide) Advertiser (Australia)

only point to ways in which Tibbies bond to humans in what appear to be "matches made in Heaven." I can only relate experiences with my own mind-readers, and I can only cite testimony from people, whether long-time or first-time owners, who are unyielding in their opinion that Tibbies intuitively understand what is in our hearts and minds. In fact, the breed's success in therapy work is ascribed to the ability to sense and respond to human emotion. If Tibbies were human, we would label them compassionate or tender-hearted.

Sensitivity has a flip side. A human may be so sensitive that he or she overreacts to a situation; we call such people nervous or "high-strung." A Tibbie may be similarly overly sensitive. They may become distraught by events such as a family argument or bereavement. All of my own Tibbies are clearly distressed by negative emotion, but each responds differently. Some dash over and excitedly try to lick our troubles away while others stay away but are visibly shaken. Even if your Tibbie displays occasional sensitivity of this type, do not become alarmed. The Tibetan Spaniel is a resilient creature and soon recovers.

Acrophilia (Love of Heights)

According to tradition, the Tibetan Spaniel in Tibet surveyed the surrounding countryside from atop the roofs of monasteries or houses. Owners universally agree that their Tibbies gravitate to high places where they patiently watch for, well, whatever catches their interest. Every single Tibbie owner in the world can tell a story about his or her Tibbie's love of heights, whether he perches atop a sofa or walks up a mountain or, in the case of Mrs. Berg's Bertha, climbs a tree. One afternoon, during the apple harvest, Mrs. Berg moved the ladder from one apple tree to the next only to discover that Bertha had scaled the ladder and sidled out onto a branch! Here is another of Bertha's tales.

Bertha's High Adventure

In order to open a window high in her dairy barn, Mrs. Berg climbed to a high beam via a ladder on the barn wall. Straddling the beam, she had crept about halfway across the expanse of the barn when she was struck by an eerie feeling that someone was watch-

ing her. Looking over her shoulder, she was horrified to see Bertha nonchalantly following her along the beam. Stunned, Mrs. Berg could not conceive how Bertha had managed to climb the vertical ladder. Although terrified for her puppy, Mrs. Berg was helpless; at three stories above the barn floor, she was unable to let go or turn around. She had no choice but to continue, with Bertha tagging along, until she reached the window ledge.

Watchdogs

As their ancestors in Tibet were, my Tibbies are all-seeing and all-hearing. They alert me when anyone approaches on the lane to our remote farmhouse or when other trespassers, such as deer in the garden or 'possums on the back porch, invade their territory. The watchdog instinct is a decided advantage in the modern world as it was in the ancient.

Luckily, most Tibbies seem to intuitively discriminate between situations that require an alert and those that do not, and you can easily train a watch-Tibbie to shut off the alarm on command. After a few minutes of suspicious eyeing, Tibbies happily accept a sincerely friendly stranger, but they are not easily deceived. Although a Tibbie's job is only to warn you of possible danger, at least one Tibbie has proven his mettle as a bona fide guard dog.

Oscar, My Hero

Oscar is a Tibbie whose tail stops wagging only when he's asleep. He has never met anyone or anything he didn't like. Living in the country, we have only one neighbor. The only other living creatures around are deer and rabbits.

While I was planting tomatoes in the garden one spring day, Mikey, my one-month-old son, slept in a baby seat under a nearby tree. Oscar was in the house, watching us through the patio screen door. As I filled my watering can, I heard thunderous growling and barking. I was momentarily stunned because I had never heard Oscar growl! Dropping the watering can, I spun around to see Oscar lying on top of my tiny baby. Oscar's teeth were bared, and a scruffy stranger was backing away from him.

I ran and knelt by the baby and petted Oscar. The stranger mumbled that he was looking for "John Brown" and then turned and left quickly. It was then that I noticed that Oscar had ripped the screen away

"Hermes" (Simpasture Julien) enjoys the company of "Isa," a Dogue de Bordeaux puppy. They belong to Raymonde DuFourg (France).

from the metal door frame so that he could get outside to protect Mikey.

Since that day, I have never again heard Oscar growl at anyone or anything. Although he places himself between any of my children and strangers and watches carefully, he never utters a sound. Oscar is a show champion, but that isn't what makes him My Hero.

Contributed by Cindy Chrisos (U.S.)

> *I can honestly say had it not been for these darling little dogs coming into my life, I would not have the drive or determination that I continue to have to this day.*
> Toni Anders-Tumlin (U.S.)

Tibbies and Children

Children are attracted to Tibbies, perhaps because of their approachable size and monkey-like faces, and most Tibbies are genuinely fond of and patient with children. While visiting another couple on a bleak winter evening in the Netherlands, the Steurbaut's Tachy was drafted to entertain the couple's six children. Placed on a cushion, the children brushed, combed and blow-dried Tachy and adorned her with little bows and barrettes. "Dear, patient Tachy kept the children busy for more than two hours, and you can imagine that not everything was done gently," remembers Mrs. Steurbaut. "When at last it was bedtime for the children, Tachy literally heaved a deep sigh of relief. Tachy is truly a tolerant Tibbie!" Tibbies like Tachy are often used in therapy programs for sick children.

LIFE ON THE FARM

A gale shrieks between the barn and cottage. A northwester driving the sleet horizontally along. By the back door two German Shepherds curled against the storm, tails over their noses, backs white with sleet, eyes slitted against the cold. They will never move. As close to us, their masters, as they can loyally get, braving all discomfort. Opposite the back door is the hay barn warm and dry. All over stepped heights of bales are spread our Tibetan Spaniels. Asleep or awake they will notice the slightest occurrence in the cottage. They sit with half-closed eyes and wait, warm and dry, contemplating...the pathetic spectacle of the two German Shepherds whose intellects are obviously so much smaller than their own.

Life is made to be savored; one must keep occupied; so much to do, so much to see. Pass by the horses and cows. Cats are prickly and unchaseable. The ducks and poultry are the donors of prized "pic-nics" to be transported high up into the hay barn, held between little paws and opened delicately by the so useful undershot jaw and suckled dry at leisure. Then on to the sheep, unhasty gentle creatures made of a size for a Tibetan to talk to. Climb on to the bales which make the lambing pens so one can watch the lambs. Life is most enjoyable.

Contributed by Lyn R. M. Donaldson (U.K.)

Occasionally, a Tibbie is disinterested in and ignores small children. A Tibbie that feels threatened by an over-exuberant child, or overwhelmed by a group of children, may try to hide or may bark at them. It is extremely important for children to be taught how to interact with a Tibbie (or any other dog) and for Tibbie puppies to be socialized with children.

Tibbies and Other Pets

Tibbies often share their territory with other animals—including other dogs, cats, ferrets, parrots, farm animals and horses. By all accounts, Tibbies get on famously with all manner of creatures great and small.

Tibbies are at home in the country and the city. *Karen Chamberlain ills.*

Generally speaking, Tibbies are "big dogs" in a small body. Most have little fear of big dogs and get along well with them. My own Tibbies play equally well with their large cousin, a Standard Poodle, as they do with their smaller cousins, the Pugs. However, you should be aware that this lack of fear means that a Tibbie will challenge a big dog as readily as a small dog and may, as a result, be hurt. One owner recalls her Tibbie lunging at the throat of a Bernese Mountain Dog and hanging on tenaciously as the placid Berner strolled away. Another Tibbie, not so lucky, took on a large stray dog, only to lose an eye in the fracas that followed. It is up to you to exercise common sense when your Tibbie is around big dogs since he may not, for once, act very intelligently.

Adaptability and Versatility

The Tibetan Spaniel is versatile in his outlook on life. A penthouse in New York City, a country estate in New England, a dairy farm in the North, a house in a Midwestern small town, a mobile home in the Deep South, a ranch in the California high desert—all are homes where American Tibbies live happily. They adapt well to any living arrangement (except a kennel) in just about any climate. When the temperature surpasses 90° F, my Tibbies become slothful, preferring to lounge near the air conditioner. When it plunges below 0° F., they prefer to snooze by the fireplace. But, come to think of it, they are not so different than me.

Traveling by paw, pony or yak in caravans across Tibet and China, the historical Tibetan Spaniel was an adventurer. Perhaps that is why almost all modern Tibbies enjoy a journey. Their great curiosity awakens and their keen senses take in all around them. But, whether on a walk around the block or a cross-country trip, the main reason that Tibbies are always happy to go is because they are going with us.

A Walk in the Country

The Tibbies, off lead, gallop ecstatically up the steep incline behind our farmhouse to the 50-acre hay meadow atop the crest of the hill. There, they cavort in the tall grasses, streaking back and forth and up and down, traveling ten times further than Chris and I as we trudge along. They stop and listen to the deer and bird sounds from the forest flanking the lower edges of the meadow—heads high, ears perked, eyes trained on something invisible to us. Chasing and tumbling over one another, they dash on, sometimes rolling downhill in their headlong rush. We reach the great black oak in a saddle of the field and sit to rest. All around us, the Tibbies rest, too—hindlegs stretching out behind, tongues lolling. Everyone has a drink from the canteen.

Time to go. Down the hillside to the path into the forest between the high meadow and the low meadow, the Tibbies sniff groundhog burrows, woof at a deer that crashes deep in the forest and dodge the blackberry briars. The wild turkey feeder is a fascinating object that requires investigation and brings everyone to a halt. "Come on!" we call and whistle. The Tibbies sail down the forest path to overtake us, smiles all over their faces. Two miles pass by and, as we come to the end of the forest path and round the old barn, the Tibbies have tuckered out. Heads and tails droop. They file through the gate, lap some water and heave a great sigh as they curl up together. Time for a nap.

A Closing Thought

Since the letter "B" is not native to the Finnish, the nickname for the Tibetan Spaniel in Finland is *tipsu*. From an anonymous contributor, calling himself Dog-Fani, comes this anagram that succinctly sums up the appeal of the Tibetan Spaniel:

Täydellisin (The most perfect)
Ihnin (The most wonderful)
Parhain (The best)
Suloisin (The sweetest looking)
Uskollisin (The most faithful)

Translated by Elizabeth Worthington

The Tibetan Spaniel

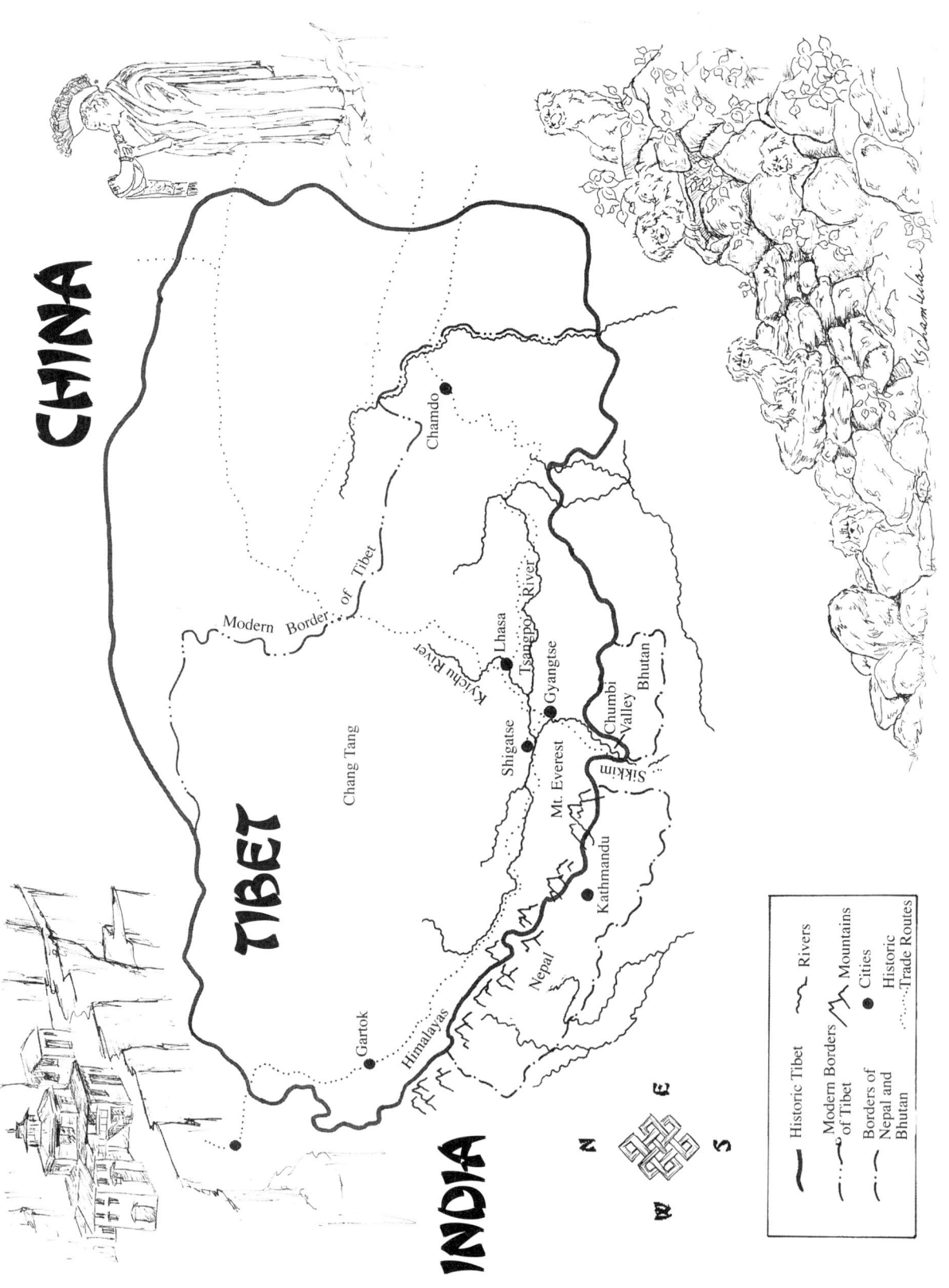

Karen Chamberlain ills.

Chapter Two

The Tibetan Spaniel in His Homeland

The Watcher

A Tibetan Spaniel is poised on the wall of a gompa (monastery) perched on a hillside. Gazing out on the surrounding rugged countryside from this vantage point, his eyes are slitted against the chilling wind that whips the prayer flags overhead, rushing their messages heavenward. The Himalayas, sacred mountains, rise white and lifeless from the horizon. His body tenses and he leans forward into the wind; his mane lifts from his back. A plume of dust raised by plodding yaks appears in the far distance. He barks to alert the Tibetan Mastiffs on the ground far below. A cacophony drifts up to his aerie as all the monastery dogs rush to challenge the intruders and the curious monks in their maroon robes pause to investigate the approaching caravan....

This is the most beloved image of the Tibetan Spaniel, an image that is invoked every time the family Tibbie climbs to the highest place he can find and gives voice at the approach of a stranger. Sadly, it is an image from the Tibet of the past. Spunky Tibetan Spaniels no longer patrol monastery walls in the clear, thin atmosphere on the roof of the world.

In 1950, China invaded and occupied Tibet. The years since then have seen destruction visited not only on the Tibetan people and their culture, but on their dogs as well. Ten years ago, breed enthusiasts in the West believed that the Tibetan breeds had virtually disappeared from their homeland. Reports circulated that the Chinese had systematically exterminated Tibet's dogs, whether mongrel or pure-bred, ostensibly as a public health measure but actually, others say, out of spite against anything Tibetan. It seemed clear that the dogs in the West and those that refugees brought out of Tibet were all that remained in the world.

On a 1993 visit to Tibet, Dr. Toodie Connor (U.S.) was surprised by the number of dogs she encountered. Besides the mongrel dogs roaming in packs and barking at night, she saw many small dogs, that were obviously pure-bred, and often heard them barking in the houses she passed. All appeared to be well-cared-for, and she was told that they were very valuable. Among the small dogs she saw were two Tibetan Spaniels, a sable and a tricolor, the former spotted at Samye Monastery and the latter with an elderly couple in Lhasa.

Like Dr. Connor, other knowledgeable travelers report sighting the occasional Tibetan Spaniel in Tibet, as well as surrounding countries. Although its numbers are greatly reduced, the breed has somehow managed to survive. Although reports such as these offer us a glimmer of hope, we must not lose sight of the fact that the Tibetan Spaniel, along with the Tibetan people, still faces extinction in his homeland. His plight should make us all the more committed to preserving the breed in the beautiful, natural form that Tibet has given us.

THE ROOF OF THE WORLD

Nearly everyone who falls in love with the Tibetan Spaniel eventually becomes curious about Tibet. Not a few of the Tibetophiles among Tibbie owners later profess that their interest grew from idle curiosity about their dogs' origin into a rewarding study of Tibet and, often, newly evolved political convictions.

The Tibetan Spaniel originated in the region historically known as Tibet, an area in Central Asia roughly one-third the size of the contiguous forty-eight States in the U.S. The breed was also found in adjacent areas including Nepal and Bhutan. To fully appreciate the Tibetan Spaniel, it is helpful to know something about the geography of the land in which the breed evolved, as well as the history and culture of the people who created it.

The Tibetan Plateau

Surrounded by inhospitable deserts to the north and a ring of mountain ranges on the west, south and east lies the Plateau of Tibet, a vast tableland 14,000 to 18,000 feet above sea level. The Himalayas bordering Tibet on the south are crowned by Mt. Everest. Called Chomolungma by Tibetans, Everest, at 29,028 feet, is the highest mountain in the world. It is sobering to realize that even the valleys of Tibet are higher than the highest peaks in North America and Europe, and it is not difficult to conceive that, for centuries, her natural boundaries effectively isolated Tibet far above the surrounding countries.

Summer temperatures on the Tibetan Plateau range between 32° F to 50°F while winter averages only -4° F to 14° F with plunges to -40° F. Rendered all the more bitter by relentless winds, snow and ice prevail for the eight months of winter. Paradoxically, the sun can deliver a severe burn due to the thin atmosphere.

Southern Tibet, the most populous area, receives annual precipitation between 20 and 60 inches per year. Contrasted with 60-80 inches in the mountains themselves, precipitation in the vast shadow of the mountains amounts to fewer than 10 inches per year. Perhaps the only advantage of this unforgiving environment is that the cold, dry climate retards the growth of bacteria.

Hydrographic features of the Tibetan Plateau include rivers and lakes. The principal river is called the Tsangpo in Tibetan, but it is more usually known as the Brahmaputra outside Tibet. The Tsangpo flows west to east across the country, passes south of the capital at Lhasa and then turns south, traversing the southern mountains to India and Bangladesh where it joins the Ganges and eventually debouches into the Bay of Bengal. The Plateau is also the source of other great Asian rivers, including the Huang He (Yellow) and Chang Jiang Rivers of China and the Salween and Mekong of Southeast Asia.

The northern half of Tibet, an area of nearly 400,000 square miles, is dominated by the Chang Tang, a great desert dotted with shallow salt lakes. With one of the harshest climates on Earth, the Chang Tang is home only to waterfowl and a few plants. Nomads who collect salt and borax skirt its southern fringes.

Wedged between the Chang Tang and the Himalayas is the narrow arc of land that supports most of Tibet's life—human, animal and plant. Arid, gravelly land in the west gives way to grassland in the east. Here, junipers, poplars and willows grow among the grasses that support herds of sheep and yaks essential to the Tibetan lifestyle. In the short growing season, farmers raise hardy domestic crops such as the barley that is the staple grain of the Tibetan diet.

In the crystalline clarity of the rarefied atmosphere, the ranges of the south provide spectacular scenery but support little or no plant or animal life. However, thousands of feet below their peaks, a small, well-watered area in the southeast supports a variety of animal life and lush alpine and tropical plantlife. Forests, nonexistent elsewhere in Tibet, flourish here. The flowers and shrubs growing here, such as gentian, edelweiss and rhododendron, are much loved by the Tibetan people.

Native fauna include the *kiang* (wild ass), Tibetan antelope, Tibetan hare, wild sheep and rodents. The magnificent snow leopard is endangered; only 2,000 remain in the world. Domestic animals include yak, horses, goats and sheep. Of the latter, the ubiquitous yak is the most useful to Tibet's people. A large, long-haired and long-horned ox, the yak is a source of power as well as food.

The Changing Surface of Tibet

For centuries, humankind made relatively little impression on the formidable surface of Tibet. The mountainous terrain, severe climatic conditions and reliance on human-power and yak-power hindered public works projects. Furthermore, modifying the landscape in any significant way was resisted out of religious scruples. Traditional forms of land transportation were by horseback and foot, and water transportation was by wooden ferry or coracle (a skin boat).

Recently, roads, bridges, airstrips and other infrastructure improvements have begun to appear in Tibet. Trucks and buses now ply the rudimentary road system, while hydroelectric plants supply electricity to major population centers.

THE TIBETAN PEOPLE

Relatively few westerners have ever seen Tibet. Until this century, Tibet was nearly always closed to outsiders, and Lhasa was termed "The Forbidden City." In fact, a romanticized version of Tibet was the model for "Shangri-La," a word now synonymous with a heaven on earth, from James Hilton's *Lost Horizon*.

Though Tibet was never a heaven on earth, her people had developed a peace-loving culture, unique in all the world. Sadly, those still living in Tibet are threatened with genocide, economic deprivation and destruction of their culture and language.

The Tibetan Spaniel in His Homeland

Demographics

Today, the population of Tibet, as defined by the Chinese, is thought to be 2.25 million. Most of the people are Tibetan, an ethnic group that resembles Native Americans in appearance. However, a growing number of ethnic Chinese, who recently began moving into Tibet, now comprise the majority in some areas.

The Tibetan people are well-known for their friendliness, sense of humor and curiosity. Although they are physically sturdy, resilient and well-adapted to life on the oxygen-poor roof of the world, life expectancy is probably less than 60 years. Infant mortality is thought to be one in six.

The language of the native people is Tibetan. Its alphabet is based on Sanskrit, the ancient language of India.

With the exception of a strip along the Tsangpo and its tributary, the Kyichu, the Tibetan Plateau is sparsely populated with fewer than two people per square mile. The populous area in the south averages 60-125 people per square mile. This area includes Lhasa, the capital and largest city (pop. 343,000). Besides Lhasa, the principal towns and cities in Tibet are Shigatse, Gyantse, Tsetang and Chamdo.

Lifestyles

For centuries, life in Tibet changed little. Indeed, the reports of western travelers visiting Tibet in the 18th and 19th centuries were much the same as those who visited shortly before the Chinese occupation in 1950. Since China embarked on the assimilation of Tibet, her policies have radically altered the lives of Tibetans. It may be useful to compare life in historical Tibet with that in contemporary Tibet.

One-fifth to one-third of men and many women in historical Tibet lived out their lives in Buddhist monasteries. These varied in size from a few monks to many thousands. The average monastery

Companion dogs often lived in wealthy Tibetan homes, as seen in this photo taken during the the first Everest Expedition, 1921. C.K. Howard Bury photo. Reprinted with permission of the Royal Geographic Society.

perched on a hillside, above a rural village or settlement, and consisted of buildings that functioned as temples, chapels, chanting halls, workrooms, school rooms, dormitories, kitchens and so on. The monastery's companion dogs roamed at will among the buildings.

Together with the monasteries, a class of aristocratic landowners controlled the wealth of historical Tibet. These landowners lived in colorful, multi-story houses. Activities centered around the enclosed courtyard where women worked and children played. Rooftops were used for storage and the display of the prayer flags. Household goods and furniture were plentiful, and seasonal flowers in pots decorated the dwelling. Most wealthy homes had one or more small dogs as pets and watchdogs.

The rest of the people were peasants, traders or nomadic herders. Peasants usually farmed a plot of their own, as well as working on the estates of the great landowners. Nomads herded sheep and yaks on the grasslands and collected salt and borax in the Chang Tang, while traders plied the ancient Asian caravan routes.

Travelers to historic Lhasa may have marveled at the sights, such as the Dalai Lama's 13-story Potala Palace with its 1,000 rooms, but had little favorable to say about most of the city. Provisions for sanitation were nonexistent, and few early travelers neglected to mention the filth and squalor of Tibetan towns and villages. Then as now, scavenging packs of mongrel dogs roamed the streets. Edmund Candler, a correspondent who visited Lhasa in 1904, wrote: "When one leaves the broad avenues between the walls of the groves and pleasure-gardens [of the environs of Lhasa], and enters the city, one's senses are offended by everything that is unsightly and unclean. Pigs and pariah dogs are nosing about black oozy muds. The houses are solid but dirty...."

Today, two lifestyles of old Tibet, the religious communities and landowners, have effectively disappeared. Between 1959 and 1975, almost all of Tibet's 6,500 monasteries were destroyed. Since 1980, China has permitted a few monastic sites to be restored, mainly to cater to the tourist trade.

Although the landowners have been displaced and the monks all but eliminated, the bulk of the country's wealth still resides in an elite class. Ethnic Chinese now control Tibet's economic activity. Most ethnic Tibetans are excluded from all but menial occupations in a manner that has been likened to apartheid.

The trappings of domestic life in secluded villages, where the peasants still farm small plots of land, have changed little since the occupation. Rural villages consist of mud or mortarless stone dwellings of one or two stories, often surrounded by a two to three foot wall. Each family's fuel supply of yak dung and brush is stored atop the house's flat roof. Attached to tree branches on the roof or to lines strung between houses flutter prayer flags. The household dogs watch for intruders from roof and yard. Inside, livestock occupy one area of the house, usually the lower story in a two-story home, while the family's living quarters occupy another area. The focal point of the living space is the cooking fire. Furnishings are few, and the family sleeps on the floor around the fire. Dark and smoky, the door and uncovered holes in the roof are the only sources of natural light and ventilation. Lacking any source of heat, other than the cooking fire, Tibetans wear many layers of clothing rather than adding fuel to the fire. These dwellings afford scant comfort to their inhabitants during the harsh winters.

Like that of the peasants, the nomadic lifestyle has remained largely unchanged over the centuries. Herders, who live in tents made of black yak hair, move their dwellings and herds to follow the supply of grass. Tibetan Mastiffs, some wearing yak hair collars, guard the camp and help protect the livestock.

Today, Lhasa consists of two sections—the historic city plus the new section, which is dominated by concrete apartment buildings built for Chinese immigrants. A few Chinese-built hotels cater to tourists. There is even a Holiday Inn®. Although improvements in public sanitation have been made elsewhere, native Tibetans living in the historic section make do without electricity or running water.

As it has been for centuries, *tsampa* (roasted barley flour), moistened with tea to form balls, is the staple of the Tibetan diet. Butter tea, a thick drink made by churning hot tea with rancid yak butter and salt, accompanies meals. *Chang* is Tibetan beer. Yak cheese and meat, mutton, rice, potatoes, Chinese vegetables and a few fruits, such as dried apricots, are found in Lhasa's marketplace today.

Tibetan Buddhism

In his book *A Strange Liberation*, David Patt calls Tibetan Buddhism the "unifying cement of society that pervaded every aspect of the spiritual, cultural, and economic life of the country." Buddhism remains the life blood of the Tibetan people, and a discussion of their lives is incomplete without noting the influence of Buddhism.

Buddhists believe that every creature, human and animal, is invested with a soul and that, upon death, the soul migrates into another creature. Each adherent aspires, through merit attained by good works in this lifetime, to move further along the path toward Buddhahood, or enlightenment.

> ## WHO IS THE DALAI LAMA?
>
> His followers believe that each Dalai Lama ("Ocean of Wisdom") is the reincarnation of Chenrezi, the Buddha of Mercy, founder and patron deity of Tibetans. When a Dalai Lama dies, the child into whom his soul has migrated is sought. When he is identified, the new Dalai Lama is trained to become the spiritual leader of Tibet.
>
> The First Dalai Lama was born in 1391. The Fifth Dalai Lama (born 1616), called the Great, achieved pre-eminence among Buddhist leaders in Tibet. He is remembered for the construction of the Potala Palace in Lhasa. In addition to his accomplishments as a leader, the Thirteenth (born 1876), also called the Great, was fond of animals and owned many dogs, including Tibetan Spaniels.
>
> The Fourteenth (and current) Dalai Lama (born 1935) became the 15-year-old ruler of Tibet shortly before the Chinese occupation. During a Chinese crackdown in 1959, he escaped to India with 100,000 followers and established a democratic Tibetan Government-in-Exile. The 1989 Nobel Peace Prize recognized his nonviolent struggle to end China's rule of Tibet and his work on behalf of Tibetan people worldwide.

Before the destruction of Tibet's monasteries, at least one son out of every Tibetan family became a Buddhist monk. Thousands were sheltered in great Buddhist centers such as the Jokhang in Lhasa, Drepung, Sera, Ganden and Tashilhunpo. Such monasteries were centers of learning and housed much of the nation's cultural wealth. *Tankas* (paintings mounted on silk brocade and hung as banners), statuary, prayer wheels and murals decorated interiors lit by yak butter lamps. All of this sacred art as well as irreplaceable texts, painstakingly copied out by hand or handprinted with wood blocks, were lost or stolen when the monasteries were destroyed.

When speaking of Tibetan Buddhism, the term "lama" is often used. Lamas are religious teachers. *Incarnate* lamas have already attained enlightenment but have chosen to be reborn in order to help others. Two important incarnate lamas are the Dalai Lama and the Panchen Lama.

Everywhere in historic Tibet were the outward signs of religious devotion. In addition to the monastery buildings and the everpresent monks in their orange and maroon robes, prayer flags, prayer wheels and rosaries, reliquary shrines called *chortens* (*stupas*) and religious inscriptions on rocks were constant reminders of the role of Buddhism in Tibetan life.

Decades of denial of religious expression do not appear to have reversed centuries of Buddhist belief and tradition. For example, the devout are still seen circumambulating (a ritual of walking or prostrating around a shrine), prayer wheels and rosaries in hand, just as they did when Stuart and Roma Gelder visited Tibet in the early 1960's and later wrote this account in their book, *The Timely Rain*: "We came upon a delightful scene by the ford at the back of the Potala where there is an ancient *chorten*. A grey-haired old lady was walking round it clockwise—in the prescribed ritual—twirling her beautiful, small silver prayer wheel and murmuring prayers as she went. A tiny, fluffy white puppy trotted close at her heels. When he was tired he sat down, faced the other way and waited for his mistress to come round again. When he got his breath back, he joined her devotions once more."

TIBET'S PAST

Before the Chinese takeover, Buddhism so thoroughly dominated society that the government of Tibet was a theocracy. The Dalai Lama was both the secular and religious leader. The current Dalai Lama, now in exile in India, is still revered by the Tibetan people and reviled by China. Even as I write this chapter, China has announced another crackdown to quash the Dalai Lama's influence in Tibet, a country he has not seen in 36 years. To understand how such singular devotion came into being, let's look back to Tibet's past.

Transformation to Theocracy

At the outset of the 7th century, the Tibetan Plateau was inhabited by numerous warlike tribes of nomads. They possessed no written language and practiced an animistic religion called Bon. Physically isolated from the rest of the world, the centuries-old Chinese and Indian civilizations, to the east and south, had little touched the way of life on the Tibetan Plateau.

In 640, a ruler named Songtsen Gampo unified the tribes of central Tibet and established his capital at Lhasa. For the next two centuries, the warrior class that he created carried on a campaign of military expansion that culminated in Tibet's emergence as the dominant military power in central Asia. In addition to exercising control over trade routes, Tibet annexed parts of China and exacted tribute from her rulers. In 821, the Chinese and Tibetans negotiated a treaty that recognized sovereignty of the two states and set boundaries.

Songtsen Gampo's reign is also remembered because two of his wives, Chinese and Nepalese princesses, introduced Buddhism to Tibet. Elsewhere, Buddhism had already existed for a millennium during which differing philosophies had evolved. After a great debate in 792, Tibetans chose to adhere to Indian teachings and rejected those of China. The development of the Tibetan alphabet at this time enabled translation of Buddhist scriptures from Sanskrit into Tibetan. Long after Buddhism declined and virtually disappeared from India, its land of origin, the Tibetan translations were preserved.

Just as the indigenous religions of Europe influenced the beliefs and rites of early Christianity, Bon remained in the cultural memory of Tibetans and colored their practice of Buddhism. Ostensibly due to the pressures of Bon, as well as resentment of the growing political and cultural influence of the monasteries, unified Tibet broke up temporarily in 842. By 1000, however, Buddhism's revival had finally begun to transform Tibet from a militaristic into a pacifist state.

Over the succeeding centuries, monasticism became the backbone of Tibetan society, and four orders developed. The most recent of these is called the Geluk. Founded late in the 14th century, the Gelukpa, or Yellow Hats as they are sometimes called, sought to reform Tibetan monasticism. In the 17th century, the Gelukpa achieved pre-eminence among the Tibetan orders under the leadership of the Fifth Dalai Lama and his Mongolian supporters. The Great Fifth's successors became the secular as well as religious leaders of Tibet.

Foreign Intrusions

As the Dalai Lama consolidated his position in Tibet, the expansion-minded Manchus seized the Chinese throne. In 1720, they launched an invasion of Tibet. From this point on, Chinese *ambans* (commissioners) resided in Lhasa to further Chinese interests. While the peace-minded Tibetans tolerated the Chinese officials as a pragmatic response to a powerful, militaristic neighbor, China interpreted their presence as the Tibetans' acknowledgment of Chinese suzerainty. Nonetheless, Tibetan life went on as it had for centuries, without regard to the *ambans*.

In the late 18th and 19th centuries, the British, by then established in India, repeatedly tried to interest Tibet in trade missions—to no avail. The Tibetans were politely disinterested, and the British never reached Lhasa.

Although the "Hermit Kingdom" was effectively closed to foreigners, bits of information gleaned from travelers, ranging from 17th century missionaries to 19th century eccentrics, gave tantalizing glimpses of Tibet and her "Forbidden City." As part of a project called the Great Trigonometrical Survey, the British employed a group of Indian explorers called *pundits* to survey the Indian subcontinent and beyond. By 1850, the survey teams reached the foothills of the Himalayas and, in 1852, determined that Peak XV on the border of Nepal and Tibet was the highest mountain on Earth. Peak XV was soon renamed Mt. Everest. In 1865-66, a pundit in disguise reached Lhasa after walking 1,580 miles (measured in 3,160,000 carefully counted paces) from Sikkim, an Indian state south of Tibet. When, in 1904, another group of British travelers set out from Sikkim en route to Lhasa, the information provided by this pundit proved valuable.

The Path to Invasion (1904-1950)

At the outset of the 20th century, events elsewhere in the world at last compelled Tibetans to parley

While in Lhasa with the Younghusband Expedition, Lt.-Col. F. M. Bailey acquired a Tibetan Spaniel, seen here in his lap (lower right). When the Mounted Infantry left Lhasa the capital, Lhasa the Tibbie walked over the mountains to India. He emigrated to Britain in 1905. *Reprinted with permisson of HarperCollins Publishers.*

THE LEGEND OF THE PRAYER DOG

An everpresent symbol of Tibetan Buddhism, the prayer wheel is a hollow metal cylinder that turns on a rod fitted through its center. Inside the cylinder, a scroll inscribed with prayers is wrapped tightly around the rod. Handheld prayer wheels are spun by a circular motion of the hand aided by the centrifugal action of chain and weight attached to the cylinder. Larger wheels, such as those found mounted in monasteries, may be five feet or more in height.

Tibetan Buddhists believe that, as the wheels spin, the prayers enclosed within them speed toward heaven and that the numerous prayers dispatched in this manner are as efficacious as those that are voiced. The customary prayer is *Om mani padme haum,* which means "Oh God, the jewel in the flower of the lotus," a reference to the Buddha.

Many references to the Tibetan Spaniel repeat a persistent legend that they turned the great prayer wheels in Tibetan monasteries where they lived and that, as a result, they were called "Prayer Dogs." Given the size of the monastery wheels, some writers theorized that the little dogs turned the wheels by means of a treadmill. No evidence to support this legend exists. Perhaps some imaginative breed enthusiast hoped to promote the Tibetan Spaniel by spinning a charming myth out of romantic notions about the mysterious spiritual life of Tibet.

Inspired by some coveted object that I possess or by my request for some measure of obedience, my own Tibbies often sit up and "pray" to me. With their front paws touching, they gesticulate zealously and smile impishly. Since I did nothing to teach them this form of devotion, perhaps there is some truth to the legend after all, and they are the "Prayer Dogs" of Tibet!

---

with the British. With the tangible weakening of the Manchu (Qing) Dynasty in China, the British feared that the Dalai Lama, who had turned aside their overtures for trade relations, was leaning toward an alliance with czarist Russia in order to throw off Chinese influence. To avert a Russian alliance, the British mounted a military/political expedition to force its way to Lhasa. This was the controversial Younghusband Expedition that is often credited with "opening" Tibet to the West.

Crossing the Jelap La Pass (14,390 feet) from Sikkim into Tibet in the dead of winter, the Expedition reached Lhasa several months later, but not before an abortive attempt at resistance left 600 Tibetans dead. By the time the British reached Lhasa, the Dalai Lama had escaped to Mongolia. Although the threat of Russian influence turned out to be unfounded, the British gained a trade mission at Gyantse, which continued in operation until 1947.

To protect their interests in Asia, the British swiftly negotiated two agreements on the status of Tibet. Anglo-Chinese and Anglo-Russian accords, signed in 1906 and 1907 respectively, recognized China's political control over Tibet. Tibet did not sign the agreements. No longer concerned about British or Russian interference, China invaded and occupied Tibet in 1910. Once again, the Dalai Lama escaped Lhasa—this time to India. Although they annexed several Tibetan provinces, the Chinese were soon distracted by events at home—namely a revolution—and temporarily lost interest in Tibet. With China's departure, the Dalai Lama returned and declared independence for Tibet. When Chinese leaders refused to sign an agreement on Tibet, the British concluded that they had forfeited their suzerainty and concurred that Tibet was autonomous.

The next several years were peaceful in Tibet. China was preoccupied with domestic matters, and the First World War had little impact on the roof of the world. Beginning in 1921, several expeditions, mounted to conquer Everest, added to the meager store of western knowledge about Tibetan geography and culture. Although British trade and diplomatic contacts continued throughout this period, few other travelers were permitted to visit mysterious Tibet.

After the Second World War, events in the outside world once again came to bear inexorably on Tibet. In 1947, British India's long struggle for independence was achieved, and the country partitioned into the states of India and Pakistan. The next several years were a troubled period for the region.

Two years after Indian independence, in China, Communist forces finally defeated the Nationalist regime. Rather than stay at home and repair the ravages of years of warfare, the new leaders of China turned their eyes to Tibet once more. China's burgeoning population required room for expansion. With the British departure from India, Tibet's ties to the west had been severed and her only defense against China had vanished. At the close of 1949, the People's Liberation Army was poised on the borders of Tibet.

A Tibetan woman carries her particolor Tibetan Spaniel in 1924. *Bentley Beetham photo*

Chinese Occupation (1950 to the Present)

When the Chinese invaded Tibet in 1950, they encountered little resistance. The Tibetans had little with which to resist and were, after all, a people dedicated to religion. A recent film entitled *Tibet—The End of Time* characterizes this period, "Genocide would descend upon Shangri-La—a holocaust breaking the peace and silence of a world that hardly knew the sound of a machine, let alone a machine gun."

Although Tibet promptly appealed to the United Nations (U.N.), India, herself vulnerable and intimidated by China, urged the U.N. to table the matter. Faced with resistance from the Communist bloc, the U.K. and the U.S. acquiesced to the Indian position. The U.N., already embroiled in the Korean conflict, conceded. Meanwhile, Tibet was forced to agree to accept Chinese hegemony in return for a pledge to preserve the Tibetan religion, culture and political system. In the wake of the U.N.'s non-response, the Chinese moved 20,000 troops into Lhasa in 1951.

Punctuated by occasional protests and a failed revolt, an uneasy standoff continued until 1959 when the Chinese responded to a protest by launching the wholesale subjugation of Tibet by the destruction of her culture, religion and ethnic identity. The Dalai Lama fled with 100,000 followers to India where he formed the Tibetan Government-in-Exile.

The overthrow of the Tibetan government in 1959 presaged the forced assimilation of Tibet into China. This was the period when landowners were displaced and most of the monasteries and their irreplaceable contents were destroyed, their occupants imprisoned or dispersed. In 1965, China sliced away sections of historic Tibet and renamed central Tibet the Xizang or Tibetan Autonomous Region. The chaos and destruction of the Cultural Revolution, 1966-1976, spilled over into Tibet.

Beginning in 1978, China appeared to restore a few religious and economic freedoms in an attempt to pander to world sentiment and thereby advance her political and economic interests. Since then, however, the Chinese have repeatedly "cracked down" on Tibetans who protest Chinese repression.

The pre-conquest population of historic Tibet is thought to have been 6 million. The Tibetan Government-in-Exile estimates that 1.2 million ethnic Tibetans have died as a result of the Chinese takeover. Human rights violations such as imprisonment, torture and execution of political dissidents are well documented. Population control measures that are tantamount to genocide, the denigration and suppression of the Tibetan language and culture, and the enormous influx of Chinese immigrants to control Tibet's economic life are the elements of Chinese policy in Tibet.

The Government of Tibet in Exile

The government of the Dalai Lama is now termed the Government of Tibet in Exile and is based in Dharamsala, India. On behalf of Tibetan people in the homeland and in exile, the Dalai Lama continues to work tirelessly to achieve the independence of Tibet through nonviolent measures. To represent the interests of the Government-in-Exile, an Office of Tibet is located in many major cities throughout the world.

Most Tibetan refugees live in India but substantial communities exist in other countries, including Switzerland and the U.S. These refugees have endured great hardship in their efforts to transition to life outside Tibet while struggling to preserve their native traditions.

THE TIBETAN DOGS

We come now to the question of the Tibetan dogs. How have the history and culture of Tibet's people impacted canine Tibetans and vice versa?

Observations

It has often surprised me, as both a student of history and an animal-lover, how infrequently the domestic animals of a people are documented. With a few exceptions (notably Egypt), we humans are usually so anthropocentric that we neglect to mention the existence of the animals that surround us, work for us and give us pleasure.

It would have been hard for western travelers to ignore the presence of dogs in Tibet. Even Marco Polo's account of his travels between 1271 and 1275 notes the huge guard dogs he saw as he skirted northern Tibet on the Silk Road to China. In 1811, an eccentric named Thomas Manning reached Lhasa disguised as a Chinese. "The avenues are full of dogs," he observed as he commented on the pitiful spectacle of Lhasa's mongrels, as did Edmund Candler who accompanied the Younghusband Expedition in 1904. Visiting Lhasa in 1987, Blake Kerr described packs of dogs still roaming the streets: "A lone, primal howl came from the alley. The howl was joined by frantic, high-pitched barking from a pack of Lhasa Apsos, Tibetan spaniels, and terriers that seemed to be fighting to the death. Dogs ruled the [Tibetan section of Lhasa] at night. Alone and in packs, their individual and collective yelps ebbed and swelled in a canine chorus."

Although these packs of loose dogs (called *YunKyi* in Tibetan) and huge guard dogs (*DoKyi* in Tibetan, Tibetan Mastiff in English) are often noted, any mention of companion dogs is conspicuously absent from early travelers' accounts. Either they were not allowed to see, or did not consider noteworthy, the charming dogs then inhabiting Tibetan homes and monasteries. In fact, the arrival of 20th century travelers who chronicled their adventures in photographs gave us our first glimpses of the little dogs, with confident faces, who shared their Tibetan masters' homes.

Dogs in Buddhist Thought

The Buddhist faith of the Tibetans is one reason that we are blessed with Tibetan Spaniels and other Tibetan breeds. Out of the belief that every creature possesses a soul that migrates into another creature upon death arises the Buddhist prohibition against killing and, as an extension, a toleration of and kindness toward all creatures. Indeed, every Buddhist realizes that his or her soul may have occupied a dog in a previous incarnation and may yet occupy a dog in the next. The good life that an owner provides his or her dog may improve its prospects for a future incarnation further along the path to Enlightenment by preventing the sins of a past life that lead to its present incarnation as a dog!

In Buddhist symbolism, a lion following at Buddha's heels, much as a dog follows its master's steps, signifies the triumph of peace over violence. It was also thought that a small dog was transformed into the lion depicted as Buddha's steed in sacred art. Thus, the small companion dogs of Tibet may have been bred in the image of Buddha's spirit-lion. I can easily imagine my Tibbies as *senge* (lion in Tibetan) with their scowling foreheads, magnificent manes, and leonine postures.

The "Damci" on these Bhutanese stamps is the Tibetan Spaniel. The King of Bhutan once owned a Tibbie he called "Khomto" (my little baby). During a visit to Bhutan in 1985, Mr. David Lang (U.K.) saw several Damcis in the role of family companion but none living in monasteries.

Evolutionary Ideas

Evidence suggests a large number of breeds developed in Tibet. Over time, enthusiasts of five of these breeds have succeeded in bringing individuals out of Tibet or adjacent regions and building a viable population in the West. The five breeds flourishing outside Tibet are the Tibetan Mastiff, Tibetan Terrier, Lhasa Apso, Shih Tzu and, of course, Tibetan Spaniel. Enthusiasts of the rare Kyi Apso, a large Tibetan breed, are starting along the same path.

This tricolor was photographed in Lhasa, in 1993, where he was seen in the company of his owners, an elderly couple. He appears to be a purebred Tibetan Spaniel. *Toodie Connor, DVM photo*

It is highly likely that the small Tibetan breeds are somewhat related, perhaps the descendants of a common ancestor. Many people have speculated at length upon their origins, and I recommend Ann Wynyard's *Dogs of Tibet and the History of the Tibetan Spaniel* for a stimulating account of the debate. In addition to gleanings from written accounts and art, the science of genetics sometimes gives us tantalizing clues that these breeds sprang from a common ancestor or from one another. For example, a Lhasa Apso litter sometimes includes a little "prapso" (from "perhapso") puppy, indistinguishable from a Tibetan Spaniel, while Tibetan Spaniels always breed "true"; this suggests that the Tibetan Spaniel is the forebear of the Lhasa Apso. While it may be fun to toy with these ideas, it is unlikely that anyone can ever prove the way in which the Tibetan breeds evolved.

Similarly, it is unlikely that we will ever know for certain whether other Asiatic breeds, such as the Pekingese or Japanese Chin, are related to the Tibetan Spaniel or other Tibetan breeds. Proponents of the Tibetan Spaniel have long insisted that the Tibetan Spaniel is the ancestor of the Pekingese. In 1909, Mrs. McLaren Morrison, an early expert on our breed, wrote confidently: "The Thibet Spaniel is the true ancestor of the Pekinese, Japanese and English Toy Spaniel, of that there really can be no doubt and, as such they are doubly interesting." At the same time, other authorities asserted with equal assurance that Chinese dogs were the ancestors of the Tibetan dogs. As support for their arguments, both cited the reciprocal transport of small "lion dogs" as gifts between the Chinese and Tibetan rulers. Opinions as to which group of people initiated this trade may depend on which cultural group the writer favors.

Here is my own opinion about the evolution of the Tibetan Spaniel. It may be equally unproven, but it makes sense.

My Theory on the Origin of the Tibetan Spaniel

Many thousands of years ago, naturally occurring mutations and the harsh environmental conditions on the Tibetan Plateau combined to produce smallish dogs with moderately short muzzles. This happened long before any group of people had started calling themselves Tibetan or Chinese or much else for that matter.

In accordance with Mother Nature's "survival of the fittest" rules, some of the traits that we now see in the Tibetan Spaniel evolved in response to the environment:

- *thick double-coat and snowshoe-like gloves for warmth and water-proofing in the harsh winters,*
- *harefoot for speed over short distances, as well as dexterity and surefootedness in the steep, gravelly terrain,*
- *low-built, sturdy construction for strength and stability (rather than speed), and*
- *oval eyes that close like slits for protection against wind, blizzards and dust storms.*

Life was tough for human and dog alike, but these hardy little dogs endured because they were both useful and appealing. "Useful" because they were good watchdogs, body warmers and vermin-catchers. "Appealing" because both puppies and adults possessed those baby-like qualities to which human beings are drawn by some deep-seated psychological need. And besides, they did not eat much!

At first, the useful and appealing traits were perpetuated by natural selection and the random mating choices of the dogs themselves. Much later, their human companions developed an understanding of "breeding" dogs for certain qualities, just as they had figured out how to breed their sheep, goats, yaks and horses. Consistent with the relative isolation of their humans' tribes, pockets of these small dogs developed independently of one another across Central Asia. They varied in appearance from pocket to pocket, but a resemblance was evident. As tribes made contact, traded with one another and later allied themselves to form countries, their dogs interbred and a more consistent appearance spread over wider geographic areas. Nonetheless, the original genes were still in the gene pool and recessive traits periodically reappeared—and still do!

Much later, as Buddhism and its symbolism emerged, the faithful throughout Asia seized on some of the small dogs walking around and maybe even "improved" upon them so that they more closely fit the image of Buddha's lion dog. Or, maybe the little dogs inspired the idea of the lion dog in the first place. Who knows?

As political and trade relations developed between what were, by now, the countries we call Tibet and China, a reciprocal exchange of dogs commenced, possibly as early as the 9th century, and continued into the 20th century. Beyond this exchange between ruling classes, propagation and trading of small Tibetan and Chinese dogs continued as it had for centuries.

The dogs traded between China and Tibet varied in what we today call "type" but undoubtedly resembled today's Tibetan Spaniel more than today's Pekingese, Pug or Chin. With the ascension of the Manchus to the Chinese throne, in 1644, the Chinese breeds began to differentiate more noticeably as certain qualities, such as the short muzzle and bowed legs, were exaggerated by natural and artificial means. The Chinese breeds exaggerated in this manner and brought to Tibet after the 17th century may have influenced the Tibetan Spaniel just as the Tibetan Spaniel had earlier influenced the Chinese breeds. I think that we can conclude confidently that the Tibetan Spaniel is related to other small Tibetan breeds and that he is probably a principal contributor to the Pekingese and perhaps to other Asiatic breeds as well.

The Role of Dogs in Society

It has been suggested that Tibetan Spaniels were "sacred" in historical Tibet. As reliable a source as Mrs. F.M. Bailey, whose husband accompanied Younghusband and who lived in the area for many years, debunked this idea. Perhaps some romantic-minded westerner, fascinated by their origin in the monasteries of mysterious Tibet, innocently embellished their role. Or, more likely, someone created this story, like that of the "Prayer Dog," hoping to promote the breed's popularity. However, it is true that most wealthier families and monastic communities kept one or more small dogs. Even the Thirteenth Dalai Lama, an animal lover, owned Tibetan Spaniels!

Valued as watchdogs, bed warmers and companions, the dogs were allowed free run of the house or monastery and often accompanied their masters on journeys and pilgrimages. Heinrich Harrer, who spent seven years in Tibet during and after the Second World War, recollected seeing pet dogs circumambulating the Lingkor, a pilgrimage route around Lhasa, along with their masters and mistresses.

A fondness for dogs proved to be common ground in contacts between British and Tibetans. Although the Tibetans were always reluctant to part with their dogs, several British officials and other visitors managed to acquire Tibetan Spaniels, as well as other Tibetan breeds, while in India. The "types" of Tibbies acquired by the British varied considerably; some had longer muzzles than others, some were larger than others and so on. Curious about which "type" Tibetans preferred, the British learned that smaller Tibetan Spaniels were favored over the larger. Although Tibet, then as now, had no formalized standards for her breeds, Tibetans could readily identify a quality Tibbie. Doma of Ladkok, acquired by Dr. A.R.H. Grieg in the 1920's, was reputedly the ideal Tibbie according to the Tibetan concept of excellence.

It is often written that Tibetans are the only Asian society that harbors genuine affection for dogs similar to that of western societies. With all the hardships Tibetans have endured over the past 50 years, the loss of their dogs may seem a trivial event in the larger scheme of things. But, imagine your feelings as you watch your pets weaken and die from lack of food. Imagine standing by, helpless, while an invader systematically destroys the dogs in your neighborhood. Perhaps you can somewhat understand how these losses further demoralized the Tibetan people.

The fact that any of the small breeds has survived at all—despite famine, economic deprivation and political and cultural upheaval—speaks volumes about the position of dogs in Tibetan society. It is yet another example of the tenacity of Tibetans in their effort to preserve their cultural identity. Dr. Daniel Taylor-Ide (U.S.), conservationist and frequent visitor to Tibet, reports that a small group of dog lovers in Lhasa hopes to rehabilitate the Tibetan breeds. In 1992, the mayor of Lhasa remarked to Dr. Taylor-Ide, "Tibet has made three great exports to the international world: her religion, her carpets, and her dogs. Religion and carpets are doing well. Now we must take action about our dogs." Let us hope that these people and like-minded Tibetans are able to save the Tibetan Spaniel in his homeland.

The Tibetan Spaniel

Chapter Three

The Tibetan Spaniel in the United Kingdom

To Tibet, we owe the origin of the Tibetan Spaniel. To the U.K. and her breeders, we owe its growth and present-day status outside of Tibet. The British were the first to bring the Tibetan Spaniel to the West and, after a couple of false starts, they developed the breed into the viable and healthy population which exists today.

While cultivating their own lines, British breeders supplied foundation stock to the rest of the world and set the example for the new breeders who followed in their footsteps. Tibetan Spaniel breeders all over the world admire British Tibbies, and it is not uncommon for enthusiasts to undertake what may best be described as "pilgrimages" to the U.K. to meet her breeders and see dogs.

Since the World Wars each marked a near-to-extinction decline of the Tibetan Spaniel in the U.K., the history of the breed there divides readily into pre-World War I, between the Wars and post-World War II periods. The 50 years since the end of the Second World War may be divided into periods before and after the Tibetan Spaniel Association (TSA) was formed in 1958.

BEFORE THE FIRST WORLD WAR

During the 19th and first half of the 20th centuries, many British citizens traveled to India to serve in the military or in civilian administrative or commercial functions. Among these are the people whom we must credit for first bringing the Tibetan Spaniel from its Himalayan homeland to Great Britain.

Mr. John C. White, C.I.E. is the first Englishman known to have owned a Tibetan Spaniel. As a government official, Mr. White traveled extensively in the Himalayan region. While in Nepal in 1884, he acquired what he termed a "Palace Dog," a black and white male named Boojum. Whether Boojum was a true Tibbie has been debated. Differences in appearance (e.g., length of muzzle, overall size, varying colors and markings) are seen in photos of Tibetan Spaniels preserved from this period. Mr. White's Boojum may have been a Nepalese version of the Tibetan Spaniel.

Wedged between Nepal and Bhutan, on the flanks of the Himalayas that form the southern border of Tibet, Sikkim was one of many Indian principalities. While serving there, in 1888, Mr. White acquired a black puppy on the Tibetan "frontier." There is no question that this male, named Tibet, and his mate, Tabitha, were Tibbies. Mr. White owned their descendants for many years.

In an article written for *The Kennel* (1911), Mr. White praised Tibbies as "unusually intelligent and quick, very affectionate and adaptable, excellent watch dogs." The temperaments of Mr. White's predominantly black Tibbies were clearly on a par with the dogs we know today. Although his Gangtak Tibbies no longer figure in today's pedigrees, Mr. White contributed to our early knowledge of the breed.

The daughter of an aristocratic family and a great dog lover, Mrs. McLaren Morrison often traveled to India with her husband and, while there, acquired several Tibbies. She became the most influential of the owners from this early period. After bringing specimens from India around 1895, Mrs. McLaren Morrison became, in 1898, the first to exhibit the breed in Britain. She was indisputably the most prolific writer to champion the Tibetan Spaniel in the early years of this century.

While a tiny group, including Mrs. McLaren Morrison, labored to establish the breed in Britain, events in the Himalayas hinted that more specimens might soon become available. In 1904, the Younghusband Expedition entered Tibet and reached Lhasa, the first Westerners to reach the "Forbidden City" in 50 years. As an outgrowth of the negotiations, the British established a trade mission at Gyantse in Tibet. In his 1911 article for *The Kennel,* Mr. White observed that, "Really good specimens [of Tibetan Spaniels] are

In 1906, Mrs. McLaren-Morrison wrote that black and white Tibbies "are now fairly familiar to show visitors." This Tibbie appeared in an article on Tibetan breeds in the Kennel Encyclopedia (1911).

very rare, and the owners are unwilling to part with them." Although the trade mission operated until the British left India, in 1947, only a few Tibbies exited Tibet during all those years. However the relations first established early in the century enabled British officials who were serving in the area to later bring Tibbies home to Britain.

In 1906, Mrs. McLaren Morrison wrote this entry for James Watson's *The Dog Book:* "The monasteries of Tibet enclose many beautiful specimens of this fascinating breed, and the monks know their value well. The black and white and the black and tan variety are now fairly familiar to show visitors, who however, have yet to learn that self-coloured sable specimens as well as those of rich tan and ruby as well as brown etc., should also soon be found at our shows. In conclusion let me assure the reader that these various little Asiatics are of a most loving and devoted disposition, showing great sagacity and by no means difficult to rear in our climate where they are therefore able to be our constant companions. To know them is to love them! One can but trust that soon that they will have the position in England and also in America which they so truly deserve." When Mrs. McLaren Morrison wrote this passage, there were, she says, 50-60 Tibbies in Britain and she anticipated continued growth in the breed. By 1911, the Tibetan Spaniel, Lhasa Terrier, and Other Foreign Dogs Club formed to promote the interests of these breeds. It was short-lived.

BETWEEN THE WARS

The Tibetan Spaniel effectively died out in Britain during the First World War. Since there were so few kennels, an outbreak of a contagious disease, such as distemper, or the loss of an important dam or a litter or two would have been a serious setback. The upheaval of the war years undoubtedly contributed to the decline as well.

For many years early in this century, Will Hally wrote a column in *Our Dogs* in which he followed the progress of Tibetan breeds. Writing in 1915, only six years after Mrs. McLaren Morrison's optimistic remarks, Mr. Hally commented, "...Tibetan Spaniels are doing little more than holding their own" and, by 1921, he lamented, "I cast regretful eyes at the apparent extinction of the Tibetan Spaniel...." In 1925, Mr. Hally remarked that the breed would probably never again attain the level that had inspired Mrs. McLaren Morrison's hopeful outlook in 1910.

The Grieg Tibbies

Since the breed population in the U.K. was decimated during the War, the only recourse for replenishing the breed was to import new stock from the Himalayas. This was not as easy as it sounds. Although the idea that Tibetan Spaniels were considered "sacred" has been refuted, neither were they strays to be picked up and carried away from the streets of Himalayan villages. As the intervening years roll away, the stories passed down to us that describe how Tibbies came into the hands of the British, in India, have taken on a distinctly romantic tone: a gift from no lesser person than the Thirteenth Dalai Lama to F.M. and Mrs. Bailey, the gift of the Maharajah of Sikkim to Col. and Mrs. E. B. Wakefield, and this little story of canine intrigue.

The Covered Basket

During the 1920's, Dr. A.R.H. Grieg worked as a physician in India, and her work sometimes took her to the frontier of Tibet. One night, an emissary brought Dr. Grieg a covered basket. Inside were two puppies. The puppies, she was assured, would bring her luck if she took good care of them. But, the emissary warned, she must not let the puppies be seen until she was out of the country. The aura of secrecy convinced Dr. Grieg that her benefactor had stolen the puppies, a Tibetan Terrier and a Tibetan Spaniel, from a monastery.

These Tibetan Spaniels, owned by J.C. White, appeared in the *Kennel Encyclopedia* (1911). Mr. White acquired his Tibbies on the Tibetan frontier. Note the differences in type.

The Tibbie puppy, called Doma, grew to a 5-pound, reddish gold sprite. In her book The Tibetan Spaniel *(1972), Phyllis Mayhew wrote that Doma "was aloof and regal if she felt that way, but her eyes could sparkle with intelligence and impishness if the occasion demanded.... Indian judges of the time expressed surprise and wonder that such a little gem had ever been allowed to leave Tibet."*

The Dr. Grieg of this story sent her mother, Mrs. A.R. Grieg, several dogs she acquired while in India. These included Tibetan Spaniels, Tibetan Terriers and Lhasa Apsos. Exhibited under the kennel names of Ladkok and Lamleh, the Grieg Tibbies resurrected the breed in Britain. By 1929, Mr. Hally wrote in his column, "...in reviving what threatened to be a completely 'lost' breed in this country, I do congratulate Mrs. Grieg on her enterprise."

Growing Pains

Mrs. Grieg's "enterprise" seeded other new kennels of Tibbies between the wars. The most notable of these was the Fanthorpe kennel belonging to Rev. and Mrs. Stutely Abbott. Mrs. Abbott's Fanthorpes Nanki Poo, a red and white particolor, had a son called Skyid. As you will later read, Skyid is the only Tibbie from the Griegs' pre-war bloodlines that figures in the pedigrees of today's Tibbies.

By 1934, the Tibetan breeds were sufficiently numerous to warrant formation of the Tibetan Breeds Association. Representing the Tibetan Spaniel, Tibetan Terrier, Lhasa Apso (also called the Lhassa Terrier) and Shih Tzu, the Association's mission was to develop Breed Standards. These Standards set forth the ideal characteristics of each breed, the goals for which breeders should strive and the criteria by which judges should evaluate exhibits.

Tibetan Spaniel entries in shows of the 1930's were meager by today's standards but considered respectable at the time. Eight Tibbies competed at Crufts in 1936. The principal exhibitors during this period were Mrs. McLaren Morrison (after forty years still the breed's avid supporter), the Griegs, Mrs. Abbott and Mr. W. H. Lopwood.

Britain's dog press of the 1930's did not neglect the Tibetan Spaniel. Besides continuing coverage of Tibetan breeds in *Our Dogs, Hutchinson's Dog Encyclopedia,* issued in serial form during the mid-1930's, provided information about the Tibetan Spaniel and may have been responsible for the pervasive Prayer Dog legend: "Many Tibetans keep a small Tibetan Spaniel and train it to turn the prayer-wheel—hence they are often called 'Prayer Dogs'. Prayers are written on parchment or paper and put into a revolving box. Every time the box revolves the Tibetan considers that all the written prayers have been duly said...instead of turning the box himself he trains his little Spaniel to do the work. Thus he reaps the benefit from the saying of the prayers without any exertion on his part...!"

Tibbies descended from those sent to Britain by Dr. A.R.H. Grieg in the 1920's reintroduced the breed there. Except for one dog, the line died out during the Second World War.

THE TIBETAN DILEMMA

No history of our breed, during its first 40 years in Britain, would be complete without explaining the issues that were debated during that period. Stated simply, they were:

- Is the Tibetan Spaniel a distinct breed?
- If a distinct breed, what is the breed's correct type? In other words, what should a Tibetan Spaniel look like?
- Is the Tibetan Spaniel the ancestor of other Tibetan breeds and/or of other Asian breeds?

A Breed Apart?

What seems so patently obvious to us now—that the Tibetan Spaniel is a pure breed apart from other breeds—was not taken for granted when the first Tibbies arrived in Britain. The controversy had already commenced, by 1904, when this passage by Mrs. McLaren Morrison appeared in *The Twentieth Century Dog* by Herbert Compton: "The natives of the frontiers of Thibet know well the value of these dogs, and *they are as recognized as a breed* [my emphasis] as, say, the King Charles is with us." In the same source, Mr. Compton continues, "Mr. H.C. Brooke, another high authority on foreign dogs, considers the Thibet spaniel is quite *a distinct breed* [my emphasis] and thinks the specimens exhibited show a marked type of their own." That the authors made these assertions indicates that some readers would not have considered Tibetan Spaniels a pure breed.

Although the Tibetan Spaniel was accepted as a distinct breed, debate over differentiating the other Tibetan breeds persisted well into the 1930's. Although most of the dispute concerned the breeds we now call the Tibetan Terrier, Lhasa Apso and Shih Tzu, the Tibetan Spaniel was caught up in the debate simply because it shared the same land of origin. As an example, Mr. Hally wrote in a 1934 column, "The Tibetan Terriers and Tibetan Spaniels are being affected by the prejudiced judging because of confusion over the Apso-Shih Tzu breeds.... These are definitely different breeds and so there is no excuse for anyone not being aware what the respective standards are.... Both Tibetan Terriers and Tibetan Spaniels are quite non-controversial as the public are realizing, even if the judges are failing to do so." In her book *The Dogs of Tibet and the History of the Tibetan Spaniel,* Ann Wynyard acknowledges Mr. Hally's contribution in preserving the history of the breed by writing about Tibetan Spaniels so faithfully in the period between the wars. Further, she credits him with "[achieving] acceptance of the idea that the various Tibetan breeds with which we were dealing were not, as it then seemed to some people, simply variations of type within one single breed, but were a number of totally different breeds."

The confusion over the Tibetan breeds was compounded by conflicting nomenclature both in Tibet and in Britain. The Tibetans identify dogs more by function than appearance, and names for each breed apparently differed. Furthermore, one can easily imagine regional variants of these names throughout the Himalayas. Writers familiar with the Tibetans' names for their dogs have variously identified the Tibetan Spaniel as the *Jemtse Apso* (scissored dog), *Gyakhi* (Chinese dog), and *Zim-kyi* (bedroom dog). However, the naming problem seems to have troubled the Tibetan Spaniel least of all the Tibetan breeds. In English, it has been consistently called the Thibet, Tibet or Tibetan Spaniel since the late 19th century. Whichever English-speaking person first called the breed a "Spaniel" may have done so because of its silky, flat-lying coat, likening it to the smallish spaniels, originally used to flush birds but then (as now) enjoyed as pets.

What is the Correct Type?

"Type" is a word used by dog breeders and exhibitors to mean the sum of the traits that characterize a breed and differentiate it from all others. A breed's type is an ideal described in its Breed Standard, the set of guidelines by which breeders breed and judges judge.

The Tibetan Spaniel had been shown in India since the first years of this century, and the formalized Breed Standard adopted by the newly formed Tibetan Breeds Association, in Britain, was nearly identical to the standard of the Indian Kennel Club. Nonetheless, several questions about the qualities that characterize the ideal Tibbie were passionately debated during the formulation of the British Standard. Emotions ran high because the decisions could effectively set one breeder's stock over that of another.

There is no question that Tibbies from the 19th and early 20th centuries varied in appearance. Not only were several colors and varied markings seen, but traits such as overall size, ear carriage and shape and length of muzzle also differed. The tasks before the Association's committee were to generalize which features distinguished and typified the Tibetan Spaniel and then to discriminate quality from lack of quality.

Lady Freda Valentine, who was present, recalled that the question of drop-ear vs. prick-ear was the most hotly contested because some of the Grieg Tibbies had prick-ears. In her Foreword to Mrs. Wynyard's book, she wrote, "The matter was settled by the Committee agreeing to the charming lift of the ears next to the head."

Although the resulting 1934 Standard required pendant (drop) ears, it allowed considerable variation in weight, from five to 14 pounds, in recognition of small examples such as the Griegs' Doma of Ladkok. However, all four of the British Standards to date, including the 1934 version, clearly penalized traits such as a "broad flat face" so as to clearly differentiate the Pekingese from the Tibetan Spaniel. Chapter 12 further discusses these Standards.

Which Came First?

Common sense dictates that small Asian breeds that bear some resemblance to one another probably owe their existence to a common ancestor in the misty past. Today, most people concede a relationship between the Tibetan Spaniel, other small Tibetan breeds and the Pekingese.

An interesting but fruitless debate over which breed developed first has occupied many enthusiasts of Asiatic breeds during this century. Is the Tibetan Spaniel the ancestor of the Pekingese or the Pekingese the ancestor of the Tibetan Spaniel, or do they both descend from a common ancestor? Is the Lhasa Apso the ancestor of the Tibetan Spaniel or vice versa? And so on.

As early as 1908, Mrs. McLaren Morrison, the first breed expert, wrote in the *Kennel Encyclopedia,*

TIBETAN SPANIEL FOREBEARS

The four unrelated dogs whose names appear in bold and italic print in this diagram are forebears of all Tibetan Spaniels in the West today. Dolma, Lama, Potala and Garpon were brought to Great Britain from India shortly after the Second World War. Skyid is the only Tibbie descended from the pre-War British Tibbies that figures in the pedigrees of today's dogs. Note the brother-to-sister and even mother-to-son pairings from which today's Tibbies descend.

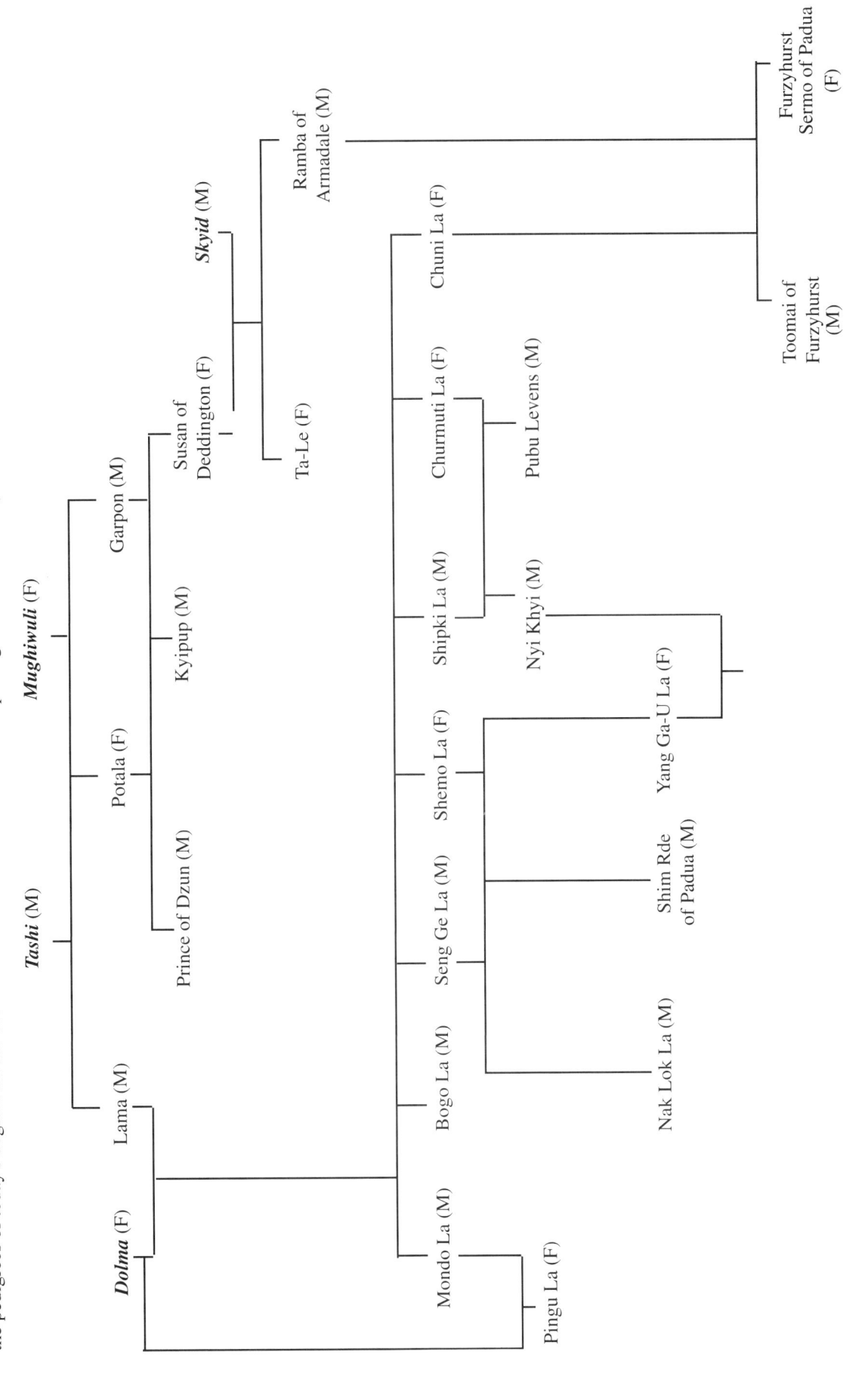

THE SEARCH FOR NEW BLOOD

All registered Tibetan Spaniels in western countries descend from five dogs—one descended from those brought to Britain after the First World War and four (including three siblings) brought to Britain after the Second World War. After considerable effort, a few other Tibbies were added to this small gene pool.

YEAR	NAME	ORIGIN	OWNER
1968	Dikki Dolma	India	Joyce (U.K.)
1968	Yasodhara	India	Wynyard/Forbes (U.K.)
1969	Jawalakhel Dorji	Nepal	Tamura (then U.S.)
1970	Honeybun	Hong Kong	Hacker (U.S.)
1971	Dido	India	Whiting (U.S.)
1971	Bimbo	India	Whiting (U.S.)
1973	Tashi Dordja of Khumbila	India	Perkins (U.S.)

"It is stated with some authority that the Tibet Spaniel, known for hundreds of years in the monasteries of Tibet, is the original ancestor of the Pekingese, Japanese [Chin], and English Toy Spaniel." In the same publication, another author wrote, "There now comes the question as to how far Tibet has derived her smaller breeds from China.... It may be that China's small dog, the Pekingese, found its way by caravan to Tibet...and has in time degenerated to the present type of 'Tibetan Spaniel'.... [The] origin of the 'Spaniel'...is most likely traceable to Chinese importations, unless it can ever be authentically proved that it is the other way around."

Most reasonable people now agree that the matter of which breed was the more ancient can never be resolved definitively one way or the other. Which way you lean probably depends on whether you view the Pekingese as an "exaggeration" of the Tibetan Spaniel or the Tibetan Spaniel as a "degeneration" of the Pekingese. My own theory on this subject appears in Chapter 2.

POST-WAR RENAISSANCE

The Second World War, once again, devastated the Tibetan Spaniel in Britain. Phyllis Mayhew, who had admired the breed since the late 1930's, wrote: "The breed was doing well [before the War] and it seems incredible that with such a long lived virile breed that it should have virtually died out in...six or seven years.... Litters were bred in the early part of the war, and one wonders what became of the puppies. Mrs. Grieg's dogs were all lost in a severe outbreak of hardpad [distemper], a great tragedy for the breed as well as Mrs. Grieg. Other kennels were given up and the inmates scattered as pets and lost from the breeding point of view. I had a puppy on order at the outbreak of the war which I had to cancel as I knew my Pekingese kennel would have to be drastically reduced under war time conditions...."

The Emigrants

By the end of the war, only one known representative of the pre-War lines remained—a substantial red-colored dog called Skyid, the son of Fanthorpes Nanki Poo. If the Tibetan breed was to survive in Britain, Tibet or India must provide more dogs.

Mughiwuli and Tashi

In his book Past Imperative, *Sir Edward Wakefield recounts his first encounter with a Tibetan Spaniel during luncheon with a high Tibetan official in 1929. "I was entranced by the Gyaki (Tibetan spaniel) which was his constant companion and shared his bed and board," Sir Edward writes, "It was literally a lap-dog for, when he was sitting, it lay across his hands concealed in the broad sleeves of his robe. An animated hot-water-bottle, it kept him warm by day and by night." Nearly a decade later in 1938, Lady Wakefield was given a bitch by Dr. Khanshi Ram, the Trade Agent at Gartok, in western Tibet. The little Tibbie, Mughiwuli, was born in northern India of parents from western Tibet.*

Mughiwuli became an Indian champion and reputedly charmed all who met her. One of her devotees was the Maharaja of Nabba, Sir Pratep Sing, Malvendra Bahadur. In anticipation of a breeding, Dr. Ram arranged to borrow a male Tibetan Spaniel, called Tashi, from the monastery in Tashigong across the border in western Tibet. The loan of the Maharaja's own Rolls Royce enabled Mughiwuli to travel in style for a rendezvous with Tashi in Simla.

Mughiwuli gave birth to eight puppies in two litters with Tashi, the first born in 1941. One of these puppies, a sable male called Lama, emigrated to Britain with the Wakefields when they left India, in 1946.

Dolma's Story

When the Maharaja of Sikkim asked him in what way he could reward Sir Edward Wakefield for a service rendered, Sir Edward mentioned that Lady Wakefield would like to have a Gyakhi bitch. In his book Past Imperative, *Sir Edward explained, "Gyakhis are the treasured pets and watchdogs of Tibetan monasteries, and the monks are no more ready to part with a Gyakhi than is a desert Arab to part with his mare. I did not know it at the time but the Maharaja was a patron of the monastery at Phari Dzong in the Chumbi valley of South Tibet...and had no difficulty in obtaining a young Gyakhi bitch for me. I had forgotten all about my suggestion to the Maharaja when, some months later, his emissary, clothed in a long broad-sleeved robe, arrived at my house in New Delhi. He held in both hands a purple silk cushion, and on the cushion, lay a small golden-haired Gyakhi. Her name was Dolma and she was about four months old."*

Dolma was a dainty Tibbie, much like the famous Doma of Ladkok, reddish-colored with a bright expression accentuated by the lift of her ears. Accompanying the Wakefields back to England in 1946, she became an ancestress of today's Tibbies.

Toddles

It is often surprising where Tibbies turn up. When the Germans retreated from Baghdad, in 1917, they left behind a reddish gold female Tibetan Spaniel. She probably arrived in Baghdad via caravan, where she had been adopted by the German Flying Corps. Luckily, Toddles, as she was soon named, passed into the hands of Col. A. W. Hawkins and, in due course, landed in England. Confirmed to be a Tibbie, she was the Hawkins' beloved pet until her death at age 18. Since the only other Tibbie in England after the decimation of the breed during the First World War was also a female, Toddles sadly never had Tibbie puppies. Yet another line was lost to posterity.

Nonetheless, Toddles had a lasting influence on the breed. Like countless owners before and since, Col. and Mrs. Hawkins found that life without a Tibbie is never the same. Years after Toddles' death, while posted in India, they heard about Mughiwuli's litter and bought two of the puppies—a red male they called Garpon and his black-and-tan sister named Potala.

Garpon and Potala made the trip to Britain with Col. and Mrs. Hawkins in 1946, the same year their brother Lama and the unrelated Dolma returned home with the Wakefields. These four Tibbies, along with Skyid, the sole survivor of the pre-War lines, became the ancestors of the British lines we know today, and these British lines have seeded virtually every other line in the world outside India and Tibet.

The New Generations

Considerable inbreeding (mother to son and sister to brother) was necessary to build the breed. In the early generations, the potential for producing defective puppies as a result of inbreeding was great.

GB Ch. Amcross Vosta Kushi Kee, born in 1975, was bred by Mr. and Mrs. D. Foster and owned by Dierdre Jenkins and M.C. Hourihane. He was a top-winning Tibbie and an influential sire. *Diane Pearce photo*

GB Ch. Langshi Super-Ted, bred and owned by Julie Carter, is the top-winning British Tibbie. He has won 23 C.C.'s, seven Bests in Show at club championship events and Best in Show at the British Utility Breeds Association Show. *John Hartley photo*

However, pairing these close relatives also quickly identified dominant traits among the wildly varied types and colors represented by the five foundation dogs. At one extreme was Skyid: foxy red, large and heavy-boned with a long muzzle, long coat and pronounced undershot bite. At the other extreme was Dolma: light reddish gold, small and dainty, with moderate coat. In between were the Mughi-wuli-Tashi puppies: all similar in type with moderate bone, balance and longish muzzles, but varied in color with Potala's black-and-tan, Lama's sable and Gar-pon's bright red. The variations in type seen in these forebears emerge even in today's Tibbies. You can see large pups or dainty pups, long muzzles or short, legs long or short, coats heavy and sparse—even in the same litter and even if it is intelligently line-bred! Variation in type is one of the challenges and intrigues of our breed.

Tibetan Spaniels were never easy to obtain, but political events in the Himalayan region, during the late 1940's and 1950's, made them impossible to find. India's independence and subsequent civil troubles, along with the departure of the British, followed by the Chinese occupation and eventual takeover of Tibet quashed hopes for obtaining Tibbies to reinforce the new lines developing in Britain.

The little Tibbie could have perished in the sweep of world events. Fortunately for us, he did not. I am sure that it was ever in the minds of these early breeders that some tragedy—such as an outbreak of disease, an accident or the appearance of a defect—could check their progress or even, as had happened twice before, devastate the modest population of Tibbies. So they understandably compensated for the lack of specimens by inbreeding to produce as many litters as possible from each good dam. There was simply no other way to assure the breed's survival.

The Wakefield Tibbies, whose names were all followed by La (the Tibetan word for "mountain pass"), and the Hawkins Tibbies seeded other early kennels including:

Furzyhurst (Hervey-Cecil)
Kye-Ho (Peach)
Padua (Braye and Elam)
Ramblershot (Dudman)
Rosaree (Hubberstey)
Szufung (Battson)
Traza (Thirlwell)

With the growth of new kennels, competition at shows increased until, as the first decade of the post-war period waned, most large Championship shows offered classes for the Tibetan Spaniel.

GB Ch. Reinbridge Simba at Souska, bred by D. Chapman and owned by Ian Blackshaw is a six-time winner of top sire awards.

The Tibetan Spaniel in the United Kingdom

(Left) 1993's top brood bitch, GB Ch. Wildhern Winter Jasmine, was bred by Linda Micklethwait. *Diane Pearce photo*

(Right) GB Ch. Tyesholme Ensign, bred and owned by Major and Mrs. J.E. Tye, won Best of Breed at Crufts, the U.K.'s most prestigious show, in 1994. *Diane Pearce photo*

(Left) GB Ch. Shamau Trangka La (left), her son, daughter and grandpuppy, all bred by Maureen Sharp, are descendants of GB Ch. Shamau Tranka, the first particolor to be awarded his title (1973). Miss Sharp specializes in "partis."

Jane Lilley's GB Ch. Kensing Currant Bun won the Bitch C.C. at Crufts in 1994.
Peter Diment photo

THE MODERN ERA (1958 TO PRESENT)

In 1958, the Tibetan Breeds Association (founded 1934) disbanded in favor of separate clubs for the four breeds, and the Tibetan Spaniel Association (TSA) was formed. At that time, only 58 Tibetan Spaniels were registered in the U.K. Even today, Tibbie registrations account for about one-quarter of 1% of the 180,000 dogs registered in the U.K. each year.

The formation of the TSA marks the beginning of the modern era of Tibetan Spaniels in the U.K. The renaissance continued as new breeders came on board and developed new lines. As registrations grew, the breed qualified to compete for championships; this in turn sparked further interest in the breed. Revised Breed Standards, including an Illustrated Standard, were developed and adopted. Membership in TSA grew and, as Tibbies gradually became more evenly distributed throughout the U.K., regional clubs formed to serve local needs.

Evolution of the Breed Standard

After a quarter century under the original 1934 Breed Standard, the newly formed TSA promptly adopted a revised Breed Standard in 1959. Revised again in 1975 and 1986, successive Standards altered or clarified requirements and addressed points omitted in earlier versions. Examples of key revisions include weight, height, preferred type of bite and eye shape. Although they vary slightly, the world's Tibetan Spaniel Breed Standards are substantially based on the U.K. Standard.

The Show Scene

To qualify for his championship, a British Tibbie must win three Challenge Certificates (C.C.'s) from three different judges. At least one of these must be awarded after the dog is one year old. Championships first became available in 1960, when the Kennel Club granted "separate breed status" to the Tibetan Spaniel and allocated four sets (one each for best dog and best bitch) of C.C.'s based on the 1959 registration of 58 Tibbies. In 1965, the Kennel Club increased the C.C. allocation when registrations jumped to 154. By 1994, Tibbies were allocated 31 sets of C.C.'s.

In 1961, GB Ch. Rowena of Padua, owned by Misses Braye and Elam (a descendant of Chuni La, a daughter of Dolma and Lama) became the first Champion in the U.K. In her book, Phyllis Mayhew tells the story that Tenzing Norgay of Mt. Everest fame, himself an authority on Tibetan breeds, complimented Rowena as a "lovely specimen of her breed and as near perfection as any he had seen." In Rowena's pawprints have followed 263 Tibbies who have become GB Champions through the end of 1994.

Another coveted award is the Junior Warrant (J.W.). In 1965, Sivas Lakshmi, bred and owned by Sara Selby, won the first J.W. awarded to the breed. (Chapter 12 further explains the British championship requirements and the J.W.)

Today, 80-100 Tibbies compete at 30 Championship shows that offer classes for Tibetan Spaniels each year. One of these is the TSA's all-Tibbie Championship show, an annual event since 1968. Several Tibbies have won top honors in the Utility Group (the British equivalent of the American Non-Sporting Group), starting with GB Ch. Windamere's Lho-Zah-Mi, owned by Mrs. G. S. Vines, in 1977. In 1990, GB Ch. Langshi Super-Ted, bred and owned by Julie Carter, won Best in Show at the British Utility Breeds Association Championship show.

In 1967, TSA's first all-Tibbie Open show, an annual event ever since, took place with record entry of 130. Entries at other Open shows, one or more of which occur every weekend, vary considerably but may average about 12 Tibbies. Although no C.C.'s are given at this type of show, several Tibbies have won Best in Show at Open shows.

The TSA and Regional Clubs

The stated mission of the TSA is to "encourage responsible ownership and breeding to the Kennel Club standard of Tibetan Spaniels, and to further these objects by organizing shows, educational events, and other appropriate activities." With only 87 members in 1965, membership in the TSA mushroomed to nearly 400 by 1975. Since then, it has remained fairly stable at slightly over 400 members. Foreign memberships currently comprise about 10% of the total.

In addition to hosting its annual Championship and Open shows, TSA awards several trophies each year to recognize special achievements. These include the TSA Points Trophy, Eulyn Stud Dog Trophy, Sivas Breeders Trophy, Rosaree Brood Bitch Trophy and the Individual Points Trophy. Other activities include conducting a judges' education program, maintaining a Code of Ethics, encouraging testing for genetic diseases and coordinating rescue and re-homing activities. *Tibetan Tidings* (a yearbook), a newsletter and the *Illustrated Breed Standard* are informative publications.

To meet the needs of local enthusiasts, five regional clubs have formed in the U.K. The South Western and Northern Tibetan Spaniel Clubs formed in 1971 and 1974 respectively. The Tibetan Spaniel Club of Scotland, the Northern Ireland Tibetan Spaniel Association and the South East and Anglian Tibetan Spaniel Club followed suit in the 1980's. Besides providing a forum for sharing information and resources, regional clubs sponsor competitive and social events. All host Open shows, and four of the five host annual all-Tibbie Championship shows.

A trio of recent Amcross Tibbies: GB Ch. Amcross Machaya with two of her puppies were bred by Dierdre Jenkins and M.C. Hourihane. V. Hourihane photo

Breeding Notes

Many breeders have joined the ranks in the past thirty-five years. Bridget Croucher, TSA's Honorary Secretary, estimates that about 100 members (one quarter of the membership) are active breeders. However, most kennels remain small, yielding only one or two litters per year. Here is a sampling of U.K. kennel names since 1958:

Amcross (Jenkins, Hourihane)
Balgay (Young)
Braeduke (Wynyard)
Carretero (Carter)
Caselden (Rose)
Clydum (Simper, Scoates)
Colphil (Butler)
Deanford (Keen)
Eulyn (Donaldson)
Langhsi (Carter)
Mingshang (Mayhew)
Kensing (Lilley)
Parkplace (Dalrymple-Hay)
Shamau (Sharp)
Simpasture (Beale)
Sivas (Selby)
Taimani (Wilson)
Tsingay (Atkins)
Tyesholme (Tye)
Whitewisp (Grounds)
Wildhern (Micklethwait)
Windameres (Vines)

From the early 1960's, several U.K. kennels have exported Tibbies to other countries. Kennels in Finland, Sweden, the U.S., Australia, New Zealand and, recently, Slovenia and South Africa were seeded by Tibbies from the U.K.

One sought-after bloodline has been Braeduke Tibetan Spaniels, started in 1962 by Ann Wynyard. Through Mrs. Wynyard's efforts, litter sisters imported from India and the offspring of American imports, from India and Hong Kong, added new genes to the older British lines and, from there, the genes traveled into lines in other countries as well. Mrs. Wynyard has also been responsible for much of our breed literature. Her books, *The Dog Directory Guide to the Tibetan Spaniel* (1974, 1980) and *Dogs of Tibet and the History of the Tibetan Spaniel* (1984) are "must reading" for enthusiasts.

GB Ch. Tiggy of Wildhern was top brood bitch for 1991. She is owned by Linda Micklethwait.
Diane Pearce photo

ISSUES FOR THE TWENTY-FIRST CENTURY

As they approach the turn of the century, the principal concerns facing the U.K.'s Tibbie owners are to maintain the genetic health of the breed, to continue judges' education and to provide re-homing for unwanted Tibbies.

Breed Rescue

The TSA coordinates breed rescue in the U.K., with backup provided by the regional clubs. Although rescue is a high priority, coordinators gladly report that few Tibbies require re-homing each year. Most breeders take back and re-house their own stock. Where this is not feasible, young Tibbies are relatively easy to place. It is more difficult to find homes for elderly Tibbies, even those that are healthy and have many years of companionship left.

Judges' Education

The TSA publishes a list of judges whom the organization would support to judge the breed classes. Many of these are "specialist judges" who judge only the Tibetan Spaniel. Many are themselves breeders. However, some exhibitors are frustrated that the Best of Breed Tibetan Spaniel too often fails to advance in higher level competition—even here in the land of the breed's renaissance. The judges' education program in the U.K. is described in Chapter 12.

Health Concerns

The British Veterinary Association/Kennel Club Committee (BVA/KC) does not consider any inherited disease to be prevalent in U.K. Tibbies. An inherited condition called juvenile nephropathy (progressive nephropathy or congenital kidney disease) has prompted the Kennel Club to advise the TSA to "monitor the incidence of this disease at an early stage when appropriate action could be taken to limit the perpetuation of the problem." Data on the incidence of the disease is being collected. In addition, the TSA encourages members to seek veterinary advice and, in the case of puppies that die, to determine the cause via post mortems.

Due to reported cases of progressive retinal atrophy (PRA), a hereditary disease that leads to blindness, U.K. breeders are encouraged to have their Tibbies tested before breeding. Voluntary compliance by serious breeders is thought to be successful. In addition, the Kennel Club records on a puppy's registration certificate whether the eyes of the sire and dam have been tested. The TSA PRA Register, produced each year, publicizes the results of eye tests in an effort to prevent further propagation of the disease.

Chapter Four

The Tibetan Spaniel in the United States

In her book entitled *Thin Air,* Constance Bridges Jones recounts how she acquired her Tibbies, Mu and Tashi, during a visit to Tibet in the 1920's. Enchanted by Tibetan Spaniels seen in the private chambers of a High Lama in Tibet, Mrs. Jones set out to find puppies, which she called Tibetan or Lama "pugs," to take home with her. Luckily, she found a male, said to have arrived on a caravan from Lhasa, and then a female, offered by a Chinese merchant. "The male puppy had a fierce frown and was energetic; the female was gentle and confiding and sat motionless whenever one put her down," Mrs. Jones wrote. After a year of travel, the puppies arrived in the U.S. Sadly, Tashi died without offspring. However, when her photograph appeared in the *American Kennel Gazette,* 14 years later, Mu was described as still "as lively as a puppy" and a "beloved tyrannical dowager."

Although Mu was the first documented American Tibbie, the real story of the Tibetan Spaniel in the U.S. does not begin until many years later.

EARLY AMERICAN TIBBIES

In 1966, Leo Kearns of Connecticut purchased a Tibetan Spaniel. Imported from the U.K., Mr. Kearns' new Tibbie was a bitch that he named Doghouse Dream Baby ("Missy"). Two years later, her litter by GB Ch. Yakrose Chiala of Amcross, imported from the U.K., marks the start of the history of the Tibetan Spaniel in the U.S.

Before Mr. Kearns' fortuitous purchase, a few other Tibbies had found their way to the U.S. Like Mrs. Jones' Mu and Tashi, some of these came directly from Tibet or adjacent regions while others originated in the U.K. Occasional rumors about Tibbies that returned with American servicemen remain undocumented. Although four litters were reportedly born before Doghouse Dream Baby's litter, the puppies from these earlier litters have not been traced.

When Mr. Kearns bought Doghouse Dream Baby, very few references to the Tibetan Spaniel had appeared in the American press. In a 1933 article in the *American Kennel Gazette,* Margaret Hayes described Tibbies as "charming," "greatly prized," "active," and of "extraordinary intelligence." And, in a 1937 article, the Hon. Mrs. Eric Bailey related the tale of Lhasa, the Tibbie her husband acquired while in Tibet in 1904. When the Second World War enveloped Britain and swept away the Tibbies there, the American dog press fell silent on the subject of the Tibetan Spaniel and remained so as British breeders struggled to rebuild the breed during the post-War period. It is not surprising that Mr. Kearns knew little about Tibbies when he first saw Doghouse Dream Baby.

Mr. Kearns, along with his friends and acquaintances, soon succumbed to the charms of the breed. When demand outstripped supply, he and his initiates launched a campaign of importation to introduce new bloodlines for their breeding program. Although a few Tibbie litters were born elsewhere in the U.S. during the late 1960's and very early '70's, we owe our thanks to this Connecticut group for launching the breed.

THE ROAD TO RECOGNITION

In 1971, Jay Child showed her Ciceter Norbu at a rare breeds match. Although she faced no competition, the little Tibbie won a pink ribbon. This was the first exhibition of a Tibbie in the U.S., and the experience motivated Mrs. Child and others in the Connecticut group to take several steps on the road to American Kennel Club (AKC) recognition for the Tibetan Spaniel. It was to be a long road.

Getting Organized

Before recognizing a breed, the AKC requires that several conditions be met. To meet the requirement

51

The dog in this photo, taken in 1917, has many of the hallmarks of a sable Tibetan Spaniel. The neck appears to carry a mane, the muzzle is short and cushioned, and the ears, paws and fringes are characteristic. Could this be the first American Tibbie? *Susan and Christopher Miccio Collection.*

for a national breed club, the Tibetan Spaniel Club of America (TSCA) was formed in 1971. Including Mr. Kearns, the "Founding Father," there were fourteen charter members. Until 1983, ownership of a Tibetan Spaniel entitled the owner to TSCA membership.

TSCA's initiatives in the 1970's and early '80's were strategic measures to solidly establish the Tibetan Spaniel and, at the same time, to convince the AKC of compliance with its recognition requirements. Since AKC requires a breed registry, one of the new TSCA's first actions was to establish a Stud Book. Its purpose was to document the "foundation stock" for the breed. To be eligible for eventual AKC registration, all Tibbies born in or imported to the U.S. were registered in the Stud Book.

Besides those clustered in the Connecticut area, other Tibbies and their owners scattered around the U.S. yielded additional registrations and new members for the TSCA. Among these were Tom and Florence Whiting's Tibbies acquired while they lived in India, Lily Tamura's Nepalese-born Tibbies and Marguerite Perkins' Tibbie, born in a Tibetan refugee community in India.

As further evidence that American Tibbie owners were committed to firmly establishing their breed, regional Tibbie clubs (now defunct) formed during the 1970's. A bimonthly newsletter was begun in 1971 to connect widely dispersed TSCA members.

Early Shows

TSCA sponsored its first all-Tibbie "specialty" match in 1972. These matches provided not only competition but also a forum for sharing information and social interaction among American Tibbie owners. Now AKC-approved National Specialty shows, these annual all-Tibbie competitions continue to the present-day.

The creation of a club championship program in 1976 helped to standardize the concept of quality in the breed and, at the same time, recognized those who attained these quality standards. Witneylea Kulha, bred by Mrs. A.L. Weller (U.K.) and owned by Joan Child, became the first to append TSCA Champion to his name and was a leading stud dog in his day. In all, 55 TSCA Champions were named in the eight years from the program's incep-

Constance Bridges Jones with Mu, her Tibetan Spaniel, as they appeared in the *American Kennel Gazette* of September 1, 1937. *Courtesy of The American Kennel Gazette. Underwood and Underwood photo.*

> **FOUNDATION STOCK IN THE U.S.**
> **1971-1985**
>
> Registrations in the TSCA Stud Book show the origin and growth of U.S. foundation stock. Of the 749 Tibbies registered, 88% were U.S.-born. However, 14% were either themselves imported from the Himalayan region or the U.S.-born puppies of such imports.
>
> *U.S.-Born Puppies*
>   from parents born in U.S., Canada, Netherlands   567
>   from parent(s) born in Nepal, India, Tibet   91
>   TOTAL U.S.-BORN   658
>
> *Imported Puppies/Adults*
>   from England, Canada, Netherlands   81
>   from Nepal, India, Tibet   10
>   TOTAL IMPORTED   91

tion until the AKC's championship program supplanted it in 1984.

Since they were not eligible to compete in AKC shows during the early 1970's, Tibbies competed in "rare breed" shows. A milestone on the road to recognition was reached in early 1977 when the AKC approved the Tibetan Spaniel for obedience competition and for conformation competition in the Miscellaneous class. Competition in this class was a precursor to the "regular" classes where the Tibbie would be eligible for AKC championship.

Occasional articles in the dog press attempted to promote the breed to the American public. For example, a 1974 article called the Tibbie "one of the world's most winsome dogs," "treasured pets of the Tibetan nobles for untold centuries," and "a symbol of [the] Buddhist virtue 'to cultivate a heart of love'." Like others of the period, this article perpetuated the myth that Tibbies turned prayer wheels in their native land. Despite this type of publicity and the continued growth of the breed's population, the Tibetan Spaniel remained a *rara avis* in the U.S. Few people other than dog breeders and exhibitors were acquainted with the breed.

Recognition At Last

Under the persuasive leadership of then TSCA President Phyllis Kohler, the long road to recognition finally came to an end. In 1983, the AKC approved the TSCA Stud Book and Breed Standard and authorized the Tibetan Spaniel to compete in regular conformation classes, beginning in 1984. The breed was assigned to the Non-Sporting Group.

Culminating the 12-year effort, eleven Tibbies trotted into the ring in Savannah, Georgia on January 6, 1984. Soon-to-be Am. Ch. Calamalca Cassidy won Best of Breed and went on to place third in the Non-Sporting Group, the breed's first Group placement. Days later, "Casey," bred by Helen Almey (UK) and owned by Herb and Betty Rosen, became the first Tibbie awarded his AKC championship. The first female to win her championship was Am. Ch. Bim's Twin Socks Kamla, R.O.M., bred by Tom and Florence Whiting and owned by Mallory Driskill.

A spate of articles in the dog press touted the Tibbie as "easy keepers," "hardy and rugged," "extremely intelligent, sweet-natured and affectionate, family-oriented and very trusting of other dogs and people," "long-lived," "devoted," "extremely tolerant" and as a breed with a "merry, mischievous heart and spirit." The publicity attending the announcement of impending recognition increased public awareness and intensified breeder interest. Many of

Leo Kearns, the "Founding Father" of the Tibetan Spaniel in the U.S., with GB Ch. Yakrose Chiala of Amcross, imported from M.C. Hourihane and D. Jenkins (U.K.). *Courtesy of the Tibetan Spaniel Club of America.*

Bimbo, born in India in 1967, was brought to the U.S. by Tom and Florence Whiting. He added new genes to the breed in the 1970s.

today's established breeders acquired their first Tibbies around the time of recognition.

Wherefore a Tibbie?

Most American Tibbie breeders started with other breeds, large and small. The diverse list of breeds includes herding dogs such as the Welsh Corgi and Shetland Sheepdog; hounds such as the Basset and Beagle; working dogs such as the Great Pyrenees and Siberian Husky; terriers such as the Australian and Norfolk; non-sporting breeds such as the Lhasa Apso and Schipperke; sporting dogs such as Irish and Gordon Setters; and toy breeds such as the Shih Tzu and Pug. That the Tibbie is loved by owners of such diverse breeds bespeaks their universal appeal.

One breeder says he wanted a "cuddly" breed, another a "quieter" breed and another a "compact" breed. Others loved the "face to die for" and the "exotic and elegant look." However, to people who show dogs, the single most attractive feature of the breed was his easy-care, "shake-and-show" coat. This enables owners to show their own dogs, without professional help.

Perhaps the most memorable reason for choosing the Tibbie came from a breeder who said, "I wanted a dog that my sporting-dog husband could like. At first, he pretended he wasn't interested. Now, the Tibbies own him!" Is it any wonder that, once in the house (and generally on the bed), the Tibetan Spaniel usually replaced his owner's former breeds?

POST-RECOGNITION (1984 TO THE PRESENT)

Registrations of Tibetan Spaniels made substantial gains after recognition, peaking in 1987. In 1990 and 1991, registrations once more spurted upward and then leveled off.

TSCA membership has paralleled the breed's growth. At the time of recognition, members were clustered in the northeastern and mid-Atlantic States with a substantial pocket on the West Coast. Soon, a substantial new group grew in the Midwest, as well as new toe-holds in the West.

At the midpoint of the 1990's, Tibbie owners are more widely distributed throughout the U.S. than ever before. The major concentration has expanded up and down the East Coast, all the way from New England to Florida. Populations in the Midwest, Pacific States and Texas have grown, while those in the Southwest remain stable.

Breeding Notes

After an influx of new breeders around the time of recognition, the number of U.S. litters produced has climbed at a slow pace. Both new and established breeders have concentrated on line-breeding American stock. However, a few dogs imported from the U.K. and Finland have supplemented American genes. Among the British kennels contributing were Braeduke (Wynyard), Kensing (Lilley) and Wildhern (Micklethwait).

To encourage quality breeding, the TSCA introduced a Register of Merit (R.O.M.) program to award titles to sires and dams who produce champion progeny. In 1987, TSCA published the first *Tibetan Spaniels in America* yearbook covering 1984-1986. These biannual yearbooks recap titles awarded and display photos and pedigrees submitted by owners whose dogs have attained titles. Other educational efforts in the post-

GB, Am. Ch. Braeduke Dung-Ka, bred by Ann Wynyard (U.K.) and owned by Phyllis Kohler, is a top producer. Siring 46 champions in the U.S. and U.K., Dung-Ka's descendants literally cover the globe.

The Tibetan Spaniel in the United States

Am. Ch. Calamalca Cassidy, bred by Helen Almey (U.K.) and owned by Herb and Betty Rosen, became the first AKC champion Tibetan Spaniel in 1984. *Meyer photo*

The first female Am. Ch. was Bim's Twin Socks Kamla, ROM, bred by Tom and Florence Whiting and owned by Mallory Driskill. *Charles Tatham photo*

Am. Ch. Phylmarko Shan-Hu, bred and owned by Phyllis Kohler, sired 18 champions. He is a son of GB, Am. Ch. Braeduke Dung-Ka.

Am., GB Ch. Kensing Rusk, ROM, bred by Jane Lilley (U.K.) and owned by Richard and M.C. Jeffery, was 1985 Westminster winner and a top producing sire. *Ashbey photo*

Am. Mex. Ch. Ambrier's Amazing Pumpkin, ROM is the top-producing American sire with 25 champion progeny. Bred by Mallory Driskill and owned by his breeder and Betty Rosen. *Rich Bergman photo*

Am. Ch. Ambrier's Pass the Buck, ROM, bred by Mallory Driskill and owned by Barbara Berg, has 17 champion offspring to his credit. *Lloyd W. Olson Studio photo*

U.S. REGISTRATION OF TIBETAN SPANIELS
1984-1993

Since the AKC first recorded registrations for the Tibetan Spaniel in 1984, 967 registered litters have been born in the U.S, and a total of 2397 Tibetan Spaniels (both U.S.-born and imported) have been registered.

YEAR	AKC RANK	DOGS	(LITTERS)
1984	115	113	(51)
1985	113	129	(44)
1986	109	177	(78)
1987	109	210	(84)
1988	109	184	(72)
1989	107	192	(113)
1990	100	284	(104)
1991	102	354	(139)
1992	102	371	(136)
1993	103	383	(146)

recognition period have included production of the AKC Breed Video on the Tibetan Spaniel and publication of the first breeder's directory in 1988.

Today, 50-60 breeders are active in the U.S. Most are small (one to three litters per year). A sampling of American kennel names, past and present, includes:

    Aki Shima (Berg)
    Ambrier (Driskill)
    Bet'R (Rosen)
    Boda (Howard, Herman)
    Deetree (Robinson)
    Dragonsong (Bradbury)
    Jemari (Jeffery)
    Jo'Jevon (Child, Wright, Crofts)
    Phylmarko (Kohler)
    Tamzil (Craven)
    Tibroke (Dickeson)
    White Acres (Tyte)
    Winsum (Preston)

The Show Scene

Having achieved its goal of recognition, one of TSCA's new goals was to give a National Specialty show. On its way to attaining this goal, TSCA hosted a series of AKC-sanctioned matches between 1985 and 1991. Under AKC rules, a national breed club must complete this requirement before permission for a National Specialty show is granted.

Generally speaking, entries in conformation competition in All Breed shows remained small during this period. An American championship requires 15 points, including two "majors" (three to five points) earned under two different judges. Since the number of championship points awarded depends on the number of Tibbies competing in the show, exhibitors often banded together to make "majors." Group placements were fairly rare. Only a few Tibbies competed in obedience trials.

The 1990's opened with another first for the breed; Am. Ch. Kensing Pongo R.O.M., bred by Jane

Am., Ber., Can. Ch. Fairstar Cho-Sun, bred by Mrs. F. McCartney (U.K.) and owned by Herb and Betty Rosen, was the first Best of Breed winner at Westminter (1984) and an influential sire in the 1980s. *Wm. P. Gilbert photo.*

Am., GB, Can. Ch. Amscor Solo Man, ROM, bred by V. Hourihane (U.K.) and owned by Herb and Betty Rosen, was a Group winner and Best of Breed at Westminster in 1986 and 1987. *Ashbey photo*

AMERICAN TITLE HOLDERS 1984-1994		
YEAR	CHAMPIONSHIP	OBEDIENCE
1984-1986	156	6
1987-1988	116	4
1989-1990	151	5
1991-1992	187	1
1993-1994	190	2
TOTALS	800	18

Lilley (U.K.) and owned by Richard and M. C. Jeffery, became the first Tibbie to win Best in Show at an American All Breed show. Later that year, the first American-bred Tibbie to attain this distinction was Am. Ch. Jo'Jevon Distant Thunder, R.O.M., bred by J. Wright, Y. Crofts and J. Child and owned by White Acre Kennels, Reg. Group placements became more frequent.

In 1992, 125 Tibbies, an unprecedented number of entries in an American show, met in Kentucky to compete in the first AKC-approved TSCA National Specialty show. Accustomed to the small entries in All Breed shows, American enthusiasts were thrilled by the sight of so many Tibbies ranging from puppies to veterans. The annual Specialty shows allow breeders and exhibitors dispersed across the U.S. to meet and "talk Tibbie" as well as compete for coveted placements in a sweepstakes (a puppy showcase) and in the big show itself. Other activities on the Specialty agenda include announcement of the Register of Merit (R.O.M.) certificates for champion-producing sires and dams, social and fund-raising activities, educational seminars and eye examination clinics.

Competition in obedience has remained sparse in the 1990's. However, in 1994, Am. Ch. Jemari Joyous Pippin, N.A., bred by Richard and M.C. Jeffery and owned by Karen Chamberlain, became the first Tibbie to win an agility title. In 1995, Am. Ch. Santera Spitnimage Tumblweed, T.D., bred by Sandra Novocin and owned by Anette Kittleson, became the first American Tibbie, and possibly the only Tibbie in the world, to win a tracking title!

ISSUES FOR THE TWENTY-FIRST CENTURY

Asked to express their views about the future of our breed, certain themes emerge in the concerns of American owners. The principal issues facing Americans in the 21st century are:

- preventing breed exploitation,
- re-homing and rescue,
- preserving the "natural" Tibbie, and
- maintaining genetic health.

Breed Exploitation

Those who newly discover our breed usually marvel that the Tibetan Spaniel is the "best-kept secret" in the world of dogs. In many ways, this statement is true. Many American owners worry that any

Am. Ch. Tashi Tamara of Northwood, ROM, bred by Jeanne Holsapple and formerly owned by Pamela Bradbury (now owned by J. Wright, Y. Crofts and J. Child), has 10 champion offspring. She is the daughter of Tashi Dordja, a Tibbie brought from India by M. Perkins. *K. Booth photo*

The Tibetan Spaniel

Group placing Am. Ch. Ambrier Breakin' All the Rules, ROM, bred by Mallory Driskill and owned by Kay Dickeson, has nine champions to her credit. *Don Petrulis photo*

Am. Ch. Tibroke's Glimpse of Stocking, ROM, bred by Barbara Berg and Kay Dickeson, is a top-producing dam, owned by Mary Garrett Bodel. *Wayne Cott photo*

Am. Ch. Jo'Jevon's Distant Thunder, ROM, bred by J. Wright, Y. Crofts and J. Child and owned by White Acres Knls., Reg., was the first U.S.-bred Best in Show winner and twice Best of Breed at Westminster (1991-'92). *The Standard Image© Photo*

Am. Ch. White Acres Press One, bred by White Acres Knls., Reg., and co-owned by the breeder and Don and Patti Kelley, counts among his wins Best of Breed at Westminster (1994) and two all breed Bests in Show. *The Standard Image© Photo*

Am. Ch. Ambrier's Tsand this Bud for You, bred by Mallory Driskill and Kay Dickeson and owned by Sandra Lidster, won Best of Breed at the 1994 National Specialty. *Joe Rinehart photo*

Multi-Group winner Am. Ch. Tiblaterr's Dressed Tuth Nines, bred by Robert and Martha Brewer and owned by Arlene Tanel, was Best of Breed at Westminster in 1995. *Bill Meyer photo*

publicity (such as this book!) poses a risk to the breed. The risk is that publicity may set in motion a chain of events that leads to popularity and exploitation of the breed.

When the AKC recognized the Tibetan Spaniel in 1984, the joy of attaining a long-sought goal was tempered by the fear that recognition and its attendant publicity would inevitably lead to exploitation. This concern is as valid now as it was in 1984, and most American breeders are rightfully leery of anything that risks popularity and its dire consequences.

TSCA has sought to prevent exploitation of the breed by promoting ethical breeding practices, assuring that Tibbies are placed only in good homes and promoting spaying or neutering of dogs not destined for a breeding career. Since the AKC requires that a national breed club maintain a majority of breeders and exhibitors in its membership, TSCA's membership requirements are the strictest in the world. For example, applicants must demonstrate a substantial commitment to the breed (e.g., exhibiting the breed for two years) and pledge to abide by a Code of Ethics.

The Tibbie is still relatively "unpopular" in the U.S.—in the sense that the public is largely unaware of the breed. Attrition has tended to stabilize the number of active American breeders, and large-scale breeding has not taken hold. Based on the number of litters born, the Tibbie ranks number 103 out of the 137 breeds recognized by the AKC at the close of 1993.

Besides its naturally low rate of reproduction, the breed's low growth rate in the U.S. is influenced by the difficulty of placing the youngsters. Breed enthusiasts are still shocked whenever someone who is not a dog breeder or exhibitor identifies a Tibetan Spaniel.

Am. Ch. Tiara's Double Bubble of Tabu, bred and owned by Becky Johnson, is a Group winner and was Best of Opposite Sex at the first TSCA National Specialty (1992). *Bill Meyer photo*

Even ten plus years after recognition, the average American has never heard of a Tibetan Spaniel and, even when face to face with one, rarely recognizes him for what he is.

To Tibbie or Not to Tibbie

Jim Milke recalls approaching a couple while walking his two Tibbies, one sable and the other black-and-white, in a park. The woman stopped and, admiring the dogs, asked what breed they were. Accustomed to this query, Mr. Milke politely replied that his dogs were Tibetan Spaniels. "No, they aren't!" her husband interjected, "I know what they are. They're mixed Pekingese." Taken aback, Mr. Milke explained that the Tibetan Spaniel is a distinct breed, thought to be the forerunner of the Pekingese. "No, it isn't!" the husband retorted, "They're mixed Pekingese, and that's it." With this pronouncement, he marched off, a look of smug self-assurance on his face, leaving Mr. Milke with a look of astonishment on his.

Knowledgeable breeders understand that little or no profit is made in the ethical breeding of dogs. While they may complain about placing puppies of a breed that has no name recognition and, moreover, is usually confused for some other breed, they concede that difficulty in selling puppies has a plus side. Since profit-motivated dog breeders who run "puppy mills" want frequent, large litters and easy sales, small litters and difficulty in selling the puppies has, for the most part, discouraged their interest in the American Tibbie.

Re-Homing and Rescue

The TSCA Code of Ethics requires member breeders to re-home Tibbies whose owners are unable

Am. Ch. Ambrier Boda Zelicious Zima, bred by Shirley Howard, Kathy Herman and Mallory Driskill and owned by Mallory Driskill, was Best Puppy at the 1995 TSCA National Specialty. *Jeane Harkins photo*

to keep them. Although voluntary compliance with this provision is thought to be successful, abandoned Tibbies are sometimes found in animal shelters. In addition, a number of "lost" Tibbies are found wandering each year. More troubling are isolated cases of Tibbies discovered in deplorable conditions.

In response to renewed concerns about Tibbies needing re-homing, TSCA formalized the Tibetan Spaniel Rescue Service in 1992. Regional rescue coordinators, appointed by the club, rely on volunteers to supervise their local areas. Acting on their own initiative, these volunteers alert anyone who may come in contact with a lost or abandoned Tibbie (e.g., shelter operators and veterinarians) that rescue is available. One such volunteer, Shirley Howard, distributes fliers displaying pictures of Tibbies to shelters in three Midwestern States and relies on them to contact her if they take in a dog that even "remotely resembles" a Tibbie.

The "Natural" Tibbie

Shown in the Non-Sporting Group, the American Tibbie appears in the ring with glamorous breeds such as the Lhasa Apso, Standard and Miniature Poodles and Bichon Frise and visually striking breeds such as the Dalmatian and Bulldog. Although a judge compares the Tibbie to its own Breed Standard and not to the other dogs in the ring, the perception remains that the Tibbie is "competing against" these breeds.

Concerned that breeders and exhibitors would be tempted to gain a competitive advantage by converting the "natural" Tibbie into an overcoated and overgroomed breed, the American Breed Standard endorses the natural coat and expressly prohibits trimming other than the underside of the paws. This strict presentation requirement was designed to forestall any attempt to cultivate exaggerated coats and/or to introduce elaborate trimming and styling.

TSCA resolved to enforce the "natural" presentation standard by educating judges and exhibitors. Anticipating impending recognition, TSCA distributed

Am. Ch. White Acres Fame N' Fortune, bred and owned by White Acres Knls., Reg., won Best of Breed at the 1995 TSCA National Specialty. *Animal World Studio photo*

Phyllis Mayhew's "Interpretation of the Standard" from her book entitled *The Tibetan Spaniel* to licensed judges of Tibbies for their use as a guideline to supplement the new Breed Standard. The first judges' seminar took place in 1984. A decade later, the TSCA published the *Tibetan Spaniel Illustrated Breed Standard*, partly in an effort to reinforce the "natural" presentation.

It is fair to say that most U.S. exhibitors comply with the spirit of the Standard and present their Tibbies in unaltered condition. Nonetheless, established breeders and exhibitors must continue to educate new breeders and exhibitors, as well as judges, to appreciate the elegant understatement of the natural coat.

Genetic Health

Although healthy and long-lived, a number of problems that are influenced by heredity have been reported in American Tibbies. Although all evidence indicates that these illnesses are extremely rare, breeders must nonetheless learn how to prevent them in order to protect the future health of the breed.

In the early 1990's, American breeders were saddened to learn that some imported and American-bred Tibbies carried the gene for progressive retinal atrophy (PRA). Since these Tibbies had been used in American breeding programs, TSCA responded by disseminating the pedigrees of the affected dogs, establishing a PRA Registry and exchanging information with European clubs. The American Registry, which is voluntary, records and publishes the names of Tibbies *that have tested clear for PRA*. Other initiatives included a seminar on eye diseases and publication of facts about PRA in the club newsletter.

Although indisputably a tragedy, the outbreak of PRA served to alert American breeders to the risk of this and other hereditary diseases. Rather than lapse into isolationism, it is important to continue this invaluable international cooperation and coordination on all health issues. Each individual breeder must also take an active part in preventing propagation of genetic diseases.

Chapter Five

The Tibetan Spaniel Around the World

In an effort to form a world-wide network of people who own and breed Tibetan Spaniels, the Tibetansk Spaniel Klubb (TSK) of Sweden recently contacted all known clubs that represent the Tibetan Spaniel and, where no club exists, individual owners from that country. By early 1995, 18 countries had joined the Tibetan Spaniel International Group. It appears that the time for such an international organization is ripe. Increasingly, Tibetan Spaniel breeders and owners are realizing that they have interests and concerns in common with breeders and owners in other countries as well as their own.

After a brief overview of the breed's status worldwide, the remainder of this chapter describes the status of the breed in selected countries. These thumbnail sketches focus on the growth of the breed and, as a gauge of the country's stewardship of the breed, on the activities of the breed club. I also asked breed enthusiasts, from each country, to address the issues that face the Tibetan Spaniel of the future—that is, their hopes and fears for the future of the breed in their countries.

THE WORLD AT A GLANCE

Finland ranks first in the world in annual registrations of Tibetan Spaniels, the eighth most popular breed there. Norway, the U.K. and Sweden form a bloc in which the breed flourishes while, in several other European countries, smaller but solid populations are entrusted to a few dedicated owners and breeders. Although some European owners are relatively isolated in their own countries, such as those in Italy and Slovenia, there is ongoing international communication among many European enthusiasts.

Travelling west across the Atlantic, the U.S. population of Tibbies approaches that of Norway and the U.K. but is much less numerous in proportion to her human population. Elsewhere in North America, Canada has few Tibbies, and I have no information on Mexico.

Crossing the Pacific Ocean to the southern hemisphere, Australia and New Zealand maintain steady populations of Tibbies, despite a sense of being somewhat "cut off" from the rest of the Tibbie world. However, new initiatives may soon better link the Tibbie people "Down Under" with those in North America and Europe.

I have been provided little information on Tibetan Spaniels in South America, Asia and Africa. With the exception of South Africa, where a lone breeder struggles on, the organizations that replied to my inquiries indicate no Tibetan Spaniel activity in their countries.

In most countries, the Tibetan Spaniel is represented by a club that also represents an assortment of other Tibetan or Asian breeds. A representative or committee within the club may provide a focal point for Tibbie interests and issues. In most countries where Tibbies are more numerous, a breed club dedicated to the Tibetan Spaniel has splintered from the multi-breed club.

Let's now take a look at some of the countries where Tibbies live.

AUSTRALIA

Australia is made up of six states, a territory and a capital district, each of which has its own kennel organization. These eight organizations are members of the Australian National Kennel Council (ANKC), the federal governing organization. The ANKC reports that annual registrations of Tibetan Spaniels Australia-wide averaged 185-188 during the 1990's.

Breeding Notes

Most Tibbies live in the southeast in the states of Victoria (where there are about 15 breeders) and New South Wales (where there are about 12 breeders). In the state of South Australia, the sole breeder is Ken Talbot (Toreana). Across the continent, several owners, with about 20 Tibbies among them, and lone breeder Cindy Stack (Wencyn) live in vast Western Australia. Only a few breeders live in Queensland in the northeast, and only two owners reside on the island state of Tasmania to the south. I have no information from the Northern Territory.

As a country of continental proportions, Australia has faced problems similar to those faced in establishing the Tibetan Spaniel in the U.S. and Canada—small numbers and great distances.

Aust. Ch. Toreana Junki, bred and owned by Ken Talbot, is the current top-winning Australian Tibbie.

Myra Livett (Leagay) imported the first Tibetan Spaniels, Aust. Ch. Skelbeck Cherry Bud (a bitch) and Braeduke Numa (a dog), to Australia in 1974. Delma Clatworthy (Koorabar) also imported a pair in 1974. Both pairs produced their first litters in 1975, with Mrs. Clatworthy's litter the earlier by seven weeks. Among the programs that commenced in the late 1970's and early '80's were Judy Gard (Barrajy), Mrs. J. L. Mahony (Tygil), John Jones (Karakorum) and Mr. Talbot. Several of these programs were based on U.K. and New Zealand imports as well as Australian-bred stock. A recent arrival is Aust. Ch. Braeduke La-La Babu, bred by Ann Wynyard (UK) and imported by Michele Waterman (Buquet).

In addition to the established kennels mentioned above, several new Australian breeders are getting started. Most breeders are small, producing one or two litters each year. A sampling of Australian kennel names, past and present, includes:

> Barrajy (Gard)
> Beauandel (Fenwick)
> Buquet (Waterman)
> Koorabar (Clatworthy)
> Karakorum (Jones)
> Leagay (Livett)
> Toreana (Talbot)
> Tygil (Mahony)
> Wencyn (Stack)

The Club Scene

Due mainly to Australia's state-based kennel organizations, several clubs represent the Tibetan Spaniel. These include the Tibetan Spaniel Association of Victoria, Inc. (founded 1995), the Oriental Breeds Association of Victoria, Inc. (1994) and the Asian Dog Breeds Club of New South Wales, Inc. (1966).

Aust. Ch. Tygil Dikki, bred by Lorna Mahony and owned by Judy Gard, won Best of Breed at Royal shows seven times. He also has five Best in Group awards. "Harry," remembers Judy, "was a great ambassador for the breed and perfect gentleman."

The Tibetan Spaniel Around the World

Aust., N.Z. Ch. Braeduke Ming-Mo, bred by Ann Wynyard (U.K.) and owned by Ken Talbot of South Australia, counts among her descendants 28 Australian champions. *Ann McSweeney photo*

The first club dedicated solely to the Tibbie, the newly-formed Tibetan Spaniel Club of Victoria has 70 plus members Australia-wide and is the only all-Tibbie club in the southern hemisphere. Its mission is to promote responsible ownership and breeding. The 50-member Oriental Breeds Association of Victoria, Inc. represents 14 breeds, among them the Tibetan Spaniel. Five hundred miles away in New South Wales, 15 of the 87 members of the Asian Dog Breeds Club of NSW, Inc. own Tibbies. Australia's breed clubs share useful veterinary information as well as show results, training tips, poems and stories and social notices in their newsletters.

The Show Scene

Regardless of where a Tibbie is shown, uniform ANKC rules for attaining his Australian championship apply. The best of each sex is awarded a C.C., and each C.C. is worth a total of six points plus one point per dog defeated. A championship requires 100 points with a maximum of two C.C.'s from a single judge.

The NSW club sponsors two shows each year, and each features one of its breeds. The Tibetan Spaniel Feature Show took place in 1995 and drew an entry of 40 Tibbies. At present, the largest Tibbie entries occur at Royal shows, one in each state each year. The prestigious Royal Melbourne, where 6,096 dogs competed in 1994, is one of these. In their first showing in Australia, in 1979, two Tibetan Spaniels were exhibited at the Royal Melbourne. In 1994, 53 Tibbies competed. Traditionally, the Royal shows have been the rare occasions on which widely dispersed breeders and exhibitors were able to meet and discuss Tibbie matters. Other than the Royal shows, a typical Tibbie entry in a show in eastern Australia averages 10-25, but a western show may draw only one or two entries. All Tibbie owners in Australia are doubtless hopeful that the first all-Tibbie Championship show will take place in the near future.

Formerly shown in the Non-Sporting Group where it was "lost" among larger and/or more showy breeds, the Tibetan Spaniel was transferred to the Toy Group in 1985. Although the breed is certainly more successful in the Toy Group, many exhibitors nonetheless express frustration that the Tibetan Spaniel wins too few placements in Group competition. With the greater consistency in the appearance of Australian Tibbies and increased number of competitors as well as improved judges' education, exhibitors hope that the Tibetan Spaniel's chances in the Group will improve.

Aust. Ch. Chakpori Dolma, bred by Anna de Jager (N.Z.) and owned by John Jones, of New South Wales, won Best of Breed at the Tibetan Spaniel Feature Show in 1995. *Barbara Kilworth photo*

Thoughts on the Future

Of chief concern to Australian owners and breeders are breeder ethics, judges' education, better communication within Australia and closer ties with the international Tibetan Spaniel community. Although many breeders voice concern about injudicious breeding practices, health issues do not crop up in discussions as they often do in Europe and North America. For example, there have been no documented cases of PRA and breeders do not routinely obtain eye examinations before breeding. As Australian enthusiasts prepare to celebrate the silver jubilee of Australian Tibbies, there appears to be a rejuvenated commitment to our breed and optimism about the Tibetan Spaniel's future in the land "Down Under."

BELGIUM

The Société Royale Saint-Hubert, the national kennel organization of Belgium, registered only 63 Tibetan Spaniels in all of the years between 1980-1993. Happily, three litters were born in 1994 alone.

Breeding Notes

The only known breeders of Tibetan Spaniels in Belgium are Magda Vuylsteke-Briers (Falconsnest) and Ilse Mittemeijer (Tiara-Su). Mrs. Briers first imported breeding stock from the Sommerlysts kennel (Denmark) about 1990. She has also imported from the v. 't Burgstse Hof kennel (Netherlands). The Tibbies now owned by Mrs. Mittemeijer were brought from the U.K. by their former owners, Pauline Smith and Edith Atwell.

The Club Scene

The Tibetaanse Rassenclub van België (Flemish) or Club des Races Thibétaines de Belgique (French), founded in 1969, represents the Tibetan Spaniel in Belgium. Mrs. Mittemeijer and Mrs. Briers are the only members who own Tibbies. The club publishes a newsletter, sponsors social activities, and conducts ringcraft classes. It also promotes its breeds by sponsoring an "Exposition de Club," where C.A.C.'s are offered, and awards an annual club championship in each breed.

The Show Scene

Entries at large Belgian shows average 10-12 Tibbies, including some entries from outside Belgium. Since so few Tibbies are shown in this part of Europe, judges' education is considered a priority.

WORLD REGISTRATIONS IN 1993

Registration data are the only available gauge of Tibetan Spaniel population. While useful as an indicator for comparing populations among countries, do not base conclusions about actual populations on these data. Here is a sampling of worldwide registrations:

Australia	185*
Canada	6
Denmark	46
Finland	1150
France	62
Germany	5
Ireland	150*
Netherlands	12
New Zealand	59
Norway	430
South Africa	1
Spain	10
Sweden	327
U.K.	386
U.S.	383

*Average

Belg., Neth., Ger., Int., Lux. Ch. Sommerlyst's Mishog Nag Po, bred by Ragnhild Poulsen (Denmark) and owned by Magda Vuylsteke-Briers, is the top-winning Belgian Tibbie.

Thoughts on the Future

Like others who have struggled to introduce the breed to their countries, Belgium's owners are puzzled by the lack of interest in a breed with such a charming personality. There is no demand for puppies, and most must be placed in surrounding countries. Nonetheless, they hope that Belgium's proximity to countries where interest in Tibbies is growing (such as France and Germany) will ultimately encourage the growth of the breed in Belgium as well.

CANADA

It is fair to say that Tibbies have never "caught on" in Canada, which is sad considering that the climate there is ideal for a cold-loving breed. Barbara McConnell (Pechenga), who produces the bi-monthly newsletter, comments that the Tibetan Spaniel has only a "tenuous toe-hold." In the 1990's, registrations average 20 puppies per year.

Breeding Notes

The breed started in Canada during the 1970's with British stock owned by Elaine Vaughan (Rowfant). The Canadian Kennel Club (CKC) recognized the breed in 1980, after the requirement for foundation stock of 25 Tibbies was met by nine imported dogs and sixteen Canadian-bred puppies. Jenny Chalmers (Tritou) brought in other British Tibbies, and Diane Lilley (Timothy) later took on Mrs. Chalmers' stock. Lois Tryon (Tryon) and her daughter Pat Antliff were also involved in establishing the breed during the 1980's.

Today, the few Canadian breeders each produce only one or two litters per year. Litter registrations peaked at eleven in 1988. In the '90's, registered litters average only six per year.

The Club Scene

The Tibetan Spaniel Club of Canada (TSCC) was founded in 1979. The TSCC's objectives are to protect and promote the breed. Although its members number 25-30 (mostly in Canada with a few in the U.S. and U.K.), the club is not recognized by the CKC and does not host matches. However, its newsletter links widely dispersed owners, breeders and exhibitors.

Can. Ch. Seng Gay of Rowfant, owned by Pat Antliffe, was the first Tibbie to be awarded a Canadian championship.

The Show Scene

Tibbies are exhibited at fewer than one in ten Canadian shows. Entries average only two Tibbies, and the largest entry has been ten (back in 1988). Despite the small number of Tibbies competing, 58 have become Canadian champions, and many have won Group placements. The Tibetan Spaniel is shown in the Non-Sporting Group. The first Tibbie exhibited in Canada was Can. Ch. Tritou Ha-Na, bred by Jenny Chalmers and owned by Diane Lilley. The first to win his championship was Can. Ch. Seng Gay of Rowfant, bred by Elaine Vaughan and owned by Pat Antliff. The second, Can. Ch. Timothy's Bam-bi, bred by Diane Lilley, still holds the record as Canada's top winner (set in 1980); he was also the first to place in Group-level competition and the first Group winner. Tritou Jeremy, bred by Jenny Chalmers and owned by Donna Bradley, was the first C.D. The highest score in obedience was achieved by Can. Ch. Pechenga's Tibouchina, C.D., T.T., bred by Ms. McConnell and owned by Joanne Baal. Some Americans show in Canada, and a few Canadians in the U.S.

Thoughts on the Future

The status of the Tibetan Spaniel in Canada today is the same as it was 15 years ago. The immense distances separating small pockets of Canadian Tibbies

Int., Dan., Lux., Ger. Ch. U Wong of Jo-Gua-Kang was bred by Irmgard Weinekamp (Germany) and is owned by Bente Rytter Jørgensen.

impedes growth and improvement of the breed. Breeders rarely use distant breeding stock, and exhibitors rarely travel to distant shows. In fact, if the CKC adopts proposals to require "major" wins in awarding Canadian championships, the few Tibbie exhibitors may not be able to gather the entry required for a "major."

While Canadian enthusiasts appreciate that their small numbers have spared them many of the problems that go along with popularity (e.g., increased health risks, less friendly competition), a little growth spurt would nonetheless be welcome. "We are very vulnerable," explains Ms. McConnell, "If only one person decides to drop out of the breed, a major part of the fancy dissolves. I would like to see just enough increase so that we could feel secure."

DENMARK

Denmark has a solid and growing population of Tibbies. In the '70's, registrations averaged little more than two per year. Dropping out 1980 (when none were registered) and 1989 (when registrations spiked to 41), registrations averaged 12 per year in the 1980's. However, beginning with 1989, average annual registrations have jumped to 50. It is estimated that 400-500 Tibetan Spaniels make Denmark their home.

Breeding Notes

The first breeding stock in Denmark was probably a pair that Ann Wynyard (U.K.) sent to Kurt Brendstrup, in 1966. Although litters were born to this pair, the breeding history of Danish Tibbies really began with Bente Rytter Jørgensen (Tenzing), in 1976. Mrs. Jørgensen's first import was Fanfare for Skya Snar, a bitch bred by Constance van den Boom, from the Netherlands. She also imported stock from Germany, including Int., Ger., Dan., Lux. Ch. U Wong of Jo-Gua-Kang, bred by Irmgard Weinekamp, and later from Mrs. Wynyard. Besides Mrs. Jørgensen, there are now about 15 registered kennels plus several private breeders in Denmark.

The Club Scene

The Fællesklubben for Junderacer uden Specialklub, a club for breeds that do not have sufficient numbers to form their own club, represents the Tibetan Spaniel. An elected breed coordinator oversees matters related to the breed. About 35 members own Tibbies.

Bred by Mrs. Jørgensen, Int. Ch. Tenzing Losang is also a champion in Denmark, Germany, the Netherlands, France, Monaco, Italy and Austria as well as winner of numerous prestigious shows.

The Show Scene

A typical Tibetan Spaniel entry at a Danish show in 1994 was 16 Tibbies. Since quarantine restrictions have been lifted, Tibbies from Finland, Sweden and Norway are now allowed to travel to shows in Denmark. Danish Tibbies are also exhibited outside Denmark.

Thoughts on the Future

Speaking for Danish enthusiasts, Ragnhild Poulsen, the breed representative, comments that the Danish breeder's top priority must be to maintain the breed's charming temperament, without which the Tibetan Spaniel is not a Tibbie. Next, sound health is important. Although no Danish Tibbie has been diagnosed with PRA, eye examinations, within the year prior to breeding, are mandatory. Third, maintaining the breed's natural beauty is important. And finally, all of the above should be accomplished, Mrs. Poulsen warns, without in-breeding or very close line-breeding.

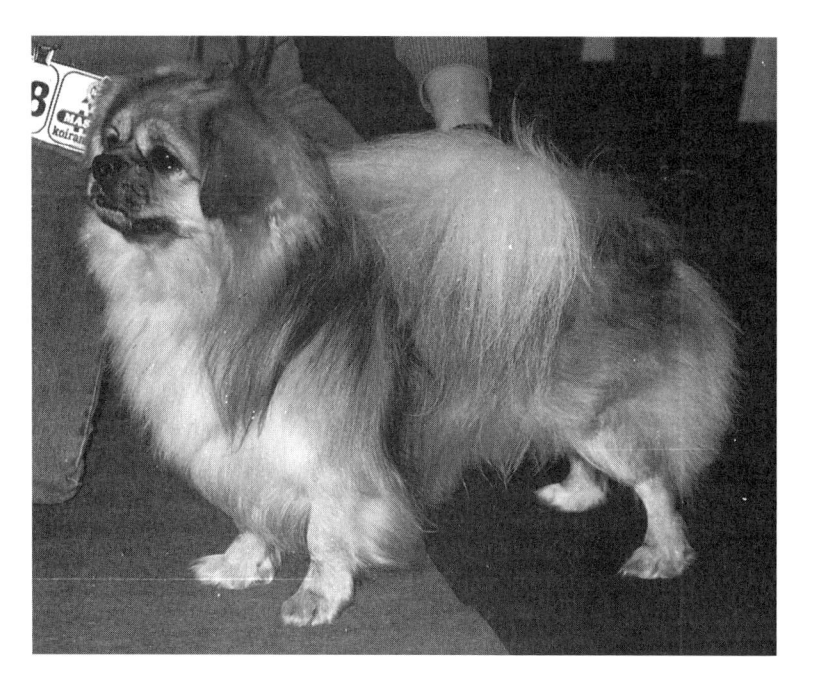

Int., Fin. Ch. Milarepa of Zlazano, bred by Paula Kangassalo and owned by Maija Perttola, is a top-winning Finnish Tibbie. *Venäläinen photo*

FINLAND

Currently, the Tibetan Spaniel is the eighth most popular breed (in terms of registrations) in Finland. Over the last decade, registrations have averaged nearly 1,100 per year. Known as Suomi to her residents, Finland may be the only country in the world where the Tibetan Spaniel is widely recognized outside the ranks of dog breeders and exhibitors.

Breeding Notes

Not so long ago, the Finnish public thought that Tibetan Spaniels were Pekingese, as they do everywhere else. The first Tibbies arrived in Finland in 1964, imported from the U.K. by Paula Kangassalo (of Zlazano). By the end of the decade, four Finnish breeders were active. In the past thirty years, Finnish breeders have tapped many prominent British lines as well as lines from Sweden, Denmark, the U.S. and Ireland.

YEAR	TOTAL IMPORTED
1964-73	32
1974-83	32
1984-93	66

Although a few breeders produce large numbers of puppies (ten or more litters per year), most are small (one to three litters). I am also told that most Finnish breeders are young people. As you may surmise, based on the number of registered Tibbies, there are many breeders in Finland. Of the 225 breeders listed in the 1993 yearbook, about 75 are the most active. A complete list is available from the breed club. Here is a sampling of Finnish kennel names, past and present:

Central Point (Keskinen)
Chu-Shun (Sarin)
Fieldlan (Karlström)
Habanas (Amperla)
Jadelia (Rautapuro)
Lecibsin (Kuusisto)
Olazza (Pekkanen)
Polarsun (Kinnari)
Saffron (Linnus)
Sajasan (Vestelin)
Seduhin (Säviaho)
Silences (Viitala)
Tashi-Gong (Venäläinen)
Toyway (Leiviskä)
Zlazano (Kangassalo)

The national kennel organization, the Suomen Kennelliitto (Finska Kennelklubben), awards the coveted Vuolasvirta prize to meritorious breeders. Among those honored have been Orvokki Keskinen (Central Point), Salme Vestelin (Sajasan), Erro and Kirsti

Fin. Ch. Chu-Shun Lejja, bred by Eeva Sarin and owned by Tiina Pentinmäki, was top-winning Finnish Tibbie in 1994.

Karlström (Fieldlan), Pirrko Linnus (Saffron), Katriina Venäläinen (Tashi-Gong) and Jouko Leiviskä (Toyway).

The Club Scene

The Suomen Tiibettiläiset ry (a club) formed in 1971 to represent Tibetan breeds. The Tiibetinspanielit ry, a sub-group devoted to the Tibetan Spaniel, formed in 1978. In 1993, the Tiibetinspanielit ry was authorized to be the sole representative of the breed. Its 1,700 members include pet owners as well as breeders and exhibitors.

As examples of its activities, the club organizes competitive and social events, monitors the health status of breed, recommends puppy prices and stud fees, advises on reproductive matters, plans judges' education and tracks the progress of the breed. The club yearbook publishes judges' critiques as well as photos, pedigrees and the results of health examinations. The club's superlative quarterly magazine is of interest to all members—pet owners as well as breeders and exhibitors. Its contents range from the *Jami* cartoon strip by Päivi Leppikangas to show results to informative articles. Each issue contains about 60 photos of Tibbies.

The Show Scene

Finnish exhibitors enjoy three Specialty shows each year. Entries in these and other large shows exceed 100 Tibbies, with the record at 155. Entries average 45 Tibbies at smaller national shows and 70 Tibbies at international shows. Respected specialist (breeder) judges from the U.K. are often invited to judge Finnish shows.

Conformation competition is predictably fierce. From 1964-1994, about 420 Tibetan Spaniels became Finnish champions. It is estimated that about 10-20 Finnish Tibbies participate in obedience and agility competitions, and Tibbies accompany several junior handlers into the ring.

Thoughts on the Future

The top-priority issues among Finnish enthusiasts are breeder ethics and health. The breed club's breeding regulations are comprehensive. For example, in any year, no one stud dog should father a number of puppies greater than 3% of the previous year's total registrations. This provision reduces the risk of any one popular stud dog transmitting a genetic problem to a large proportion of Tibbie puppies. The breeding regulations also require eye and patellar exams of prospective sires and dams. Although these regulations are voluntary, the breed club publishes a list of PRA-checked Tibbies and the results of patella and hip examinations in its magazine and yearbook.

PRA is the health issue most discussed in Finnish Tibbie circles at the moment. Nine cases have been diagnosed in Finnish dogs. This is a small number considering the Tibbie population there, but some breeders voice concern that other Finnish Tibbies may be carriers. In 1988, more than 100 Tibbies' eyes were examined; today, about 250 examinations take place each year. Although a total of 1300 exams have been conducted, only about 15% of litters are born to sires and dams that have both been examined in the previous two years. The breed club hopes to improve these statistics by persuading the national kennel organization to make eye examinations mandatory (as was recently done in Sweden).

Other conditions causing concern are patellar luxation and progressive nephropathy (PNP). Out of 800 Tibbies whose patellas have been examined, most results were normal or only mild luxation. Hip results have been good, and only three cases of PNP were identified.

It is oddly satisfying to know that there is a country in which lay people actually understand what a wonderful breed the Tibetan Spaniel is. And yet, sadly, we all know that the popularity of a breed puts it at risk. I speak for enthusiasts everywhere in expressing the hope that the popularity of the Tibetan Spaniel in Finland does not lead to its exploitation and in wishing the Tiibetinspanielit ry success in its efforts to promote ethical breeding and maintain the health of the Finnish *tipsu*.

FRANCE

Growing steadily in the 1990's, registrations of French Tibbies average 168 puppies per year. Imports average two per year.

Breeding Notes

Although a number of British Tibbies were exported to France in the early 1970's, the first Tibetan Spaniel of known origin was registered by the Société Centrale Canine (SCC), France's national kennel organization, in 1973. However, little progress was made until, in 1981, Mrs. Brouilly (de Rongbuk) and Simonne Chauvin-Daroux (de la Nerto) commenced programs with imports from the U.K. Raymonde Dufourg (Wand'Ioni) followed suit shortly afterwards.

By 1987, twelve breeders were active. The SCC's statistics now show these numbers of breeders producing one or more litters:

YEAR	BREEDERS*
1991	43
1992	55
1993	58

*These figures may be slightly inflated by "one-litter-only" breeders.

The Club Scene

The Club des Chiens Tibétains de France (CCTF), which also represents the Lhasa Apso, Shih Tzu and Tibetan Terrier, is the national breed club for Tibetan Spaniels. Although CCTF has existed for about ten years, the SCC, France's national kennel organization, recognized the club only in 1994. A two year probationary period will end in 1996. (Before 1994, the Club des Chiens du Tibet, which is no longer affiliated with the SCC, represented the breed.) About 100 of CCTF's 500 members own Tibbies, and a few of these are active breeders.

Besides publishing a newsletter, *Le Lien Tibétain*, CCTF organizes social and competitive events. CCTF also hopes to hold eye examination clinics and provide educational opportunities for judges in the near future.

The Show Scene

In 1981, the first Tibbie to win a French championship was Fr. Ch. Ramdouk, a female brought from Nepal and owned by Elizabeth LeCoq. The first male champion was Int., Lux., Fr. Ch. Tomaran's Gwe-N-Daw, bred by T. Sergeant and owned by Mrs. Chauvin-Daroux. Although the number of entries in French shows is unpredictable, 22 Tibbies were entered in CCTF's first Nationale d'Élevage (specialty show), in 1994. Other major shows may attract 10-20 Tibbies. Although most of the Tibbies exhibited are French, the largest shows also draw foreign entries. Fourteen Tibetan Spaniels were awarded French championships from 1989 through 1993; 14 French-registered Tibbies were awarded International championships during the same period.

Thoughts on the Future

One of CCTF's first undertakings has been to convene a committee to formulate a "coherent breeding policy to educate

Fr. Ch. Échoubi de Tatsienlou, bred and owned by Sylvie Sanchez, was top Tibbie in 1992 and Best of Breed at CCTF's first Nationale d'Élevage.

The current generation of German Tibbies is represented by these Amrita's puppies born in 1994. They were bred by Wilhelm Fleuchaus.

breeders [by] helping them build sensible breeding programmes avoiding the use of bloodlines with suspected inherited diseases or serious physical faults...." The proposed policy includes a grading system for prospective sires and dams, based on criteria such as eye examinations and show wins. Since continental judges evaluate the mouth strictly, one point that the committee hopes to address is the improvement of the mouth. Another point concerns permissible color designations for the breed. Although no documented case of PRA has been found in France, French breeders also consider health issues a high priority.

The number of Tibbies exhibited in France is just beginning to expand. It is gratifying for breeders and exhibitors to meet people who now recognize the Tibetan Spaniel. On the other hand, French breeders and owners are aware of the risks of rapid breed growth. Although the breed's start in France was erratic, the *épagnuel du Tibet* now appears to be on solid footing.

GERMANY

With registrations averaging only 13 per year in the last three years, the Tibetan Spaniel has only a toe-hold in Germany. This is somewhat surprising since, when Mrs. Wynyard's *Dogs of Tibet and the History of the Tibetan Spaniel* was published, the breed seemed to be off to a good start in Germany. Given the small population, it is understandable that *Der Tibet-Spaniel* is not well-represented at shows; five to seven Tibbies is a good entry.

Breeding Notes

Although Tibbies were in Germany by 1970, it is not known which was first or when the first litter was born. For several years, Irmgard Wienekamp (Jo-Gya-Kang) imported many Tibbies from breeders in the U.K. and established a solid program that produced top winners including Bente Rytter Jørgensen's Int., Ger., Dan., Lux. Ch. U Wong of Jo-Gua-Kang (Denmark).

It is not clear how many Tibbie breeders are in Germany today; information from one breed club indicates that fewer than five members are breeders. Wilhelm Fleuchaus (Amrita), one of the active breeders, imported his first bitch, Flahs of Eulyn, in 1968.

The Club Scene

One of the three clubs that represent the breed is the Internationale Klub für Tibetische Hunderassen e.V. (KTR). Founded in 1967, the KTR also represents the Tibetan Terrier, Lhasa Apso and Tibetan Mastiff. The stated purpose of the KTR is to "unite friends, owners and breeders of Tibetan dogs, who have made it their goal to contribute to the understanding of the history, the cultural significance and the traditional types of Tibetan dog breeds...and to support the breeding of Tibetan purebred dogs for the purpose of the preservation and future security of their healthy constitution, their characteristic appearance and their special nature." Twenty-four KTR members are Tibbie owners from within and outside Germany.

Consistent with its objective, KTR's breeding regulations are comprehensive and reflect the membership's concern over health issues. For example, the regulations on genetic diseases require eye examinations before every breeding, no longer than eight weeks before breeding for a bitch and no longer than six months before breeding for a dog, through eight years of age. Breeders are required to report cases of genetic diseases such as PRA and hip dysplasia. These reports may be released to other KTR members for breeding purposes and are regularly published.

IRELAND

The annual registration of Tibetan Spaniel puppies over the past three years has averaged about 150, the strongest showing since the Irish Kennel Club, the national kennel organization, first recognized the breed in 1968.

Breeding Notes

Aileen Young (Balgay), from Scotland, may be credited with introducing the breed to Irish show rings when she traveled there to campaign her dogs in the 1970's. In fact, her Ir. Ch. Balgay A-Li-Ka-Li was the first Tibbie awarded an Irish championship. M. C. Moorhead (Benagh), the first Irish breeder, brought in her foundation bitch, Clawson Me-Tsag, from the U.K. in the 1970's. Before Miss Moorhead's early death, Benagh Tibbies were exported to the U.K., Canada and Finland. In the late '70's, Peggy Walsh and Betty Flynn (Waesfjord) and Peter Murphy (Kilmologue) commenced their programs. Mr. Murphy, who recently died, helped many of today's active kennels get started by generously placing fine Tibbies with them.

Today, about ten active breeders are members of the Tibetan Spaniel Association of Ireland. Most of these breeders are small, producing only one or two litters per year. Here is a sampling of Irish kennel names, past and present:

Amichiri (Mulcahy)
Avigdor (Moran)
Benagh (Moorhead)
Brooklodge (Buckley)
Kilmologue (Murphy)
Lahume (Hurley)
Milbetan (Clancey)
Waesfjord (Walsh and Flynn)

The Club Scene

Formed in 1982, the purpose of the 35-member Tibetan Spaniel Association of Ireland is to promote the breed for showing and breeding. In 1994, the Association's first breed seminar included workshops on judging and heredity. In the same year, the Association sponsored the first eye examination clinic for Tibbies, and 60 Tibbies tested clear for PRA. The Association also produces a newsletter/yearbook.

Ir., GB Ch. Brooklodge CoCo's Clown, bred by Vivien Buckley and owned by Kathleen O'Sullivan, was Annual Champion of 1992. Rob Richardson photo.

The Show Scene

The largest showing of Irish Tibbies may be seen at the Association's yearly Championship show where 70-90 entries compete for honors. A large entry of 50-60 Tibbies competes in the annual Open show. The St. Patrick's Day show in Dublin, the most prestigious Irish show, has recently attracted entries of 60-70 Tibbies. The 24 all-breed Championship shows in Ireland each year typically draw an entry of about 30 Tibbies. Besides these shows, Tibbies compete in a Championship show for the Utility Group breeds.

Two Green Stars, the Irish C.C.'s, are offered for the Tibetan Spaniel entry at almost all Championship shows. One is awarded to the best unbeaten dog and the other to the best unbeaten bitch. Each Green Star is worth one to ten points. To attain an Irish championship, a Tibbie must win Green Stars worth a total of 40 points, and at least four of the Green Stars must be "major" Stars worth five to ten points each. The calculation of the point value of a Green Star offered at a given show is based on the number of dogs and bitches shown that day, but also considers the previous year's entries in the breed. In a nutshell, the greater the number of last year's entries, the greater the number of entries required for a major Green Star this year. Of the breeds in the Irish Utility Group, the Tibetan Spaniel has the greatest number of entries.

As of this writing, 54 Tibbies have won Irish championships. In 1978, the first Irish-bred champion was Ir. Ch. Waesfjord Little Yellow Peril bred by Mrs. J. Wynne Jones and owned by Peggy Walsh and Betty Flynn. After Ir. Ch. Ballymore Tarim, a black-and-tan bitch owned by Peter Murphy, became the first Tibbie to win a Utility Group (1977), four others have won Group competition. As yet, none has broken through to win an all-breed Best in Show.

A coveted title is the Irish Kennel Club's "Annual Champion" awarded to the top-winning dog or bitch that has garnered at least 30 points. The 1994 Annual

Ir. Ch. Avigdor Jussina, bred and owned by Anthony Moran, won her title at Ireland's first international show. She is a daughter of GB, Ir. Ch. Avigdor Justin, the first Irish-bred Tibbie to win both titles.

Champion was Ir. Ch. Milbetan Spooky, bred and owned by Mr. and Mrs. Michael Clancey.

Since Ireland and the U.K. both require strict six-month quarantines for incoming dogs, exhibitors from other countries rarely show in Ireland or the U.K. However, because they have the same restrictions, Irish and British exhibitors show in each other's countries. Three Irish-bred Tibbies have attained titles in both countries. Ireland's first-ever international show, held in conjunction with the 1995 Congress of Judges, hosted by Ireland, drew an entry of 27 Irish and British Tibbies. Given the quarantine restrictions, it remains to be seen whether Ireland will further participate in international shows.

Northern Ireland

No discussion of Irish Tibbies would be complete without including Northern Ireland. Although her dogs are under the jurisdiction of the U.K.'s Kennel Club rather than the Irish Kennel Club, Northern Ireland's breeders work closely with those in the south and have contributed to breeding programs in the south—beginning with Phyllis McAfee (Carnam) who imported her first Tibbie in 1968. About four breeders are currently active in Northern Ireland.

Exhibitors also patronize one anothers' shows. The only show in Northern Ireland that offers C.C.'s for the Tibetan Spaniel is at Belfast where about 50 Tibbies compete. The second big event for Tibbies is the Northern Tibetan Spaniel Association's yearly Open show (see Chapter 3). Ir., GB Ch. Wandwend Zasha, bred and owned by Kathleen Lowe of Northern Ireland, recently finished her dual championship.

Thoughts on the Future

In discussing the breed's future in Ireland, Evelyn Hurley, Honorary Secretary of the Tibetan Spaniel Association of Ireland, praised the quality of Irish Tibbies. Cautioning breeders not to be mislead by talk of "old-fashioned" vs. "modern" traits, she expressed her hope that Irish breeders continue to study the Standard and preserve the traits that distinguish and elevate the breed, such as the silky coat, harefeet and small, elegant head.

THE NETHERLANDS

The Raad van Beheer op Kynologisch Gebied in Nederland, the national kennel organization of the Netherlands, registered the first *tibetaanse spaniel* in 1970. It is estimated that there are only 150-175 Tibbies in the Netherlands, a country of 15 million people (that's one Tibbie to every 100,000 people). From 1984 through

Bred by Mr. and Mrs. W. G. Dick (U.K.), Neth., Ger., Belg., Swiss, Fr., Lux., It., Int. Ch. Niord Riccardo is owned by Ria Kavelaars-van Loenhoet. He has won many prestigious European shows.

GETTING STARTED

In Italy, the Club Cani Compagnia (Companion Dog Club), founded in 1962, represents 37 breeds including a sub-group of Tibetan breeds. Of its 1,000 members, only Adriana Tarsi owns a Tibbie. In fact, she imported two of the three Tibbies registered in Italy since 1991. Ms. Tarsi, who remarks that she has never seen another Tibbie at an Italian show, also shows her Tibbies in France, Monaco and Switzerland.

Although a few litters were produced from U.K. imports in the late 1970's, the last Tibbie registered in Italy, before Ms. Tarsi's first Tibbie, was in 1980. Ms. Tarsi hopes to begin a new generation of Italian Tibbies because, like many of us, she has fallen in love with the breed that she calls "a fun-loving creature that fills your day with thousands of special and pleasurable moments."

As of this writing, eight Tibbies live in the neighboring country of Slovenia—thanks to the efforts of Primoz Peer (Rombon). After falling in love with a Tibbie he saw at a show, Mr. Peer spent four years studying the breed and seeing as many Tibbies as he could, a feat which was, he writes, "not at all easy—the nearest Tibbies lived 700 miles from Slovenia." He then imported a bitch from from Ann Wynyard and a dog from Helen Forbes (U.K.). Their first litter was born 1993. Another male, Tackalla Ku-Be-Ra, bred by Mrs. Hazelwood (U.K.), has since joined the group. At present, Mr. Peer is the only active breeder in Slovenia but hopes that two other owners will soon have their first litters.

The Klub za Tibetanske pasme Slovenije, formed in 1992, represents five Tibetan breeds. The club's purpose is to collect information about the breeds, cooperate with foreign clubs, establish responsible breeding programs and help new owners, breeders and judges. The club's first specialty show took place in 1993. Mr. Peer, who exhibits in several countries, writes, "Showing Tibbies in our area is sometimes quite unrewarding but sometimes quite funny. In Slovenia, Austria and Italy, almost every judge is looking at the first, second or third Tibetan Spaniel they have seen in [their] lives."

As an active family with a five-year-old, the Peers take their Tibbies on outings to the nearby Alps, on shopping trips and to their son's kindergarten, where the Tibbies have made many friends among the children. Although Mr. Peer recommends the breed whole-heartedly, he adds, "I hope that Tibetan Spaniels will never become a fashionable breed—a situation that has ruined so many [other] breeds."

Int., It., Social Ch. Tenzing Loh-Cha-Mo bred by Bente Rytter Jørgensen (Denmark) and owned by Adriana Tarsi, is the first of a new generation of Italian Tibbies.

Int., Slovenian, Austrian Junior Ch. Helfor Norbu, bred by Helen Forbes (U.K.) and owned by Primoz Peer, is the first Tibbie to win a Slovenian championship and sired the first Slovenia-bred litter. *Carol Ann Johnson photo*

A daughter of the famed Niord Riccardo, Neth., Belg., Lux. and Int. Ch. Mani-Padme v. 't Burgstse Hof, bred by Mrs. Kavelaars-van Loenhoet, follows in her father's pawprints.

1993, 101 Tibbies were registered, of which 16 were imported. Registrations during the 1990's have averaged 16 per year.

Breeding Notes

The first Tibbie in the Netherlands may have been "Yoyo" who arrived in 1964 with Ms. M. A. de Jong-van Zeventer. Yoyo was purchased as a pet in the U.K. Mr. Post imported the first Tibbies for show and breeding purposes in 1969. To begin her breeding program in 1970, Constance van den Boom (Fanfare), who died in 1995 at the age of 86, imported the first of many Tibbies from the U.K. Active in Tibbies until 1983, Mrs. van den Boom specialized in the black-and-tan, and her well-travelled Tibbies collected many European titles. The first litter born to Neth., Hung., Fr., Swiss, Int. Ch. Braeduke Sivas Supi Yaw Lat, Mrs. van den Boom's first bitch, in early 1971 marks the real start of the history of the Tibetan Spaniel in the Netherlands. At about the same time, Misses Iwes (Markley) and Rob Schipper (Bhoeddha) also began their breeding programs with imports from the Braeduke kennel.

Today, about four breeders are active (one to two litters per year) in the Netherlands, and three families had their first litters this year. From 1984-1989, only one or two litters were born each year. However, beginning in 1990, the number of litters has increased to four or five each year. Dogs imported from the U.K. and Denmark as well as Dutch-born Tibbies are used in recent breeding programs in the Netherlands. Dutch kennel names, past and present, include:

Bhoeddha (Schipper)
Fanfare (van den Boom)
Markley (Iwes)
Tamashing Dumra (Heltzel)
Top of the World (Tijman)
v.d. Beekjeshof (van Beek)
v.'t Burgstse Hof (Kavelaars-van Loenhoet)
Varja (Moes-Korver)

The Club Scene

The Tibetan Spaniel is represented by the Pekingees- En Dwergspanielclub (Pekingese and Miniature Spaniel Club). Founded in 1931, the club represents rare breeds such as the Havanese, Coton de Tulear, Xolitzcuintle and Peruvian Hairless as well as the Tibetan Spaniel. About 17 of the club's 500 plus members own Tibbies. The main purpose of the club is to help those interested in breeding to improve the breeds, not to multiply them.

Neth. Ch. Cuckoostone Ying Chen, bred by Audrey Williams (U.K.) and owned by Thea Heltzel, was top Tibbie at the Netherland's most prestigious show 1989-1991.

The Show Scene

To become a Dutch champion, a dog must win four C.A.C.'s (some C.A.C.'s count as two and some Reserve C.A.C.'s count as one C.A.C.), and the last C.A.C. must be after the dog is 27 months old. The first Dutch-born champion was Neth. Ch. Fanfare for Jam-Po, bred by Mrs. van den Boom.

Today, entries at most shows vary between two and six Tibbies. The largest entries are in the twice-yearly shows sponsored by the breed club. The aim of the spring show is fun and public education, whereas the fall show is more serious. A judge from the U.K. or Ireland is often invited to preside. About ten Tibbies enter these shows—a large entry for the breed but not enough, unfortunately, to qualify for a C.A.C.

Thoughts on the Future

Hannie Tijman-Logtenberg, breed correspondent for *De Hondenwereld* (a dog magazine), sums up her hopes for the future of the breed in the Netherlands, "I would like for the Tibetan Spaniel to be more known in our country but not with the excesses that sometimes happen when a breed becomes popular."

NEW ZEALAND

The New Zealand Kennel Club, Inc. reports that annual registrations have recently averaged about 70 Tibbies.

Aust., N.Z. Ch. Tensing Kye-Mo, bred by Judy Cassells and owned by Ken Talbot (Australia), was born in New Zealand's first particolor litter.

Breeding Notes

The first Tibetan Spaniel to arrive in N.Z. was Rosaree Cho-Kor-Gye, bred by Mrs. E. Hubberstey (UK) and brought in by Valerie Williams from the U.K. in 1972. Mrs. Williams' mother, Win Alexander (Wintersweet), began the first breeding program in N.Z. Judy Cassells (Tensing) started in 1978 with an Australian import followed by imports from Mrs. Wynyard (UK). Vivian Hartley (Aztlon) began her program in 1981 with N.Z.-bred Tibbies and later imported Tibbies from several U.K. lines, including several from Mrs. Wynyard. In the mid-'80's, Mr. Prendeville also imported several Tibbies from the U.K. As the years passed, Mrs. Hartley's Aztlon kennel has supplied other N.Z. kennels with foundation stock, and Aztlon Tibbies have been exported to Australia and the U.S. The partnership of Mrs. Hartley and Anna de Jager (Chakpori) has produced 46 champions.

It is believed that fewer than ten breeders are active in N.Z. today, including some who are starting new programs. A sampling of kennel names, past and present, includes:

Akeara (Van Gelder)
Azienta (Allison)
Aztlon (Hartley)
Chakpori (de Jager)
Potala (Walsh)
Wintersweet (Alexander)

The Club Scene

Twelve of the 96-member Asian Breeds Club, Inc. own Tibbies. The Tibbie members' chief "Tibbies only" activity is a "Fun Day" where owners of pet Tibbies are encouraged to join in. Contests include "Fluffiest Tail," "Best Harefeet," and "Best Ear Fringes." Every Tibbie takes home a prize.

The Show Scene

Each year, the club hosts two Championship shows, an indoor winter show, coinciding with the "National" in Wellington, and an outdoor summer show around Christmas, as well as one or two Open shows.

To attain a N.Z. championship, a Tibbie must win eight C.C.'s under at least five different judges. One C.C. must be won when the dog is at least one year old. Major events, such as club Championship shows, attract about 15-18 Tibbie entries. The record entry is 26.

N.Z. Ch. Aztlon Wizard, bred by Vivian Hartley, has won many group placements and the first Best in Show at an Open show. *Steven Mathie photo*

Unlike neighboring Australia, N.Z. Tibbies are shown in the Non-Sporting Group. Formerly overlooked in Group-level competition, more N.Z. Tibetan Spaniels are winning Group placements due, Mrs. Hartley believes, to greater depth of quality on the part of the exhibits and also to greater understanding of the breed on the part of the judges.

Thoughts on the Future

Among the concerns of N.Z. enthusiasts are breeder ethics and judges' education. Speaking as President of the Asian Breeds Club, Mrs. Hartley remarks, "Here in N.Z., we feel cut off from the rest of the world, and we are always thrilled to hear of people bringing Tibbies in and enjoy hearing from others with interest in the breed." However, fearing that the Tibetan Spaniel will be bred indiscriminately, Mrs. Hartley adds this cautionary note: "No one should breed without knowing what is back of the parentage and only the highest possible quality dogs and bitches, with no health problems, should be used for breeding." She hopes that the future Tibbies of N.Z. will be "strong, healthy, happy little dogs with wonderful personalities."

NORWAY

In 1994, the Tibetan Spaniel is the 15th most popular breed in Norway. Annual registrations average 449. Although many Norwegians now recognize *tibber*, it is still not the usual breed that one passes on the street.

Breeding Notes

Tibetan Spaniels got their start in Norway in 1974 when Arvo and Solveig Smedstuen (Dea Divina) and Rune Lerudsmoen (Rumens) imported their foundation breeding stock from Sweden and Finland. The first Tibbie registered in Norway was Braeduke Rje-Tse, a U.K. import, in 1976. A litter born in 1975 was the first to be registered

Today, it is thought that about sixty breeders are active in Norway, but the number is difficult to estimate since some breeders do not have kennel names. A sampling of Norwegian kennel names, past and present, includes:

Margibo (Gaardsmoen)
Muskoko (Mörk)
Sagaland (Strand)
Sakya (Olsen)
Shangri-La (Løkke)
Tusitalas (Holt)
Yotonos (Engebak)
Zolo (Kverndokken)

The top-winning Norwegian Tibbie of 1994, Int., Sw. and Nor. Ch. Sagaland's Z-Mar-Tell is bred and owned by Gerd and Kjell Strand. "Martell" has won 10 Best in Shows and, in 1994, was #12 on the all-breed list of top-winning dogs in Norway. *Hans Sonne Rasmussen photo*

The Club Scene

The club that represents the Tibetan Spaniel is the Norsk Miniatyrhunde Klub (Norwegian Miniature Dog Club). In 1993, 150 Tibbie owners were members of this club. The club hosts one all-Tibbie Open show each summer, an event in which 50-60 Tibbies compete.

The Show Scene

To win a Norwegian championship, three C.A.C.'s are required, each of which must be given by a different judge and one of which must be won at a Norsk Kennel Klub (NKK) show. About ten NKK shows take place each year.

It is not unusual for 50 plus Tibbies to compete in the prestigious NKK show in December, where the Best of Breed is awarded the title Norwegian Winner of the year. At other shows, Tibbie entries fluctuate between 10-80 dogs. In the past five years, Tibbies have been very successful in Group-level competition. The first Norwegian-bred Group winner (1980) was Muskokas Piro Piccolo, bred by Berit Mörk and owned by Randi Eriksen. Many Tibbies also appear in obedience, agility and junior handling events.

Thoughts on the Future

Karin Olsen, the breed representative for the Norsk Miniatyrhunde Klub, cites health issues, including PRA and progressive nephropathy, as the chief concern and top priority of Norway's enthusiasts. Currently, the NKK permits registration of a puppy without proof of examination of the parents' eyes. However, a request to make eye examinations mandatory (as has been done in Sweden) is now pending with the NKK. Ms. Olsen reminds us, "To breed a puppy that is healthy and has good temperament is most important. If the puppy also becomes beautiful, it is nice but not the most important thing."

SWEDEN

According to the Svenska Kennelklubben, Sweden's national kennel organization, 19 Tibetan Spaniels were registered in 1956. In 1993, 327 were registered, making Sweden one of the top producers of Tibetan Spaniels. Although the breed is popular, it is not so numerous that Tibbies are recognized as readily as breeds such as Poodles or Fox Terriers.

Breeding Notes

The first Tibetan Spaniels imported to Sweden from the U.K. arrived in 1955 from the Furzyhurst (Hervey-Cecil) and Hawkins kennels. Progress was slow until Marianne Braune (Krysants) and Gunhild and Einar Johannson began their programs in the late 1960's. Mrs. Braune's program, begun in 1967, seeded many new kennels in the '70's. Four kennels that began in 1970, among them Börje and Monica Herjeskog's Strömkarlens and Lisbeth Sigfridsson's Ulvus, caused a surge in registrations in the early '70's. Since then, a steady stream of new breeding programs have been built on stock from Sweden, the U.K. and Fin-

---

BA-DAM

Nalinas Ba-Dam, a bitch owned by Karin Olsen, was diagnosed with PRA in 1987. Ba-Dam was six years old. Looking back, Ms. Olsen says that she is comforted knowing that Ba-Dam's misfortune ultimately benefited others. The Norwegian Veterinary College used Ba-Dam in training new eye technicians, and her case inspired Dr. Ellen Berkås to initiate a study of PRA-affected Tibbies in Norway and Sweden (1986-1993). When Ba-Dam died, her eyes were donated to Dr. Berkås' investigation.

Ms. Olsen strongly believes that breeders of all countries must cooperate in the effort to eradicate this disease in Tibetan Spaniels. Chapter 11 discusses PRA.

Int., Nor., Sw. Ch. Zollis Han-ne-Krogh, bred by Monica Zollfrank-Larsson and Bjorn Larsson (Sweden) and owned by Gerd and Kjell Strand, descends from British lines. *Studio S photo*

S.A. Champions Dyffydd's Khenpo, Dyffydd's Ching Chang, bred by Jane Fawcett, and Crisnibek Tom-mee, bred by Mrs. R. M. Genes (U.K.), were owned by Jane Fawcett. *Visual Concepts Photography CC photo*

STRUGGLE IN SOUTH AFRICA

Tibbies first arrived in South Africa from the U.K. in 1975. During their first decade there, fluctuating registrations averaged ten per year, peaking at 23 in 1977-78. Beginning in 1986-87, registrations declined sharply and never recovered. Only one Tibbie was registered 1990-1994.

When Jane Fawcett (Dyfydd) re-homed two Tibbies in 1982, she knew nothing about the breed but soon found herself captivated. At that time, two or three breeders were active, and Ms. Fawcett began a modest program of her own, acquiring Tibbies from the other breeders and importing from the U.K. In the end, misfortune undermined her efforts.

As of this writing, it is believed that only 17 Tibbies remain in South Africa. No litters have been born in the past five years. In fact, Balgay Koo-Lin of Chuma, a puppy bred by Aileen Young (U.K.) and owned by Ms. Fawcett, is believed to be the only unspayed bitch in South Africa. To reach her new home in 1994, she endured a 20-hour flight from freezing winter to hot summer.

"I will try never to be without a Tibbie again. I love them," Ms. Fawcett writes. However, a breeder in South Africa must be sustained by love alone. Since the breed is unknown and thought to be cross-bred, it is impossible to sell puppies. Good homes must be found, and all of the breeder's expenses are out of pocket. Unfortunately, prospects for the future of our breed in her country are gloomy, and Tibbie enthusiasts all over the world can only sympathize with Ms. Fawcett's lonely struggle.

land. Swedish Tibbies have been exported to Finland, Norway and, recently, Australia.

Today, more than forty breeders are active in Sweden. Swedish kennel names, past and present, include:

- Bellissimas (Hansson)
- Bibaccs (Rosén)
- Bio-Bio (Molin)
- Body Rock (Andersson)
- Hårskas (Winberg)
- Jannocks (Hägglund)
- Krysants (Baurne)
- Lässebackes (Ödmans)
- Mavibos (Olsén)
- Nalinas (Reis and Karlsson-Reis)
- Ramblers (Enstad)
- Rhengold (Wolfsberg)
- Strömkarlens (Herjeskog)
- Ulvus (Sigfridson)
- Zibbans (Sellén-Andersson)
- Zollis (Zollfranck-Larsson)

Sw., Dan. Ch. Bio-Bio's Ballerina Girl was second on the list of top-winning Swedish Tibbies in 1994. She is bred and owned by Lisa Molin. Per Undén photo

The Club Scene

The Tibetansk Spaniel Klubb (TSK), with a membership of 941 members in 1994, is the breed club. TSK requires members to follow Svenska Kennelklubben's rules, register puppies, maintain purebred lines and provide humane care and treatment. "Puppy-farming" is forbidden. It is believed that Swedish breeders adhere to these rules and, to date, inspectors from the Svenska Kennelklubben have reported no problems among Tibbie breeders. Most of TSK's efforts in recent years have been directed toward health concerns.

The Show Scene

To win a Swedish championship, three C.A.C.'s under two different judges are required. There are many competitive opportunities for Swedish Tibbies. The average number of Tibbies entered in an all-breed show in Sweden is 25, but a respected breeder judge may attract up to 90 entries. As many as 120 may enter one of the five or six all-Tibbie shows that the TSK hosts each year. In addition, the annual Tibethund show features all five of the Tibetan breeds.

From 1967 to the present day, about 350 Tibbies have become Swedish champions. During the past few years, Tibbies have been more successful in Group-level competition. Int., Nord. Ch. Zollis A-Bra-Ham, bred by Monica Zollfranck-Larsson, is the all-time top-winning Swedish Tibbie and also a top-producing sire. The TSK recently published a book of champions to summarize the competitive achievements of Swedish Tibbies.

Int., Nordic, Fin. Ch. Bio-Bio's Ivanhoe was the top-winning Tibbie in Sweden in 1994 and #8 on the all-breed top winners list in 1995. In addition to winning many prestigious shows, he was the first Tibbie invited to compete in the Champion of Champions show. "Ivanhoe" is owned by Lisa Molin. OBC photo (Denmark)

The Tibetan Spaniel

Sw. Ch. Rhengold's Lotus is the #3 top-winning Tibbie in Sweden during 1994. She is bred and owned by Britt-Inger Wolfsberg. *Per Undén photo*

Int., Sw. Ch. Bibacc's How High the Moon, bred and owned by Sune and Ann Rosén, is on the list of top-winning Swedish Tibbies for 1994.

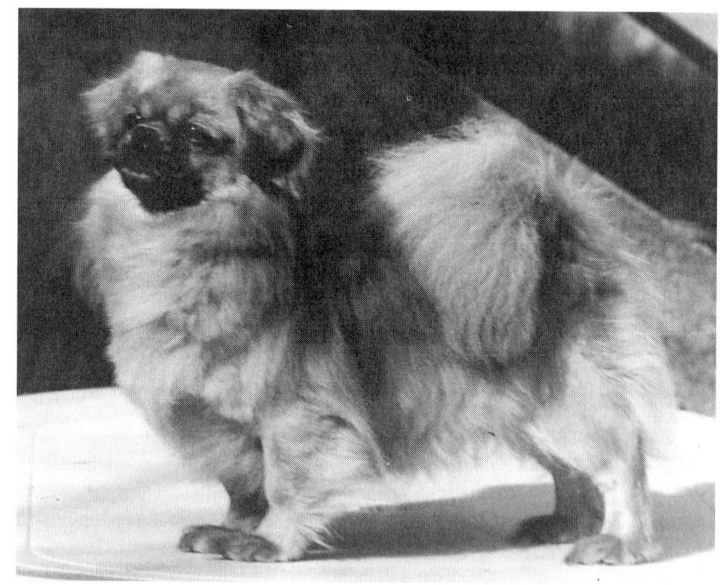

Sw. Ch. Rhengold's Kalejdoskop, bred by Britt-Inger Wolfsberg and co-owned by Ms. Wolfsberg and Paul Stanton, won Best of Breed at the 1994 Tibethund show.

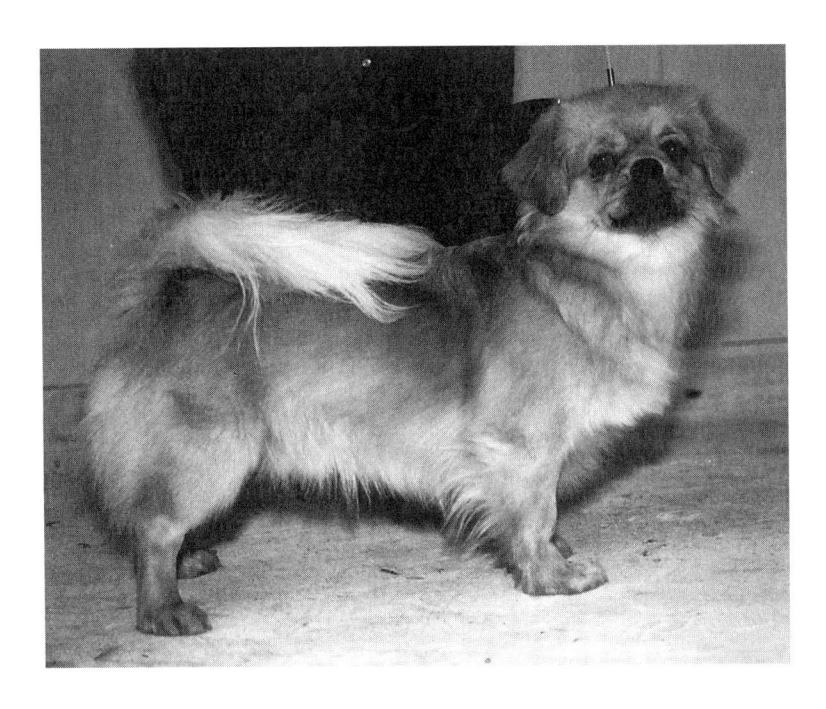

Shown here at nine months old, Sw., Nor. Ch. Body Rock's Neil Young, bred and owned by Richard Andersson and Stellan Ytterström, is the first Tibbie to win Best in Show at a Swedish all-breeds championship show.

Thoughts on the Future

Sweden has suffered the highest incidence of PRA among her Tibbies as a result of line-breeding carriers and extensive use of stud dogs that were carriers. Sadly, inheritance of the disease was not understood; breeders were advised only to avoid repeating a mating that produced PRA-affected offspring, but not to avoid breeding the carriers to other mates. In response to the resulting crisis, the TSK began a campaign to identify affected dogs and carriers. Effective in 1994, the Svenska Kennelklubben permits registration of a Tibetan Spaniel puppy only if both parents' eyes were examined within a year of the breeding *and* neither:

- shows any sign of PRA,
- has any earlier progeny affected by PRA, nor
- has a father, mother, brother or sister with PRA.

This policy was implemented at TSK's request.

TSK arranges eye examination clinics in several locations in Sweden each year and underwrites part of the cost for members. Exams are recommended for Tibbies up to eight years old and for pets as well as breeding stock. Each year, TSK publishes a list of confirmed cases as well as known carriers. The club also sponsors seminars.

The TSK is spearheading an effort to join Tibbie owners and breeders worldwide in the Tibetan Spaniel International Group. "In Sweden, Tibetan Spaniels have had serious problems with PRA. But we are recovering slowly by breeders being honest and open and by following the health program," writes Inga Enstad, President of the TSK, "The PRA problem is the main reason [for] our appeal to all other countries. ALL TOGETHER we must work against PRA!" Once a network is in place, other health issues and concerns of universal interest can be shared among enthusiasts.

Karen Chamberlain ills.

Chapter Six

The Tibetan Spaniel at Work and Play

"At work?" you ask, "What kind of work can a little dog like a Tibetan Spaniel do?" The Tibbie's intelligence and sturdiness make him a superlative companion to you, and that is his life's work. From around the world come stories of the creative ways in which Tibbies and their humans enjoy one another's company and the ways, both dramatic and subtle, in which Tibbies serve humanity.

What your Tibbie can achieve is limited only by your imagination. I hope that this chapter, my favorite, will open your mind and heart to the possibilities of companionship with your Tibetan Spaniel.

IN COMPANIONSHIP TO HUMANITY

"Very sporting little dogs," is what the British call Tibbies. This is not meant to imply that Tibbies are hunting dogs (although some could be), but refers instead to their adventuresome spirit, their enthusiastic approach to life and their willingness to tackle new tasks.

A Dog for All Seasons

I have long suspected that the Tibetan Spaniel has something of every breed of dog in him. Pigeon-holing the multi-faceted Tibbie according to preconceptions about small, charming dogs is short-sighted and denies the promise of his complex personality. Stories from around the world confirm my suspicions. For example, Cobi and Bert Greve (The Netherlands) believe that they own...

A Tibetan Greyhound

Some years ago, Mr. and Mrs. Greve decided to choose a smaller, but sporty dog to go along with their two Salukis. In view of the rarity of the breed in their country, they were lucky to soon find a Tibbie puppy called Varja Amiro. After a slow start in a "puppy course," Amiro surged ahead of his classmates to pass his final exam at the top of his class. Encouraged by this outcome, the Greves enrolled him in an obedience course, where he also turned in a solid performance and good scores. Meanwhile, Mr. and Mrs. Greve began Amiro's show training, and he rewarded them by winning Dutch, Belgian and International championships. A couple of outings in the agility ring showed that the athletic Amiro would tackle any sport. Ah, but Amiro was capable of much more!

One day at the track, after all the Salukis and Sloughis had finished running, someone pointed to Amiro and jokingly suggested, "Now let's see what he can do and then we'll go home." Everyone was startled—everyone, that is, except Amiro. Having accompanied his housemates to the track many times, he knew exactly what to do and, more than anything, he wanted to try. And he's off! Just like the Salukis, he coursed energetically, his rear legs stretching out behind and his forelegs gulping the air ahead. Around the track he flashed, eager for a chance to grab that fake hare at the end of the race.

Amiro's family enjoys vacationing in forested areas where rabbits frolick provocatively nearby. Ever ready to take up the challenge, Amiro pursues them enthusiastically cross-country. As far as he is concerned, coursing is the greatest fun in the world. There he goes again!

The fastest Tibbie in history? Certainly, GB Ch. Sivas Mesa would be a contender for the title. At a meet in Yorkshire, many years ago, his owner and breeder Sara Selby challenged the scornful owners of two racing Whippets. It comes as no surprise to those of you with speedy Tibbies that Mesa streaked across the finish line six lengths ahead of the Whippets!

Originally, a Spaniel (from the Old French word *espaigneul*) was a hunting dog whose specialty was flushing birds, and this meaning survives in the names of breeds such as the Cocker Spaniel. No one knows exactly when or why our breed was designated a Spaniel. Rather than a reference to any hunting prowess, the name probably sprang from our breed's resemblance to European toy breeds descended from the hunting Spaniels, pet dogs with drop ears and silky coats, much in the same way that the Pekingese and Japanese Chin were once called the Pekin Spaniel and Japanese Spaniel.

Yet, some Tibbies still have the hunting instincts of their remote ancestors—the wolves and early dogs. Debra Bennett (U.S.) reports that her cat-like Tibbie climbs into the bird feeder to capture birds, while David Parry (U.K.) reports that his Tibbies adroitly flush birds in the field. In fact, not unlike my Tibbies who flush wild turkey, Mr. Parry's two bitches Tess (Little Miss Prim and Proper) and Little Digger (Kyimna Sweet Angelica) may be...

True Spaniels?

One evening in early summer, we were enjoying a short moorland walk. We had allowed the two oldest bitches, Tess and Little Digger, off their leads. Bouncing (a word more suited to Tibbies than bounding) about in the heather, they were busy "putting up" grouse and catching moths. Since their bouncy action hampered their progress through the endless shrubbery, I was confident that I could easily outpace them and that they could not get into any trouble and so we watched their play with relish.

Up ahead, I spotted rabbits and they were...chasing one another? Not on your life! It was Tess, the youngest bitch, who had climbed a drystone wall some four feet high in pursuit of game. I vaulted over after her and, with a bit of a sprint, stopped her short in her tracks. Fortunately, Tess is not as wayward as some and came quickly once she saw and heard me near. I picked her up and dropped back over the wall. Five minutes later, prim and proper Tess shot off again, disappearing into the last of the heather before we reached the car. Seven pounds of dog soon appeared dragging three pounds of grouse!

Over two yards, Tibbies are amongst the quickest around, even if they have some difficulty gripping with slightly undershot jaws. Sometime later I was to see just how quick their reactions can be. We were sitting in the garden. The dogs were all out, lounging and sniffing around. In a flash, Little Digger leapt into the air and caught a house sparrow in flight. I had to see it to believe it!

Contributed by David Parry (U.K.)

Tibbies are also good farm dogs. Barbara Berg (U.S.) reports that her Tibbies love the barn most of all—climbing in the rafters, playing in the hay and hunting mice. Several of her Tibbies have also proven themselves good herding dogs. When milking time rolls around, they trot into the pasture with the Corgi and Australian Cattle Dog to bring home the cows. Of course, the cows know the way home but, when one strikes out in the wrong direction, the Tibbies are perfectly capable of turning her around. They use all the herding moves—back and forth, crouch and watch, creep and stare. Intelligent beings that they are, Mrs. Berg believes that the Tibbies learned the routine by mimicking the herding dogs. Ragnhild Poulsen (Denmark) writes that her daughter's Tibbie, Tes-La (Dan., Ger. Ch. Sommerlyst's Assam Tes-La), often helps her move sheep: "I walk in front, the sheep after me, and behind Tes-La circles and pinches the hocks of the sheep if she thinks they are too slow!" Joel and Peter DeCloux (U.S.) owned a Tibetan Cattle Dog called...

Cowboy Moose

For some time, Moose had observed the cattle comings and goings on the neighbor's farm with casual interest. One day, some steers breached their fence and wandered into the DeCloux vegetable patch. After phoning his neighbor, Mr. DeCloux called Moose. Under the neighbor's doubtful scrutiny, Moose quickly separated and cornered the lead steer. Darting back and forth and nipping at his heels, Moose moved the steer in classic herding

The Tibetan Spaniel loves outdoor exercise. *Nan Kilgore Little ills.*

I'd rather be skiing

Susan Miccio ills.

style—classic, that is, other than constantly bouncing to see over the tall grass. All the while, in classic Tibbie style, he talked to the lead steer to make sure his instructions were understood. He did not consider his job done until all of the steers were safely back in the neighbors' barn.

Tibbies do not lack for tenacity in pursuit of objectives. In fact, I wonder if my Bear is a...

Tibbie or Terrier?

On a twilight stroll down the farm lane with my husband, Bear's sharp ears detected a sound in the brush and set off in pursuit of a small animal which, as Chris soon learned to his dismay, was an odoriferous skunk. Despite receiving a dose of the skunk's medicine, Bear persisted in running the creature to ground where he received yet another dose—right between the eyes. Still, he would not relent. Digging furiously at the burrow's entrance, he repeatedly poked his head into the opening and eventually wedged his shoulders in as well. When, at last, my husband's whistle overcame his Tibbie/Terrier tenacity and he trotted homeward, Bear was not the least bit chastened by his experience. My husband and I, on the other hand, endured months of "breathtaking" experiences each time Bear got the slightest bit wet!

Hiking, Jogging and Skiing

Tibbies love the outdoors, and hiking is a pastime enjoyed by Tibbies and their owners all over the world. A fit Tibbie is also a fine jogging companion. His natural trot perfectly matches an easy jogging pace. Of course, if he puts his four-paw drive in gear, he easily outpaces most of us. When you consider how small a Tibbie is, his endurance is phenomenal, as in the case of...

Ranger Lady

As the daughter of a forester, Julie Hall is a lifelong outdoorswoman. Lady, Ms. Hall's Tibbie, also reaped the benefits of a active lifestyle. They routinely jogged together—three to five miles each day. They also backpacked and enjoyed family camping trips in the high country of the American West. Although Lady usually traveled on her own four paws, she could be seen perched atop her owner's backpack whenever sharp shale, covering the trail, would have damaged her paws.

When Ms. Hall spent her summers on duty in a fire tower in the Sawtooth Range of Idaho, Lady did her part as well. Sitting for hours atop the perimeter wall of the fire tower, she surveyed the surrounding countryside, her sharp eyes following the everpresent gophers, ears pricking at the forest sounds and nose testing the wind. It does not require a great leap of imagination to picture Lady atop a monastery wall in the far mountains of Tibet.

Tibbies love cool weather and, in the winter, Ms. Hall and Lady switched to cross-country skiing. In fact, in all the cold and mountainous nations of the world, owners and their Tibbies enjoy skiing together. On outings with his Tibbies, Jim Milke (U.S.) makes the trail for Becky and Ernie. Becky is content to follow his lead, while the more independent-minded Ernie forges her own way. Plowing through drifts until she can no longer move, Ernie backs out and trails her owner for a while. When she gets her second wind, she charges off by herself again.

Swimming and Boating

Some literature suggests that Tibbies do not care for water. Since my own Tibbies ignore all toys lobbed into the pond and are highly insulted if plopped into the surf, I was inclined to accept this premise as fact until I began to hear stories about Tibbies and water sports. Barbara Berg, for instance, reports that all of her fourteen Tibbies enjoy a summertime swim in the creek. One called Tailor (Am. Ch. Aki Shima's Tailor Made), a bit of a show off, likes to dive from the rocks into the cool water. From Texas come snapshots of a bevy of Tibbies lolling on a raft and enjoying the occasional dip in their backyard pool.

Of course, not all water sports require getting wet. The DeCloux Tibbie, Moose, was an inveterate sailor. Sitting fearlessly on the bow of the family sailboat as the boat was underway, he preferred to remain dry unless swimming were absolutely necessary to stay near his family. When he takes them canoeing, Jim Milke's Ernie and Becky repose contentedly amidships where a canopy, à la Cleopatra's barge, offers respite from the fierce sun. While living in Hawaii, Toni Anders-Tumlin and her son, Michael, sailed in the Pacific with a seafaring Tibbie called George (Am. Ch. Tuwin Phylmarko Ala George). Mrs. Anders-Tumlin says that George "would gingerly run to the opposite side of the bow whenever he heard the coursing word 'tack' yelled out. Needless to say, he did a lot of 'tacking' in his day, but, to him, it was all a great game!!"

"Othello" (Gatak's Othello) hitches a ride on a board while out for a swim. He belongs to the Proescher and Fleuchaus (Amrita's) families (Germany).

"George" (Am. Ch. Phylmarko K-ung Tzu of Tuwin) sails off Hawaii with his pal, Michael Tumlin. "George *loved* to sail and swim," writes his owner, Toni Anders-Tumlin (U.S.) *Toni Anders-Tumlin photo*

On the Move

Personally, I cannot leave the house without at least one Tibbie-in-tow. Like me, many owners take their Tibbies everywhere, and most Tibbies love to go along for a ride. However, all modes of transport are acceptable to Tibbies. Moose, for example, enjoyed a leisurely horseback ride. In a daypack on her owner's back, with the zipper pulled up and a sunscreen over her head, Julie Hall's Lady bicycled around town and country. Snuggled in the cab of a "big rig," Princess travels everywhere with her truck-driving owners, Fred and Patricia Webb (U.S.), putting as much as 40,000 miles a year under her paws.

When Gary and Linda McDermaid leave home for Sunday brunch, they take along Abbey (Chumbi Dragonsong Satin). As a weekend pilot, Mr. McDermaid flies single engine, four-seater aircraft to their destination. "Abbey likes to be high up," he says, "whether it's in the plane or on the back of the sofa." The McDermaids pronounce their Abbey "an ideal little dog" and declare that their friends have all fallen in love with her.

It is true that, wherever they go, Tibbies are ambassadors for our breed. When Pamela Basile and her Gianni go shopping at Saks Fifth Avenue in New York, the staff are enchanted by the winsome, well-behaved Tibbie. Mrs. Basile's husband, Dr. John Basile, sometimes takes Gianni along on the daily commute to his office in the city, where she sits atop his desk and greets his patients. Gianni is not on the only Tibbie with professional responsibilities. Meet...

"Abbey" (Chumbi Dragonsong Satin) prepares for take-off. The pilot is owner Gary McDermaid (U.S.).

Sherpa Good, Queen's Counsel

Sherpa Good, Q.C., may be, we believe, the only practicing Tibby lawyer in Canada. Each day, Sherpa commutes to the office with his senior partner and favourite owner Donald Good, Q.C. After greeting his other favourite person, Lori, the receptionist and computer secretary specialist, Sherpa bounces upstairs where he hopes the staff will share their morning muffins with him. After his "coffee break," Sherpa returns downstairs to take up his post.

Sherpa guards Donald at work as fiercely as he does at home. He is especially alert to protect his colleagues against delivery men and couriers, some of whom, for reasons known only to Sherpa, he regards as dangerous enemies. Has anyone succeeded in persuading a Tibby to be docile and obedient? If so, I, and the Kingston delivery and courier men, would like to how to do it.

The above submitted by Lin Good, unwilling servant of Sherpa who merely tolerates me as the person who washes him, grooms him, disciplines him (or tries to do so), redeeming myself only by feeding him.

Games and Competitions

Tibbies love to play all kinds of games and this personality trait gives us yet another opportunity for their companionship. The Chamberlain Tibbies, Pippin (Am. Ch. Jemari Joyous Pippin, N.A.) and Whimsi (Am. Ch. Nittni's Whimsical Creation, N.A.), enjoy a variety of organized games with owners Karen and Scott (U.S.). In fact, they love to go to...

Summer Camp

At "Camp Gone to the Dogs," a recreational camp for dogs and their owners in the U.S., Pippin tried on a lot of hats. On the Terrier course, her gay tail and powderpuff

"Sherpa" Good, specialist in canine law, contemplates a difficult case at the office of his partner (and owner), Donald Good, Q.C. (Canada).

pantaloons were distinctly un-Terrierlike as she popped over the jumps and disappeared into the tunnel. Nonetheless, the Terriers awarded her "Honorary Terrier with the Fuzziest Cheeks" for her performance in "going-to-ground." Later, observing the sighthounds running on the lure course, Pippin became so excited that she began to vibrate. When her turn finally came and the lure took off, Pippin sprinted after it with all her heart. With each stride, her tail wound and unwound like a spring. For her enthusiasm, she received an award of "Honorary Miniature Sighthound."

Alas, Pippin was not so successful at all the games. In the game of Flyball, the player places his forepaws on a treadle which catapults a ball into the air. Using his hindlegs to propel himself, the dog jumps to catch the ball in midair. Unfortunately, Pippin's twelve pounds would not trigger the ball, so she eagerly jumped on the treadle with all four paws. The ball shot upward but, without the leverage of her hindlegs, Pippin could not jump for it. Up, up, up and over her head it went, time after time. Frustrated Pippin had a few words to say about that!

Besides showing their Tibbies in conformation and obedience competitions, the Chamberlains have discovered their Tibbies' aptitude for competitive agility events. Pippin and Whimsi are the first American Tibbies to win agility titles, and Chamberlains have become agility instructors themselves.

IN SERVICE TO HUMANITY

Companionship with your Tibbie can be more than fun and games. Many owners have found yet another dimension to the multi-faceted Tibetan Spaniel—the work Tibbies do in service to humanity.

To This Breed I Owe So Much

In October 1984, I purchased a Tibetan Spaniel dog named Barrajy Achates, and I called him Beau. Beau and I went everywhere together, and I guess he almost became my shadow. I later purchased a lady friend for Beau. Barrajy Demelsa, as she was called, did not take to me for a while as she was not used to the company of a man. However, Beau must have told her, 'He is OK for a feed and a pat' as Demelsa soon became very close to me.

At three AM one day in November 1986, I was awakened with extreme pain across the shoulders and violent temperature changes. Added to this, Beau was scratching wildly at my chest and whimpering. At the foot of the bed, Demelsa was pirouetting and whining.

"Pippin" is ready for camp. *Karen Chamberlain ills.*

As much as I growled at him and pushed him away, Beau continued his relentless scratching and whimpering. In an effort to get some relief, I pushed him off the bed, but to no avail as he jumped straight back on the bed and continued to scratch at my chest. At this stage, Beau was almost driving me insane with his persistence. Desperate for relief, I was able to reach the phone and ring my daughter Julie. I told her that I was having another muscle spasm, as this was what I thought I had, and besides, I added, Beau is almost driving me crazy. Fortunately for me, Julie treated my illness seriously and phoned for an ambulance while my son-in-law Charles rushed to help me.

I remember being wheeled into the casualty section when I arrived at the hospital. From that point on, I can recall nothing until I felt my whole body jump followed by a burning sensation across my chest. I remember opening my eyes and saying, "What the bloody hell is going on?" A voice replied that everything is OK and, when I looked in the direction of the voice, I saw six medical personnel at the end of the bed.

As you have surmised, I had not suffered a muscle spasm but a heart attack. For a short period, I had been clinically dead until revived by a defibrillator. After open heart surgery and a triple bypass, I can now report that all is well with me.

Had Beau not been so persistent with his scratching and whimpering, I would have tried to endure the pain as I had done on two previous occasions.

It was only his added agitation that spurred me to call Julie. Beau will be eleven years old this year.
TO THIS BREED, I OWE SO MUCH.
TO THIS DOG BEAU, I OWE MY LIFE.

Contributed by Michael Fenwick (Australia)

Healing

Those of us who are owned by a Tibetan Spaniel know that Tibbies sense and respond to signs of physical or emotional discomfort in their humans. Like Mr. Fenwick's Beau and Demel-sa, they require no special training or inducement to respond to people in need. Which of us has not experienced a Tibbie's healing powers after a long day at work, in bed with the flu or during a time of grieving?

Toni Anders-Tumlin (U.S.), who has suffered from lupus for nearly 20 years, credits her Tibbies with helping her fight this disease. "[My Tibbies] are a continuing part of my daily therapy. I can honestly say had it not been for these darling little dogs coming into my life, I would not have the drive or determination that I continue to have to this day. They have truly been instrumental in maintaining my health both mentally and physically."

Tibbies are especially devoted to the bedridden. When her father was suffering from the last stages of bone cancer, Beverly Burney (U.S.) recounts how her Kimba (Windweiler's Kimba v. Bev), a male Tibbie, became his constant companion. For endless hours, Kimba lay in a chair next to her father's bed and watched over him with undivided attention.

Breeders report that Tibbies placed in families with disabled children or adults often have a exceptional effect on the well-being and outlook of the disabled person.

Gabby, Hero Tibbie

Since she was 12 years old, Terri Smith has suffered from an illness called myalgic encephalomyelitis. Confined to her bed and in constant pain, young Terri longed for a dog, a friend to help her pass the long hours. After screening several breeds, she settled on the Tibetan Spaniel.

Having just retired from her show and breeding career, Aust. Ch. Toreana Yana Su, soon to be called Gabby, was bred by Ken and Pam Talbot (Toreanna). Gabby was almost six years old when she met 14-year-old Terri. "Within five to ten minutes she was acting like we were long lost friends," remembers Terri. It was love at first sight.

Gabby was the perfect choice for Terri. Sensing Terri's pain, she intuitively understood that she must be gentle. When Terri was able to sit up in her wheelchair for brief periods, Gabby snuggled in her lap. When Terri was in bed, Gabby cuddled with her. Watching over Terri as she slept and pacing outside the door whenever Terri took a turn for the worse, Gabby dedicated her life to her young mistress. She took her job seriously. "Whenever I went to hospital, Gabby would get so upset that I'd have her brought [there]," remembers Terri, "Gabby has even tried to get rid of the doctors when she thought they were trying to hurt me."

In May 1992, Gabby's devotion and service to Terri were officially recognized when she was named a "Hero Dog" by the South Australia Foundation. In the "Heroes Escort" parade through the streets of Adelaide, South Australia's capital, Gabby rode proudly in Terri's wheelchair. Although Terri was unable to be present for her Tibbie's hour of glory, Gabby brought home the medallion and certificate presented to her by the Lord Mayor.

"Gabby," Hero Dog, with her owner, Terri Smith. *Courtesy of* The (Adelaide) Advertiser *(Australia). Chris Mangan photo*

"Sparkie," a Hearing Dog for the Deaf, lives with Mrs. Dorothy Sharpe (U.K.). Sparkie awakens Mrs. Sharpe each morning. He also alerts her to the doorbell, telephone, cooker-timer and smoke alarm. *Courtesy of Hearing dogs for the Deaf (U.K.) Photo by Albert Rigby A.R.P.S., A.P.A.G.B.*

Today, Terri's condition is improved, and her family credits Gabby with lifting Terri's spirits and encouraging her to fight the debilitating ailment. As for Terri, she sums it up with, "She's a GREAT dog!"

Hearing Tibbies

Three Tibetan Spaniels are currently serving as Hearing Dogs for the Deaf (H.D.F.D.) in the U.K. Sparkie, Sally and Star each graduated from a four-month training course where canine candidates learn to alert their hearing-impaired owners to everyday sounds. The cost of training each Hearing Dog is £2500 (about U.S. $3700) and is funded through private and corporate donations. Trainees are chosen for their high intelligence, friendliness, willingness and, of course, keen hearing and responsiveness to sound.

The H.D.F.D. Tibbies, like other Hearing Dogs, provide their owners with an increased sense of confidence, self-esteem and well-being. They also help to counteract the isolation and loneliness experienced by many hearing-impaired people. Allowed to accompany their owners into shops and restaurants and to travel free on various British transport systems, these Tibbies contribute to their owners' independence outside as well as inside the home.

When visitors arrive at Eileen Boath's home, they ask her Tibbie Sally to "Fetch Eileen." Sally also alerts Mrs. Boath to the doorbell, telephone, alarm clock and smoke alarm. Sally was donated by Tibetan Spaniel Rescue, and a corporate sponsor paid for her training. "[Sally is] a very caring, hard working loveable Rascal," Mrs. Boath writes, "The more work Sally gets, the happier she is. [She] keeps me fit going for walks. I love her dearly as she loves me."

Community Service

Owners and their Tibbies contribute to the communities in which they live in many ways. For example, Martha Rosner (U.S.) and Lita (Tibroke Nirvana, C.G.C.) visit schools as part of a program to teach children the responsibilities of pet ownership. Many other Tibbies and their owners find pet therapy a rewarding form of community service. Pet therapy brings together pets with people who would not otherwise have a chance to experience the special bond between human and animal beings. Tibbies work their wonders in facilities such as nursing homes for the elderly or disabled, rehabilitation units, and hospitals for veterans, children or the mentally ill. Their monkey faces, small size, silky coats and sweet dispositions appeal to patients of all ages.

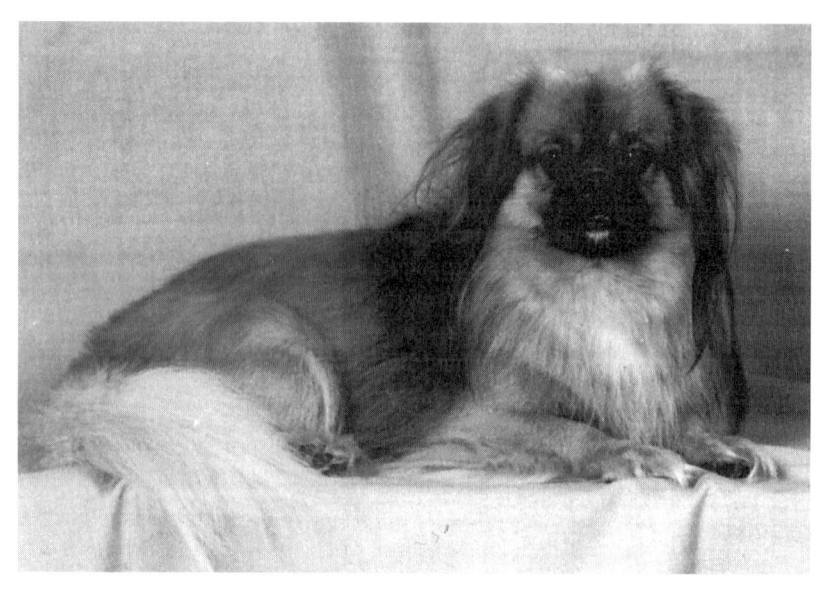

"Justin" has accompanied his owner, Joan Shaw (U.S.), on therapy visits for more than a decade. *Nanette Stewart photo*

Mrs. Helen Brown enjoys a Tibbie's attentions. Owned by Alfred and Mary Ann Umble, "Wisk" was groomed for therapy work from the day he was born. He paid his first visit on his first birthday (the minimum age) after passing his test only a day earlier. *Alfred Umble photo*

Arlene Tanel (U.S.) remembers a visit to an outpatient cancer treatment center. There, a young girl about ten years old was undergoing chemotherapy, a treatment lasting five hours. She was clearly despondent. Arlene's Tibbie, a registered therapy dog named Kylee (Tashi Tai Kylee, C.G.C.), bounced in, spotted the child and darted to her. Leaping into her lap, Kylee circled once and laid down. The child passed the hours playing gently with Kylee, even begging Arlene to allow Kylee to stay through lunch. By the time her treatment was over, the little girl had been transformed to a happy, animated child despite her ordeal.

The Program Director of the cancer treatment center recognizes the tremendous positive influence of Arlene's Tibbies and the other therapy dogs that visit the unit. In general, facilities are more receptive to therapy dogs now than they were only a few years ago. Joan Shaw (U.S.), whose Tibbies Justin (Am. Ch. Tudorwell's Justin Tyme) and Felicity (Am. Ch. Hiwind's Felicity Kendal) were registered as therapy dogs in the mid-1980's, recalls that some hospitals turned down her offers to visit, citing concerns about sanitation. Today, the tireless efforts of pet advocates and pet-friendly members of the medical community are changing these attitudes. Rod Beckstead (U.S.), founder of Comfort Caring Canines, recalls that each facility his organization has approached has reacted differently. In one case, a children's hospital reluctantly agreed to pet visits only after one of its own professional staff had lobbied a full year to persuade them. However, an enlightened administrator at another facility impatiently interrupted Mr. Beckstead, after only thirty seconds of his pet therapy pitch, saying, "Just tell me what I have to do to get these dogs in here!"

Once their paws are in the door, professional staff and patients alike react positively to Tibbies and eagerly anticipate their visits. Becca and Ernie, proudly chaperoned by Jim Milke (U.S.), visit several facilities including psychiatric hospitals and nursing homes. After only one visit to a facility, the Program Director wrote in praise of the "girls" and invited them back as soon as possible. During an initial visit to a psychiatric ward, Danny (Am. Ch. Bet'R's Standing Ovation, C.D.), owned by Mr. Beckstead, coaxed an obviously troubled but undiagnosed young man into revealing that, as a child, he had often hidden in his dog's doghouse to escape abuse suffered at the hands of his father. This revelation, in the presence of the psychiatrist, convinced

Young Dante Jones, a patient at St. Louis Children's Hospital, meets "Holly," owned by Chris Curtis (U.S.) *Chris Curtis photo*

the formerly skeptical professional staff to thereafter welcome Danny's visits with open arms.

If you would like to become involved in pet therapy, find out whether a program to promote the therapeutic benefits of the human-animal bond exists in your area. Such a program is the Pets Active Therapy (PAT) scheme in the U.K. Even where no formal program exists, as in Australia and New Zealand, Tibbies paying therapy visits have been well-received.

In the U.S., most visits to facilities are arranged by pet therapy organizations. These include Therapy Pets International, Therapy Pets, Inc., Comfort Caring Canines, Pet Partners program of the Delta Society, and the Therapy of Unique Canine Helpers (TOUCH) program of Support Dogs, Inc. Community-based pet therapy groups (which may be affiliated with an organization named above), kennel clubs and animal welfare organizations may also sponsor visits. These organizations depend on volunteers; none charges for its services.

Besides arranging visits, American pet therapy organizations carry insurance to cover accidents or other problems that may occur during visits. Since some dogs are not suited to therapy work, these groups wisely screen volunteers and provide training to prepare for visits. For example, many organizations require that your dog pass the AKC's Canine Good Citizen (C.G.C.) test (see Chapter 10). Others require more extensive training. Chris Curtis (U.S.), Tibbie owner and Program Coordinator for TOUCH, explains the program's comprehensive 12-week training course. After canine candidates are screened to assess out how well they tolerate noise and discomfort, they learn basic obedience commands. Next, the course acclimates the dogs to hospital equipment and conducts simulated facility visits. Meanwhile, medical personnel help owners understand hospital protocols. The course concludes with a performance test for the dogs and a 50-question test for their owners.

Waiting Patiently

A 21-year-old soldier lay comatose in a veteran's hospital. The staff had tried everything to stimulate his injured brain but with no response. So, when Holly, a soft and silky particolor Tibbie, came to visit the patients, the nurses asked her owner to bring Holly to see the young man.

When placed at the foot of his bed, Holly tiptoed over the gastrointestinal and other tubes cluttering the bed to take her place at his side. A nurse placed the young man's hand next to Holly and said, "We've brought a puppy. Can you feel her?" Ten minutes passed. Then fifteen. Holly remained immobile, wait-

"Cakes," owned by Billie Ponton (U.S.), routinely visits a hospital for patients with severe mental illnesses. *John Ashbey photo*

ing patiently. His hand moved. He touched her. He caressed her.

Holly (Tiara's Holiday Party, C.G.C.), owned by Mrs. Curtis, is the first Tibetan Spaniel to complete the TOUCH course. Her owner considers Holly a "natural" for therapy work. "She does it from her heart and soul, not just to appease me," Mrs. Curtis says, "There's never a person who's a stranger to her. She always seems to know what to do." She adds that Holly, like other Tibbies, may sometimes be aloof toward strangers in other settings but never when she is on duty as a therapy dog.

Although most therapy Tibbies love their work and have an admirable amount of stamina, end a visit whenever your Tibbie becomes tired and always be on guard for discomfort that patients may unintentionally inflict. Billie Ponton (U.S.) and her Tibbies regularly visit a psychiatric hospital where patients with a variety of severe mental disorders are treated. Once, while Cakes (Jo'Jevon's Strawberry Shortcake) happily nestled on a patient's lap having her ears and chin scratched, Mrs. Ponton noticed the Tibbie's eyes widen. The patient's harmless scratching had become a stranglehold on her neck. Mrs. Ponton and an aide worked to pry Cakes away from the patient—all the while speaking in soothing tones to avoid alarming the patient. Through it all, complacent Cakes, a very "laid back" Tibbie, did not utter a protest.

Although many patient visits take place in a central lounge or in their rooms, some visits involve specific therapeutic goals under professional guidance. For example, in a rehabilitation unit, a therapist may request that a Tibbie play a game of fetch so that a stroke victim can exercise a weakened hand. The Tibbie's bouncy retrievals, smiling face and shining eyes give the patient incentive to play the game and distract him from the discomfort. In the neurological unit of a children's hospital, a child's responses, such as tracking the Tibbie's movement with the eyes or reacting to the feel of the coat, may help staff assess the child's recovery from brain surgery.

Karen Chamberlain (U.S.), a speech pathologist, asks Pippin (Am. Ch. Jemari Joyous Pippin, N.A.) to perform specific tasks with her patients. When programmed to say commands that a patient selects, electronic speaking devices enable severely disabled children and adults who cannot speak to communicate with Pippin. Despite the device's nonhuman, electronic "voice," Pippin understands commands such as "Sit" and "Come." The delight of the patients who "speak" to Pippin through the device is obvious. Less apparent is the self-esteem that they gain from their interaction with her. A 12-year-old girl summed it up, "Pippin is the first one that listens to me because she wants to, not because someone told her to."

Lightning:
A Christmas Story

Christmas is three days away. Holiday decorations adorn the

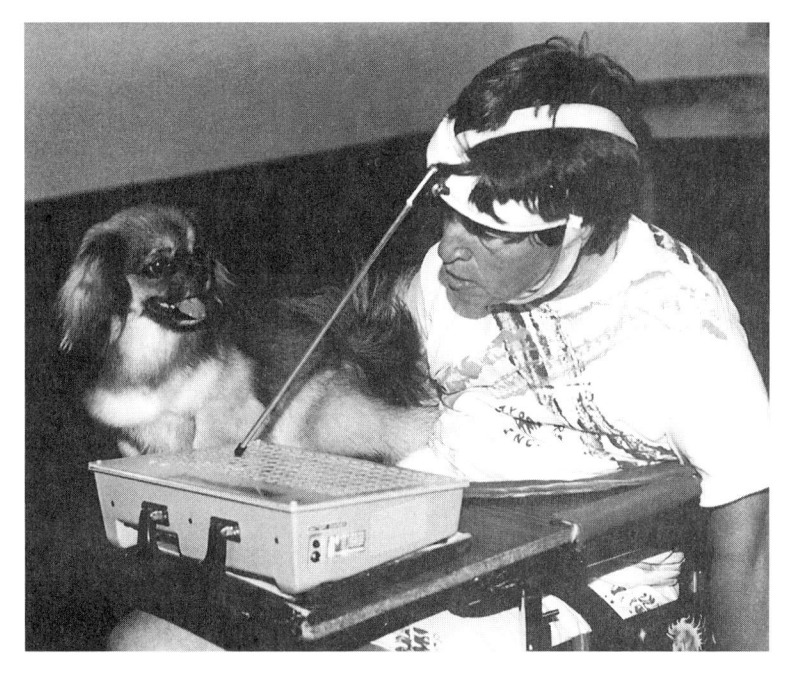

Emilie Smith communicates with an electronic speaking device. When Ms. Smith speaks, "Pippin" listens. *Scott Chamberlain photo*

recreation room where, near the center, an elderly woman slumps in a wheelchair. The fingers of one hand clutch a handkerchief. Her other hand is clenched in a fist. Her body is rigid; her downcast face is furrowed with anger and fear.

The Activity Director watches the woman sadly. Placed in the nursing home by her family only an hour earlier, the woman has become withdrawn, silently rebuffing the staff's efforts to comfort or distract her. Cradled in the Activity Director's arms, Lightning approaches the woman in the wheelchair. He wags his tail tentatively and sniffs. The Activity Director says, "I've brought someone to see you. This is Lightning. He lives here, too." With that introduction, she gently places Lightning in the woman's lap.

Stretching up, Lightning plants an irresistible Tibbie kiss on the woman's cheek. Instantly, her arms

encircle and clasp him to her body. As she lowers her cheek to receive more kisses, her feelings of sorrow and abandonment well to the surface. She cries. Her fist unclenches; the fingers tightly grasp the soft fur of his mane. But Lightning understands. He cuddles to her and kisses her sweetly and will stay with her as long as she needs him. That's his job.

Lightning (Beckstead's Midday Siesta) is owned by Ruth Mumbauer, RN. (U.S.).

A Courageous Undertaking

"Dogs have been my hobby since age twelve and I've been a paramedic for fifteen years," explains Meranda Rodehaver (U.S.). "I began to wonder what contribution that I, as a Tibbie breeder, could make to my community and, at the same time, whether I could do more to save lives outside of my own profession." Long aware of the role of dogs in recovering victims of disaster, Mrs. Rodehaver's experience in rescue operations and emergency medicine give her a natural interest in search and rescue dogs. Studying her own Tibbie, Chip (Westview Sport Shot of Marvek), convinced Mrs. Rodehaver that Tibbies are ideally suited for certain kinds of rescues. Her husband Bill, a specialist in disaster communications and Chip's best buddy, agrees wholeheartedly.

A Tibbie's harefoot makes him exceptionally sure-footed, Mrs. Rodehaver explains. That trait, together with his small size, stability, fearlessness and love of climbing, give the Tibetan Spaniel a natural advantage in working on sites covered with rubble and debris where victims may be trapped in tiny crevices. The Oklahoma City bombing tragedy springs to mind. The Tibbie's sensitivity to human emotion, as well as the uncanny bond he forms with his owner, heightens his responsiveness. Add to these qualities the Tibbie's keen sight and hearing and you have the formula for a dog who can work quickly in situations where every minute may mean the difference between life and death for a disaster victim.

Chip has accompanied Bill Rodehaver on train and aircraft disaster simulations and demonstrated his aptitude in agility training. Aside from the fact that Chip does not conform to the expected image of a search and rescue dog, detractors sometimes point to the breed's independence as a drawback. Mrs. Rodehaver replies, "How can you lump every Tibetan Spaniel together in one category? They are individualistic!" By identifying each Tibbie's strengths and weaknesses and developing a training plan based on positive methods, she is convinced that each will realize his potential. I wish the Rodehavers and Chip the best of luck in their future training together.

Closing Thoughts

My congratulations to all the owners whose Tibbies are serving their families and communities in innovative ways. Having read this chapter, I hope that you, too, will look at your Tibbie with new eyes. Remember that his potential as a companion is limited only by your imagination.

Three Words from a Tibbie

I had worked with four-year-old Jason in a Family Day Care program for children with special needs for about a year and a half. A charming child with big blue eyes and light brown curly hair, Jason suffered from muscular dystrophy and spina bifida. Although he could move only his fingers, he was very bright and he loved to draw, his little hand in mine guiding the brush over the paper. He always drew the same thing—a dog.

It was raining when I picked Jason up, but the happy light in his eyes warmed the day. He was to spend the day with my Tibbie Sophie (Aust. Ch. Toreana Szo-Fei). Sophie loves children, and they always run and play together. But this little boy was strange, sitting there quietly on my knee. Sophie became distressed and tried to jump up to him. "Come and play!" she seemed to shout.

Jason was not too keen on this jumping little dog, but Sophie soon settled quietly on the couch next to us and interested herself in the "doggie" slippers on Jason's tiny feet. Slowly, she inched toward Jason. When I placed his small hand on her, the tail started to wag! The little boy beamed. "She is so soft," he whispered. Then laughed, "What a cold nose!" "Why is it cold?" "Why is her tongue pink?" And a thousand other questions.

As the day went by, Jason fed Sophie biscuits and brushed her with my help. He loved the way she talked to him, like Tibbies do, and they became firm friends. I was amazed that she was so loving, tender and gentle with him. She now understood that he was a special little boy. Could he come and see his friend Sophie again, Jason asked when it was time to go home. Sure thing, I promised.

Shortly afterward, I had to go into hospital myself and, when I returned home, I learned that Jason had passed away. When I was fit again, I kept my promise. Looking down at the small grave, Sophie in my arms, I thought of the happy day we all spent together. As Sophie licked the tears from my face, to say "Jason is well again now, Mum," I placed the flowers down. The card said three words...

"*Love from Sophie*"

Contributed by Joan Aspinall
(Australia) in memory of Jason

Karin Olsen ills.

Chapter Seven

Finding Your Tibetan Spaniel

Have you found something about the Tibetan Spaniel that appeals to you? His small size and cute face perhaps? His cleverness or mischievousness? His rarity and mysterious past? His aptitude for therapy work? Or, is your child pressing you for a pet dog?

Whatever the reason for your interest in a Tibetan Spaniel, choosing a breed and then selecting a dog is a complex decision that you should consider seriously. Just think, if your child is just starting school, the Tibbie puppy that you buy now will probably be your family pet until your child finishes college! This is a long-term commitment to another living being as well as a significant investment of time and money.

DECIDING ON THE BREED AND THE BREEDER

One advantage of choosing a pure-bred dog, as opposed to a mixed breed, is the pure-bred's predictability. While all members of a breed are certainly not clones, they are generally consistent in size and appearance. Moreover, there is a general theme in the breed's personality.

None of a pure-bred dog's inherited traits of appearance or personality is inherently "good" or "bad"— just different from those of another pure breed. The Tibetan Spaniel is what he is and whether he is the right breed for you depends on your personality as well as his!

Are You Right for a Tibetan Spaniel?

"After 15 years, I still find them intriguing and absolutely enchanting. It's partly their complete self-importance," says Barbara McConnell (Canada) who adds, "but you can never dominate a Tibbie and, if that's what you need to do, then Tibbies aren't the right breed for you." Ms. McConnell's remarks are echoed by many owners around the world. As wonderful as Tibbies are, the Tibetan Spaniel is not the right breed for everyone.

The average dog owner thinks that it is easier to live with a breed that is calm and easygoing. Most Tibbies have a moderate energy level and, although they get excited about something new in their environment, they settle down quickly. No problem so far!

For ease of training, the average dog owner also prefers a breed that is moderately intelligent and fairly dependent on people. Rather than being dependent, most Tibbies are mildly to extremely independent. Are you patient enough to train a dog that may not be slavishly eager to please you, that "tests" you and that requires constant motivation? Are you willing to learn positive training methods? Tibbies are also very intelligent. They learn quickly and are creative problem-solvers (or, as some would say, "scheming"). Are you creative enough to live with a dog that may be one step ahead of you? Are you ready for a dog that demands stimulation, but is easily bored? In other words, do you have the sense of humor and persistence to match wits with a Tibetan Spaniel?

While dog owners usually agree that small dogs are easier to live with than large ones, many people are inconvertibly wedded to the idea of a big dog. Will everyone in your family accept a small dog?

The next consideration is very important, so be honest with yourself. If you have a very small child, do you believe that he or she is old enough to understand how to be gentle with a Tibbie? Can he or she be taught not to shriek, flail the arms, run at, pull on, poke or tease the Tibbie? Does he or she reliably close outside doors or gates? Although most Tibbies are wonderful with children, a home with very young or excitable children may not be best for a Tibbie.

To maintain his health, a Tibbie deserves excellent veterinary care and high quality food. His other needs include grooming supplies, a crate, collar with ID tags, lead, licenses, etc. Do you have the means to supply his needs? Although he is easy to groom, in comparison to other breeds, he nonetheless requires routine care. Can you spare a few minutes each day to

Mary Browning ills.

brush him and a hour or so every week or two for other grooming tasks? Can you tolerate some shedding in your home?

A lonely, housebound Tibbie is a despondent dog. Do you have the time and inclination to exercise a Tibbie? Can you give a Tibbie the affection and companionship that he craves?

Get to Know Tibbies

Reading this book is a good first step in getting to know Tibbies. Find out as much about the breed as possible even before you visit a breeder. One place to see Tibbies is at a dog show where you may be able to meet their owners, too.

If you are convinced that you and a Tibbie were made for each other, the next step is to find and convince a Tibetan Spaniel breeder!

Why a Breeder?

Obtain your Tibbie only from an ethical breeder. Concerned breeders believe in placing puppies directly in homes rather than selling them to "middle-men" who operate for profit. That is why it is extremely unusual to find a Tibbie in a pet shop. Further, ethical breeders screen potential owners to assure that the puppy will live in a good home, and they take time to educate new owners about caring for their Tibbie. An ethical breeder's primary concern is the welfare of his or her Tibbies and not any profit to be made. In fact, reputable breeders consider themselves very lucky to break even.

How to Find a Breeder

The best source for breeder information is the club that represents the Tibetan Spaniel in your country. For example, the Tibetan Spaniel Club of America publishes a breeder directory. (A list of club addresses appears at the end of this book.) Another source of information is the national kennel organization in your country; your local kennel club may be able to help, too. Advertisements that appear in periodicals dedicated to dogs are another source.

In countries where Tibbies are fairly numerous and geographic distances are fairly small (such as Finland and the U.K.), you may be able to find a breeder close to your home. In other countries, however, breeders are less evenly distributed. In the U.S. and Australia, for example, you may need to travel a great distance to a meet a Tibbie breeder.

How Do I Choose a Breeder?

From your very first contact with a breeder, you should look for evidence that he or she is ethical and responsible. It is critically important that you, as a potential buyer, do your part to discourage unethical and irresponsible breeders by refusing to patronize them.

The growing popularity of a breed typically spawns profit-seeking, disreputable breeders and has proven a curse for many dog breeds. "Puppy mills," where large numbers of puppies are bred for profit, exist in the U.S. and other countries. Typically, these mills are operated by unethical and/or ignorant breeders who acquire mediocre individuals of a popular breed and breed them indiscriminately, without regard to pedigree or health. Dogs live in appalling conditions, lacking adequate housing, food and veterinary care. Dams are required to produce more litters, at a greater frequency than is considered humane, and dogs that have outlived their usefulness as breeding stock are callously destroyed. Many puppies are never registered.

Sadly, the heedless propagation of genetic disorders degrades the overall health of breeds exploited in this manner. Puppies that have never had the benefit of proper care and socialization are sold to pet retailers who resell them to uneducated and ill-prepared consumers. Many are ultimately abandoned, which in turn contributes to the horrific numbers of dogs destroyed in shelters each year.

Since profit-motivated animal breeders want frequent, large litters and easy sales, the Tibetan Spaniel's low reproduction rate has to some extent discouraged them. In countries where the breed is relatively unknown, Tibbie puppies are difficult to sell and this too has dampened their interest. However, as the Tibetan Spaniel becomes more widely known, unethical breeders may proliferate. Therefore, be vigilant and discerning when you choose a breeder. Here are some guidelines.

A breeder should exhibit knowledge of the breed and show interest in sharing that knowledge with you. Does the breeder specialize in Tibbies? Does the breeder show his or her Tibbies as a way to assess their quality? Does he or she belong to dog-related organizations and/or subscribe to a breeder's Code of Ethics?

Is the breeder as curious about you as you are about him or her? Expect an ethical breeder to ask you questions about your family, your home, your other pets, your experience with dogs, your reason for wanting a Tibbie and your idea of a good relationship with a dog. The sad truth is that many people have inappropriate reasons for wanting a dog, and/or they have unrealistic expectations of the responsibility of owning a dog. So, if it seems that the breeder is downright nosy, remember that he or she is quizzing you only to make sure that you will give a Tibbie the love and care that he needs. Placing puppies is as much a part of an ethical breeder's job as raising them.

An ethical breeder understands that Tibbies are neither happy nor well socialized when isolated in a kennel. Look around. Does the breeder allow you to see where the dogs live? Are the premises clean and safe? Do you see evidence that the Tibbies are accustomed to a homey environment? Are the Tibbies clean, happy and well-adjusted?

An ethical breeder will not consider selling a Tibbie puppy before eight weeks. In fact, most prefer to wait until the puppy is about ten weeks old because Tibbies mature slowly. Most are reluctant to place a puppy during holidays, such as Christmas, because of the stress on the puppy. Some refuse to sell a Tibbie to a home with small children. Others require that the home have a fenced yard. Remember that the ethical breeder cares more about his or her Tibbie's welfare than about your preferences. That is the way it should be!

Raising a Tibbie puppy (or two) is a great joy, but also a great responsibility. *Herb Rosen photo*

AN OWNER'S CODE OF ETHICS

1. I accept a life commitment for the Tibetan Spaniels that I own. If I find that it is absolutely necessary to give up any of my dogs, I will first consult the breeder of my dog and make proper arrangements for my dog's future care.
2. I will maintain a high standard of health and care for my dogs at all times. I will properly house, feed and exercise them and seek veterinary help when needed.
3. I will obtain routine preventative health care for my dogs, including immunization and deworming, following the advice of my veterinarian.
4. I will not allow my dogs to roam at large or to cause a nuisance.
5. I will provide my dogs a means of identification at all times.
6. I will discourage my dogs from fouling public places, and I will clean up after them.
7. I will spay or neuter any dog sold to me as a companion.
8. I will always conduct myself in a manner that reflects credit on dog ownership and sets a good example for others.

An ethical breeder wants to make sure that you understand how to take care of a Tibbie. Does he or she volunteer advice and information and, in turn, answer your questions fully and willingly? At a minimum, the breeder should provide you with a record of the Tibbie's health care, including a frank description of any known health problems in the Tibbie's family. He or she should provide feeding instructions and discuss training.

An ethical breeder should also willingly provide you with registration papers (e.g., AKC in the U.S., Kennel Club in the U.K., etc.), a five-generation pedigree (family tree) and a bill of sale (or contract) for your Tibbie. At a minimum, the contract should:

- identify the Tibbie you are buying,
- state the conditions of the sale (e.g., price)
- specify the conditions under which you may return your puppy and/or receive a refund, and
- state whether the Tibbie is being sold as companion (pet) or as a show prospect.

Finally, an ethical breeder exhibits an enduring commitment to his or her Tibbies. He or she never wants them to be mistreated, whether intentionally or through ignorance. The breeder should be as concerned about the health and well-being of puppies destined to be household pets as those being groomed for the show ring. He or she should stipulate, preferably in the contract, that you are required to spay or neuter a Tibbie sold as a companion (pet). The breeder should also inform you, preferably in the contract, that he or she will always re-home your Tibbie, even years later, if you find yourself unable to keep him for any reason. These provisions are in place to assure that only wanted and carefully bred Tibbie puppies are born and that no Tibbie is ever left homeless.

Corky

To those of us who love them, it is inconceivable that anyone in his right mind would discard a Tibbie by dumping him on the street or abandoning him at a shelter. And yet it happens.

Whenever possible, Karen Chamberlain (U.S.) volunteers at her local animal shelter. One evening she stopped by to help out and, while walking down the aisles, she was horrified to find a pitiful little Tibbie in one of the cages. Misidentified as a "mixed Peke," Corky was an intact male about five years old. His shoulder had been broken and never set, so one elbow jutted out at an angle. His coat was ratty. His nails had been neglected for so long that they had curled and embedded into his pads. His teeth were in horrible condition.

Mrs. Chamberlain was able to learn only that Corky had been shuttled from home to home during his short life. His last stay had been with an elderly couple whose home had been gutted by fire. After that, Corky was left at the shelter. The next day was to be his last.

Despite his miserable life, Corky was a sweet, loving little gentleman who only wanted to be with people who cared for him. Mrs. Chamberlain took him home and arranged for the care he needed. The veterinarian clipped and cauterized his nails and treated his pads for infection. Although most of his teeth could not be saved, those that remained were cleaned. He was neutered. Bathed and brushed tenderly, Corky's natural beauty began to shine through.

A few weeks later and somewhat recovered from his ordeal, Corky met the new family Mrs. Chamberlain selected for him. Today he lives on a small farm where he enjoys perching atop fieldstone walls to survey his territory. An elderly Doberman Pinscher is his best buddy, and "Mom and Dad" love him dearly. Corky has finally found the home that he, like all Tibbies, so richly deserves.

CHOOSING YOUR TIBBIE

If you have decided that the Tibetan Spaniel is the best breed for you, let's look at how to find the right Tibbie.

Puppy or Adult?

Raising a Tibbie puppy is a rewarding and memorable experience. I love having puppies in the house, and my memories of puppies are among my most cherished. As adorable and playful as a puppy is, not everyone is prepared to raise one, and many people do not realize all that is involved. Realistically speaking, you cannot leave a young puppy alone for more than four hours. When you are at home, a puppy requires not only lots of affection but constant supervision as well. You must take an active part in training and socializing him. You must puppy-proof your home for his safety, but, no matter what preventative steps you take, some damage to your home and belongings is almost inevitable. Besides the cost of the puppy himself, there are many veterinary and other expenses. Remember that it is completely unrealistic to expect a child to take care of a puppy's needs.

If you are reluctant to raise a puppy, you should know that adult Tibbies are often available from breeders. Adults, usually between five and seven years old, are retired brood bitches and studs whose good service their breeders are anxious to reward with loving pet homes. Younger adults whose show careers did not unfold as expected may also be available. Since the breed is so long-lived, adult Tibbies remain youthful in appearance and behavior. They are eager to become someone's pampered pride and joy and readily adapt to life in a pet home. As members of the breeder's family and former show dogs, most come to you well-trained and well-socialized.

If you lack the ability, time, patience or inclination to bring up a puppy, do not deprive yourself of the joys of a Tibetan Spaniel. Consider adopting an adult Tibbie.

What Makes a Good Pet Tibbie?

What do a Tibbie with a liver-colored nose, a Tibbie with a twisted leg, a Tibbie with "flyaway" ears all have in common? Although each has a physical flaw that disqualifies him from a show and breeding career, each is a personable, healthy Tibbie and the beloved pet of a family who would not dream of trading him for the most beautiful show specimen in the world!

Health and personality are the most important criteria in choosing a pet Tibbie. If a Tibbie has a wonderful personality and good health, minor physical imperfections that differentiate "show quality" from "pet quality" are meaningless. Concentrate on finding a reputable breeder whose knowledge and experience you can trust to help you select a healthy, happy pet.

Many people have the impression that they will select a puppy from several in a litter. This may not be possible because Tibbie litters are small—perhaps only three to five puppies—and two or more of the puppies may already be "spoken for." Further, many breeders prefer to choose the puppy for you, especially if you are inexperienced with dogs or if this is your first Tibetan Spaniel. Although the breeder's experience and understanding of young puppies is invaluable in finding a good match to your lifestyle and personality, the final decision is yours. Read on for tips on choosing a puppy.

What Do "Papers" Mean?

Here in the U.S., many people believe that a dog that comes with "papers" is a quality dog. What exactly are "papers"?

A pedigree is a form that shows a dog's antecedents back to his great-great grandparents and documents that he is a pure-bred Tibetan Spaniel. In other words, it is simply the Tibbie's family tree. The dogs named on the pedigree may or may not have been good quality, healthy Tibbies. In the hands of a knowledgeable breeder, a pedigree is a tool used to predict the outcome of breeding, but they are not usually very meaningful to a pet owner.

Also among the "papers" is an official registration document. This form means that national kennel organization in your country (e.g., the American Kennel Club (AKC) in the U.S., the Kennel Club in the U.K., etc.) has on file a record of the Tibbie's antecedents. Since breeders provide the information in the organization's records, the accuracy of the registration information depends largely on the integrity of breeders.

The national kennel organizations of some countries allow breeders to register a dog in a manner that does not permit the registration of any of the dog's future offspring. For example, the AKC terms it a "limited registration." This non-breeding form of registration is intended to discourage breeding of all but the highest quality dogs.

In a few countries, the national kennel organization does not allow registration of a Tibetan Spaniel unless certain criteria, intended as a gauge of genetic health, are met. For example, the Svenska Kennelklubben (Sweden) will not register a Tibbie puppy unless both of his parents passed eye examinations within one year before the puppy's conception. In countries where health testing is voluntary (e.g., U.S., U.K.), registration restrictions of this type do not exist, but some kennel organizations annotate the registration document with health information provided by breeders. For example, the AKC records Canine Eye Registry Foundation (CERF) numbers on its registration forms.

Put into perspective, the pedigree and registration document that a breeder gives you indicate that the dog is a pure-bred Tibetan Spaniel and that the breeder complies with the record keeping rules of the registration organization. Certainly, you should insist on receiving such "papers." However, neither the pedigree nor registration document is a guarantee of the Tibbie's overall quality and health. Ultimately, you must rely on the breeder's advice and on your own assessment to determine the Tibbie's quality. In other words, *caveat emptor.*

Among the papers you receive from the breeder are a contract, pedigree and registration document. It is important to review these documents carefully even when distracted by your new Tibbie. *Chris Miccio photo*

Evaluating Personality

If you are considering purchasing a Tibbie puppy, begin your evaluation of the puppy by letting him wander around freely while you observe his appearance and behavior. Is he alert and happy-looking? Does he behave in a confident, not skittish, manner? Is he active without being hyperactive? Next, hold out your arms and call the puppy to you. Does he come? Does he show interest in playing? Does he follow you around? Try petting him. Does he allow you to hold him without struggling? Try turning him on his back and holding him there. Does he relax after a few moments of wiggling?

What you have just read briefly introduces how to observe and evaluate a puppy's "temperament" (personality). Many dog books explain how to do this.

This puppy calmly accepts being restrained on her back. This exercise indicates that she will be an easygoing Tibbie. Familiarize yourself with temperament tests before selecting a puppy. *Chris Miccio photo*

For example, Linda Colflesh's *Making Friends* outlines an excellent procedure for temperament testing. Since it is not within the scope of this book to repeat all of the guidelines, it is a good idea to familiarize yourself with these methods before choosing your puppy.

There are some differences between evaluating an adult and a puppy. For example, an adult Tibbie will obviously be calmer than a puppy, but he should be just as alert and confident. Note that you should not expect an adult Tibbie, that has just met you, to greet you enthusiastically. Remember that an older Tibbie may be slightly aloof or indifferent toward a stranger, but he should warm up to you before very long.

Assessing Health

Are the eyes bright and the skin clear? Is the Tibbie lively? Does he appear to be well-nourished? Beyond looking for obvious outward signs of robust health such as these, your assessment of the Tibbie's health depends in large part on information from the breeder. A reputable breeder usually volunteers health information, but, if not, ask for it.

If you are buying a puppy, ask for a record of the health care the puppy has received. A veterinarian should have examined the puppy at least once. The puppy should have been dewormed and, depending on his age, given at least the first round of vaccinations. Next, ask to see both of the puppy's parents, if possible (the sire may not be there), and ask about family health history. For example, ask whether either of the parents has experienced health problems such as allergies. Ask to see proof that the parents' eyes were examined.

For an adult Tibbie, ask for a record that shows the dates of immunizations and, where rabies is an issue, a copy of the latest rabies tag and certificate. Discuss the Tibbie's own health history including dental care, surgery and/or any illnesses. Ask whether the Tibbie has any behavioral problems or quirks. For example, it would not be at all unusual for a male dog that had been used at stud to "mark" (urinate on) vertical objects in the house. In some males, habitual marking persists to one degree or another even after neutering. Discuss this matter frankly with the breeder. In addition, explore the Tibbie's family health history to ascertain whether any problems run in his line.

Assessing Show Quality

If you are considering buying a show quality Tibbie, it is incumbent on you to learn about Tibetan Spaniel conformation. You should attend many shows and study the Breed Standard as well as other available sources of information. To learn the ropes, most novices carefully select an experienced, respected breeder as a mentor.

Knowledgeable breeders understand that puppies change as they grow up. A breeder's assessment of show potential is, at best, an informed guess. Therefore, when buying a puppy as a show prospect, make sure that your agreement with the breeder specifies a remedy if the puppy does not grow up to be a show dog. Other stipulations should spell out, for example, how future breedings will be handled.

Note that breeders may be reluctant to sell a show prospect to a novice or may insist on a means of retaining control, such as co-ownership, as a condition of the sale. See Chapter 12 for more detail about selecting show prospects.

How Much Should I Pay?

Breeding dogs in an ethical manner is a expensive venture. Costs of housing and feeding, show and travel expenses, dues and fees, veterinary bills and training costs add up. In most countries, the purchase price of a Tibbie is unregulated and varies. In general, expect to pay more for a show prospect than a pet Tibbie and, perhaps, slightly more for a female than a male. The amount may vary according to the quality reflected in the Tibbie's pedigree and the breeder's reputation and location.

Matches Made in Heaven

You are reading about choosing a Tibbie, but you should be aware that the Tibbie often chooses the human, rather than the other way around! Every breeder can tell a story about the Tibbie that selected his owner with no help from the breeder. When a Tibbie meets the person with whom he wants to spend his life, a spark passes between them, and in that instant, fate takes a turn.

What About Me?

When Karen Chamberlain (U.S.) decided to buy a Tibbie, she visited the home of breeder Carole Jeffery to see her Tibbies. Although Mrs. Jeffery had no pups for sale at the time, Mrs. Chamberlain was fully prepared to wait for the perfect pup to come along. As they chatted and watched the Tibbies play, a perky little bitch, about six months old, separated herself from the others, popped into Mrs. Chamberlain's lap, bestowed a Tibbie kiss, turned and bounced off to resume playing. This little scenario repeated itself several times. As they neared the end of their conversation, Mrs. Jeffery suddenly asked, "Well, do you want the little

> ## OPERATION RESCUE
>
> Breed rescue is a program for re-homing Tibbies that are homeless or living in inhumane circumstances. Runaway or abandoned Tibbies account for some of the homeless, while others are displaced due to the death or marital breakup of their owners.
>
> Breeders must be the vanguard of the rescue effort. Homelessness is minimized if breeders place each Tibbie carefully and emphasize their willingness to re-home the Tibbies they breed. Owners should always identify their Tibbies by tag, tattoo or microchip.
>
> Breed clubs must take responsibility for co-ordinating rescue in cases where re-homing with the breeder is not possible. Compiling a waiting list of potential adopters is useful. A systematic outreach, at the local level, alerts veterinarians, animal shelters and others that may come in contact with displaced Tibbies to the existence of Tibetan Spaniel breed rescue. In countries where the breed is not recognized, photos familiarize these contacts with the appearance of the breed.
>
> Each year, only a few Tibbies needing homes come to the attention of breed clubs—even in countries where Tibbies are numerous. Sadly, as the breed become more popular, more Tibbies may require rescue services. Be prepared.

girl that keeps jumping in your lap?" Taken aback, Mrs. Chamberlain replied that she had not considered the puppy only because she had assumed that Mrs. Jeffery planned to keep her. "Well," Mrs. Jeffery shrugged, laughing, "She's obviously chosen you!" You can't fight destiny, and so Pippin went to her new home that very day.

Sometimes it seems that destiny has more than a little to do with the match between a Tibbie and his person.

Gladys and Dolly

It was hard to say anything nice about Dolly. She was not a very pretty Tibbie, and she had a cherry eye. Her personality was blah. Nobody ever played with her. Nobody wanted her.

As she worked around the house, Gladys the housekeeper became fond of all the Tibbies. She especially liked Madam, the little mischief maker who unmade the beds as soon as Gladys made them up. Wanting a Tibbie for company, Gladys decided to adopt poor little Dolly out of the goodness of her heart.

Gladys changed Dolly's life. No longer lonely and withdrawn, Dolly has become a vivacious, outgoing Tibbie. She and Gladys are inseparable. Dolly changed Gladys' life, too. Now that Dolly is there to play with, Gladys' grandchildren visit Granny more regularly. The little Tibbie that nobody wanted became the little Tibbie that everybody loves. All she needed was a true friend and a real home.

Considering the rarity of the Tibetan Spaniel, it surprises me how many of us who are "in Tibbies" found (or were found by) our first one. I can speak from personal experience about this since I found my own first Tibbie. Tibbies have walked into their owners' lives in places as far-flung as a mountain campsite in Idaho and a railway station in Kenya. Like me, these owners found their hearts stolen away by a Tibetan Spaniel and their lives have never been the same.

Glen

While walking by an empty house on a cold and wet November morning, my husband noticed a little creature huddled under a bush, soaking wet and covered in mud. A high fence surrounded the garden, and the gate was fastened. My husband entered the garden and left with a tiny puppy clinging desperately to his pullover.

The puppy was about eight weeks old. Although he was very thin, he refused to eat. The vet said that he could not eat because he had been so long without food but that, luckily, no infection was present. As we were committed to keep him, the vet felt sure the puppy would make his mind up to survive. We called him Glen.

We fed Glen with honey and milk and baby food from a spoon every three hours. After nine weeks, he was fit enough to be vaccinated and, from then on, he became stronger and stronger. A true blue in colour, Glen grew into a lively little dog, full of character, charm and intelligence. He was always on the go and a great little watchdog. Like most people who fall in love with a Tibetan Spaniel, we soon acquired a family of Tibbies. Glen played with and ruled over them all benevolently, and they loved him, too.

Except for a bit of arthritis, Glen remained healthy until advanced old age. He continued to go on walks with the family and, of course, he always enjoyed people fussing over him on these outings. When he became too tired to walk with the others, I carried him. Although he became deaf in the last year of his life, Glen watched us for signals, and the other Tibbies were a great help to him, too. One Friday morning, he suffered a stroke. After recovering slightly, he again became disoriented and weak. We could not let him lose all quality of life, and, on the following Thursday, we let Glen go to sleep forever. He was sixteen years old. I believe that a little bit of one dies with each dog, and life can never be quite the same again for any us without Glen.

I had always felt that Glen was somehow "special." He seemed to understand everything around him and sensed what was going to happen before it happened. My mother had suffered a stroke many years before and she had deteriorated mentally. I tried to warn her that Glen was getting old and we could not have him much longer, to which my mother cried, "Glen, you can't die before me. I couldn't live without you." Glen died three weeks after my mother.

I had always said that Glen would send us another Tibbie after he died. Soon after his death, we were promised a male puppy from a litter of Tibbies that were related to ours. When the puppy was eight weeks old, we traveled to Yorkshire to collect him. Arriving home, Ming the puppy trotted around the house with his newfound "brothers" and settled on Glen's beanbag. He was joined on the beanbag by Kim, Glen's buddy, who had abandoned the beanbag after Glen died. Ming and Kim slept together all night without a peep. Ming was born the week my mother died in a house numbered 17, the number of my mother's house. Deval, the name that appears on my mother's deed, also appears in Ming's kennel name, Danesteval. Added to these "coincidences," Ming possesses many of Glen's traits, and we have decided that he must be Heaven-sent.

We were never able to trace Glen's background. It was suggested that he may have been stolen and then dumped in the garden where my husband found him. He was the find of a lifetime! I think he was special because of his great devotion to us. He was always so obedient and full of love for his family. All he asked was to be with us; we were his life.

Tibetan Spaniels are a joy to own. I will always be grateful for knowing Glen because it was he who opened up a new world for us, that of the Tibetan Spaniel.

contributed by Diane Zammit (U.K.)
in loving memory of Glen

Suzy Wong

I found her one day in 1960, outside the East African Railway Headquarters in Nairobi where I worked. I had gone downstairs to the ladies restroom on the ground floor and there she was, wagging her tail and being very friendly. She tried to get back in the lift with me but I left her there. She was a Pekingese perhaps, I thought at the time, but somehow different.

When I left work to go home that evening, she was still there and, when my husband came with the car, she was quite happy to jump in with me. As she had no collar or tag, we went round to the railway houses to see if anyone there knew where she lived. But, since no one knew her, we took her home. The next day, we decided that she must go to the local Dog Pound as her owners were probably looking for her. When I handed her in, they also guessed that she was a Pekingese and that is how she was advertised on the local radio station.

At the end of two weeks, the Pound manager phoned me to say that they would have to put her to

"Suzy Wong" in Nairobi, Kenya.

sleep because no one had claimed her. "Oh, you can't," I cried, "How much will it cost me to come and collect her?" "Forty-two shillings madam," he said. So off I went with collar and lead, and she was overjoyed to see me again.

We decided to name her Suzy Wong after a film I had just seen. Her coat was a lovely colour, nearly mahogany red on her back with lighter colour on her chest and trousers and underneath her tail. She had a black shawl and some black in her tail and on the tips of her ear fringes. She seemed very different from other dogs. In that she liked fish and cream, she had the characteristics of a cat. In that she was very agile and jumped great distances from the back of one chair to another, she reminded me of a monkey or flying fox. She always wanted to sit up high so that she could see everything outside, and her hearing was so acute that she would warn us of someone's approach before our German Shepherd, Marcus, had heard anything at all.

We never found out where Suzy Wong came from—perhaps from an Asian family or member of the Chinese legation in Nairobi—or why no one claimed her when she was advertised.

Shortly after returning to England in 1966, I entered Marcus in an obedience competition, and Suzy went along for the ride. A German Shepherd judge noticed Suzy in my car and remarked, "Oh, I see you have a Tibetan Spaniel as well." "I have? Where?" I asked, baffled. The judge convinced me to get in touch with the Tibbie people to let them have a look at her, and I contacted Mrs. Ann Wynyard (Braeduke) to show her Suzy's photos. "Where did you get her?" Mrs. Wynyard asked me, "I have been trying to import one for ages and now I see this! Have you bred from her?" Knowing what I do now, perhaps I should have bred from her, but I never did.

When Suzy became old, we knew that we wanted another Tibbie when she was no longer with us, and that's how we started in Tibetan Spaniels. Suzy Wong died at age fifteen, the most enchanting little dog I had ever owned.

contributed by June Tomlinson, Breed Historian *emeritus* for the Tibetan Spaniel Association (U.K.)

Chapter Eight

Caring for Your Tibetan Spaniel Puppy

For the first year of his life, your job is to give your puppy proper nutrition and veterinary care to enable him to grow into a healthy adult. At the same time, you gently and gradually set the limits that define acceptable adult behavior. This chapter explains how to prepare for your puppy's arrival and take care of him while he's a puppy. Chapter 10 discusses training.

BRINGING PUPPY HOME

The New Puppy

I glance at the puppy snuggled in his new owner's lap. I smile and remind her, for the forty-seventh time, to please call me if any questions or problems come up. I back (reluctantly) away from the car, and Chris and I watch it pull from the driveway. I wave cheerfully. I am happy to see the puppy go to such a good home and such a nice family, I tell myself, but there's a tug at my heart and a tear in my eye just the same. Every Tibbie puppy is so precious.

A flash of memory. Another puppy snuggles on a towel in a new owner's lap—a saucy-faced little golden girl with four white paws, a splash of white on the tip of her tail and the thumbprint of Buddha on her forehead. "Not a fear in the world, this little monkey," I remember saying to Chris as he inched our compact car from the breeder's driveway. (That was before we graduated to the minivan-world of multi-Tibbies.) Kissie was my first Tibbie puppy, and, well, she taught me a thing or two....

Cute and fuzzy though he is, it is important to remember that a puppy is a baby. It is unrealistic to expect a puppy to be perfectly behaved from the moment you bring him home. He needs time to be a puppy. Although you will understandably be relieved when certain puppy phases, such as chewing and housetraining, are over, your memories of your Tibbie's puppyhood will be precious. So much so, in fact, that you may be inspired, like so many before you, to add a new puppy to your Tibbie family.

When to Bring Home a Puppy

The best time to bring home a puppy is when you can arrange to spend a few days with him. During this critical time, he has a chance to bond to you, to explore his new home and to adjust to your schedule (and vice versa). As Chapter 10 explains, it is important to establish a feeding and "potty" routine during these first few days.

Introduce the puppy to your home during a period of normal household activity and make his first few days with you as stress-free as possible. Bringing home a puppy during a holiday season is inadvisable.

Crate and Travel Kennel

Buy your basic supplies before bringing your puppy home. Your most important purchase is a sturdy crate. The crate is essential for housetraining your puppy and, after housetraining, continues its service as a "den." I prefer a crate made of wire mesh. A good size for a Tibbie puppy measures about 24" long x 20" wide x 20" high, give or take an inch here and there. Remember that a crate that is too large is not effective for housetraining, and a crate that is too small is not comfortable as a den.

When you bring your puppy home, introduce him to his crate right away. If he does not enter on his own, toss a treat inside as a lure. Let him wander in and out at will. Most owners place the crate in the bedroom at night, both to give the Tibbie a sense of belonging to the family and also to allow them to watch over the puppy. During the day, they move the crate to the kitchen or other room where the puppy will be left while they are away from home.

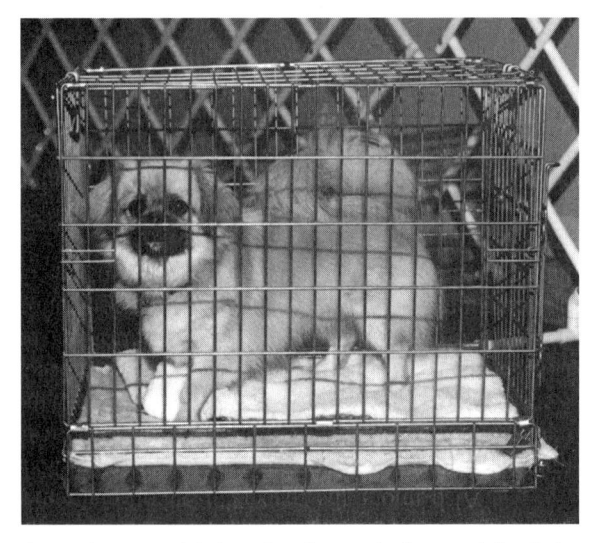

A crate is an essential piece of equipment, both as a training device and as a "den" for your puppy. The crate continues to be useful even after he grows up. At two years old, "Gizmo," owned by Linda Couchon, still fits perfectly in his. *Scott Chamberlain photo*

Some people believe that closing a dog in a crate is inhumane. It would be if the dog were left in the crate for excessively long periods of time or if the crate were too small or unsanitary. However, when the dog is given a clean crate of the correct size and plenty of exercise and free time with his family, crating is not only humane but actually gratifies the dog's inborn need for a den. As a training aid, use of crates has helped to reduce the numbers of dogs returned to breeders or abandoned by dissatisfied owners.

I Love My Crate!

When Gary and Linda McDermaid (U.S.) brought home their Tibbie Abbey, they decided not to use the crate in which breeder Ruth Mutschler had housetrained her. However, Abbey reacted to the loss of her crate by becoming skittish and insecure, and the McDermaids soon restored the crate to its place. "She regards it as her sanctuary," says Mrs. McDermaid, "And she is very protective of it. If the cats go in, she plops on top of them!" Although Abbey is grown now, the open crate remains next to the McDermaid's bed, and Abbey divides her time equally between bed and crate. Whenever she needs a bit of peace and quiet, Abbey retires to her crate and, making a mound of the blankets, perches atop them in typically Tibbie fashion.

Also consider buying a travel kennel. These are usually made of molded plastic, vented, with a latching wire door and handle for carrying. They fit into a car more easily than a wire crate. An average-sized woman can readily carry the size suitable for most Tibbies.

Toys

Tibbie puppies are intelligent and require stimulating activities. Toys contribute to physical and mental development and distract busy puppies from destructive pastimes. Chew toys, fuzzies (such as stuffed animals) and balls are Tibbie favorites.

Before giving your Tibbie any item to play with, consider whether the toy is potentially harmful. For example, an object with strings or small pieces, that he may pull off and swallow, may be dangerous. Do not give your Tibbie old shoes or socks as toys; he is not able to differentiate between your good shoes and your old shoes!

Chew toys are essential during your puppy's teething phase, which may last until he is one year old, and continue to contribute to his dental health throughout his life. Dogs love chew toys made of rawhide and usually prefer them to those made of nylon or other non-natural materials. Many owners, including myself, have used rawhide chew toys without incident. However, some owners avoid them out of concern that chunks torn away from the toy may choke or cause an internal obstruction. In the past, illnesses were rumored to be caused by toxic substances reportedly used in manufacturing poor quality rawhide toys. If you choose to use rawhide chew toys, select a high quality brand that is so thick and large that your Tibbie must work on it for a long time. Do not choose small "chips" or "knots" that he can tear up and consume in a short time. Keep an eye on him. If he softens a piece that he can pull off and swallow, cut it off with scissors. Similarly, when you notice that he has reduced the toy to a size that he could swallow, remove it.

Never give your Tibbie real bones, especially pork or poultry bones, since they may splinter and cause serious injury or death.

Collar and Lead

For puppies under four months, choose an expandable collar that you can "let out" as the puppy grows. Test the collar to make sure that it clasps securely. Do not use a "cat collar" or other collar with an elastic inset. Avoid collars with decorations that a puppy could pull off and swallow.

Once the puppy is nearly adult size, select a good quality collar. Although plastic clasps are adequate for small puppies, I recommend a metal buckle collar for Tibbies over six months old. Rolled leather collars do not damage the mane/shawl and are inconspicuous.

Caring for Your Tibetan Spaniel Puppy

Sagaland's Z-Mar-Tell, age seven weeks, bred and owned by Gerd and Kjell Strand (Norway). *Studio S photo*

Ishido and l'Yezo de Tatsienlou, at three months, bred by Sylvie Sanchez (France).

Tashi-Gong Caroline, bred by Katriina Venäläinen and owned by her breeder and Maija Venäläinen (Finland), enjoys a bed of pansies.

The collar should fit snugly so that your Tibbie cannot "slip" it (by backing out), but you should be able to easily slip your fingers under it. A too-tight collar can choke your Tibbie or damage his trachea. Your Tibbie should wear his collar, fitted with an identification tag, at all times.

For a starter lead, choose a lightweight lead about four feet long and fitted with a snap-bolt. After the puppy is accustomed to the starter lead, consider buying a retractable lead. These come in various lengths up to about 20 feet and are excellent for training. Regardless of the type of lead that you use, be aware that a boisterous Tibbie puppy can wrest it from your hand in a moment. Always hold the lead in a secure manner and be attentive.

Chapter 10 explains lead training.

Other Supplies

Select metal or ceramic (rather than plastic) food bowls for a puppy. Separate bowls for food and water are easier to handle than a feeder with two wells. Grooming supplies are discussed in Chapter 9.

Puppy-Proofing Your Home

As a puppy owner, you should consider both the dangers that your home poses to your puppy and damages your puppy may inflict on your home. Do not underestimate a Tibbie puppy's ability to get into trouble!

To protect your puppy, conceal electric cords or gather them up out of reach and secure with a twist-tie. Move all houseplants beyond his reach. Assure that no cleaning solutions or other poisonous household products, such as pesticides, are at puppy level. Close exterior doors securely and keep them closed at all times.

To protect wood furnishings, apply a product such as Grannick's Bitter Apple™ to susceptible targets such as chair legs and the lower edges of cabinetry. Always keep loose articles, such as your eyeglasses, out of reach. To minimize damage from housetraining accidents, consider applying a protectant product to fabrics.

If you need to temporarily confine your puppy to certain areas of the house, such as the kitchen, consider installing a baby gate or purchasing a portable, folding pen.

Chapter 9 describes adequate fencing and other precautions designed to protect your Tibbie while he is outside. Chapter 10 discusses housetraining accidents and problem behaviors such as destructive chewing.

RAISING YOUR PUPPY

As a rule of thumb, a Tibbie's puppyhood lasts one year. No magical transformation occurs on his first birthday, but one year is a useful approximation. During this first year, he grows rapidly and requires special nutrition to build his body. Psychologically, he requires a broad range of experiences to nurture his developing personality.

Handling Your Puppy

It is important to learn how to correctly pick up and hold a Tibbie puppy so that you do not hurt him. Since his body is immature, hold the puppy in a manner that supports both the forequarters and hindquarters, but does not strain or damage any of his musculoskeletal structures.

Lift your puppy by clasping him around his rib cage and supporting his hindlegs. Picking him up in any other manner, such as lifting him by his forelegs, may cause pain and injury.

The owner places her fingers so that the puppy's elbows are held tight against the puppy's chest wall. *Chris Miccio photo*

Caring for Your Tibetan Spaniel Puppy

The two important points about holding a Tibbie puppy are to support his hindquarters as well as his forequarters and to hold his elbows tightly against his chest wall at all times. If the puppy is small enough to be supported with one arm, brace his body snugly between your arm and torso so that his rump rests in the crook of your elbow and the hindquarters and abdomen are supported by your forearm. Support his forequarters by wrapping your hand around the front of his body so that his chest and upper forelegs rest on your hand. If you wish, support his dangling paws with your other hand. Another way to support the forequarters is to rest his chest on your palm but place *only* your forefinger between his forelegs and hold his elbows tightly against his body with your thumb on one side and your ring and little fingers on the other side. As the puppy gets older and heavier, a two-handed approach is required. Wrap one arm around his midsection to anchor the forequarters and support his hindlegs with your other hand.

Since a young puppy's "elbow" joint may be easily damaged if it is stretched away from the body, never support the puppy's forequarters by placing your entire hand, palm up, beneath the puppy's body so that your fingers and thumb push the elbows away from the body. Never pick up and/or hold your puppy facing you, each of his "armpits" resting on the joint between your thumb and hand, in the way that we hold human babies. Since this hold pushes the elbows away from the body and your puppy's whole weight rests on the weak structures beneath his elbows, holding him in this manner risks pain and permanent damage.

It is extremely important to teach children how to pick up and hold a puppy properly. Chapter 10 discusses socializing children and puppies.

Naming and Identifying Your Puppy

A Tibbie usually has two names—his call name (the one you use everyday) and his registered name (the official name on his papers). Your Tibbie's call name is a personal choice; my only advice is that it should be short. The official name is subject to a few more rules. For example, it must be unique; you probably would not be permitted to register your Tibbie with only a simple name like "Princess." In addition, the breeder may want you to use his or her kennel name, as part of the name, and he or she will explain how this is done. The national kennel organization that registers dogs in the country where you live may impose additional rules. For example, the AKC limits the length of the name to 25 characters (including the spaces between

---

SAMPLER OF TIBETAN NAMES

For those of you who may like to choose a Tibetan name for your Tibbie, here are some interesting ideas.

artful	*chang-po*	lion	*seng* (or *senge*)
baby	*cunu*	lioness	*sengemo*
bear	*dom*	little	*cun-wa*
beautiful	*dze-pa, bzanba*	merry	*krulop*
beloved	*cespa*	partner	*kaya*
best	*donno*	plump	*rompo*
big	*chhem-po*	precious	*rincen*
candy	*kanda*	puffball	*pabu*
dear to hold	*ceba*	puppy	*kyigu*
delight	*dgaba*	rainbow	*jalus, ja*
dog	*kyi*	silk	*dar*
doll	*miu*	small	*cinba*
dragon	*druk*	smile	*dzum*
faithful	*dadpa*	snow	*kaba*
gentle	*ampo*	snow leopard	*zigsa*
ghost	*mimayin*	star	*skamar*
gold	*ser*	sugar	*kara*
good	*don*	sweetheart	*dodgrogs*
honey	*ransi*	tickle	*kitsi*
hope	*rewa*	tiger	*stag*
lady	*jomo*	treasure	*ter*

109

Saffron Phutnam, at age three months, bred by Pirkko Linnus (Finland) *Mikko Mäntyniemi photo*

words), and the Société Canine Centrale of France requires that the names of all puppies registered in a given year begin with the same letter.

As soon as you decide on a call name, buy an identification tag that shows the Tibbie's name, your name, address and telephone number. Since the ID tag is the quickest way for other people to identify him, he should wear it on his collar at all times along with any required licenses (such as rabies). Tattoo and microchip are permanent forms of identification that are always present, even when the dog's collar is accidentally or intentionally removed. Most national kennel organizations now require a permanent form of identification.

Taking Your Puppy to the Veterinarian

The breeder should provide you with a health record for your puppy. Depending on his age, he should have received at least the initial series of immunizations and deworming.

Visit your veterinarian shortly after bringing the puppy home. In fact, the agreement that you and the breeder signed may require a veterinary evaluation of your puppy within a specific time frame. During this first visit, your veterinarian examines your puppy, apprises you of any health problems that he or she may find and explains preventative health care. It is extremely important for you to follow through on the entire course of immunizations your veterinarian recommends since your puppy is not fully protected against disease until all of the injections are complete.

If you do not already have a family veterinarian, Chapter 11 suggests criteria for choosing a veterinarian and explains preventative health care. Chapter 13 explains congenital conditions sometimes found in Tibbie youngsters.

Feeding Your Puppy

Your puppy should be eating solid food before you bring him home. The breeder should explain what and how to feed your puppy, because it is important to keep your puppy on the breeder's diet temporarily, according to the schedule he or she suggests, to avoid stomach upsets. The breeder will also probably give you a small supply of food. If you prefer to feed another brand or form of puppy food, transition from the breeder's diet slowly.

The food you feed your puppy, for the first year of his life, should be a premium brand specifically formulated for puppies (sometimes called a "growth" food). Do not feed cheap brands or food formulated for other life stages. If you feed a premium quality puppy food, dietary vitamin or mineral supplements are usually unnecessary.

The form of food preferred for puppies, as in other life stages, is dry food. Select a small size chunk. If your breeder suggests mixing in some canned food,

Bioko's Clipper, at age four months, bred by Christina Käglefeldt and owned by Lisa Molin (Sweden).

Baron von Dunning of Alan-Li, age eight months, bred by the author and owned by Rev. and Mrs. William Dunning (U.S.) *Chris Miccio photo*

follow his or her advice and gradually change over to an all-dry diet.

For treats, I suggest a small biscuit formulated for puppies by a manufacturer of premium food. You may be tempted to treat your puppy with human food, but try to resist. Besides the upset it may cause, feeding table food encourages begging and finicky eating.

Much of the information that applies to adult diets also applies to puppy diets. For more information about canine nutrition, see Chapter 9.

Exercising Your Puppy

Your Tibbie puppy needs moderate physical exercise to strengthen his bones and tone his muscles. Walking uphill and downhill is especially good for Tibbies. Ample physical exercise reduces the mischief your puppy makes ("A tired puppy is good puppy"), and he is less likely to indulge in problem behaviors. However, while he is a baby, avoid exercise that stresses or traumatizes his joints, such as jumping from furniture.

Your intelligent Tibbie puppy also requires stimulating mental exercise. The psychological drive to play is especially strong in Tibbies, and puppies as young as eight or nine weeks begin to play games. Playing games such as "fetch" builds the bond between you and your Tibbie and lays the groundwork for future training. Playtime is the perfect time to begin teaching your puppy basic commands such as "Come."

Chapter 10 explains how to train your puppy and to handle puppy behaviors such as chewing.

The Tibetan Spaniel

Karen Chamberlain ills.

Chapter Nine

Caring for Your Adult Tibetan Spaniel

For all the pleasure they give us, we owe our Tibbies the best possible care. This chapter addresses everyday life with your adult Tibbie. Feeding, grooming, exercising, and traveling with him are among the topics. We'll talk about the special needs of the geriatric Tibbie, and close with some thoughts about saying good-by to a special friend.

GROWING UP

From the time you bring home a puppy until he is a year or so old, your Tibetan Spaniel is busily growing up. He passes through several developmental "phases." In addition to physiological changes, his range of experiences expands and his adult personality is shaped by environmental as well as hereditary factors.

You may hear people say that the Tibetan Spaniel matures slowly. This means that a Tibbie may not attain a fully adult appearance until he is two or three years old. However, other physiological and mental changes that signal impending adulthood, such as puberty, occur on a par with other small breeds.

Changes in Appearance

Most Tibbies are born with a very blunt muzzle which lengthens as they grow. The lower jaw continues to grow for a longer time than the upper jaw. Whereas a young puppy's "bite" may start out level (upper teeth meet lower teeth on the same plane) or overshot (upper teeth extend beyond lower teeth), the slowly growing lower jaw may gradually change the bite to undershot (lower teeth extend beyond upper teeth). A puppy that starts out with a slightly undershot bite may develop a more pronounced undershot bite as he grows. It is unlikely that a level or undershot bite will become overshot.

The sharp baby teeth fall out between four and seven months and are gradually replaced by permanent teeth. The eruption of molars in the back of the mouth may crowd the incisors until they become crooked. Some of the molars may be misaligned, too. The movement of teeth may continue well into adulthood; the one-year-old with perfect dentition may have crooked teeth by age two or three years.

The period during which a puppy is teething is trying for Tibbie and owner alike. Like other teenagers, the Tibbie is growing rapidly. His skull is larger in proportion to his body than an adult's head and body. The body and legs look too long and the chest too narrow; overall, nothing seems in proportion. In dog jargon, a teenage dog as "has no body" but will hopefully "grow into himself."

As he grows out of his gawky stage, between six and twelve months, he reaches adult weight. His chest broadens and the muscles of the foreleg and shoulders tighten and add muscle. His hindlegs also gain strength and tone. The spine may become less noticeably protuberant as the musculature around it develops. By the time he is a year old, the sum of his parts seems to add up to a balanced whole.

Meanwhile, the puppy's coat also transforms slowly. Most sable Tibbies are born dark and lighten into their adult color before they are one year old. The white markings they had at birth, such as socks or a Buddha mark, usually disappear or diminish in size. The plush puppy coat also falls away during the first year. Some young Tibbies replace it with a silky pre-adult coat, but many sport a sparse coat for several months. Their "undressed" state only intensifies the gawky, teenage look. Although a young puppy may sprout little trousers, the ear fringes, gloves and mane/shawl usually do not fill in until much later. In fact, many mature males do not attain manes of leonine proportions until two, three or even four years of age. Be patient.

Changes in Behavior

Between nine and twelve weeks, your puppy is in a developmental stage during which fears may be easily and indelibly imprinted. In a temperamentally sound puppy, positive experiences during this period lay the foundation for a well-adjusted adolescence and adulthood. As he approaches puberty, the dog becomes progressively bolder and more adventuresome. As an adolescent, he loves you but willfully tests the limits you set for him,

Sometime before his first birthday, your male puppy stops squatting and begins to lift his leg to urinate. This is the most noticeable sign of male puberty. Others include experimental mounting and territorial marking. Unless he is neutered early, these hormonally induced male behaviors may become habitual.

A female puppy's attainment of puberty, signalled by the onset of her first heat cycle (season), usually occurs between seven and twelve months. When the cycle begins, her vulva swells followed by a bloody discharge. Although the discharge may last only a couple of weeks, the cycle itself lasts for a period of three to four weeks. During a part of this period, she is fertile and, if afforded the opportunity, permits mating. Unless she is spayed, these seasons recur every eight to 14 months (or so) with each season posing the risk of a pregnancy. Chapter 12 further describes the heat cycle.

FEEDING YOUR TIBBIE

For health conscious people, nutrition as a means of preserving health and promoting longevity is an absorbing interest. Good nutrition and weight maintenance have been credited with reducing health problems such as heart disease and cancer in humans. Just as interest in human nutrition has grown in recent years, more attention has been focused on pet nutrition and research has provided many new and reliable food products for dogs.

Everyone agrees that a well-nourished, fit Tibbie is longer-lived and better able to fight health problems. However, owners express a wide range of views as to what exactly constitutes good nutrition for a Tibetan Spaniel. Pronounced with the voice of conviction, all of these clashing opinions reflect canine nutrition issues being debated among the larger group of all dog owners.

In a sense, I am glad to hear so many opinions because they indicate that some Tibbie owners are thinking about nutrition, rather than just buying the cheapest can of dog food in the grocery store. Although it is not within the scope of this book to address all of the issues, this section may help you cultivate a taste for Tibbie nutrition.

The general guidelines in this section apply to all ages. However, the special needs of puppies are discussed in Chapter 8, older Tibbies later in this chapter and breeding stock in Chapter 13.

What Do Tibbies Need?

All Tibbies need protein, fat, carbohydrates, vitamins, minerals and water. These are exactly the same nutrients that we humans need. That, however, is where the similarity ends.

> *A man is always in trouble, and a dog is always hungry.*
>
> Tibetan proverb

The idea that dogs need the same foods that we do is a myth, and just because a dog food resembles human food does not mean it is the best food for your Tibbie. (Besides, much of what we eat is no good for us either!) Another myth is the idea that dogs are carnivores. Dogs are omnivorous, which means they eat everything, not just meat. In their native Tibet, Tibbies subsisted for centuries primarily on a staple diet of *tsampa* (barley flour moistened with yak butter tea). While it is true that a Tibbie likes meat flavors, an all-meat diet would not furnish the nutrients he needs. For example, an all-meat diet contains too much phosphorous but too little calcium.

Which Brand of Food is Best?

While some Tibbies are finicky about their food, most gladly consume anything. My Bear is a veritable vacuum cleaner, gliding his mouth over the floor and sucking in any debris, food item or otherwise, that happens to be in the way. At the other extreme, Barbara McConnell (Canada) describes how one of her Tibbies approaches a treat: "[He] sticks his lips forward like little fingers so the treat doesn't touch his tongue. He drops it on the ground and studies it before he tries to eat it and, when he eats it, it is mincingly."

Unlike Ms. McConnell's Tibbie, most Tibbies are undiscriminating, and it is we owners who must select the best possible food for them. My recommendation is to feed a premium brand of commercial dog food that states it provides complete and balanced nutrition for your dog's life stage (puppy, adult, senior). Dog food manufacturers in the U.S. are not allowed to display this claim on their products unless the food has been tested, according to procedures approved by the American Association of Feed Control Officials (AAFCO).

One nutrient that dogs require is protein. Protein is essential for growth and replenishment of body tissues. The percentage of protein usually recommended for the maintenance diet of an adult dog (any breed) is 20%-28%—a wide range met by almost all brands. Current research indicates that the higher the protein's *quality*, the less *quantity* of it a dog requires to meet his nutritional needs. Highly digestible protein is considered to be the best, and the most digestible protein sources contain the greatest variety and quantity of the amino acids. High quality protein also results in firmer, smaller stools. Feeding your Tibbie a premium brand assures that he receives high *quality*, not *quantity*, protein as well as the other nutrients he needs,

Some dog foods come in "flavors" or in fancy shapes and bright colors. Despite advertisers' claims, features like these are not important. Do not allow your personal preferences to dictate what you buy for your Tibbie! Base your choice on the food's nutritional content and research backing up the manufacturer's claims. Although premium brands usually cost more, they may be less expensive in the long run because they are the highest quality (most digestible) and "nutritionally dense" foods. Do not be penny-wise and pound-foolish when it comes to feeding your Tibbie.

Which Form of Food Should I Feed?

Dog food comes in three forms: dry, moist and canned. The main difference in them is in the amount of water they contain. Dry food averages 9% water, moist food 35% water and canned food 75% water. The dry matter in all three types is made from meat, meat byproducts and grain.

Veterinarians and most American Tibbie breeders recommend dry food. Since it contains the least water, dry food costs less to feed. To receive the same amount of nutrition, a Tibbie would have to eat nearly three times more canned food than dry food. Since many Tibbies have dental problems, dry food helps prevent tartar buildup on teeth and is better for the gums.

The two methods of manufacturing dry dog food are baking and expansion (or extrusion). In the former method, ingredients are baked together on a sheet and then broken into bite-size pieces. In the expansion method, the ingredients are mixed and cooked at a high temperature, then pressed through a form and dried to create the shapes you see in the bag. The final step is to spray the chunks with fat or a similar substance to make them more tasty. Several American breeders voice the opinion that baked food packs more nutrition, per pound, and is less likely to cause gastrointestinal upsets than expanded food. Others disagree and exclusively feed expanded food.

One owner remarked that she gives her Tibbies canned food because she herself likes meat. Others prefer canned food because the Tibbies seem to enjoy it more. If you feel this way, my advice is to give your Tibbie little balls of premium canned food as a treat but to rely on dry food as his primary nutrition source.

Protein Content and Source

The traditional recommendation for an adult Tibbie is a "low protein" diet. The belief that Tibbies need low protein may have grown as a result of gas-

---

PEPPI'S PALATE

We once gave a very dear family friend the gift of an orange-colored dog puppy that she called Peppi. To Jenny, the little fuzz-ball became the Centre of the Universe and, not surprisingly, very spoiled. As Peppi became older, he became very fussy about what he consumed. Roast Chicken became a bore, Braised Steak was ignore, and anything that vaguely resembled traditional dog food was frowned-upon. Though driven crazy trying to find dishes to satisfy his discerning palate, Jenny eventually found the ideal menu: Bananas, Madeira Cake, Spaghetti Bolonaise, and Rice Pudding. After all, why should one eat Hamburger when one can have Veal?

At the time, Jenny had a son who lived in the U.S. Once a year, her husband and she left Peppi with us for four or five weeks while they visited their son. Though I must admit that Peppi thrived on Jenny's fine cookery, it was always surprising how quickly he adapted to an "ordinary-dog-diet" while in our care. Nonetheless, Jenny could never believe that her Peppi ate dog food because, as soon as she returned, he insisted on the customary haute cuisine from his chef.

Contributed in fond memory of Jenny
by Anthony Moran (Ireland)

trointestinal upsets caused by diets with a high meat content. Such "rich" meaty diets (including homemade ones) were popular in the past, and they were unsuitable for many dogs. It is possible that the Tibetan Spaniel, a breed that evolved on a carbohydrate-based diet, was likewise intolerant of meat-rich diets. Today, most owners report that Tibbies thrive on premium commercial dog foods and confidently declare that their Tibbies have "cast-iron" stomachs.

I am inclined to believe that the improvements in dog food, based on nutritional research, have relieved any protein-related problem that the breed may have experienced. However, if you are concerned about protein levels, the prudent course is to feed your Tibbie high quality protein, such as that found in premium brands of dog food, but at the low end of the range of recommended minimum levels. This approach satisfies both current nutritional science as well as traditionally held beliefs.

Besides meat, some commercial dog foods contain soy (from soybeans) as a protein source. Some Tibbie owners opt to avoid soy while others report no problems with feeding soy-based food. Since some health problems were thought to be linked to soy, certain manufacturers claim that their products are soy-free. Whether soy is as high in quality (digestible) protein as meat-based foods has also been debated. Recent research indicates that soy is not responsible for bloat, loose stools, skin allergies or zinc depletion. If you are considering feeding soy-based food, you may wish to contact the manufacturer to determine whether feeding trials have been conducted and whether the protein was found to be of high quality,

Lamb and rice diets are very popular. Although corn is the usual grain found in dog food, rice is a highly digestible carbohydrate for dogs. Lamb is promoted by manufacturers as a "hypoallergenic" protein source. Lamb-based food may help your Tibbie if he is allergic to the other meat ingredients (such as beef or chicken) that are more usually found in dog food. However, if he is not allergic to these ingredients, the lamb is no more beneficial than other protein sources. In fact, the trend of feeding a lamb-based diet, whether or not a dog is actually allergic to other protein sources, has now precluded the use of lamb in most dietary trials for food allergies and forced manufacturers to develop foods based on alternative protein sources such as rabbit or venison. (Chapter 11 explains dietary trials.)

Preservatives

Another issue in canine nutrition concerns the safety of preservatives and additives such as BHT and BHA. The jury is out on this issue. Some owners opt to limit the preservatives and additives that their Tibbies consume, although most commercial products contain these substances.

Remember the Water

Dogs need water to maintain their body temperature and to help the kidneys and other organs process food. They require about two to three times more water than the food they eat. Generally, dogs fed a dry food require more than dogs fed a canned food.

Always keep plenty of fresh water available for your Tibbie. If he travels with you, offer him water on long trips and when the weather is warm. Non-spill water dishes make travel easier.

Supplementation

If you feed a premium brand of dog food, your Tibbie probably does not need any supplementation because premium foods usually meet or exceed the required levels of vitamins and minerals for dogs. If you are concerned about the adequacy of your Tibbie's vitamin/mineral intake, consult your veterinarian and, if needed, improve your pet's diet.

Never feed your dog calcium supplements unless directed by a veterinarian. Serious side-effects include improper bone growth and arthritis.

Adding oil (such as cooking oil) to dog food is a traditional recipe for conditioning the coat and skin. This practice is not recommended because the fat in the oil may contribute to digestive upsets such as pancreatitis. In lieu of adding oil, talk to your veterinarian about a supplement that provides the beneficial fatty acids without the excess fat.

Should I Vary the Diet?

We all tend to anthropomorphize Tibbies to one extent or another—to think about them, speak to them and treat them as though they are human. Personally, I am not offended by this behavior unless it results in failing to give them the kind of care that, as another species, they need.

The usual reason that we humans feel compelled to vary our dogs' diet is that we ourselves like variety. We call variety the ""spice of life" and the allusion to food, in this saying, has at its root our love of the delights of the palate. The truth is that varying your Tibbie's diet can upset his stomach and/or make him a finicky eater. Maintain one basic food in your dog's diet and, if you wish, vary his treats now and then.

When to Feed

When you feed your adult Tibbie depends on your circumstances. Many people successfully feed their Tibbies dry food "on demand" or "free-choice"—that is, food is available at all times. This method is easy on you but can be a problem if your Tibbie is a glutton, an anoretic, on a special diet or requires monitoring for some other reason.

Experts often recommend that you feed twice a day, usually morning and evening, at about the same times. Leave the food for 10-20 minutes, and then pick up anything left over. This is a little more work for you, but your Tibbie quickly learns what to expect and finishes his meal promptly.

How Much to Feed

Energy needs vary based on several factors. Expectant and nursing mothers, growing puppies, seniors and moderately active young adults require different caloric intake to support their activity level. Anyone who has ever watched a Tibbie mother nurse her pups intuitively realizes that she needs more calories (in fact, two to four times more) than the sire snoozing on his pillow. Similarly, anyone whose ancient Tibbie sleeps all day understands that the old dog requires fewer calories than a growing puppy.

Luckily, dog food manufacturers have done the complicated calculations on our behalf. First, feed an age-appropriate premium brand of food; the manufacturing process will already have taken into account the normal differences in requirements, based on age. Second, feed the recommended quantity for your Tibbie's weight. Finally, monitor your Tibbie to determine whether any adjustment is needed.

Foods to Avoid

Do not feed table scraps. These are often high in fat and may cause diarrhea or other gastrointestinal upsets.

Do not feed natural bones, especially poultry or pork bones, whether raw or cooked.

Do not feed raw or undercooked meat or eggs due to the risk of salmonella.

Storing Dog Food

Store dry food in a tightly closed container. Dry food may become rancid if stored too long or in a location that is too warm, and rancidity destroys vitamins A and E. If the food does not smell fresh, do not use it. If you feed canned or moist food, be sure to seal and refrigerate unused portions.

Obesity in Tibbies

Perhaps the first dietary advice for Tibbie owners to appear in print was Mrs. Geoffrey Hayes' comment, in her 1932 article entitled "The Many Breeds of Mysterious Tibet," in *Our Dogs*. She wrote, "Like all Tibetan dogs, the Spaniels are inclined to become very stout, and should be kept on a short and scanty diet; though this is difficult as they are terribly greedy and will do anything to get extra titbits." Mrs. Hayes is correct that Tibbies are greedy for treats. When denied, our resourceful little climbers have occasionally been known to take matters into their own paws; the neglected sandwich disappears from the table and the overlooked bowl of milk is deftly emptied of its contents!

About one-third to one-half of all dogs that veterinarians see are overweight. For every excess pound of fat, an overweight dog's heart must pump blood through seven additional miles of vessels!

Tibbie adults generally manage their food intake well. Left to their own devices, they eat just enough to maintain a normal, stable weight. A Tibbie may gain weight because his energy output has decreased rather than that his food intake has increased. If he is otherwise healthy, more exercise may help. Walk him a couple of times a day, and play games in the house. If you are feeding more than the amount of food recommended by the manufacturer, reduce the amount to the suggested level. Or, if you are an indulgent owner, as I am, cut out excessive or fatty treats. If these measures fail to result in weight loss, consult your veterinarian about a prescription diet. Because they contain more fiber and less fat than maintenance diets, reducing diets deliver fewer calories while assuring that your Tibbie gets all the nutrients he needs.

Prescription and Special Diets

Just like humans, sick dogs often require a special diet. Some conditions that may call for special diets include kidney disease, liver disease, heart disease and diabetes. Generally speaking, commercially manufactured prescription foods designed to meet the needs of sick dogs are available from your veterinarian and are much easier than preparing homemade diets. For more information about health problems in Tibbies, see Chapter 11.

Summary

- Use only a premium brand dry food. Food containing high quality (not quantity) protein delivers more nutrition and results in a smaller stool. Food in a dry form is better for your Tibbie's teeth and gums and easier on your wallet.

- Feed an age-appropriate food. Adults need a maintenance diet.
- Do not feed "people food."
- Maintain proper weight through diet and exercise.

GROOMING YOUR TIBBIE

Many people choose the Tibetan Spaniel as a pet or show prospect because he is easy to groom. Unlike many breeds, a Tibbie requires no trimming (as in Poodles) or stripping (as in Terriers).

Routine grooming includes brushing, bathing, nail-trimming and teeth-cleaning. You also need to pay special attention to breed traits (characteristics that are considered unique to the breed), such as the double coat and gloves. Note that Tibbies may be fussy about their trousers. If his trousers are untidy, your Tibbie may sit down and refuse to move until you clean them up!

People who show Tibbies often call them "shake and show" dogs or "easy keepers." If you are interested in showing, remember that the Breed Standard requires you to show your Tibbie in his natural coat. That means no trimming, teasing or other exaggeration.

Brushing

A daily brushing controls shedding, keeps your Tibbie's coat in good shape, and gives you a chance to check for fleas or other irritants. My Tibbies rush to me at the sight of the brush, each clamoring to be first. After they are brushed, the little hams strut around, eyes shining, to show off. I think that they enjoy their daily brushing mainly because it is a time for special attention from me.

Brush gently and only in the direction the hair grows. Ordinarily, you should not brush out the undercoat. However, during seasonal shedding, brush deeply to remove as much of the undercoat as you can. Since your Tibbie will lose his undercoat anyway, brushing it out minimizes shedding in the house.

Even well-groomed Tibbies sometimes develop mats (tangled clumps of hair) in the silky fringes around the ears, in the trousers and under the belly. A mat may also form anywhere your Tibbie has been scratching. When you find a mat, grasp the hair between the mat and the skin so that you do not hurt the

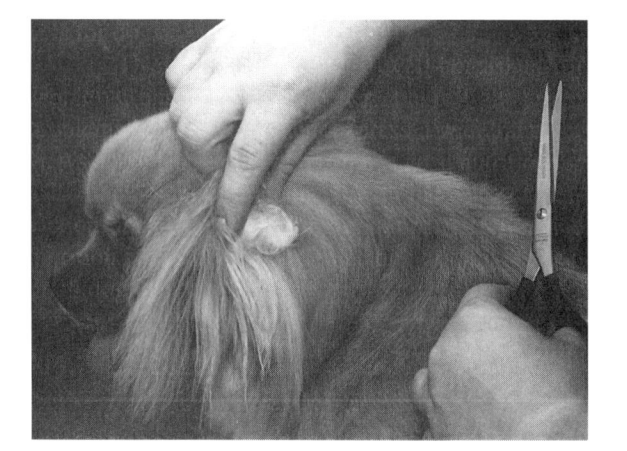

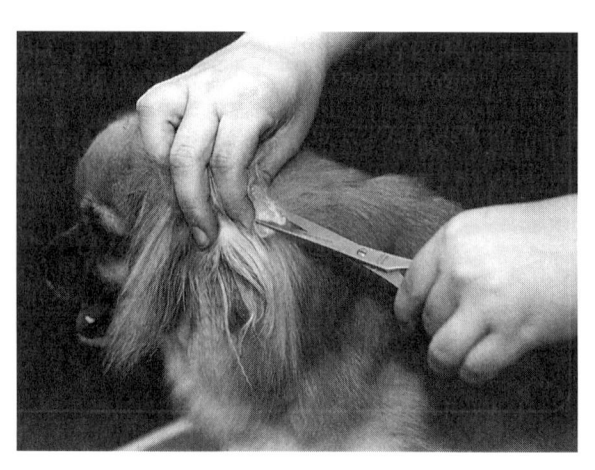

> ### GROOMING SUPPLIES
> - Pin brush—small size, bristles tipped with little balls or rounded tips
> - Metal comb—with or without handle, widely-spaced teeth
> - Flea comb—extra fine
> - Scissors—blunt-tipped
> - De-matting tool (optional)
> - Nail trimmers—preferably guillotine-type
> - Nail file
> - Styptic powder
> - Cotton balls
> - Eye ointment
> - Mineral oil
> - Washcloth
> - Shampoo—good quality mild, preferably oatmeal-based
> - Conditioning rinse (optional)
> - Conditioner spray (optional)
> - Toothbrush—dog's, child's, or fingertip
> - Toothpaste made for dogs
> - Ear cleansing solution for dogs

Mats may form in silky ear fringes. If you cannot tease a mat out, cutting into it with scissors may loosen it. *Scott Chamberlain photos*

dog. If the mat is small, you may be able to tease it out with your fingers, a comb or a de-matting tool. Pre-soaking the mat with conditioner sometimes helps. If you cannot tease it out, cut (blunt-tipped scissors only!) into the mat in the same direction that the hair grows and try again. If the mat is too large, too close to the skin or too stubborn, clip it out completely.

To softly accentuate the mane, trousers or other fringes, lift the hair away from the body and mist with water. Let dry without brushing, then brush the fringes in the direction the hair grows. Do not "tease" or otherwise exaggerate the mane or fringes.

Bathing

A Tibbie likes to be clean. You may notice them grooming themselves like a cat, even licking a paw and wiping it across the face! Unless he has encountered something smelly, romped in mud or otherwise become unduly dirty, bathe your Tibbie only every couple of weeks. More frequent bathing can give him a dry coat and itchy skin.

This Tibbie relaxes while her paws are trimmed. Trim only the fringes growing between the pads! *Scott Chamberlain photo*

1. Brush as directed above. Remove any mats before you shampoo.

2. To protect the ears and eyes, put a cotton ball in each ear and apply a little mineral oil or eye ointment to the eyes.

3. Soak the coat all the way through to the skin; make sure that the water penetrates the undercoat. Use fairly warm, not hot, water. Avoid the eyes and hold the ear leather against the head as you spray water in that area.

4. For routine bathing, choose a mild shampoo. I like an oatmeal-based shampoo that soothes the skin and leaves a pleasant fragrance. Start at the head and work toward the tail. To avoid tangling the silky outer coat, squeeze the shampoo through the coat in the direction that the hair grows, rather than scrubbing it in. Make sure you lather all the nooks and crannies. If you are using a flea or other specialized shampoo, follow label directions.

5. Rinse thoroughly, all the way to the skin and underneath the belly as well as on top. Failing to rinse all the shampoo out of your dog's coat causes itchiness.

6. Whether to use a conditioning rinse depends on the texture of your Tibbie's coat and your preference. A rinse may soften coarse-textured coats but make silkier coats limp. In lieu of a rinse, a spray conditioner gives a little extra silkiness to the coat.

7. Do not shampoo the face. Dampen a cloth with warm water and go over the face and ears.

8. Before removing the dog from the tub, squeeze out as much water as you can. If you feel suds in your fingers, re-rinse.

9. Wrap the dog in thick towels and squeeze gently to remove excess water. Do not rough up the coat. If the weather is warm, the Tibbie can air-dry. In cool weather, use a blow dryer. Take care not to let your Tibbie, especially the seniors, get chilled.

Caring for the Paws

Since some Tibbies do not want you to touch or hold their paws, start paw care while your Tibbie is young. I think that some Tibbies have ticklish paws. My Bear, for example, vigorously resists paw care by dancing around and jerking his paws away from me.

Many dog care books suggest ways to gradually train dogs to accept paw care. One suggestion is to place the Tibbie where he is off balance. Some owners hold their Tibbies in their arms while trimming their nails. Alas, I am not that coordinated, so I place my dancing Bear in the laundry tub. While he is distracted by thinking about the impending bath, he forgets about his paws for awhile. Another method that has worked for me is to calm your dog with a massage technique, such as the Tellington Ttouch™. As a last resort, ask your veterinarian for a medication to sedate your dog. A *slight* sedative, used once or twice, may allow your

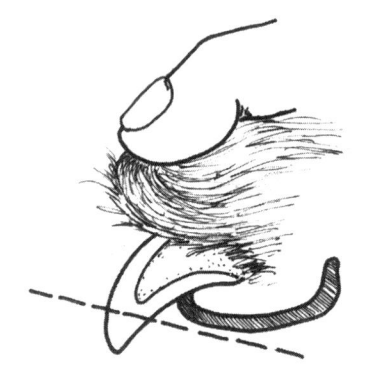

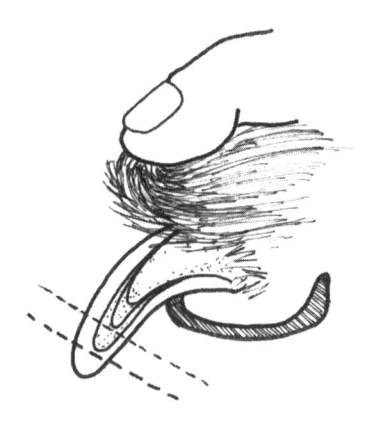

Holding your Tibbie's "glove" back, clip the nail in the location shown, taking care to avoid the triangular "quick." If your Tibbie's nail grows overlong, clipping the tip will induce the "quick" to gradually recede. *Karen Chamberlain ills.*

Tibbie to learn that paw care is not painful and even earns him a treat.

Since the Tibetan Spaniel's glove is considered a breed trait, *please do not trim the fringes growing from the tops of the toes. However, do trim the hair that grows between the pads.* Left long, the hair between the pads collects mud, burrs, salt or whatever debris the Tibbie steps in. It may cause discomfort and foster fungal growth between the toes. You may detect a moldy smell to the paws of a Tibbie whose pad hair has been allowed to grow long. I keep the pad hair trimmed except during snow season, when I leave it a little longer for protection against cold.

To trim the hair between the pads, first separate and hold the fringes that grow from the tops of the toes out of the way. Using blunt-tipped scissors, trim the hair growing between each toe pad, scissoring from the nail toward the center pad. Next, trim the hair growing between the center pad and the toe pads. Be careful not to nip the pads themselves! If your Tibbie becomes rambunctious, take a break and play a game. Resume trimming when he calms down.

Tibbie nails seem to grow very fast. Overlong nails make walking uncomfortable and can split or be caught and torn. Unless your Tibbie's nails wear naturally due to lots of exercise, trim them every week or two. I prefer guillotine-type trimmers. Many Tibbie nails are light enough for you to see the pink, triangle-shaped "quick" within the nail. Clip the nail as shown, avoiding the quick. When you cannot see the quick through a dark-colored nail, clip between the curve of the nail and its tip. Rather than accidentally nip the quick, be conservative. If you nip the quick and the nail begins to bleed, push the nail into styptic powder. After trimming the nails, take a moment to file away the rough edges.

Cleaning Teeth

Since many Tibbies have the crowded mouth of short-muzzled breeds and may experience dental problems, you should routinely clean their teeth to help avoid bad breath and tooth loss. Accustom your Tibbie to dental care while he is young. In the long run, a quick scrubbing every day (or at least two or three times a week) is better than a thorough cleaning once a month.

You may use a toothbrush made for dogs, a child's toothbrush, a fingerbrush that fits over your fingertip or a gauze pad wrapped around your forefinger.

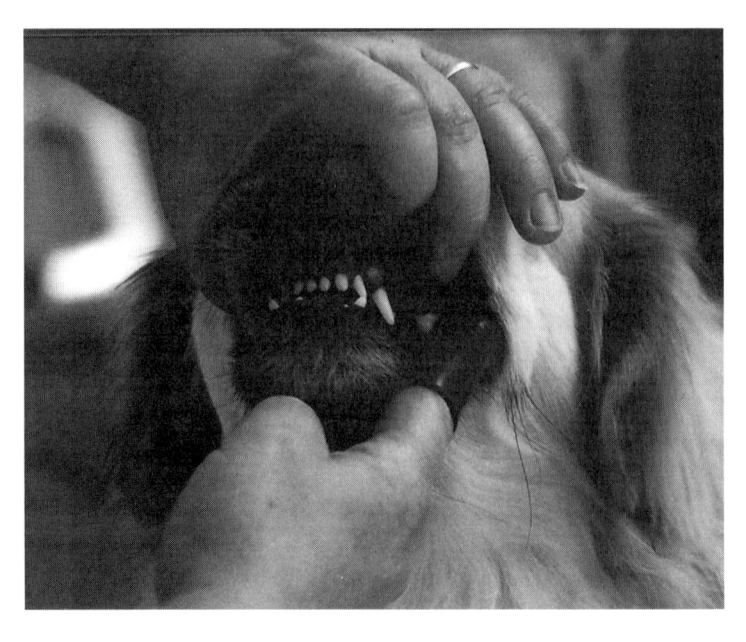

"Bear" enjoys having his teeth brushed with a fingerbrush. Here, I am working on a molar that is particularly susceptible to tartar buildup. *Chris Miccio photo*

Use only a commercial enzyme-action toothpaste made for dogs. (Human toothpastes are harsh and distasteful to dogs.) Moisten the brush and apply the paste. Push back his lips, and brush the top and bottom teeth, inside and outside surfaces, on one side. Reapply paste, and repeat on the other side of the mouth. Brush each side for at least 30 seconds. If your Tibbie wiggles, tuck him under your arm and use that hand to hold back his lips. There is no need to rinse out the paste.

My Tibbies enjoy their dental care. In fact, Bear likes the toothpaste so much that he once ate a tube of it that I carelessly left in plain view.

Caring for the Eyes

Some Tibbies "tear." If your Tibbie has weepy eyes, gently cleanse the area each day using a cloth moistened with warm water. Commercial products to diminish tear stains are available. Follow the label directions carefully, and do not allow the solution to enter your Tibbie's eye.

Caring for the Ears

For routine ear care, gently swab the external ear surfaces using a cotton ball moistened with warm water or mineral oil. An occasional cleaning of a more thorough nature may help prevent certain infections. Instill an ear cleanser made for dogs, and follow the label directions carefully. Remember that the ear is a delicate organ! Do not push anything into your dog's ear. If you are unsure how to clean the ears, ask your veterinarian to demonstrate.

Grooming Checks

As you groom your Tibbie, you can check for external parasites or outward signs of potential problems.

- Look for fleas or dark specks of "flea dirt" where the tail meets the back or under the belly. An extra fine flea comb is handy for detecting flea dirt and fleas, but it will pull out the undercoat.
- Check for hidden ticks by raking your fingers through the coat. Be especially thorough around the head, neck, ears and under the collar.
- Inspect the mouth while you brush the teeth. Your Tibbie's breath should be fresh, the gums moist and pink, with no signs of bleeding or inflammation, and the teeth shiny and white with no yellow or crusty deposits.
- Examine the ears when you bathe your Tibbie. They should look clean and smell fresh.
- Examine the eyes. They should be clear and clean. If your Tibbie tears mildly, there should be no pronounced stain nor any sign of redness or inflammation.
- Observe the skin and coat condition. The coat should be shiny and soft with no sign of flakes or patchy hair loss. There should be no lumps or bumps under the skin. Be sure to check around a female's nipples.

If you detect any sign of abnormality, consult your veterinarian. See Chapter 11 for more information.

LIVING WITH TIBBIES

Whatever kind of home you have—whether a city apartment, a suburban house, a farm or a grand estate—the Tibetan Spaniel fits in. Living in your home satisfies his need to be near you,

Indoors

Long after you stop worrying about housetraining or puppyhood naughtiness, your Tibbie still appreciates his open crate in the family or bedroom so that he can nap in his "den" whenever he likes. He also welcomes a dog bed placed slightly out of the mainstream of household traffic, but where he can still keep an eye on the family. He may also make a bed of a basket of fresh laundry or curl up atop your pillow. A spot next to a window, from which he can observe his territory, satisfies his watchdog aspirations, and plenty of toys provide entertainment.

Assure that no safety hazards such as poisonous substances (antifreeze, pesticides, household cleaners) or poisonous houseplants are within his reach. Do not leave doors ajar. Remember that a Tibbie can both climb and open doors!

Although Tibbies are a naturally clean breed, your dog may occasionally make a mess. For example, ours routinely trail in mud from their morning walk. When we rehabbed our farmhouse, we considered the Tibbies. Instead of carpet on high traffic areas, we installed vinyl sheet flooring with a wood grain pattern that disguises dirt and makes clean-up easy. If your floors are wood or concrete, consider sealing them. For carpeted areas, we chose durable commercial-grade carpet made of synthetic fiber because these fibers, such as olefin, are less likely to absorb stains and odors. A tightly woven low pile is less likely to harbor fleas. If your carpet is made of natural fibers, consider treating it with a soil and stain resistant compound. Area rugs that you can easily remove for cleaning are another carpeting option. In choosing carpet color, consider one that camouflages hair and dirt. The multi-colored loops in our carpet match our sable Tibbies perfectly.

Outdoors

As mentioned earlier in this book, a resourceful Tibbie's independent nature and curiosity may result in escape and possible tragedy. When fencing an outdoor exercise area for your Tibbie, bury at least 12 inches of wire fencing at the base of a wood or wire fence so that a Tibbie trying to tunnel out will hit wire instead of soil. Our wood stockade fence is four feet high, but some owners recommend a six-foot fence and others recommend covered runs. If you construct a wooden fence, avoid using pressure-treated wood because the chemicals used to treat the wood are toxic. If your fencing material is wire, assure that the metal is a type that is both sturdy and durable. A "chicken wire" fence, for example, is so thin that a Tibbie can easily chew through it. Other types of metal may rust and break away, leaving a gap through which your Tibbie could wiggle his way to the outside. The mesh in a wire fence and the spaces between the pickets of a wooden fence must be small enough that a Tibbie cannot squeeze through them. Also, your gate should be tight-fitting and latch securely. Periodically inspect the fence for needed repairs.

The invisible fences currently in vogue are promoted as an aesthetic alternative to conventional fencing. While they keep your Tibbie on his own turf, they do not prevent stray dogs or people from trespassing onto your property. I do not endorse their use. If you must use an invisible fence, keep your Tibbie under constant supervision. Do not use a tie-out. Apart from the dangers of dogs and other trespassers, a Tibbie on a tie-out may strangle or be injured.

Assure that your Tibbie has a sunny or warm place for shelter in cold weather and a shady place to rest in hot weather. During the hot days of summer, in the high desert of California, Jody Thomas' Tibbies enjoy a roll and a splash in the baby pools that she scatters around the tree-shaded property. Provide a dry refuge for rainy days.

Inspect your property to assure that no poisonous plants or other hazards are present because you never know what trouble a Tibbie will get into.

Whoopi's Midnight Adventure

It was nearly midnight in the dead of winter. Snow covered the yard and dog run. While out in the yard for a sniff around before bedtime, Whoopi decided to visit the dog run. Wiggling through the chain link fence that separates the yard from the dog run, she next decided to investigate the shed in the dog run. In pursuit of some quarry, known only to her, she crawled into a small gap between the shed and the fence. As she inched along, the space became more and more narrow. Finding herself wedged in, she panicked and tried to back out but, in her frantic attempt, flipped herself onto her back. Then she began to scream as only Tibbies can.

Following the cries, Ruth Mutschler (U.S.) and her nephew quickly found Whoopi, who promptly stopped crying, but they could not reach her. After clearing the shed, they carefully measured the distance from the corner of the shed to the all-black Tibbie, all but invisible in darkness. Working with a power saw from inside the shed, Mrs. Mutschler's nephew opened a hole through the wall at a spot near where Whoopi was trapped on the other side. With a little tugging and coaxing, she emerged, shaken but uninjured.

Exercising

Whether you live in city or country, exercise your Tibbie daily by walking or actively playing with him. Chapter 6 pointed out several kinds of activities for Tibbies and their owners. Have fun, but always be on the lookout for dangers.

Although some of the stories in this book are about off-lead activities, never allow your Tibbie off-lead unless he is perfectly trained and in an area where there is absolutely no danger from other people, animals or traffic. Always obey leash laws, and clean up after your Tibbie.

Do not allow him to become overheated or to gulp large amounts of water right after exercise. Watch out for substances that may injure or irritate his paws such as hot road tar or lawn pesticides in the summer and rock salt in the winter.

Traveling with Tibbies

Most Tibbies enjoy traveling with their owners and vice versa. Their small size makes them perfect traveling companions.

The Accident

While they were traveling on vacation, John and Pamela Basile's car flipped three times and came to rest upright in a ditch at the side of the highway. Although the doors popped open and gas began to leak, the car did not break up, which may have been the only thing that saved their lives. Momentarily too stunned to move, Dr. and Mrs. Basile were helpless to stop their terrified dogs, riding loose in the backseat, from escaping through the open doors.

Two young men, who stopped to help, managed to catch the Collie, but the Tibbie, Gianni, disappeared into the high brush along the road. Sore but otherwise unhurt, Mrs. Basile was terribly distraught by Gianni's loss. When the couple's offer of a substantial reward was publicized over the area's radio and TV stations, cars lined the highway at the site of the accident and people could be seen combing the nearby hills, but there was no sign of Gianni.

Several days later, Gianni decided to be found. Six miles from the accident scene, she walked up to a man mowing his lawn and announced her presence by licking his leg. The widespread publicity paid off, and the Basiles were soon speeding toward the man's home. Knowing that her Tibbie would refuse to eat or drink, Mrs. Basile brought along a batch of Gianni's favorite meatballs.

Although this story has a happy ending, it might not have. After this harrowing experience, the Basiles now buckle their dogs into safety restraints made for pets. A Tibbie loose in the car may interfere with your ability to drive and thus endangers you, as well as himself. Although it is great fun to ride with your Tibbie asleep next to you or excitedly watching the sights go by, it is safer to confine him to a travel kennel.

Other travel tips are:

- always carry fresh water,
- always call ahead to make sure dogs are allowed at overnight accommodations, and
- never leave your Tibbie in the car on a warm day.

Holidays with Tibbies

Tibbies are part of the family and, as such, a part of holiday celebrations as well. Curious about anything new in their home, your Tibbies may break, chew and/or swallow tree ornaments and other holiday decorations. Holiday treats and feasts are also potentially dangerous. Alcohol and chocolate, for example, can be poisonous to dogs. Many cases of gastrointestinal upset have resulted from raids on the dining room table or fatty treats proffered by kindly relatives.

Although Tibbies usually love company, too much confusion can be stressful. Make sure that your Tibbie has a quiet haven for respite from the revelry.

Sternly's First Christmas

Anticipating a pleasant afternoon of holiday tree-trimming, Pamela Bradbury (U.S.) carefully un-

Barbara Bradbury's (U.S.) Sternly poses with Santa Claus and a Welsh Corgi buddy. *Alex Smith photo*

packed her collection of antique glass ornaments. Intrigued by the novelty of a tree in the living room, nine-month-old Sternly sat nearby, contemplating each shiny object that she placed on the tree, Mrs. Bradbury next unrolled a glittering garland and began to drape it from branch to branch. The garland's dangling end teased Sternly like a fishing lure. In a flash, he leapt to the bait. Grabbing the end in his mouth, he spun around to escape with his prize. Down tumbled the tree behind him, shattering ornaments and scattering the shards far and near. Delighting in the chaos, Sternly began running in circles around his squealing mistress, the garland that trailed from his mouth ensnaring Mrs. Bradbury and binding her to the overturned tree. The garland spent, Sternly dropped the end and sat, smiling impishly as he watched his mistress struggle to disentangle herself.

Sometime later, when calm was somewhat restored, Mrs. Bradbury reprimanded Sternly, but not too sternly of course; after all, she reasoned, it took a clever Tibbie to pull such a stunt. Fortunately for Sternly, Santa, too, forgave his naughtiness.

CARING FOR THE SENIOR TIBBIE

The Tibetan Spaniel is noted for his longevity. American Tibbies live an average of sixteen years, but longer-lived individuals are often reported here in the U.S. and elsewhere. Although modern veterinary medicine and improved nutrition contribute to longevity, even historical Tibbies lived well into their teens. Lhasa, the Tibbie who came out of Tibet with the Younghusband Expedition (1904), lived to the ripe old age of 18 (see Chapter 3). Since Tibbies are long-lived, most owners are destined to care for a geriatric dog.

The Active Senior

Tibbies reach "middle age" roughly around age ten, give or take a year or two, and they rarely show any significant signs of aging until they are between 12 and 14 years old. Even at this age, many Tibbies look and behave much like young adults. Owners agree that most healthy Tibbies, when afforded the opportunity, remain active companions until they are quite advanced in years.

Mrs. High's Elderly Gentlemen

Mrs. Rita High (U.K.) writes "I have been possessed by Tibbies for over 20 years.... I am 83 years old and several years ago I decided I would have no more puppies...but I would take on the care of older dogs needing it." Since that decision, Mrs. High has re-homed several Tibbies between ten and 13 years of age. Her first, a 12-year-old blind Tibbie, came from the Battersea Dogs Home, an organization that has rescued and re-homed unwanted dogs since 1860. Others came from elderly owners who had died or become unable to care for their Tibbies.

Senior Tibbies gracefully adapt to their new home with Mrs. High. Her latest adoptees are Ross and Simon. When they first met, Mrs. High recalls that Simon (the Extrovert) leapt onto her lap and gave her a "good slobber." He now sleeps with her every night. Ross (the Rascal) was more subdued. Only after grieving his former mistress for many months did he greet Mrs. High with "wagtails and waggle-bots."

Always interested in the care of elderly and psychiatric patients, Mrs. High has been active in the Pro Dogs National Charity and its PAT (Pets Active Therapy) scheme for many years. Ross and Simon accompany her on weekly visits to a geriatric hospital. In addition, they have appeared on television programs, in promotions for the Society for Companion Animal Studies publication on the benefits of pet ownership for the elderly and in articles on pet loss and bereavement in the Daily Mail *and* Dogs Monthly. *In short, Mrs. High's elderly gentlemen now have a second career—that of canine celebrities!*

Growing Old

As your Tibbie moves from the middle to senior years, his activity level diminishes. He slows down, plays less and with less vigor and loses stamina. He tends to take long naps in warm places, and he is stiff when he gets up. He may become a little grouchy and less tolerant.

His coat becomes gray, starting usually on the face and then spreading over the body. It may also become thinner and drier, no longer silky and smooth like a youngster's coat. Mats seem to develop more readily.

The senses also decline. He may not hear you as well, or perhaps he decides to ignore you better. He may bark at phantom intruders. Just like older people, his eyes no longer focus perfectly, but he usually sees well enough to get around even after his eyes turn pearly grey due to the aging of the lens. Later, a cataract may render his lens opaque, and he loses his vision.

He may lose a tooth or a few, especially the incisors in front. The remaining teeth may become brownish, and the gums may recede.

The older Tibbie sometimes puts on weight. At the same time, subtle changes in the body's shape give him a less robust appearance. He may suffer periodic stomach or bowel upsets. Diseases associated with old age, such as diabetes and kidney problems, may develop.

What you have just read may be the typical and inevitable signs of aging, but you can help make your Tibbie's later years comfortable and rewarding.

"Ross" and "Simon" pose with Mrs. High in a publicity shot. *Publifoto, Ltd. photo*

Nourishment for the Body

The feeding guidelines earlier in this chapter are sensible for the healthy senior Tibbie as well as younger adults. However, bear in mind that, as his activity level diminishes and his metabolism slows, a senior Tibbie needs fewer calories. Since obesity contributes to heart disease and other problems, reduce his caloric intake to keep his weight down. Pamper him with extra affection rather than extra treats.

Commercial diets formulated for otherwise healthy seniors are now available. These diets are slightly higher in fiber but lower in protein, fat, calcium and salt than maintenance diets for younger adults. The lower protein content may aid in preventing or delaying the onset of kidney and other diseases. Discuss your senior's need for a specially formulated diet with your veterinarian.

If diagnosed with certain diseases, your Tibbie may require a special diet. In the "good old days," you would have prepared the special formula at home. However, a suitable prescription diet may be available from your veterinarian.

Other Kindnesses

Like some older people, older dogs are "set in their ways." Since changes in daily routine may unnecessarily stress them, follow a regular schedule for feeding, exercise and bed times. Try to find the least stressful alternatives to changes in his routine. For example, when you go away on vacation, consider hiring a pet sitter instead of placing him in a boarding kennel.

Moderate exercise keeps an older Tibbie's joints supple and muscles in tone. As a general rule, exercise him as much as he tolerates comfortably, but be aware of physical limitation or risk of injury that his age may impose. For example, he should no longer be allowed to jump off furniture. If he suffers from certain diseases (such as heart conditions or intervertebral disc disease), your veterinarian will advise you on a safe exercise program.

Just like many old people, an old Tibbie is sometimes unable to control elimination as reliably as a young adult. Thinking back, it is as though he is a puppy again. Recognizing that he may need to urinate more frequently, take him out more often—especially before bed and first thing in the morning. Be tolerant of the occasional mishap.

Grooming is very important to an elderly Tibbie's comfort. He may need a bath more often. Choose shampoos that soothe and moisturize his skin and brush him often to distribute oils through his dry coat. Carefully remove mats. Since he may no longer tidy himself up, keep the anal area clean. Trim his nails

At age 16, "Sunny" (Am., Ber., Can. Ch. Fairstar Cho-Sun ROM), owned by Herb and Betty Rosen (U.S.), is in declining health and passes his days taking long naps. Nonetheless, whenever his youthful "rival" is around, Sunny assumes the alert, dignified bearing of a "top dog"—if only for a few minutes. *Scott Chamberlain photo*

often since an old dog's nails tend to wear less than a young dog's nails. Be gentle and affectionate as you groom your old Tibbie.

Pet supply manufacturers have recently introduced products beneficial to senior dogs such as "egg crate" matting and heating pads safe for dogs. Soft beds for sore joints and warm places to lay down are a kindness to your senior Tibbie.

Nourishment for the Spirit

Your elderly Tibbie requires more than your attention to his physical needs. You must not neglect the nourishment of his spirit. Even as his health begins to fail and his discomforts to multiply, a Tibbie's perception of his rank in the household remains intact. His pride often outlasts his physical vigor, and he struggles to maintain an aura of dignity. Regardless of age, he needs your affection the same as always. Ignoring him, or lavishing affection exclusively on the younger household dogs, is unkind. Think back to past achievements and honor him for his glory days.

Prevention and Treatment of Illness

Some problems commonly attributed to "old age" result from disease, not from a natural aging process. You may be able to prevent some of these problems or, if not, they may be curable or at least treatable. Cancer, kidney, liver and heart disease are the most common life-threatening illnesses in senior dogs. Of the conditions that cause discomfort, but are not life-threatening, the most common is arthritis. Medication for heart conditions, cataract surgery and pain-relievers for arthritis are examples of treatments that may improve the quality of your Tibbie's life and possibly prolong it. Techniques such as the Tellington Ttouch™ may help make your senior more comfortable.

Preventative health practices are as important for elderly Tibbies as young ones. The golden years are not the time to slack off! The most important measure to ensure your senior's well-being is semiannual veterinary checkups. Visiting the veterinarian twice each year, instead of once, increases the odds that he or she can treat an illness or injury before it worsens.

At home, check for signs of possible health problems while grooming and clean his teeth regularly. The importance of dental care for older dogs cannot be understated since infections may spread throughout the whole body. Be alert for signs such as:

- weight loss,
- lumps,
- loss of appetite,
- increased thirst,
- frequent urination or straining,
- labored breathing,
- lameness or limping,
- exhaustion,
- diarrhea or vomiting, and
- bad breath, reddened gums, or other signs of dental disease.

Chapter 11 discusses preventative health practices and illnesses reported in the Tibetan Spaniel.

The Last Years

Although most elderly Tibbies remain healthy until advanced old age, care-giving may eventually become difficult. Adjustments in your life may be necessary—such as walking your Tibbie more often, giving him medication every day or gracefully accepting the occasional accident in the house. Today's dog owners are reportedly more willing to accept a measure of inconvenience in their lives and to pay for the veterinary care that older dogs need. They are less likely to euthanize or abandon an elderly dog who, with care and treatment, may have many comfortable, happy years left to give. I hope that each of you is a devoted owner who needs only to reflect on the great pleasure that your Tibbie has given your family to know that caring for him in his old age is the right thing to do.

As told by two such devoted owners, Julie Hall and Norman Weinstein (U.S.), this story describes the last years of a Tibbie called...

Lady Jo

Lady Jo was always an active, healthy dog. In good weather, Julie and Lady Jo ran three to five miles each day. Even when snow blanketed the ground, Lady Jo could be seen briskly trailing Julie in the tracks of her cross-country skis. An unavoidable attack by a large dog, about three years before her death, seemed to mark the beginning of Lady Jo's decline. Her owner recalls that, after the violent shaking she suffered, Lady Jo "was never the same."

In the two years before her death, Lady Jo's coat thinned and then failed to shed at the usual time, as it had shed seasonally over her whole life. Her muzzle grayed, and abscesses formed on the forehead above her eyebrow. She lost her incisors. Benign lumps, called sebaceous cysts and lipomas, developed under her skin, and papillomas, like overgrown warts, appeared on the surface.

Although she had had a litter before she came to Julie, Lady Jo was spayed while still young. Good nutrition and an active lifestyle helped her maintain her girlish figure, at a svelte 12 pounds, throughout most of her life. But, in the last year, her appetite diminished and her weight dropped significantly.

Bright light began to bother her. When cataracts took her sight, she began walking into walls and could no longer find her food. At the same time, her hearing seemed to deteriorate, or she became more selective in what she chose to heed.

Only a year and half before Lady Jo died, stiffness developed in her hips and rear legs. Like those of an elderly person who has "crepitus," her bones seemed to grate against one another. Like people who suffer from chronic heart or lung disease, her rib cage broadened and became barrel-shaped.

The stiffness and her worsening heart condition finally slowed Lady Jo down. She lost stamina. Her movement became labored and the walks with Julie and Norman shorter until, toward the end, she struggled only a short block in a half hour.

Troubled by urinary incontinence and recurrent diarrhea, the quality of Lady Jo's life declined rapidly. When she no longer wanted to leave her bed, Julie and Norman reluctantly admitted that Lady Jo was suffering and decided that euthanasia was the only recourse.

Although she lost her trademark playfulness and seemed a little confused near the end, Lady Jo never became short-tempered. Despite her many aches and pains, she remained sweet-natured and dignified, like

WHAT THE KACHINA TOLD

in memory of Lady Jo

> when the body's weave comes
> strand by strand un
> ravelled, from the marrow
> of an elderly Tibetan
> spaniel comes
> a spirit-force
> that lives on—she
> bounds through thickets
> in more-than-human joy
> toward us—held
> forever bounding—despite
> all the world's wrong conclusions, this
> open
> leap
>
> Norman Weinstein

Lady Jo, about age 16, with Norman Weinstein.

the ancient Tibetan she was, to the very end of her life— at nineteen years of age.

SAYING GOOD-BY

Whether an elderly Tibbie passes on peacefully after a long and happy life or a young Tibbie's life is cut short by illness or injury, it is never easy to say good-by.

Good-by Dear Friend

Parti belonged to Dr. Edwin Harper (U.S.). From the moment they met, it was a match made in Heaven. Parti, a spirited young Tibbie, and the retired physician, nearing his ninth decade, were simply inseparable. Wherever Dr. Harper was, there was the serene Parti, his hand caressing her. Life ebbs. For the six months that he lingered bedridden, Parti waited beneath Dr. Harper's bed, emerging only to go outside briefly and then resuming her vigil. Inseparable to the end.

The Terrible Decision

Euthanasia, from the Greek words meaning "an easy death," is a choice that most people who love dogs face sometime in their lives. In western culture, we consider it merciful to help an animal die painlessly when the time comes. Sadly, deciding when the time has come is often difficult. We torture ourselves with doubts and questions. Is the situation really hopeless? Should I wait? Is there something else I can do?

Even with elderly Tibbies who have lived long lives, the decision is seldom clearcut, Joan Child (U.S.) remembers her struggle to decide when the time had come for her Jubilee. Blind from cataracts and deaf as well, Jubilee had been failing for years. She suffered from a neurological disorder and once bit through Mrs. Child's nails as she struggled to give a pill. And yet, Mrs. Child reasoned, Jubilee was continent, she managed to get around and she was not in pain. No, the time had not yet come.

Mrs. Child's recollection pinpoints some of the criteria that most of us apply when evaluating the

PENNI-ONE-CENT

Even though seizures had signalled something wrong in Penni's little body all during her short life, she somehow bounced back after each bout of illness. But, when she suffered yet another seizure shortly after her third birthday, Penni could not recover. Despite her vet's best efforts, her breathing became labored and her kidneys failed.

After several days of hospitalization, her owners, Barbara and Tim Balbort, decided to bring her home and, the next morning, Penni joined them in bed for a quiet cuddle. An hour later she was gone. "It was as though there was nothing wrong with her. She just slept peacefully," Mrs. Balbort says. "She knew she was going to die, but she waited until she came home so she could say good-by to us." Although two other Tibbies now live with the Balborts, Penni will always occupy a special place in their hearts.

Even though she's gone now,
her love touched not one but many.
Oh how we miss our little cuddler,
the little Tibbie we called Penni.

Barbara Balbort

Karen Chamberlain ills.

quality of our pet's life. If he is in pain, incontinent or no longer able to walk, most of us reluctantly conclude that the time for euthanasia has come. We often turn to our veterinarians to reassure us that we have made the right decision.

Remember that your Tibbie spent his life striving to be close to his family. If you have the strength, let him be near you in his last moments.

Grieving

A catch in the voice and a painful pause, the person at the other end of the line haltingly tells me how her beloved Tibbie lived and how he died, "I cried for days." "We kept looking for her in her favorite chair." "I miss him terribly." Guilt speaks, too, "It was the only time he ever went in the road." "I just lost sight of him for a second." "Maybe if I had taken him to the vet sooner." Some people have confided to me that their sorrow was so profound that they sought counselling. Later, when the treasured, aging snapshots arrive in my mail, the images of Tibbies under the Christmas tree, Tibbies asleep on the bed and Tibbies playing with the kids remind me how very special to his family each of these Tibbies was.

Over the past few years, people have begun to accept the idea that grieving for a pet is a natural, healthy catharsis and that those who grieve deserve compassion rather than scorn. The ways in which we mourn for pets are relatively undefined as compared to longstanding customs, prescribed by religious practice and culture, with which we grieve human losses. However, bereaved people often draw on these familiar practices to mourn the loss of a pet. A ritual of burial, whether in the backyard or complete with marker and flowers in a pet cemetery, soothes sore hearts. Many find solace in the longstanding and respected tradition of composing memorial poems or by publishing tributes. For example, Sir Edward Wakefield remembered the passing of Dolma, the ancestress of many of today's Tibbies, at the age of 16 years, in his book *Past Imperative:* "[Dolma's] children and grand-children and great-grandchildren have won countless awards at Crufts; and she herself ruled our Derbyshire household until, in 1962, old age led (she was a Buddhist) to her translation." Some assuage their sorrow by bringing home a new Tibbie—not, they say, to replace the lost Tibbie, because that would be impossible, but to begin anew. Others must grieve a while before opening their hearts to a new Tibbie. It does not matter how you grieve, only that you accept sorrow as a natural result of losing such a special friend as a Tibetan Spaniel.

The Vigil

He waits alone now, in the corridor outside the door, subdued.

Hours earlier, the relatives waited here, speaking in hushed tones. Inside the room, the frail figure in the bed roused slightly. Her daughter touched her hand and asked, "What can we do for you, Mother?" The whispered reply was relayed out to the corridor and down to the nurse's station. A call was made. "Hurry," the message said. He arrives. The elderly lady in the bed awakens to his compassionate gaze. She strokes his head twice and passes on.

They are gone now, his friend and her family, but Lightning remains, his head resting on his paws. Good-by, dear friend.

Karen Chamberlain ills.

Chapter Ten

Training Your Tibetan Spaniel

Although he learns very easily and quickly, the Tibetan Spaniel has a reputation for being difficult to train. Why the apparent inconsistency? To train a Tibbie, you need to understand the way he thinks and then apply some basic Tibbie psychology!

Tibbies enjoy trying to outwit us. The more training is like a game of wits, the more the Tibbie has to think. The more a Tibbie has to think, the better he likes training. The more he likes training, the better he learns.

THE BASICS

A few simple principles apply to all training—whether you are housetraining a puppy, practicing routines for competition or teaching your Tibbie "tricks."

Why Train a Tibbie?

While researching for this book, I was dismayed to learn that many owners fail to teach their Tibbies even the most basic commands. While few people disagree that large breeds require training, many owners see little compelling reason to train their Tibbies.

The main reason to train your Tibbie is for his own safety. The second leading cause of death in the Tibetan Spaniel is accidents. Training your Tibbie to respond to basic commands, such as "Come" and "Stay," could save his life!

Good training fulfills your Tibbie's need to please you, builds his confidence, reins in his independence and stimulates his intellect. He is secure and self-assured. He is predictable and reliable around strangers and in unfamiliar situations. You can take him anywhere and do anything with him. *In short, the second reason to train a Tibbie is to make him a better companion.*

The Positive Training Method for Tibbies

The only way to teach a Tibbie is to give him the opportunity to succeed and to immediately receive a reward for it. Since dogs best learn a task by doing it, you must devise a way for him to do what you ask of him so that you can reward him. For example, when you say "Come" and then lure him to come to you with a treat, you give him an opportunity to succeed. When he comes to you and receives his reward, he forms a concrete concept of the correct response to "Come." Each time he comes and you reward him, the response becomes more firmly rooted and his confidence grows. He will eventually come reliably on command.

When you begin to train a Tibbie, whether a puppy or an adult with no previous training, reward even tentative, minimal successes. This encourages the Tibbie to think about what he did to deserve the reward. That is what you want—a Tibbie that thinks! When he begins to perform more consistently, withhold the reward until his performance improves slightly. In this way, you teach the desired behavior gradually with success all along the way.

Just as you reward the performance of good behavior, you should reward the absence or cessation of undesirable behavior. For example, when a barking Tibbie quiets on command, reward him.

To borrow a phrase from the fitness craze, "Use it or lose it!" Reinforce important lessons by continuing to practice the skills often throughout the lifetime of your Tibbie. For example, each time you let your Tibbie out the door, tell him to "Sit/Stay" until you open the door and give him permission to go out. Someday, this simple exercise may save him from bolting out the door and into the street where he could be killed. As you practice, continue to reward good behavior because Tibbies are notorious for "forgetting" what they learn if they discover that there is no reward for them.

Lifelong reinforcement is a matter of getting into the habit of practicing. Scatter containers of treats around the house and then practice a couple of quick exercises whenever you have an idle moment. For example, a friend of mine keeps a jar of treats next to the microwave; while she waits the few minutes for leftovers to heat or popcorn to pop, she and the Tibbies practice a "Sit/Stay" or two. Conveniently located caches of toys make it simple to have a quick game of "Fetch" to sharpen retrieval skills. A walk is also a perfect time to practice.

Making Friends, by Linda Colflesh, is an excellent source of information about positive training techniques proven to work with independent-natured Tibbies.

The Principles of "Correction"

Many people are quick to "correct" and "punish" misbehavior, but slow to praise and reward good behavior. Allowing a Tibbie to fail and to receive punishment teaches him only what you do not want him to do. As intelligent as he is, your Tibbie cannot figure out what he must do to merit praise. By punishing him for his failures and not rewarding his successes, he learns only to distrust you.

Whether correcting or rewarding your Tibbie, you must be prompt! The instant he performs well, reward him. The instant he thinks about misbehaving (you can often tell from the expression on his face), correct him and redirect his energy into a behavior that you can reward. Give him a reward the moment he improves.

If you do not catch a Tibbie "in the act" of misbehaving, you achieve nothing by scolding him. He does not have the foggiest notion why you are displeased, and your misbehavior will only teach him to avoid you.

Let me emphasize, at this point, that a training method based on force is wrong for Tibbies. Anyone can put on a choke chain on a Tibbie, jerk him around and force him to submit. However, I assure you that bullying a Tibbie always backfires. He will learn to resist and distrust you. Although people attracted to Tibbies rarely set out to mistreat them, a lack of understanding of positive, inducive training techniques and of the Tibbie personality may, nonetheless, lead to undesirable results.

How the Tibbie Personality Influences Your Training Strategy

The Tibbie personality traits that most influence how we train them are independence, intelligence and sensitivity.

SMART LIKE A FOX

We have had four pet foxes and varying breeds and crossbreeds of dogs. The only breed even faintly up to the high intelligence and ingenuity of a fox is the Tibetan Spaniel. Foxes cannot be trained as a working breed of dog can, because they know men are fools; fools ought to be humoured, and to humour you (albeit laughing at your childlike pleasure) a fox may let you believe you've trained him to perform a few little tasks which do not exert or annoy him too much. This too is the attitude my Tibetans hold. Now I understand what a clown I am to them, we all deal famously. I ask, they condescend, I am overcome with delight, they puff and chuckle and nudge each other over their joke.

Contributed by Lyn R. M. Donaldson (U.K.)

The classic independent canine does not care about your opinion of him. He wants his own way, and he does not think he needs you to get it. Period. Given a choice, he would rather strike out on his own than stick by you. Training an independent dog is more challenging than training one who craves your praise, and most Tibbies are moderately to extremely independent.

Most Tibbies are also highly intelligent. Intelligence can be both an advantage and disadvantage in training. The smart Tibbie quickly figures out how to accomplish an objective and you can readily capitalize on these natural abilities. On the other hand, the smart Tibbie soon becomes impatient with long sessions and bored with repetition.

I wish I had a dime for every time a Tibbie owner has said to me, "She knows what to do, but she just doesn't want to do it." How true! *To train the independent, intelligent Tibetan Spaniel, you must capture his attention and then creatively sustain his interest.* Be inventive, not rigid, in your approach. Employ a variety of training techniques in a variety of settings.

To motivate a Tibbie, tempt him with something more stimulating and tangible than praise alone. Almost all Tibbies respond to "food" and/or "play" motivation. For example, using a treat as a lure, to induce the Tibbie to do what you want, is a valid training technique for independent-minded dogs. Do not allow anyone to convince you otherwise; "praise-only" training may work for some breeds, but it does not work for the Tibetan Spaniel. When the Tibbie does what you ask, the proffered treat becomes his reward. Anja

Outward displays of affection build rapport between an owner and his Tibbie. "Patches" formed an early and enduring attachment to my husband's nose and nose-tip nibbling became a mutually enjoyable pastime. *Kris Gilmore photo*

Hansson (Sweden) trained her Tibbie, Fia, using creative commands. "No matter how often I called 'Here!' Fia just sat there, like a little statue, and looked completely bored," Ms. Hansson recalls, "But then I hit upon a trick. She has real sweet tooth, and when I changed the command from 'Here' to 'Sugar bit', she came like a bullet!"

As Ms. Hansson discovered, you can capture a Tibbie's interest with a treat, but sustaining it is not so easy. The Jackpot Game, a technique that combines food and play motivation, keeps Tibbies on their toes. The "jackpot" is a very special treat in plastic bag or small container that is hidden on your person or in a convenient location. When you pull out the bag, exclaim "Jackpot!" and allow your Tibbie to eat from the bag. By varying when you reveal the jackpot, you sustain the Tibbie's interest. The Jackpot Game is especially effective for rewarding a Tibbie that has just overcome a learning hurdle or for helping a stressed Tibbie overcome his anxiety.

The Jackpot Game is an example of a strategy that appeals to a Tibbie's sense of playfulness. Since Tibbies are intelligent, games are excellent motivation for them, with or without a food reward. In fact, game-like training techniques stimulate Tibbies so much that playing the game becomes a reward in itself. Other examples of training games appear later in this chapter.

Before you hand out tangible rewards, always give plenty of verbal praise and physical affection. In this way, your Tibbie learns to associate your praise with the same feelings he experiences from treats and play.

As a species, dogs are social creatures. As hardheaded and clever as they are, most Tibbies are also sociable. Observing their behavior, Tibbies seem to be torn between their inborn self-absorption and their inborn sociability. They want to be independent of you and yet they want to be with you. They want their own way, but they also want to please you. These are conflicting psychological drives not unlike those seen in children.

Taking advantage of another inborn trait may help resolve your Tibbie's inner conflict in your favor. As a breed, Tibbies are highly responsive to non-verbal cues. To build non-verbal rapport, make frequent eye contact and exchange long, loving gazes. Smile at and caress your Tibbie. Tummy rubs are especially pleasant, and stroking the ears is very soothing for dogs. The better your Tibbie "reads" you and the better you "read" your Tibbie, the more likely he is to respond in the manner you desire.

Training Language

You communicate with your Tibbie in three ways: body language, speech and hand signals. Since dogs communicate via body language, you, too, can send your Tibbie a message with your body. A tall, straight posture and serious expression says, "I'm the boss (top dog) and it's time to do something I want you to do," whereas a crouched posture and smiling face says, "Let's play."

> *You can teach pups and children anything.*
>
> Tibetan proverb

Training speech consists of commands, praise and reprimands. Your delivery is as important as what you say. The first command to teach your Tibbie is his name. Yes, his name is a command! It means "Look at me" and "Pay attention to me," all rolled into one. After all, humans talk all the time and, since most of what we say does not make any sense to a Tibbie, saying his name lets your Tibbie know that you are talking to him. When he responds by making eye contact with you, reward him. Thereafter, begin all voice commands, *except "No,"* with your Tibbie's name.

To give a command, speak in a confident, moderate tone of voice. There is no need to yell or bark commands. Similarly, do not whine or plead. For a little puppy, you may need to give a command several times as you induce him to do what you ask. However, gradually progress toward giving a command only once, by rewarding only when he complies promptly. Repeating yourself like a parrot teaches your Tibbie that it is acceptable to ignore your voice.

Tibbies learn faster and respond more consistently to hand signals than to voice commands alone. Either make up signals or use standardized signals for commands such as "Sit" and "Stay." As examples, a signal for "Stay" may be the open palm placed in front of the Tibbie's face or the signal for "Down" may be a finger pointed at the ground. Say the voice command a fractional second before you give the corresponding the hand signal.

The trick to good training language, whether body language, voice or hand signal, is for everyone in the family (including kids!) to be *completely consistent.* "Come," "Here," "Come on," and "Come here" are not the same to canine ears. After months of waffling on my choice of "Come" commands, my first Tibbie learned to ignore them all. Eventually, I wiped the slate clean and began over. Today, this Tibbie responds only to "Over here!"

When praising a Tibbie, always use the "happy voice." This is a chirpy, usually high-pitched, excited voice issuing forth from a smiling, cheerful face. Trust me: a "Good puppy!" delivered enthusiastically in the "happy voice" is more effective that a stern, flat-toned "Good puppy."

Deliver a reprimand in a calm, low-pitched voice. Yelling or shrieking achieves nothing. Never begin a reprimand with your Tibbie's name because he should never associate his name with a negative consequence. While the traditional "No" works well in most situations, Barbara Cecil and Gerianne Darnell, authors of *Competitive Obedience Training for the Small Dog,* recommend a guttural "Ah-h-h" because, unlike "No," it is a word not heard in everyday language. My personal favorite, "Uh, uh, uh," also works well.

PUPPYHOOD TRAINING

Start training your Tibbie while he is a puppy. From the age of seven or eight weeks until he is about six months old, he soaks up new behaviors like a sponge. Establishing a positive rapport and familiarizing your puppy with good behavior patterns during this prime learning phase sets the stage for a lifetime of training successes. Conversely, poor habits learned or fears acquired at this time may be difficult to overcome later on.

Kinds of Training

Puppyhood training is geared toward building your puppy's confidence while he has fun being a puppy and you have fun enjoying his puppyhood. "Serious" training of the type taught in obedience classes should come later on.

All young Tibbies should receive these kinds of training:

- housetraining,
- socialization,
- handling tolerance,
- travel tolerance,
- lead training,
- street avoidance training, and
- basic commands.

Housetraining

The first lesson to teach your Tibbie is where and when to eliminate. Entire books have been written on this subject, and housetraining questions are among

CLEAN UP PROCEDURE

Clean up accidents on carpet and other porous surfaces, as quickly and completely as possible, to avoid stains and to remove all traces of odor that have seeped through the padding to the subfloor. Your Tibbie's nose is thousands of times more sensitive than yours; any odor tempts him to eliminate again in the same spot.

This procedure covers both old and fresh urine, as well as feces. The steps for cleaning up diarrhea are the same as fresh urine. For more information about cleaning up after your Tibbie, see *Pet Clean-Up Made Easy* by Don Aslett.

1. Are you cleaning *old* urine on carpet (or other porous surface)?

- If yes, generously apply a solution of one part white vinegar to 16 parts water (e.g., one cup vinegar to one gallon water). Leave on for four to six hours to neutralize the ammonia from the old urine. Go to step 2.
- If no, scoop up any surface matter. Blot *(do not scrub)* surface liquid with paper towels. Firmly press several thicknesses of paper towel against the surface (use your foot) to draw out liquid.

2. Are you working on carpet or other porous surface (such as seams in vinyl flooring or unsealed concrete)?

- If yes, go to step 3.
- If no, skip to step 4.

3. Are you cleaning up *immediately* after the accident?

- If yes, go to step 4.
- If no, apply a bacterial/enzyme product made for pet stains. Follow label directions carefully.

Note: These products "digest" the urine which releases ammonia and may cause an odor. Because they may leave a brownish ring, a second cleaning with a chemical deodorizer/cleaner is usually needed.

4. Apply a chemical deodorizer/cleaner made for pet clean-up. Follow label instructions. Go to step 5.

Reminder: Do *not* use ammonia!

5. Blot up the cleaner using several thicknesses of absorbent toweling. Continue until nothing further comes up.

Optional: For the most efficient, effective final cleaning, use an extraction machine. Follow the manufacturer's instructions.

6. Apply a spray deodorant or repellent.

---

the most common that puppy owners ask. Tibbie breeders assure prospective owners that Tibbies are easy to train, and I agree. It is their owners who are difficult to train!

The best way to housetrain a Tibbie (or any other dog for that matter) is crate training. Even before they can walk, tiny Tibbies propel their rolypoly bodies to relieve themselves on newspaper that breeders often tuck into one end of the whelping box. At first, they are more likely to defecate than urinate on the paper. Later, they learn to toddle to the paper when they need to urinate. Although their early efforts may be slightly off-target, their aim soon improves. Even these tiny puppies are showing the natural canine dislike of soiling their "den." Crate training exploits our Tibbies' inborn cleanliness.

Breeders often begin training unvaccinated puppies to "go" on paper because it may be unsafe for them to walk outside where they may come in contact with diseases. However, as soon as my puppies are immunized, I begin crate training so that, by the time the puppy goes to his new home, he already understands that his crate is his den and that the proper place to "go" is outside. When you bring your puppy home, it is critically important that you continue crate training. Or, if the breeder did not begin crate training, you must *promptly* begin crate training your puppy. Besides avoiding the disappointment of soiled carpet and furnishings, crate training affords your puppy another opportunity to succeed.

It is not my purpose to explain all the in's-and-out's of crate training. Most current dog care books extol the method and explain it well. In a nutshell, crate training:

- provides the puppy with his own den in the form of a wire or fiberglass crate,
- puts the puppy on a schedule that considers his age and ability to hold his feces and urine while in his crate, and
- rewards him for "doing his business" in the right place and at the right time.

Your puppy happily seeks out his den as a place of security. He instinctively understands to hold his urine and feces while in his crate, and he will hold on as long as physiologically possible. How long a puppy can hold his urine varies among breeds and individuals within a breed. A month-old Tibbie may be able to hold his urine only an hour, but, by the time he is old enough to come home with you, he may be able to wait three to four hours. As he matures, this soon builds up to six and then eight hours. It has been my experience that a six-month-old Tibbie is able to stay in his crate for eight hours, if absolutely necessary.

Dogs are very routine-oriented. Establish a schedule, and stick to it. A diary posted in a convenient location, such as the fridge door, can help you and other family members keep track of puppy's progress. Here is a possible schedule for a 16-week-old Tibbie puppy. Note that the intervals when the puppy is in his crate are about four hours and that outdoor breaks closely follow meal and play times:

7:00 AM	Release from crate and take outside. Feed. Supervise playtime.
7:30 AM	Take outside again. Nap time in crate.
12:00 PM	Release from crate and take outside. Feed.
12:30 PM	Take out again. Nap time in crate.
5:30 PM	Take outside. Feed. Supervise playtime.
6:00 PM	Take out again. Supervise playtime.
11:30 PM	Take outside. Bedtime in crate.

Longer than eight hours is too long for any Tibbie, whether puppy or adult, to stay in a crate. If you work away from home, make arrangements for your puppy to be released from his crate every four hours or so. He needs the time not only for elimination, but also for mental stimulation and physical exercise. Many owners arrange to come home for lunch, stagger work schedules with a spouse or ask responsible children or neighbors to let the puppy out and watch him while he plays. If such arrangements are impossible for you, you should not try to raise a puppy. An adult Tibbie that is already trained is a better choice (see Chapter 7).

Many books recommend taking your puppy out during the night. Although each puppy is different, it has been my experience that Tibbie puppies sleep comfortably in their crates up to seven or eight hours overnight, but only if you take them out just before bedtime and as soon as you get up. As she was giving her standard crate-training lecture to a couple who was buying one of her puppies, Carol Srnka (U.S.) remembers noticing that the wife was crestfallen. Asked what was wrong, the woman replied that she had hoped the puppy would sleep with them. Smiling, Mrs. Srnka warned that the puppy might urinate during the night but added, "It's up to you!" Although he slept with his owners since the first night in his new home, this puppy never had an accident.

When releasing your puppy from his crate, *immediately* escort him outside (under his own steam if possible) to the approved location. If you dawdle, he will piddle! To encourage him to go outside, call him by name and tell him to "Come." Use the word "Outside" to help him associate release from his crate with going outside to do his duty. With small puppies, it may help to make little running steps; they want to chase you when you run. If a puppy dribbles as soon as he sees the outdoors, leaving a little trail of droplets across the threshold, just tell him, "No" and, as soon as he squats outside, praise him enthusiastically. His control will soon improve.

Crate-trained Tibbie puppies soon adapt to relieving themselves the very instant they get outdoors, but be sure to keep them outdoors until they have also defecated. Again, greet the performance with lots of

Karen Chamberlain ills.

praise in the "happy voice." One puppy owner confided to me that her dignified husband was reluctant to praise their puppy for "going." Well, perhaps it looks a bit silly, but praising is preferable to cleaning up piles and puddles. Remember that it is more important for the puppy to understand what he does right than what he does wrong.

Consistently saying a word when he urinates or defecates teaches your puppy to associate that word with the function, and you will be able to use the word as a command. For example, if the puppy hears "Do your duty" (or my favorite, "Go pee-pee") whenever he eliminates, he will respond appropriately to a command of "Do-your-duty" some morning that you are late for work.

Once your puppy grasps the idea of outdoors as the only place to eliminate and playtime outside his crate becomes increasingly accident-free, allow him to play for longer periods and increase the time between visits outdoors. While he is playing in the house, watch him closely for signs that he is about to urinate or defecate. If he begins to sniff intensely, he is probably ready to urinate. Whisk him outside. Similarly, if he begins to circle or pace, he may be ready for a bowel movement. Tell him "No," and carry him outside right away. Remember to praise him for "going" outdoors.

If your puppy has accidents outside his crate, you may be pushing him too fast. Quickly re-evaluate his schedule before eliminating in the house becomes a habit.

Lapses will occur. Even the most fastidious housekeepers must be realistic about housetraining accidents. If you cannot tolerate an occasional accident, you should not try to raise a puppy. Scold your puppy only if you catch him in the act. *Never* punish him for accidents; just clean up the mess thoroughly (not while he is watching!), and set out to do better next time. *Always* praise him for a job well done.

If your puppy has more than one or two accidents in his crate, he may be ill or you may be leaving him in the crate too long. Rearrange his schedule for more frequent outings before the pattern becomes ingrained. Remember that your Tibbie has less control when he is ill and take him outside more often.

Installing a pet door gives your Tibbie immediate access to the outdoors and greatly simplifies housetraining. Our home has pet doors that exit to a large, fenced, graveled area, and our puppies quickly learn to use them to go out on their own. However, *never install a pet door to an unenclosed or unsecured area.*

"Ginny goes in the bathroom and pees on the bathmat all the time." Whenever I hear this complaint, or a version of it (door mat, throw rug), I ask whether the Tibbie was first trained on newspaper that was later withdrawn. The answer is usually "yes." Sometimes Tibbies learn early lessons too well. They continue to seek paper and, finding none, urinate on something that looks like paper lying on the floor. Or, they continue to go in the spot where the paper used to be. *Never paper train unless that is the only way you want your dog to relieve himself.*

Joi-Li's Bell

Due to the din of various mechanical devices around the house, Lynne Walker (U.S.) decided to train her Tibbie puppy, Joi-Li, to ring a bell whenever she needed to go out. Holding Joi-Li's paw, Mrs. Walker showed her how to tap the clapper to ring the bell. Then, she would say "Outside" and open the door. After weeks of apparently fruitless demonstrations, Mrs. Walker's husband suggested that they stop trying. "She knows what to do," he insisted, "but I don't know why she won't do it."

For three days, the puppy refused to ring the bell. On the third day, she marched up to the bell and hit the clapper with her nose instead of her paw. Now, whenever Mrs. Walker is not in sight, Joi-Li rings the bell to signal her need to go out. Like the intelligent creature she is, Joi-Li figured out that ringing the bell also elicits attention in other situations. If a tap on the clapper fails to wake her the sleeping owner, Joi-Li "whomps" the bell. With Tibbies, you sometimes get more than you bargain for.

Socialization

One way to build your puppy's confidence and stimulate his intelligence is to expose him to a variety of situations early in his life, while he is ripe for learning. This process, called socialization, should be a positive experience that teaches your Tibbie how to handle unfamiliar people, animals and surroundings.

Assure that your puppy enjoys all of his socialization experiences. Between nine and twelve weeks, a puppy is susceptible to fear imprinting—that is, learning a fear so well that the fear is difficult to unlearn. Handling a puppy's natural fears in a positive manner is explained later in this chapter.

Puppy "kindergarten" classes, which may accept puppies as young as twelve weeks, are excellent places to socialize a puppy. However, socialization should start even earlier than this. As soon as he is safely immunized, *gently* introduce your puppy to places where he encounters new smells, sights and sounds. Invite *willing* people of all sizes, shapes and both sexes to cuddle, pet and play with him. Carry some treats with you and ask friendly strangers to offer the puppy a treat.

Encountering physical obstacles helps an eight-week-old puppy learn to adapt to new objects and situations in her environment. "Whimsi" grew up to win an agility title. *Scott Chamberlain photo*

"Backyard agility" is another means of building confidence and encouraging an inquisitive and adaptable personality in your Tibbie. With your puppy's safety as your top priority, carefully introduce him to a variety of small, *sturdy* objects for him to investigate at his own pace. For example, a puppy-sized "A-frame" is easily constructed from lumber scraps and a "tunnel" is made from a waste basket with the bottom removed.

Tibbies are small, and it is natural to want to protect them from other dogs, especially larger or more assertive dogs. However, do not teach your puppy to fear other dogs by habitually picking him up and reassuring him when other dogs are around. By the same token, do not force him to approach other dogs. Instead, expose him to friendly dogs who are under control and let your puppy's natural sociability toward his own kind take over.

Socializing Children and Puppies

Be very careful when socializing a Tibbie puppy to children. Whether intentionally or innocently, a small child can frighten or physically harm a puppy. Charging at the puppy, flailing arms, striking or throwing objects at the puppy, and shouting or squealing may frighten the puppy and irreparably damage his relationship with children. Handling the puppy improperly may cause pain and injury. Likewise, a child who does not understand the natural reactions of a friendly puppy, such as licking or sniffing, may become wary of dogs. For these reasons, some breeders are reluctant to place a puppy in a home with very small children, and all responsible breeders observe how prospective owners and their children interact with a puppy.

Having issued my warning, I can now say that children who are taught to respect and cherish dogs become more responsible, perceptive and compassionate adults. It is wonderful to watch Tibbies interact with children. Most Tibbies "take to" children, and children who have not been taught to fear dogs similarly "take to" Tibbies.

Here are some tips to assure that children and Tibbie puppies get along well:

- Tibbies shy away from anyone, of any age, who "swoops" down on them. Show the child the correct way to approach the puppy—that is, slowly with hand extended so that the puppy can sniff. Caution children not to charge at or step on the puppy.

A Tibbie puppy and her pal "Buddy" enjoy a mountain walk together. "Buddy" is owned by Melanie Hensel (U.S.). *Scott Chamberlain photo*

- Show the child how to pet the puppy gently. Do not allow the child to pull on the puppy's coat, ears or tail.
- Ask the child to speak to the puppy as he or she would talk to a baby—that is, quietly and sweetly.
- Puppies have sharp teeth and nails, and it is natural for them to mouth fingers and toes. Until they are taught otherwise, puppies also like to jump up. Explain to the child ahead of time that this may happen. Control the situation so that the child is not startled and does not strike the puppy.
- Explain that it is never OK to hit a puppy.
- More often than not, a child who loves animals tries to pick up a puppy, often by the forelegs. Having turned away for only a moment, I will never forget my horror when I turned back to see one of my puppies screaming as he dangled by the forepaws from the hands of a toddler! Assess whether the child is old enough and sufficiently attentive to learn how to lift and hold a puppy properly.

Teaching Tolerance of Handling

Your puppy should learn to tolerate handling for veterinary exams, dental cleanings, medication, grooming and judging. Most Tibbies readily adapt to all kinds of handling. To take advantage of the prime learning phase, begin at the same time as crate training and early socialization.

Teach handling tolerance in short, rewarding sessions. For example, the first session might consist of placing the puppy on a sturdy table, running your hands over his body, lifting his lips and touching his teeth, holding each of his paws for a moment or two and brushing him gently. In additional sessions, gradually progress to a full grooming and full dental cleaning. Be upbeat and remember to praise and reward the puppy for his tolerance.

Anna, Christopher and Jimmy learn how to play gently with Tibbie puppies visiting their school in Virginia (U.S.)

Teaching Tolerance of Travel

Travel tolerance is taught in much the same way as handling tolerance—gradually with lots of praise and rewards. Begin by letting puppy sniff the car. Next, sit in the silent car, then sit in a running car. Progress to short rides. Soon your Tibbie dances whenever you say, "Let's go for a ride." Remember to confine your Tibbie to a sturdy travel kennel while in the car.

Lead and Off-Lead Training

When he is about eight weeks old, introduce a lightweight collar to your puppy. Keeping a Tibbie in his collar may be a challenge for the first day or two. When he forgets that he is wearing the collar, attach a lightweight lead and let him drag it around for a while, making sure that he does not become caught or entangled. When he forgets about the lead, pick it up and coax him to follow you. If he balks, use only the power of persuasion; if you constantly jerk or, worse, drag him, he may learn to resent the lead. Use the "happy voice," treats as lures, and little running steps. He soon begins to tag along.

While your puppy is still young enough to instinctively stay close by you, it is fun and rewarding to take him on off-lead walks. However, *never* allow your puppy off-lead unless you are in a completely safe area where he is not at risk from cars, people or other dogs. Start off-lead training in a confined area and be confident of your Tibbie's response to "Come" before you venture to the great outdoors. You can also easily teach your Tibbie to respond to a whistle.

Street Avoidance Training

Teaching a Tibbie to stay out of streets is a life-saving lesson. It is the only lesson that you should teach by "aversion"—that is, by deliberately instilling fear of the street. The complete procedure for teaching street avoidance is described in Linda Colflesh's book, *Making Friends.*

Basic Commands

The minimum commands that every Tibbie should know are "Come," "Heel," "Sit," "Down," "Stay," "OK" (to release from an earlier command) and "No" (or equivalent expression). Even tiny puppies love to play, to chase, to come and to follow the leader. *To begin teaching your Tibbie puppy the basic commands, capitalize on these natural tendencies so that he can succeed and receive a reward.*

Owners often complain that their Tibbies refuse to come on command. Since this is a serious, perhaps life-threatening, problem, the most important lesson he will ever learn is...

The "Come" Command

Start training your Tibbie puppy to come as soon as he is old enough to walk. Squat down at puppy level, clap to get his attention, stretch out your arms in a welcoming gesture. In your best "happy voice," say his name followed by "Come, come, come." If he does not come right away, begin moving backward, away from him, while still calling and beckoning. At this young age, his natural instinct to stay with you should take over. Or, try luring him with a treat or toy. It does not matter how you induce him to come, always reward him with a treat and exuberant praise.

As your puppy gets older, he begins to assert his independence. You call; he sits, rooted in place, staring at you or, worse, takes off in the opposite direction. You have already laid a good foundation, so do not let it go to waste. Simply switch strategies. Put him on a lead 20 feet or more in length and allow him to wander around a bit. Then call him by name and say "Come"—just once. If he refuses to come, give a quick, assertive tug on the line, but do not overdo it. As soon as he moves toward you, praise him lavishly. When he reaches you, reward him with a treat.

To reinforce the lesson and keep his interest, play some games that involve the "Come" command. If you have a partner to help, call him first to one partner and then back to the other, both partners giving him a treat and lots of praise for coming. While in the house, play "Hide and Seek"; call him after you hide and then give him a treat and lavish praise when he finds you.

In addition to rewarding your puppy for coming when called, you should sometimes allow him to resume playing or other activity in which he was engaged when you called him. If he figures out that playtime is always over when you call him, he will quickly learn to ignore you.

The next step in teaching "Come" is to touch your puppy's collar before you give him his treat. When he is accustomed to the touch, progress to snapping on his lead before you give the treat. This strategy prevents the Tibbie from turning and running away the

To teach a puppy to "Come," get down on her level and welcome her with open arms. *Chris Miccio photo*

THE SHOW-ME-AND-TRADE GAME

As one of a dog's major ways of exploring the world, it is natural for puppies to mouth anything they find in their environment. For your puppy's safety, teach him the Show-Me-and-Trade game so that he will proudly bring you the "prizes" he finds rather than hiding with them.

When your puppy picks up something in his mouth, call out "Show me!" and coax him to bring you the object. Praise him and act excited as you inspect the object, but do not remove it from his mouth. Part of the time, say "Trade" and offer the puppy an equally (or more) desireable treat or toy in exchange for the object. When he drops his object and takes your offer, praise him for trading. To encourage this behavior, remember that you must sometimes let him keep what he finds. If the importance of this game is not evident, consider...

The Close Call

"Sometimes the Show-Me-and-Trade game is a nuisance," says Karen Chamberlain (U.S.), "because my Tibbies are always bringing me things, like dirty socks, but it's important to keep praising them for showing me." Once, when Mrs. Chamberlain and Pippin were at a nursing home on a therapy visit, Pippin scooted under a bed. "I couldn't see what she was doing," Mrs. Chamberlain says, "but, when she emerged, she brought me the object she had found to 'show me.' I praised her and quickly traded a treat for the object. If Pippin had chewed on it instead of showing it to me, she would have died. She had found a patient's nitroglycerin patch."

---

moment he receives his reward, an undesirable behavior that instructors call the "Keepaway Game."

When your puppy consistently comes on command, you should occasionally withhold the treat, but ALWAYS give the praise. Never call your Tibbie and then reprimand him. Would you come to someone who is angry or upset? And never call him for something that he considers unpleasant, such as a bath. You will only teach him to ignore you. When something unpleasant awaits him, go and get him rather than calling him to you.

Start teaching the basic commands at home in an area *free of distraction*, but, when he performs well there, quickly move the training to a place with more noise and distraction, such as a park. Since play motivates Tibbies, always incorporate a little training while your Tibbie is busy having fun. For example, practice a few "Sit" and "Stay" commands while out for a walk.

Since Tibbies bore easily, keep practice sessions short; once or twice a day for five to ten minutes is far better than hour-long sessions once every week or two. Let your Tibbie become fairly proficient at one skill before you introduce the next, but, at the same time, do not belabor a point. *Always contrive to end a session with a success and lots of praise and a treat; never let it end with a failure and reprimand.*

Your attitude is important. Remember that your sensitive Tibbie can "read" you like a book. If you do not think that training is fun, neither will he. *Keep an upbeat attitude.* Do not be harsh, irritable or hypercritical. Above all, hang on to your patience and sense of humor.

Training is a family affair. Everyone must give commands, signals, rewards and reprimands in a consistent manner. Involve your children in training the Tibbie.

When he is fully immunized, you may want to consider enrolling your puppy in a puppy class. Sixteen weeks is a good age to start. *Question the school about their training philosophy. Assure that they espouse positive methods, such as those I have described, and are experienced with small dogs.* Unless you intend to compete, choose a class that is oriented to pet owners; these tend to be more fun for you and your Tibbie than a class full of serious competitors. I also recommend attending a class with a mix of dog breeds, large and small.

BEYOND BASIC TRAINING

After basic training, you may decide to continue training your Tibbie. Perhaps you want to volunteer for pet therapy and you and your Tibbie must complete an obedience course. Or, perhaps you want to compete in the "breed ring" or obedience trials or to pursue an agility title (see Chapter 12).

Training beyond basic training requires the same positive approach explained earlier in this chapter. Imaginative exercises with few repetitions, arranged in short, fun sessions turn the Tibetan Spaniel traits of intelligence and independence to your advantage. One

The Tibetan Spaniel

CANINE GOOD CITIZEN

Many U.S. Tibbies have earned the right to add the C.G.C. title to their names. The title means that they have passed the AKC's Canine Good Citizen Test. This ten-step test is designed to prove that you have your dog under control and that he will behave well at home, in public and around other dogs. Many organizations, including kennel clubs and training clubs, give the C.G.C. Test. Aspiring therapy dogs are often required to pass it as proof of their trustworthiness.

As of this writing, the Canine Good Citizen must:

1. allow a friendly stranger to approach, speak to, and shake hands with his handler,
2. allow a friendly stranger to pet him,
3. permit a friendly stranger to brush him, examine his ears and picks up his forepaws,
4. walk obediently on a loose lead,
5. calmly walk through a crowd, while on lead, without straining,
6. obey the "Sit," "Stay" and "Down" commands,
7. calm down quickly after a period of play,
8. react calmly to the presence of another dog,
9. react confidently to routine distractions, such as a jogger or bicycle passing nearby or the noise of a door slamming, and
10. remain well-behaved when left alone, showing nothing more than slight nervousness.

Programs comparable to the C.G.C. exist in many countries. They are an important element in countering anti-dog sentiment and legislation.

---

size does not fit all and neither does any one training agenda fit all Tibbies. Be flexible and creative in your strategy. Training a Tibbie is a challenge, but it can also be fun.

It is beyond the scope of this book to give indepth procedures for training Tibbies for special purposes, such as those mentioned above. Instead, this section presents a collection of stories and anecdotes drawn from the personal experiences of Tibbie owners who have ventured beyond basic training. Among the contributors are Barbara Berg (U.S.) and Emmy (Am. Ch. Tibroke's Satin Stitches), Karen Chamberlain (U.S.) and Pippin (Am. Ch. Jemari Joyous Pippin, N.A.) and Whimsi (Am. Ch. Nittni's Whimsical Creation, N.A.), Joel DeCloux (U.S.) and Moose, and other pioneers who prefer to remain unsung.

Most Tibbie owners agree that the Tibetan Spaniel's potential has barely been tapped, not because of anything inherently difficult about the breed, but because we owners are not sure how to train a Tibbie. The themes in this section may provide insight to help you succeed.

Substitute Creative Steps for Repetition

Moose amazed Mrs. DeCloux by learning how to "Sit," "Beg," "Roll over," "Dance" and "Talk"—all in one rainy afternoon. Because they are intelligent, Tibbies learn quickly but are also easily bored by conventional training exercises that depend on many repetitions. Instead, break down complex tasks into learnable steps, being careful that the steps are not too repetitive. As a rule of thumb, Tibbies tolerate about three to five repetitions. (Incidentally, we humans usually find more than five to seven "reps" tedious!)

To capitalize on the Tibbie's love of play, turning a training exercise into a game pays off. One exercise that would otherwise be hard to teach is the...

Heel!

The conventional way of teaching a dog to "Heel" is to capture his attention and then have him follow you at heel, gradually increasing the number of steps you take from two to three to four and so on. By the time Pippin and her owner were up to five steps, the Tibbie knew exactly what to do and was exceedingly bored. To counteract Pippin's boredom, Mrs. Chamberlain set up pylons and allowed her off lead. She then ran the obstacle course herself—making crazy turns and challenging Pippin to keep up. Bounding joyfully after her owner, Pippin's good "heeling" won praise and treats.

By livening up an otherwise monotonous exercise with fun heeling, Mrs. Chamberlain captured and sustained Pippin's interest and, after that, it was only a short time before she learned the serious heeling needed for the obedience ring.

Substitute Positive Method for Correction

Although your Tibbie is intelligent, you must assure that he understands exactly what you want him to do and motivate him to do it. Because most Tibbies are more-or-less independent-natured, finding a positive way to elicit and reward good behavior often requires considerable ingenuity on your part as seen in this story about...

The Sit

While teaching Whimsi how to sit during an obedience exercise, Mrs. Chamberlain noted that Whimsi's sit looked more like a frog than a dog. The frog-sit, a slope-backed posture with the hindlegs sprawled out to the side instead of an erect posture with legs tucked neatly at the sides, is a typical Tibbie posture, but obedience judges do not view frog-sitting favorably.

To show Whimsi the proper way to sit, Mrs. Chamberlain placed the frog-sitting Tibbie's front paws on a brick and held them there until Whimsi brought her hindquarters forward into a proper dog-sit. The slight elevation of the forepaws made the frog-sit less comfortable than the dog-sit. When she sat correctly, Mrs. Chamberlain praised Whimsi effusively.

Reprimanding Whimsi for frog-sitting would have accomplished nothing because she would not have known what behavior (the dog-sit) her owner wanted. In other words, Mrs. Chamberlain creatively arranged for Whimsi to succeed at a task and then rewarded her for her good behavior.

It is impossible to overstate the importance of positive reinforcement in training Tibbies, because even the simplest "correction" may have adverse consequences. Consider the case of...

The Shocking Sidewalk

A sidewalk runs along the street in front of Cody's home. A strip of grass separates the sidewalk from the streetside curb. While learning to "Heel," Cody and his owner spent part of each day walking back and forth along the sidewalk. As the days passed, Cody became bored with the repetitious lessons and began to lag. Following conventional training advice, his owner decided to change to a chain collar so that she could issue a corrective snap whenever Cody

His eye on the treat, this puppy is induced to "Sit" when the treat is lifted over his head. The treat and his trainer's praise are his reward. *Karen Chamberlain ills.*

From a sitting position, the puppy is induced to the "Down" position by lowering the treat to the ground, which causes him to follow with his nose and forelegs. *Karen Chamberlain ills.*

> **THE TEN DO'S OF TIBBIE TRAINING**
>
> DO be creative and inventive.
> DO use food and play to motivate your Tibbie.
> DO praise generously, using the "happy voice."
> DO be prompt in giving both rewards and reprimands.
> DO be consistent.
> DO teach "Come," "Heel," "Sit," "Down," "Stay" and "OK."
> DO use body language and hand signals as well as voice commands.
> DO practice often but keep sessions short.
> DO reinforce his lessons throughout your Tibbie's lifetime.
> DO end training sessions on a positive note.
>
> **HAVE FUN!**

lagged. Predictably, Cody stalled a short way down the block, and his owner gave him a gentle correction (not a vicious jerk!). Rather than step forward smartly as his owner expected, Cody leapt sideways from the sidewalk to the grass strip as though he had received an electric jolt. He stared at his owner with all the indignation he could muster. He was shocked! Appalled! Mortified!

For six months afterwards, Cody refused to walk on the shocking sidewalk in front of the house where the "incident" had occurred. Instead, he jumped to the grass strip where he remained until the house was behind him. Needless to say, his owner abandoned the chain collar correction method of training.

Not all Tibbies are alike, and some owners have reported success in improving gait through the use of gentle correction. However, exercise caution in using this method and, whenever possible, try to conceive a positive method to induce the result you want—even if it takes a little longer.

Look for New Ways to Motivate

Be constantly alert for new and creative ways to motivate. Training games, like the Jackpot and Show-Me-and-Trade Games, described earlier in this chapter, are examples of creative approaches. Vary food treats occasionally, too. Here is a story in which a trainer discovered an innovative way to motivate a Tibbie who had a habit of...

Dillydallying

In typically Tibbie fashion, Monk occasionally "tests" his owner by dillydallying during training sessions. Even though Monk knows what to do and how to do it, it is simply a question of when he is ready to do it. To speed up his response time, Monk's owner has successfully used the Make-the-Tibbie-Jealous game. When Monk dillydallies, his owner tosses the food reward Monk would have received to any dogs or cats waiting on the "sidelines." In short order, Monk realizes that he will lose his treat to a "rival" unless he moves briskly. No more dillydallying.

Avoid Inadvertently Rewarding Inappropriate Behavior

We all reward the cute actions of puppies with smiles and hugs and treats. Unfortunately, cute actions sometimes evolve into unwelcome habits. Here is how Pippin learned to...

Tell a Story

As a puppy, Pippin "talked" more or less continuously and everyone giggled over this charming and typically Tibbie behavior. However, when the talking escalated into random barking, Mrs. Chamberlain found that she had received more than she bargained for.

Besides reprimanding her for pointless barking, Mrs. Chamberlain redirected Pippin's enthusiasm by teaching her to talk only when asked to "Tell a story." By placing a bit of cheese between the pages of a book, she induced Pippin to beg for the cheese by talking. When Mrs. Chamberlain turned the page and rewarded her with the cheese, Pippin learned that she earned the treat by talking when given the command "Tell a story," accompanied by turning pages in the book.

> **THE TEN DON'TS OF TIBBIE TRAINING**
>
> DON'T forget to reward with treats and play.
> DON'T hit or otherwise "punish" a Tibbie.
> DON'T give rough corrections.
> DON'T reprimand unless you catch the Tibbie "in the act."
> DON'T ever reprimand a Tibbie that comes to you.
> DON'T become angry or impatient and don't yell, whine or plead.
> DON'T bore your Tibbie.
> DON'T continuously repeat commands and allow your Tibbie to ignore you.
> DON'T forget to praise the absence of misbehavior as well as good behavior.
> DON'T give up.

Rather than discourage Pippin's charming talkativeness, Mrs. Chamberlain decided to redirect her talent in a positive manner. Today, her "Tell a Story" trick amuses not only friends and family, but also the patients Pippin sees in her therapy work.

Reward Appropriately and Immediately

Much of what you have read encourages use of food treats and play as rewards when training Tibbies. Knowing what rewards inspire your Tibbie is half the battle.

Never try to fool a Tibbie. If you promise a treat to induce a behavior, you had better produce the treat when the Tibbie produces the behavior. Consider the case of...

The Fickle Flyball

Everyone was skeptical about Emmy playing "Flyball," a relay race where each dog jumps four hurdles to reach a box with a lever or paddle. When the dog presses the paddle with his paw, the box tosses a ball. "The minimum hurdle is 10 inches," the skeptics said, "and she is only 10 inches high." Emmy flew over the hurdles. Then the skeptics said, "She'll never get her little mouth around the ball." Once again, Emmy proved them wrong. Emmy loved to play Flyball.

One day, Mrs. Berg noticed that some of the owners occasionally replaced the ball with a treat. When Emmy saw a treat fly out, she ran extra hard and pressed the paddle. No treat. She pressed again and again but, instead of treats, balls flew out. She ignored them. Her face took on an odd expression. She urinated on the paddle, turned her back, and stalked away. Emmy never played Flyball again.

Encourage Self-Motivation

Training Tibbies requires patience. They want to work on their own schedule, not yours. Sometimes, you must simply wait until the Tibbie acknowledges that you really expect him to do what you ask. However, another approach to dawdling is to convince the Tibbie to initiate an activity himself. A Tibbie's interest is sustained longer if he thinks it was his idea to practice in the first place. Allowing him to think that he is in control of an otherwise boring situation takes advantage of his independent nature.

The self-motivation technique consists of "cuing" the Tibbie and then waiting for him to initiate the desired behavior. When the Tibbie grasps the game, the wait becomes shorter as it did when Whimsi learned to...

Play the Piano

When Whimsi was a puppy, her owner taught her to play a toy piano by banging the keys with her forepaws but, as the novelty of learning the trick wore off, Whimsi began to lose interest. She sometimes procrastinated for up to 30 minutes before consenting to play the waiting piano.

To recapture Whimsi's interest and cure her dawdling, Mrs. Chamberlain decided to try a self-motivation game. To "cue" Whimsi that it is time to play, she takes the toy piano from the closet and stands holding it. Then she waits patiently. If Whimsi procrastinates, Mrs. Chamberlain taps the top of the piano as a reminder. To signal that she is ready to play, Whimsi sits in front of Mrs. Chamberlain, and her owner responds by placing the piano on the floor. Whimsi tucks her head, places her paws on the keyboard and "plays." Her reward? Hugs and kisses and a treat.

As Whimsi learned her "cue" and began to enjoy the game, she responded more quickly. Today, she is usually eager to begin as soon as she sees her owner go to the closet. If she is engrossed in another activity, she may delay—but no more than a minute or two.

One of the biggest problems owners encounter, especially in competitive events where intermittent rewards are not permitted, is sustaining a Tibbie's interest over a long period of time. The promise of a food reward at the end of an obedience exercise, for example, is insufficient because the Tibbie's gratification is so long deferred. Using the self-motivation technique to train Tibbies for long exercises is very effective. For example, the trainer cues the Tibbie to sit in "Heel" position (to sit next to the trainer's left foot) by snapping himself or herself into the formal "at attention" posture and waits for the Tibbie to sit alongside.

Vary Routines to Inhibit Anticipation

"Anticipation" refers to a dog's tendency to complete a task before his handler has given the command or signal. More generally, however, it may refer to the intelligent, independent Tibbie's desire and ability to perform a routine on his own, as if to say, "I know what comes next. I can do it myself!" It also arises from a Tibbie's impatience with repetition.

The simplest way to thwart anticipation is to vary the training routine so that the Tibbie is never sure what comes next. For example, if your Tibbie knows ring patterns so well that he takes short cuts, vary the speed of his movement. Introducing new commands such as "Easy," for slowing down, and "Drive," for speeding up, gives him new and useful skills to master.

Tibbies are very attuned to our body language. Sometimes they tune out our spoken words and notice only the non-verbal signals we send. For example, in the "Recall" exercise, the handler commands the Tibbie to "Sit/Stay," walks away, and, after a period of time, calls the Tibbie using the command "Come." Once he has learned the "Recall" routine, the Tibbie anticipates the commands and performs the routine whether you say "Thwark!" or "Come." To induce him to tune into your words, try...

The Fruit Game

To begin the game, say your Tibbie's name, give the "Sit/Stay" command and walk away. After

Karen Chamberlain ills.

waiting, say his name and call him with "Come." When he comes to you, praise and reward him. Now return your Tibbie to his place, say his name, give the "Sit/Stay" command and walk away. After waiting, say his name and, instead of "Come," the name of a fruit, such as "Tibbie. Apple." Use exactly the same intonation and body language to say "Tibbie. Apple." that you use when you say "Tibbie. Come." Chances are that the Tibbie will trot to you, eager for his reward. Because you must never, ever reprimand a Tibbie for coming to you, show him that you appreciate his effort by chiding him mildly but humorously (e.g., "Hey, that's not what I said!") so that he is not discouraged and keeps on thinking. Remember that he does not yet know what he has done wrong.

Happily conduct the Tibbie back to his starting place. Say his name, give the "Sit/Stay" command and walk away again. After waiting, say his name and another fruit name, such as "Tibbie. Banana." Chances are that the Tibbie will trot to you again, perhaps a little less confidently but still hoping for a reward. Again, your response should be to return the Tibbie to his place and start over. Keep your attitude upbeat.

By the time you give the third or fourth fruit command, your clever Tibbie will probably recognize that you are saying something different and figure out that you want him to remain in his place rather than come to you. Reward him for this deduction and, to reinforce the contrast, resume giving the "Come" command. Play the Fruit Game whenever you think your Tibbie is tuning you out.

Since the Fruit Game is something new and out of the ordinary, it grabs your Tibbie's attention. It deliberately allows him to fail so that you can teach him to discriminate two verbal commands given in an otherwise identical manner. A similar tactic can be used in other situations where you want to teach your Tibbie to differentiate similar situations. However, always end the game with a success, never a failure.

Validate Training in Several Settings

When a Tibbie behaves perfectly in one setting, you may be surprised when, in another setting, he no longer performs. One reason may be that the Tibbie never actually learned the correct behavior; perhaps he reached the...

The Wrong Conclusion

In his first home, Cody dutifully relieved himself on newspaper and never had "accidents." But when he arrived in his new owner's home, he constantly had "accidents" next to the back door. This behavior mystified his owner until she realized that Cody had never actually learned to "go" on newspaper; instead, he had learned to "go" next to closed doors, which was where the newspaper in his first home had always been placed. "He was not being naughty," she says, "He honestly believed that he was behaving correctly." Although it required an eight-month effort to teach the new behavior, his owner eventually retrained Cody to "go" only outside.

To make sure that your Tibbie really understands his lessons, validate all training (also called proofing), whatever it may be, in several settings. Although you should begin at home, where the Tibbie feels secure and distractions are few, move the training sessions to places that are progressively more distracting.

Owners who show their dogs in conformation competition often lament that the Tibbies gait patterns perfectly at home but seem to forget everything in the show ring. Part of the solution, of course, is to train in settings other than the home, such as a handling class or a fun match. You should view your Tibbie's first few matches or shows strictly as "training" and avoid competing in important shows until he has some experience under his paws.

Acknowledge the Dominant Tibbie

When you have a multi-dog family, acknowledge the top dog's dominance. It is natural for dogs to work out their own rankings; you should not try to enforce a ranking that you prefer nor should you insist on equality among your dogs. For example, you should greet the "top dog" first, feed him first and so on. Note that dominance is not necessarily sex- or age-dependent. The dominant dog is identified by his or her behavior as in the case of...

Queen Pippin

When Pippin was a puppy, she sometimes got into mischief while her owner was at work. To solve the problem, Mrs. Chamberlain placed Pippin in her crate during the day. The other household dogs and cats ranged freely around the house.

One morning Mrs. Chamberlain tossed a dog biscuit into Pippin's crate on her way out the door. When she returned from work, she noticed that the biscuit was lying about 6 inches outside the crate. When the other dogs failed to give a wide berth to her crate and the biscuit, Pippin puffed up and stared at them in the indomitable way of top Tibbies. She also gave them a piece of her mind. For the entire day, Pippin kept the other animals away from Her biscuit, even while confined—the sign of true Majesty.

HANDLING PROBLEM BEHAVIORS

As perfect as they are, Tibbies occasionally exhibit problem behaviors. This section lists some of the problems reported by Tibbie owners (none of which is unique to this breed) along with suggestions that may help you resolve the problem.

Behavior Problems in Puppies

Barbara Balbort (U.S.), who describes housetraining her first Tibbie as a "snap," nonetheless vividly remembers the night that she returned home to find that her five-pound puppy, Penni, had climbed the three-and-one-half foot fence barring her entrance to the living room, deftly shredded all the newspaper and left puppy puddles everywhere.

Eating houseplants, shredding paper, chewing wood, digging holes, barking for unknown reasons and jumping up on visitors are examples of behaviors in Tibbie puppies. These are normal puppy behaviors. It is as natural for puppies to chew, mouth, dig and bark

> *Training a Tibbie is the challenge of staying one step ahead of him. But, with hindsight, you'll almost always realize that your Tibbie was a step and a half ahead of you all the time.*
>
> Karen Chamberlain (U.S.), 1994

as it is for them to eat, sleep and play. Nonetheless, these behaviors may become dangerous or destructive and must be curtailed.

A puppy does not intuitively know whether his behavior is or is not acceptable. Generally, the objective is not to stop a behavior altogether but to set limits on it. For example, it is unreasonable to try to stop all chewing; your puppy has a physiological need to chew for healthy teeth and strong jaws. Instead, your objective is to redirect his chewing from your furniture to approved chew toys. Similarly, it is not reasonable to try to stop all barking; your puppy is a watchdog-in-training that may someday alert you to danger by barking. Your objective is to help him to differentiate events that are bark-worthy from those that are not and then to promptly stop barking on command.

To deal with potential problem behaviors, first take intelligent, preventative measures. Until your puppy "grows out of it," a little ingenuity may prevent many predictable puppy behaviors from intensifying into dangerous or destructive problems. Examples of preventative measures include fencing your yard, teaching your puppy to "Sit/Stay" when visitors arrive, confining him to his crate for short periods when you cannot supervise him and applying repellent ointments or sprays to vulnerable belongings.

All of the principles of positive training, discussed earlier in this chapter, apply to handling problem behaviors.

Handling Fear

Puppies often show fear; it is a natural part of growing up. Your puppy may seem reluctant to approach strange people or animals. He may bark at or back away from alien objects. Moving objects or loud noises may startle him. The way you, as his pack leader, handle the situation may influence whether the fear-inducing incident is imprinted on his psyche or casually shrugged off.

One of my puppies was unnerved when she first saw her reflection in a mirror. Another was quite alarmed when she first saw a garbage can sitting at the curb. Although she had often seen the can sitting quietly in its place by the garage, she apparently viewed its presence at the curb as a dangerous situation! Obviously, these were unfounded fears and I might have been tempted laugh at them. However, Tibbies do not suffer humiliation well. Encourage the puppy to approach the object by acting interested in the source of his fear. Give a "Sniff" command in a cheerful tone of voice and talk to the object as though it were alive. A few exploratory sniffs later, your puppy will probably deduce, as mine did, that the object is harmless and go about his business unperturbed.

I was taught that a traumatic experience during a Tibbie's impressionable puppyhood may cause him to become overly fearful. While cases like this have doubtless occurred, I believe that most Tibbies are resilient. Let me give you an example. When my Patches was about 12 weeks old, he was still unsure about walking down a long staircase. Intending to coax him to follow me down the steps, I bent over to place him on the top step, and he somehow slipped from my grasp. As I watched helplessly, he rolled sideways down the staircase, plopping on each step. As if that were not enough to frighten him for life, I plunged down the steps, screeching, and scooped him into trembling hands. Although he was not physically injured, I coddled and fussed over him the rest of the night. *My* behavior could have reinforced and imprinted what was a very natural scare on his part. However, by morning, Patches had recovered and he has absolutely no fear of steps today.

Unlike Patches' tumble down the steps, the incident(s) that imprints a fear may be so trivial (at least, as far as we humans are concerned) that an owner may be puzzled when his or her puppy suddenly becomes afraid of an object or situation. While you should certainly try to spare your puppy upsetting experiences, he may nonetheless develop fears that seem wholly unfounded to you.

Putting aside the possibility that irreversible problems related to fear may arise from poor breeding, a loving, patient and skillful owner can rehabilitate an anxious Tibbie. Even an intractable Tibbie that was the victim of trauma, mistreatment or simply a lack of good training can be redeemed. The Tibetan Spaniel was bred to be an intelligent companion (see Chapter 2). When trained with a positive method that instills confidence, even a fearful Tibbie's companion instincts will surface. They are intelligent enough to know a good thing when they see it!

First in Her Class

When his only Tibbie, Princess, became clingy and lonely due to his long work hours, Paul James decided to find a Tibbie playmate for her. Moving into a home with an active owner and a younger, more vigorous Tibbie sibling was a big change for the new Tibbie, called Honey.

Although she was an adult, Honey weighed only eight-and-one-half pounds. She seemed content to eat, sleep and go out occasionally. On their first walk together, Mr. James became concerned by her uncoordinated, wobbly gait. Since she was weak and lacked muscle tone, Mr. James and his vet concluded that Honey had had very little exercise in her life.

Honey also did not understand how to cope with new people and places. In contrast to Princess' confident demeanor, Honey was timid. Princess was unflappable, but Honey startled easily. She cowered behind her owner's legs at the sound of a passing truck. When he clapped his hands as a signal for the dogs to come and play, Honey slouched into a corner and curled up, clearly interpreting his clap as a punishment. On another occasion, when she darted behind her owner and was accidentally kicked, she interpreted the kick as punishment and began to quiver in terror. Even the prospect of a treat was a traumatic transition for shy Honey. When offered a dollop of whipped cream on the tip of Mr. James' finger, Princess sniffed and eagerly lapped it up. Poor Honey looked back and forth from Princess to the dollop, and only after three tries was she able to summon courage to take it from his fingertip.

As you may expect, housetraining proved to be another problem area. Although Honey had rudimentary paper training, she was as apt to "go" in the house as outdoors.

Mr. James felt sorry for his Honey. Somewhere along the way, she had lost the curiosity, friendliness and joy that is so characteristic of Tibbies. In short, she was physically and emotionally underdeveloped.

To enrich her store of experience, Mr. James began to gently socialize Honey to unaccustomed people and places. She began taking part in family outings with determination, albeit less enthusiasm than Princess. When Mr. James enrolled her in an obedience class, Honey was puzzled at first but, under her owner's patient guidance, gradually came to understand what to do. Outdoor exercise and good food strengthened her body and mind, and her newfound self-confidence grew with each success.

Now a beautifully coated Tibbie of normal weight, Honey has blossomed into a gregarious and outgoing individual with a calm, sweet disposition. The little dog that formerly ran cowering at the least provocation graduated first in her obedience class and passed the Canine Good Citizen test. More patient and compassionate than Princess, Honey excels in therapy work with the elderly and disabled, who fondly call her their "little lover."

Scruff Shake

When you discover your Tibbie engaged in a dangerous behavior, a more serious reprimand than a simple "No" or "No substitute" may be required. When your Tibbie is in danger and "No" fails, make eye contact with him, grasp his coat at the scruff of his neck and lift his forequarters, shake him briefly, and repeat "No" or, better yet, growl convincingly at him. Since it emulates his mother's discipline, a well-delivered scruff shake almost invariably communicates to your Tibbie, "This is important! Pay attention to me!" Use the scruff shake for only the most serious, life-or-death infractions, such as bolting into the street or chewing on electrical cords. If you overuse it, its effectiveness will diminish.

Chewing

All puppies chew when they are teething. They usually target objects such as lamp cords, houseplants and furniture legs. Boredom may escalate normal puppy chewing into destructive behavior.

It's Only a Sofa

"Oh no. Look at this mess! You've ruined it! [expletives deleted]," I cried, upon returning home to find the flounce nearly torn away from my sofa and batting tumbling from rips in the upholstery. "Where are you, you bad puppy? Come here, Kissie. Bad girl, bad girl!" Kissie, who had joyfully dashed forward to greet me, now hesitated under a table, her tail wagging tentatively. I swooped down on her and scooped her up, all six pounds. I showed her the damage; "Do you see what you did? Bad girl. Bad girl." Although pinned by the shoulders with her nose pressed to the torn fabric, she nonetheless managed to turn her trusting eyes up to my teary ones. Despite my disappointment at my loss, I instantly relented as I looked into that sad little face. I scooped her up again, but this time I cuddled

Karen Chamberlain ills.

Three-month-old "Melody," owned by Becky Maag (U.S.), has been busy teething.

her and smooched her head. "I'm sorry. Poor puppy. Did you miss me today?"

What is the point of the story? One point is that, although dogs enjoy chewing their entire lives, a puppy's chewing can be a harrowing experience for owners. From the time his shark-like baby teeth erupt until his permanent teeth are in place, a period of four months or longer, even a diminutive Tibbie can inflict substantial damage. Besides demolishing the sofa, Kissie chewed nearly through the legs of several wooden chairs and left bite marks on baseboards and plaster walls. However, the main point of the story is that I failed to handle this situation correctly. I left her unsupervised in the living room and did not provide chew toys. When the damage was done, I failed to respond appropriately. What did Kissie learn from me that day? Did she learn not to chew the sofa? Absolutely not, because I did not catch her in the act. Moreover, by calling her and then punishing her when she came and by giving her mixed signals—anger one moment, affection the next—all that Kissie learned was that she sometimes cannot trust me.

Prevention is half the battle. When unable to supervise your puppy, leave him in his crate or in an area where he can do little damage, such as the kitchen. Secure electrical cords out of reach, use anti-chew products on furniture and cabinetry and remove plants and other chewables. Chapter 8 explains how to puppy-proof your home.

Another important preventative measure is to teach your puppy the Show-Me-and-Trade Game described earlier in this chapter. The idea of the game is to reward the puppy for showing you any "prizes" he finds rather than carrying them off to a hiding place for a chew. After praising him for showing you the object, you can either let him keep it or, if the object is something he is not allowed to chew, trade it for an approved chew toy. Chapter 8 discusses chew toys.

Plant-Eating

In interviewing for this book, I was regaled with stories about Tibbies eating plants—Tibbies that dig up gladioli bulbs, harvest rows of baby carrots, shred rose bushes and steal cut flowers from flower arrangements. Puppies seem to be most interested in plant-eating and therefore most at risk. Many common plants are poisonous, and it is a good idea to post a list of them on the fridge. The simplest way to avoid plant-eating is to put plants out of reach and to spray them with pet repellent made for plants. Plant-eating seems to diminish as Tibbies grow up.

Barking

Excessive barking is not often reported as a Tibbie problem. On the contrary, most owners comment that their Tibbies bark only when there is a good reason, such as someone at the door, and then quiet down quickly once the owner investigates. Occasionally, Tibbies bark at things we do not consider particularly bark-worthy, such as squirrels in the backyard,

Little "Milo," bred by Michael Fenwick (Australia), reminds us that we must place all cords out of reach. *Michael Fenwick photo*

dogs barking elsewhere in the neighborhood, or people walking by.

If you want to preserve your Tibbie's watchdog instincts, investigate the cause of the barking before you call for silence. Praise the Tibbie and then give the command, "Enough." Even young Tibbies seem to be satisfied by an owner's interest and cease barking on command or even before the command is given. If your Tibbie does not stop or resumes barking immediately, startle him into silence with a loud noise (clapping your hands, rattling a can with a few pennies in it) or a squirt of water (or half water, half white vinegar) from a spray bottle. The instant he stops barking, praise him warmly.

Escaping

Whether they accomplish it by wiggling through, climbing over, digging under or slipping by, escaping is, without doubt, the most troubling and dangerous of the Tibetan Spaniel's problem behaviors.

I have always marvelled at a mouse's ability to squeeze its body through tiny cracks and holes, and I am convinced that Tibbies are as adept as mice. One morning, I watched one of my young Tibbies squash herself flat and squirm sideways through the tiny crack between gate and fence. Once out, she chased after a squirrel. Other owners have reported a variety of ingenious escape attempts. One was astonished to discover a human-sized burrow when she observed a team of miner Tibbies emerging from an excavation under a honeysuckle vine. Several have reported Tibbies who scaled fences as high as six feet.

The (Almost) Great Escape

When my family and I moved into a house in May 1993, we knew that the house needed repair work. We decided to convert the dining room into a dog room. Although there was a dampness problem on the outer wall, we did not know at the time that part of the wall covered an old wooden window frame. The frame had been plastered over and the wood had rotted.

Due to our working habits, the dogs are often left for two to three hours in a day. One teatime we returned from work to find that the "little dears," sensing the possibility of escape, had dug a hole (!) through the rotted dog room wall. Luckily, a new dog run lay on the other side of the wall. In typical Tibetan manner, however, they did not bother escaping into the dog run once they had demonstrated that walls could not contain them.

Building the new dog run was the first job we had completed in the house—a sound decision on reflection. Of course, we now had a draught problem as well as a dampness problem!

Contributed by David Parry (U.K.)

Prevention is the only "cure" for escapist behavior. Neutering or spaying your Tibbie removes one of the most probable causes. Providing adequate fencing (see Chapter 9), closing exterior doors and taking other sensible precautions are essential.

If your Tibbie succeeds in escaping unnoticed, you must organize a search. He may travel miles in a short time or he may be just around the corner sniffing at someone's garbage. Prepare for either contingency. Take a moment to call the local veterinarian's office in case the Tibbie is brought there. Next, gather a search party. Grab the most delectable treats you have on hand (e.g., cheese, ham) and supply the searchers. Pair off the searchers so that, if a search team spots him, one of them can bring help. Establish a search pattern so that no area is overlooked. Instruct searchers to call the dog's name and then wait a couple minutes in the same spot; calling his name constantly, while moving, disorients a dog. Be sure to tell the searchers any special word, such as "Treat," to which the Tibbie responds well.

When the Tibbie is spotted, *do not chase* him or in any way behave in an aggressive manner. And, for Heaven's sake, *do not act angry!* Such behaviors may confuse or frighten him (especially if the searcher is someone he does not know), and he may run in the opposite direction. The idea is to calm him down and persuade him to come. Call him and tantalize him with the treats, tossing them toward him. If the Tibbie does not respond to these tactics, a possible alternative is to get his attention by acting excited and then running a short distance *away from him*. Since a Tibbie is highly play-motivated, he may think you are playing a game and chase after you.

If your initial reconnaissance fails to turn up the Tibbie, begin the second phase of the search. This includes contacting the local animal shelter/dog pound, posting flyers in the surrounding area, arranging an announcement on local radio, notifying all area veterinarians and running an ad in the newspaper. Alerting your post office and mail carrier is often very helpful.

When you have your Tibbie safely at home, resume work on teaching him to "Come" and correct the problem that allowed him to escape in the first place.

Jumping Up

I derive immense pleasure from a boisterous greeting from my Tibbies—even the part where they jump up and give me kisses. As someone once said, jumping up is just the dog's way of trying to put his arms around you. However, jumping up should be controllable so that people, who may not welcome the dog's advances, and small children are not charged by a bouncing Tibbie.

To defuse the explosiveness of his greeting, give your Tibbie the "Sit/Stay" command. If he jumps up, step back and give an "Off" command. If he persists, simply lift your knee to block the jump and reprimand him. (I am not suggesting that you "knee" your Tibbie in the chest as some people do to larger dogs! A Tibbie is small enough that slightly lifting your knee is sufficient to put him off balance and back on all four paws.) Place him back in the "Sit/Stay" and ignore him until you think he is sufficiently calm for a dignified greeting.

Fighting

Many (perhaps most) intact, mature male Tibbies do not tolerate the intrusions of other intact, mature male dogs on their territories. In this regard, they are no more nor less aggressive than other breeds. While some males make much noise and do little damage, others can and do inflict wounds on other males. Lacerations of the neck often occur when one male Tibbie grabs another by the neck. Eye injuries are also common.

Fights usually occur on disputed territory. If both males are on "foreign" territory, neither is likely to try to protect it. Males who challenge one another first stiffen and stare. The hackles (the mane over the neck and shoulders) may rise. They may then circle one another. While they are in this pre-fighting stance, you may be able to "jolly" male Tibbies out of the fighting mood by acting happy and yipping as Tibbies do when they play or by distracting them with food or treats. Restraining males that are posturing, such as by tightening the lead, always precipitates the fight. Similarly, crowding them in a small area brings on the hostilities.

Once a fight is engaged, there is little you can do to stop it other than to forcibly separate them. The trick is to find a way to get them apart without injury to yourself. Speaking from experience, a furious male Tibbie can inflict a serious bite on the well-meaning human hand foolishly interjected between him and his opponent. Instead, firmly grab one of them by his mane at the scruff of the neck and by the rump and quickly lift him away from the other. Do not put your hands or arms around him or within reach of his mouth, and be careful that he does not twist to bite you.

If you are lucky, a momentary lull in the fighting, when neither is grasping the other, gives you the opportunity to lift one away from the other. A garden hose may be powerful enough to separate them, but a spray bottle probably will not. One owner suggests purchasing a boat horn; its deep, loud voice may startle them long enough to separate them. Although a high-pitched screech has no effect on my males, it may work on yours. Another course of action, albeit slightly risky, is to simultaneously grasp the aggressor's scruff and very lightly squeeze his testicles, increasing pressure until he lets go and you can lift him away.

Note that striking the fighting dogs achieves nothing. In fact, it may even make matters worse because the other Tibbie may interpret your actions as supportive.

The bottom line is that it is inadvisable to own more than one mature, intact male without facilities to keep them apart. The sensible way to avoid the problem, other than keeping them apart, is to neuter males while they are young. Unfortunately, older males or males who have been used at stud may continue to start fights even after neutering. If the fighting persists, you may want to consult an animal behaviorist for further help.

Marking

Marking is a result of hormones in mature, intact males. It is not a housetraining lapse; it is the male's way of claiming his territory. Some males are more apt to mark when stressed as, for example, when another dog "invades" his territory or when he is separated from his owner. The urine of a mature male has a strong odor and color. All vertical objects, such as the corners of beds and sofas, cabinets, shower curtains and draperies, are at risk.

The only way to wholly avoid male marking is to eliminate the male hormones from the equation by neutering the Tibbie while he is a puppy. Even neutering may not "cure" older males or males used at stud. Although the frequency may decrease, these males may continue to mark occasionally out of habit, and they may be sneaky about it.

A black fluorescent light helps you locate marks. Clean them up thoroughly, and apply repellent to the area as well as any other likely targets. If you catch him in the act, squirt him with the spray bottle and scold him sternly. Another option is a belly band, a four to five inch wide fabric strip that fastens with buttons or heavy snaps. (They seem to be able to get out of elasticized bands or bands with other closures.) Place the snug-fitting band around the male's middle, covering his penile sheath. The band spares your furnishings, and the uncomfortable sensation of a "wet diaper" may eventually discourage marking.

Incidentally, females in season also tend to mark their territories, presumably to announce their availability to passing males, by urinating small amounts. However, they rarely mark inside the house.

Stool-eating (Coprophagy)

Coprophagy is somewhat common among dogs of all kinds and, I am sorry to say, many Tibbies eat their own stools or those of other animals. While cat stools hold great appeal for dogs, my own Tibbies find the rabbit and deer droppings in our meadows very tasty indeed. It has been suggested that coprophagy tends to run in families, but it appears to be fairly widespread in this breed.

One theory is that dogs are coprophagic because dams clean the nest while their pups are nurselings. Another speculation is that the dog's scavenging habits, which have served him well in the game of survival, lead to coprophagy. There is probably a grain of truth in both of these ideas. In the case of the Tibbie, I can easily imagine that the droppings of other animals provided a needed supplement in the diet of a breed that evolved in the harsh conditions on the "roof of the world."

Besides being disgusting to us humans, coprophagy may be a health hazard to your Tibbie. Ingested stools may contain parasites or cause gastrointestinal upsets. Curiously, my own Tibbies have never suffered any ill effects from this occasional dietary supplementation.

To discourage stool-eating, my best advice is to:

- feed an age-appropriate premium dog food that contains high quality (not quantity) protein (see Chapter 9),
- avoid temptation by promptly scooping up stools or otherwise denying your Tibbie access to them, and
- scold him sternly if you catch him in the act.

If he consumes his own stools, add a substance (such as meat tenderizer) to his food that further "digests" the food and may make the stool less appetizing.

Although I do not recommend it, one owner tried the following remedy. When her Tibbies continued to consume stools, even after she spiked their food with meat tenderizer, she sprinkled a few drops of "hot sauce" on the stools themselves. To her dismay, the "hot sauce" failed to repel them and they apparently relished the extra spicy flavor!

The bad news is that the experience of many owners has been that a Tibbie, indulging in this behavior, is rarely dissuaded by a scolding. Similarly, altering or supplementing the diet appears to have little impact. The good news is that several owners report that the coprophagic tendency diminishes or disappears as the Tibbie gets older.

Thunderstorms

Some owners report Tibbies that fear thunderstorms. This is not uncommon in dogs and may be more common in older individuals. It is possible to gradually desensitize a Tibbie to the sound of thunder. Tapes of thunder played progressively louder or a tennis shoe thumping in the dryer may help the Tibbie become accustomed to the sound. Another ploy is to start a game during thunderstorms. While the thunder booms, pop popcorn and distract the Tibbie by tossing the popcorn into the air as a treat. A massage technique called the Tellington Ttouch™ has helped me relax one of my Tibbies that becomes anxious not only during storms but also during Fourth of July fireworks.

As cruel as it seems, you should not comfort or console the fearful Tibbie. This only serves to reinforce his idea that thunder is something to fear. Instead, maintain a nonchalant attitude when he is fearful and praise and reward him only when he is calm.

Don't walk away from this chapter with the impression that the problem behaviors you have just read about are common in Tibbies. On the contrary, the Tibetan Spaniel is a well-behaved (if not always perfectly obedient) breed. Instead, remember that training your Tibbie in the manner that I and the other contributors to this chapter have described will enrich both his life and yours. He will thank you for it by becoming the best possible companion you can imagine.

The Tibetan Spaniel

Karen Chamberlain ills

Chapter Eleven

Your Tibetan Spaniel's Health

The Tibetan Spaniel is a long-lived and healthy breed. If given the basic care that he requires, your Tibbie should remain happy and active well into his senior years. In fact, Tibbies live an average of 16 years (slightly less for those who are not neutered or spayed while puppies), and most owners agree that an aged Tibbie's quality of life remains good until shortly before his death.

This chapter first explains how to avoid health problems through good preventative practices. No matter how careful you are, these measures cannot thwart all illness. Although it is not within the scope of this book to list and describe every conceivable illness that may affect your Tibbie, the remaining two sections summarize routine and serious health problems reported in the breed.

PREVENTATIVE HEALTH CARE FOR THE WELL TIBBIE

The key to keeping your Tibbie healthy is to prevent illness through attention to safety, home health checks and routine veterinary care.

Veterinary Manual

Since he can catch the same bugs, pick up the same parasites and have the same accidents as other dogs, the information in a home reference veterinary manual applies to your Tibbie, too. Buy an up-to-date edition, written in plain language and well-illustrated, for your bookshelf.

If an emergency arises and you cannot get veterinary help quickly, the manual may help you begin sensible treatment. Familiarize yourself with the book's layout so that you can find a topic quickly. Spend some time studying the section on first aid, and mark it with a book mark so that you can open right to it in an emergency.

Deciding when a visit to the veterinarian is necessary is sometimes difficult for owners. A reference manual helps you discriminate the normal from the abnormal, and most state explicitly which situations require veterinary attention. After visiting the veterinarian, reading the manual may help you better understand your Tibbie's condition and the care he requires.

Home Veterinary Kit

Assemble and set aside a special place for a home veterinary kit. Include these items:

- basic instruments (such as tweezers, blunt-tipped scissors),
- bandages suitable for dogs (such as Vetrap),
- skin and wound cleaner (such as Nolvasan),
- triple antibiotic ointment,
- baby aspirin,
- product for stomach/intestinal upset (such as Kaopectate or Pepto Bismol), and
- rectal thermometer.

Some of these are "human" products that you can find in any drug store or supermarket. Others, such as Nolvasan, are available from pet supply stores. Pre-assembled first aid kits for dogs are also commercially available. If your Tibbie travels with you, keep a first aid kit in the car, too.

Safety Considerations

Terrified of a thunderstorm, the Tibbie escaped a neighbor's fenced yard and plunged into the busy street. When I spotted her frantically dodging cars in the downpour, I dashed out to the street and called to her. Running to me, she leapt into my arms (and into

"Gaily" (Am. Ch. Bet'R Go Gaily Go at Rochwar), owned by Rochelle Yuspa (U.S.), undergoes her annual physical exam by Mary Beth Soverns, DVM. Annual exams are essential to early detection of health problems. *Chris Miccio photo*

my heart). Given the reduced visibility and rushing commuters, a few more minutes may have found her small body in the gutter.

Accidents, many of them near or in the home, injure and kill many Tibbies each year. Accident prevention must be a significant concern of conscientious Tibbie owners. Guidelines for creating a safe environment for your Tibbie appear in Chapters 8 and 9, and more information about accidental death and injury appears later in this chapter.

Selecting a Veterinarian

Even before bringing your new Tibbie home, line up a veterinarian to provide preventative care and to attend to any illnesses or injuries that may occur during your Tibbie's lifetime. Finding a good veterinarian is one of the most important favors you can do for yourself and your Tibbie. In most areas of the U.S., owners now have a choice of vets. Here are some tips for selecting the person to whom you will entrust your Tibbie's health care:

- Choose a vet with whom you can comfortably communicate. Does he or she explain illnesses and treatments in terms that you can understand? Does he or she listen to your concerns and observations?

- Does the vet and the staff treat your Tibbie with kindness and concern?
- Assess how well he or she manages the practice. Ask to look around. Are the premises clean and orderly? Does the equipment seem up-to-date? How quickly can you get an appointment? Do appointments flow well without rushing? Since problems invariably seem to crop up on weekends or at night, what provisions has the vet made for emergency care?
- Ask about fees for routine procedures such as vaccinations. Can you afford to give your Tibbie the care he needs?

Keep the numbers of your veterinarian, emergency veterinary clinic and poison control center posted near your telephone at all times.

Vaccinations and Annual Physical Examination

Vaccinations—It is so easy to prevent diseases that, until a few years ago, killed or disabled many dogs. More than one Tibbie breeder has lost many beautiful puppies during outbreaks of distemper and canine parvovirus in the days before vaccines were developed. Today, distemper and parvo, as well as rabies and a variety of other diseases are preventable. Your Tibbie should receive his "shots," vaccinations to immunize him against canine diseases, each year.

Veterinarians follow slightly different vaccination schedules, especially for puppies. In general, vaccinations for distemper, adenovirus (for protection against hepatitis), parainfluenza (a virus that contributes to a disease called kennel cough), leptospirosis (a bacterial infection), coronavirus and canine parvovirus are given to puppies and then renewed at least once each year.

Unlike the canine diseases named above, rabies can infect humans as well as dogs and other mammals. In the U.S., measures to control rabies usually fall under the jurisdiction of State public health departments. The first rabies vaccination is good for a year. After that, requirements vary from State to State, with some States permitting a three-year rabies vaccination.

Two other diseases for which vaccinations are available are Lyme disease (also called borreliosis, a tick-borne bacterial infection) and bordetella (a bacteria that contributes to kennel cough). We vaccinate our Tibbies for Lyme disease each spring, just before the onset of "tick season," because our farm is located in an area with a large deer population and confirmed cases of Lyme disease. Since our Tibbies are often exposed to other dogs, we also vaccinate for bordetella to protect against kennel cough. Your own Tibbie may or may not be at risk for these diseases. Of course, your veterinarian will advise you if you are unsure about the need for these vaccinations.

Dogs occasionally experience an allergic reaction to vaccinations. Although rare, reactions reported in Tibbies cause the face to swell to the point of closing the eyes. An antihistamine quickly reduces the swelling. Although the reaction may not recur, your veterinarian may decide to use another manufacturer's vaccine the next time around, to "pre-treat" with an antihistamine and/or to monitor your Tibbie after administering the injection.

Annual Physical Examination—Most veterinary practices send their clients a notice when annual boosters are due. It is important that your dog also receive a complete physical examination during this visit. These annual checkups are responsible for detecting many health problems in the earlier, more treatable phases.

As part of this exam, the veterinarian inspects your pet's eyes, ears, nose, teeth and gums, skin, coat and lymph nodes. He or she palpates the abdomen for any evidence of abnormal organs or growths, records the dog's weight, observes the gait, and listens to the heart and lungs with a stethoscope.

Take this opportunity to discuss your Tibbie's weight, nutrition, behavior or any other concerns you may have. Bring in a *fresh* stool sample to be checked for intestinal parasites (discussed later).

Spaying and Neutering

Spaying or neutering improves your dog's chances for a long, healthy life, and he or she also becomes a better pet. Spaying or neutering your pet also eliminates the risk of unwanted or accidental puppies that contribute to the tragic and costly problem of animal overpopulation.

Veterinarians recommend spaying or neutering for all dogs that are not going to be bred or that have finished their breeding careers. Similarly, ethical breeders require buyers to sign an agreement to spay or neuter Tibbies sold as companion animals (rather than as show/breeding prospects).

Spaying—Ovariohysterectomy, the removal of the female dog's ovaries and uterus through an incision in her abdomen, is commonly called spaying. The spayed Tibbie's urge to mate disappears along with her annual estrus, usually called a "season" or "heat cycle," and its accompanying bloody discharge.

Spaying before the first heat cycle, which usually occurs between seven and 12 months in Tibbies, has the greatest potential for avoiding future health problems. The spayed female is no longer at risk for life-threatening infections and tumors of the uterus and ovaries and at less risk for developing cancer of the mammary glands. This is the second leading type of cancer in all dogs, and over one-fourth of unspayed females and those spayed after their second heat cycle develop mammary gland tumors in their lifetime. About half of the tumors are malignant, and many of these spread to other organs. Cancer in Tibbies is further discussed later in this chapter.

Neutering—Orchiectomy, usually called neutering and sometimes castration, involves removing the testicles and tying off the spermatic cords through a small incision. The scrotal sac that remains eventually shrivels. Male Tibbies reach puberty at about one year of age. To avoid problem behaviors associated with

---

NORMS

Temperature	100-102.5°
Pulse	70-130 beats per minute at rest
Respiration	10-30 breaths per minute at rest
Gums	Pink and moist (not tacky)
Conjunctiva	Pink

unneutered (also called intact) males, they are usually neutered when they are about six months old.

Intact Tibbies have been known to scale six-foot fences or to dig impressive tunnels to reach a female in season. Many have lost their lives after escaping and wandering off in search of females. All of my neutered Tibbies, no longer obsessed with finding an available female, are more content and pleasant to have around. However, the longer you wait to neuter your male, the more likely that troublesome behaviors, such as territorial marking, fighting and mounting, will have become habits. Once established, neutering may not altogether eliminate such habits.

Neutered Tibbies are no longer prone to the painful prostate problems that afflict up to 60% of older, intact male dogs. In addition, neutering diminishes the risk of prostate cancer and eliminates any chance of testicular tumors. Chapter 13 discusses prostate problems.

Prevention at Home

You can contribute to maintaining your Tibbie's health by good practices at home.

Nutrition and Fitness—A well-nourished, fit Tibbie is longer-lived and better able to fight health problems. Chapters 8 and 9 discuss fitness and nutrition for puppy and adult Tibbies respectively. Here are some reminders:

- Use a premium brand dry food containing high quality, not quantity, protein. Dry food delivers more nutrition than the same amount of other forms of food (such as canned) and helps prevent tartar buildup on teeth. It is easier on your wallet, too.
- Feed an age-appropriate food. To grow properly, Tibbies under one year old need food specially formulated for puppies. After one year of age, switch to an adult maintenance diet. Food formulated for geriatric dogs is now also available.
- Do not feed "people food."
- Maintain proper weight through diet and exercise. Remember that every excess pound of fat makes your Tibbie's heart pump blood through seven additional miles of vessels!

Heartworm Preventative—Found wherever mosquitos are found, the heartworm is a major threat to dogs. If you live where heartworm is a problem, your Tibbie should take heartworm preventative prescribed by your veterinarian. In addition, your Tibbie should periodically have a blood test to assure that no inadvertent lapse in prevention has allowed the heartworm to invade his body.

Either daily or monthly doses of preventative are available. For daily doses, decide on a specific time of day so that you can more easily remember the medication. Manufacturers of monthly preventatives usually provide a set of stickers with which you can mark a specific day each month on your calendar. Many people, especially those of us in warm climates, give their dogs a heartworm preventative year-round, while people in colder climates give preventative only during the warm months when their dogs are most susceptible.

Observe Appearance and Habits—Your Tibbie's body language can tell you how he feels. Help your veterinarian diagnose and treat your Tibbie by being an observant owner who can answer his or her questions thoroughly and accurately.

- As you walk your Tibbie, watch what he does and how he does it. Any limping? Any labored breathing?
- Most dogs are on a daily schedule. Although his routine changes as he ages, a Tibbie tends to nap, eat and play at certain times. Do you notice any deviations from the usual? Is he as playful as ever or is his activity level diminishing? Is he "off his food"? Does he sleep more?
- Watch him as he eliminates. Does he urinate a normal amount and with normal frequency? Does the urine look normal? Is the stool firm and of normal volume and color? Any sign of worms? Does he strain or show any sign of discomfort?

Make a mental note of any changes you notice, and put your senses on alert. If he does not return to normal, discuss the changes with your veterinarian.

Besides being observant, regularly examine your dog for signs of trouble. Most people find it convenient to look over their dogs while grooming. Check for:

- parasites (fleas or flea dirt),
- dental problems (bad breath, inflamed or bleeding gums, brownish teeth),
- skin and coat condition (dryness or dullness, wounds, flakes, patchy hair loss, bumps or lumps on or under the skin), and
- eye and ear problems (dull or runny eyes, sore or smelly ears).

Attend to any simple problems you find, such as cleaning obvious debris from the ears and gently removing encrusted tears from the eyes. Make a habit of cleaning his teeth each time you groom your Tibbie. Chapter 9 explains these procedures.

ROUTINE HEALTH PROBLEMS

An upset tummy, a little diarrhea, an annoying flea, a cut pad—even a well Tibbie occasionally experiences such day-to-day health problems. In conceiving this chapter's structure, I was struck by the fact that some canine health problems are so routinely encountered by dog owners everywhere that no one would consider a Tibbie affected by them to be seriously impaired or in danger of losing his life. It seemed to me that discussing such predictable problems among those that are life-threatening or debilitating lends too great a weight to ordinary problems and too little weight to grave problems. Therefore, two sections address health problems—one for routine problems as they affect the Tibetan Spaniel and another for serious, but unusual, problems reported in the breed.

Generally speaking, the conditions listed alphabetically in this section are easily treated. However, you should *not* infer that these problems do not require your attention. On the contrary, any of them may become serious if neglected or if complications arise. For example, an unchecked infestation of fleas may cause serious anemia. Furthermore, veterinarians everywhere prefer that you consult them rather than allow a simple problem to worsen. Never hesitate to ask for help!

Anal Sacs

The anal sacs, located on each side of the rectal opening, secrete a malodorous substance that helps dogs mark their territories and identify one another. Normally, the sacs empty whenever your dog defecates, but fear or anxiety may also cause them to empty. Overactive anal glands are fairly common in small dogs.

If you notice a persistent odor, you may wish to express the secretions yourself. Ask your veterinarian to show you how. Do this smelly job at bath time when cleanup is easy. (Or, you can ask your veterinarian to provide this service.) Occasionally, anal sacs become impacted and/or infected, as evidenced by scooting the bottom along the ground, blood or pus. If you suspect an impaction or infection, take your Tibbie to the veterinarian.

Dental Problems

Dental health affects the general well-being of your Tibbie. Periodontal (gum) disease and infections stemming from it can contribute to serious health problems elsewhere in the body and shorten life. One owner recalls that his aged Tibbie's overall health improved dramatically only a month after his veterinarian extracted an infected tooth from which she had long suffered. "...She had more energy, a better appetite, her coat was growing in thicker and she looked and acted like a much younger dog," he marvels.

Small breeds, especially those with short muzzles, seem prone to dental problems because a full complement of canine teeth is crowded into their mouths. Look inside your Tibbie's mouth; the molars are probably crooked, and the incisors (in front) may also be misaligned. Bacteria flourish in the nooks and crannies of this type of dentition. From this bacteria, plaque and then tartar forms. If not removed, the tartar accumulates and contributes to gum disease. The gums may recede and/or become infected (gingivitis), and the teeth loosen. Consistent with this scenario, Tibbies often experience early tooth loss, chiefly of the incisors in the front of the mouth.

Some Tibbies retain deciduous (baby) teeth, often the canines, after the adult teeth come in. Since these retained baby teeth crowd the permanent teeth, making them even more crooked and subject to the problems described above, have your veterinarian remove baby teeth that do not fall out naturally.

Improving the breed's dentition, as a means of reducing tooth loss as well as enhancing the appearance of the mouth, is a concern of breeders (see Chapter 13). Meanwhile, there is much you can do to improve your Tibbie's oral hygiene and reduce the risk of dental problems. Although suitable chewables (such as dry food, dog biscuits, rawhides, hard nylon bones) help, the best way to prevent tartar buildup is to regularly clean your Tibbie's teeth with a toothpaste made for dogs, preferably once a day. In large Tibbie families where daily cleaning is not practical, try to clean their teeth at least three times a week. My Tibbies stand in line, tails a-wag, waiting their turn to have their teeth brushed. Chapter 9 explains how to clean your Tibbie's teeth.

In addition to regular cleanings at home, your veterinarian should examine and, if needed, clean the teeth thoroughly once a year. This procedure, performed under anesthesia, becomes more necessary as the dog ages.

Oral tumors are discussed under **Cancer** later in this chapter.

Diarrhea *(see Gastrointestinal Upsets)*

Fleas

External parasites that afflict mammals in nearly all parts of the world, fleas are most common in warm months. Routinely check for fleas during your dog's daily brushing. Some amazingly stoic Tibbies can be overrun with fleas and yet scratch only occasionally. On the other hand, some Tibbies react to a single fleabite with ferocious scratching and biting. In the latter case, the Tibbie is likely allergic to the flea's saliva, which makes an uncomfortable situation an untenable one. Long after the flea has gone to its just reward, the allergic Tibbie may still be scratching at the bite.

Dogs tend to scratch at fleas where they can reach them: the neck area, the back at the base of the tail and the belly. If you roll your Tibbie onto his back, you may spy a flea scurrying along in the thin hair between the hindlegs. Even if you do not see the elusive fleas themselves, tell-tale flea dirt (a euphemism for flea droppings) is irrefutable evidence of their presence. If you draw an extra fine flea comb through the coat on the back at the base of the tail and black specs collect in the teeth, your Tibbie has fleas.

To tackle fleas effectively, it is now universally accepted that you must treat the dog, the dog's premises inside the house and the area surrounding the house. Moreover, since your dog can easily pick up a flea and bring it home to your flea-free home, ward off hitchhikers by giving your Tibbie an extra spritz of flea spray before venturing someplace where other dogs are present.

It is beyond the scope of this book to discuss the pros and cons of the myriad flea products on the pet market. For reliable advice about safe flea prevention, talk to your veterinarian. *Skin Problems,* later in this chapter, provides further information about flea allergy.

Gastrointestinal Upsets (Diarrhea and Vomiting)

Although some Tibbies seem prone to gastrointestinal upsets, most owners assert that their Tibbies have "cast-iron" stomachs. Nonetheless, most Tibbies occasionally experience a bout of diarrhea or vomiting. In addition to the following information, see the discussion of *Digestive Problems* later in this chapter.

Diarrhea—Diarrhea is characterized by watery, soft and often voluminous stools. Although it may result from a simple upset due, for example, to a change in diet or a surplus of fatty treats, diarrhea may also stem from parasites, infections, malabsorption conditions, tumors, injury and intolerance or allergy to certain foods.

I am reminded of Tricki Woo, the famous Pekingese of James Herriot's novels. Mrs. Pumphrey, Tricki's indulgent owner, constantly fed him rich non-dog foods, much to Mr. Herriot's chagrin, which caused poor Tricki to suffer periodic indispositions of his gastrointestinal tract. Like Tricki's owner, you may be tempted to give your Tibbie all manner of treats. Try to resist; remember that diarrhea on the trousers is both embarrassing to your Tibbie and unpleasant to clean up. Even if you are virtuous in this regard, your Tibbie may sometimes bring diarrhea on himself by eating indigestible or spoiled items. Even if your Tibbie has an otherwise cast-iron stomach, a surefire way to induce a bout of diarrhea is to change his diet suddenly. Always introduce new foods slowly.

To treat diarrhea at home, withhold food for 24 hours, allowing only a little water or ice cubes. Give your Tibbie a dose of Kaopectate every couple of hours. According to a catalog, published by Drs. Foster and Smith, the dosage is one ml. per pound. That is about two teaspoons for a ten-pound Tibbie or three teaspoons for a 15-pounder. On the next day, allow him to eat a bland diet of rice (because it is highly digestible for dogs) and *boiled*, skinless chicken breast. Do not cook the chicken any other way, or you will make matters worse. Water is allowed. Even if you see no further diarrhea, continue feeding this bland diet and water for three days and then gradually resume the usual diet.

Although many people successfully treat cases of mild diarrhea at home, take your Tibbie to the veterinarian *immediately* if the diarrhea:

- lasts over 24 hours (due to the risk of dehydration), or
- contains traces of blood, or
- is accompanied by loss of appetite, vomiting, fever or pain.

Vomiting—Vomiting is the ejection of food from the stomach. It may be a sign of a simple gas-

---

THE WAR AGAINST FLEAS À LA 1896

Treating both the dog and his home is an old strategy in the war against fleas. Just about the time that the Tibetan Spaniel was making his way to the West with the British, this advice appeared in *Indian Notes about Dogs: Their Diseases and Treatment* by "Major C": "If a dog be much troubled with fleas, a teaspoon full of spirits of turpentine should be mixed with the yolk of each egg used for cleaning him, and at the same time his kennel must be thoroughly purified. This can be done by throwing bucketsful of boiling water repeatedly over it to kill the fleas, and subsequently painting the woodwork with spirits of turpentine. There are plenty of nostrums which will instantly kill fleas; but the difficulty is to select those which will not injure the dog at the same time."

trointestinal upset, such as that caused by overeating, or of another underlying problem, such as dietary indiscretion. Observe your dog's actions as he vomits and examine the vomited matter. This information may provide your veterinarian with clues as to the source of the problem.

A common reason for vomiting in all dogs is plant-eating. Many Tibbie puppies are plant-eaters. Grass is particularly relished but indigestible, and some common plants are poisonous. Eating spoiled food or feces may also cause vomiting. Chapter 10 discusses plant- and stool-eating.

Carsickness (motion sickness) often occurs in young puppies, but I have never seen a Tibbie who did not out grow it quickly. Before traveling with a puppy, withhold his food and pack some paper towels. Dosing with Dramamine ahead of time also helps. The dosage recommended by the Drs. Foster and Smith catalog is up to 50 mg. every eight hours.

If your Tibbie vomits once or twice and then acts like himself again, with no other signs of illness, he probably does not require any treatment. However, other forms of vomiting may indicate inflammation of the stomach (chronic or acute gastritis), gastroenteritis, poisoning or various other illnesses. Take your Tibbie to the veterinarian *immediately* if:

- you know or suspect that he has eaten something poisonous, or
- the vomiting is persistent or recurs chronically, or
- the vomit contains blood or resembles feces, or
- you observe projectile vomiting, or
- the dog loses his appetite, or
- the dog is lethargic.

Intestinal Parasites (Worms)

Despite your best efforts, you can be sure that one or more types of intestinal worms will assail your Tibbie during his lifetime. For example, tapeworms are a common intestinal parasite transmitted to dogs via fleas.

Eggs of worms, such as roundworms and hookworms, are easily detected by fecal tests. You may see the segments of tapeworms, which look like kernels of white rice, in your Tibbie's stool or around the anus. Even if you neither see worms nor have any reason to suspect worms, my advice is to take a fresh stool sample to your veterinarian, at least once a year, as part of your dog's annual checkup.

Almost any type of intestinal worm infestation is easily eradicated by the appropriate dewormer. Choosing the correct dewormer depends on determining which type(s) of worm is present. A veterinarian is in the best position to make this diagnosis. For this reason, do not use off-the-shelf dewormers. For dogs troubled with chronic re-infestations, recently developed products combine heartworm preventative and dewormer effective in controlling certain intestinal worms.

Itchy Tibbies

Tibbie owners all over the world report itchiness. The chief causes of itchiness in Tibbies are fleas and allergies. Dry skin and hormone imbalances, both of which occur fairly often in Tibbies (as they do in all dogs), also play a role. The key to relieving itchiness is to discover its underlying cause. In addition to the following information, see *Fleas, Skin Problems* and *Thyroid Problems* elsewhere in this chapter.

Today's climatically controlled homes are often dry and contribute to dry skin in Tibbies. If you suspect dry skin, try applying one of the many commercially available moisturizing products. Some are rinses applied after shampooing, and others are sprays. Be sure to follow label directions. Dry skin in dogs usually occurs in a strip down the back. To make sure that the spray gets down to the skin, rake your fingers through the coat to lift the hair away from the body and then spray.

If you see whitish, dandruff-like flakes while brushing, the flakiness may result from an underlying allergy, bacterial infection or hormonal imbalance. A type of mite resembling dandruff may be the culprit. If the underlying problem is dry skin, moisturizers may help. If moisturizers have no effect, consult your veterinarian.

Noisy Tibbies: Honking, Snoring, Snorting, Etc.

Tibbies are known for animated "talking." They employ a variety of sounds, such as squeals and grunts, to make their wishes known. Such talking is normal and one of the many charms of the breed.

Snorting a greeting is so common among Tibbies that turning the face away is a reflex reaction for most owners returning home. Although an elongated soft palate may account for snorting, I believe that a Tibbie's snorting is merely a way of clearing his nose so that he can sniff you more efficiently. In fact, owners of many breeds, whether long-, medium- or short-muzzled, report snorting as typical welcome-home behavior.

Episodes of puffing, punctuated with noisy honking sounds, are called reverse sneezing, and they occur randomly in all dogs. What triggers these episodes is unknown. Blowing in or covering your Tibbie's nostrils for a moment may stop the episode.

Snoring or honking indicates the presence of an elongated soft palate. At the top of the mouth (the palate) a section of soft tissue begins where the hard section ends. If too much soft tissue is present, as is often the case in very short-muzzled breeds, the extra tissue interferes with the passage of air between the nose and the windpipe (trachea). The results may include impaired breathing and assorted noises, such as persistent snoring and snorting. Since a Tibbie's muzzle is moderately (rather than extremely) short, his soft palate may be only slightly elongated. The occasional noises he makes are usually no problem to the dog or his owner, and his breathing is not impaired. However, if the soft palate is too elongated, it may be necessary to surgically correct the condition.

Runny Nose

A moist nose is normal for a dog; it means that the "plumbing" that produces and eliminates tears is functioning properly. A dry nose may mean that your Tibbie's "plumbing" is malfunctioning, but it does not mean that your dog has a fever. It is a popular myth that a dog with a dry nose has a fever; fever is unrelated to the nose.

A slightly runny nose is usually related to tearing, too. The nasolacrimal duct, at the inner corner of the Tibbie's eye, conducts his excess tears into his nose. That is the same thing that happens to us when we cry; our excess tears flow into our noses. Rather than delicately blowing his nose into a tissue as we do, the Tibbie snorts out the excess.

Consult your veterinarian if you notice:

- a discharge coming from only one of your Tibbie's nostrils, or
- an abnormally colored discharge from the nostrils, or
- excessive sneezing.

Teary Eyes

Many owners report that their Tibbies' eyes tear, sometimes causing dark stains under the eyes. Tearing may not be noticed until a Tibbie's face fills out between six months and two years old. Since he usually has a fuller face, a male Tibbie may tear more than a female.

In dogs, tearing is not an emotional response. Instead, it may result from air-borne irritants, facial hair or extra lashes, various defects of eyelids, allergies or a combination of these factors.

Most tearing in Tibbies is due to the natural construction of their faces. A Tibbie's lower eyelid is sometimes too "full" or bulky. The bulky eyelid may push the facial hairs growing there against the eyeball where they irritate the eye. In response, tears are produced. Since most Tibbies have tight eyelids, instead of droopy ones, the tears do not pool between the lower lid and the eyeball. Instead, most drain away normally (that is, through the nasolacrimal duct in the corner of the eye into his nose) and cause a wet or runny nose, any tears that do not drain overflow onto the face. Excess facial hairs growing at the inner corner of the eye may worsen tearing by acting as a wick that draws the tears out onto the face.

Occasional mild tearing may be only a cosmetic problem, but ask your veterinarian to evaluate the situation. More information about tearing, its causes and consequences, is found under *Eye-Related Problems* later in this chapter.

Ticks

The only aspect that I dread about the otherwise welcome advent of spring on our farm is the return of the tick. Despite our best efforts to spray our property and to mow the grass frequently, we cannot stem the tide of ticks that invades from the surrounding wilderness as soon as the weather turns mild. The plague continues throughout the summer and fall. Since our Tibbies love to run in the meadows and adjacent forests, during their twice-daily outings, part of every summer evening is devoted to scouring their bodies for ticks.

If you and your Tibbie are urbanites, you may not need to worry overmuch about ticks. Those of you who, like me, live in the suburbs or country should, at a minimum, follow a regimen of daily inspections, tick repellents and grass mowing.

It is important to work your fingers through every square inch of your Tibbie's coat, right down to the skin, as you feel for the tell-tale hard lumps. Pay special attention to the head and neck, where ticks usually migrate. Look in out-of-the-way places, such as under the collar, inside the ears, under the armpits and between the toes. A small male dog tick is often found lurking near an engorged female tick.

Other measures can reduce the number of ticks that find your Tibbie tasty. Since the likelihood of spotting a tiny deer tick (the size of the period at the end of this sentence) is nil, my Tibbies are vaccinated for Lyme disease each spring (see discussion of this vaccination earlier in this chapter). I also use a tick repellent product according to label directions. Many experts do not recommend flea and tick collars; however, Preventic®, a collar containing Amitraz, appears to be effective.

Besides treating the Tibbie, pay attention to your home. Although pesticide use is controversial, spraying the premises surrounding your home is effective in controlling ticks. Trimming the grass short deprives the ticks of a perch from which to leap onto their victims.

Vomiting
(see Gastrointestinal Upsets)

SERIOUS HEALTH PROBLEMS

Earlier in this chapter, I discussed problems that owners of Tibetan Spaniels, like dog owners everywhere, routinely encounter. This section turns to health problems that I consider to be of a serious, rather than routine, nature.

All of us are concerned about health problems which are life-threatening or of such a chronic or debilitating nature that the quality of life is diminished. However, it is not within the scope of this book to report every disease to which a Tibetan Spaniel may succumb. Instead, I have focused on illnesses in which heredity may play a role and on those that the breed seems to share with other small dogs (whether purebred or mixed breed) and with breeds believed to be related to it (such as the Pekingese or Lhasa Apso).

This section reflects up-to-date information gleaned from veterinarians, veterinary ophthalmologists and veterinary texts and journals, as well as anecdotal evidence collected from interviews and correspondence with North American and European owners of Tibbies that suffer from serious illness. Both breeders and pet owners have contributed. In addition, I have incorporated the results of a health survey conducted by the Tibetan Spaniel Club of America (TSCA) and the results of veterinary examinations collected and supplied by the Tibetan Spaniel Club of Sweden (TSK). Current data on eye problems reported to Canine Eye Registry Foundation (CERF) (U.S.) are also cited.

My reasons for describing these serious illnesses are to educate and to encourage open communication among owners. So that this section may serve as a convenient breed-oriented reference, the problems are arranged in alphabetical order according to the body system or part they affect (e.g., Digestive, Eyes).

While reading about these illnesses, remember that the Tibetan Spaniel is a healthy and long-lived breed. Let me emphasize that no evidence exists to indicate that health problems reported in this section are any more numerous in this breed than in dogs in general or in similar breeds. Furthermore, it would be wrong to infer that the problems discussed here are prevalent in the Tibetan Spaniel. On the contrary, all available evidence indicates that most of these illnesses are very rare. Rather than focusing on the incidence of these problems, the only appropriate conclusion to draw from this section is that we must be vigilant in protecting the future health of the Tibetan Spaniel and that we can protect the breed only if we are aware of the problems that *may* threaten it.

> *If a dog gets angry, his soup remains untasted.*
>
> Tibetan proverb

Causes of Death in Tibetan Spaniels

According to respondents to TSCA's health survey, the causes of death in American Tibetan Spaniels are (in order of frequency):

1. old age
2. accidents
3. heart failure
4. birth defects
5. anesthesia
6. cancer
7. kidney failure
8. birth complications
9. liver disease
10. spinal problems

It is important to note that "old age" is not really a cause of death; instead, it is cited when the actual cause(s) is unknown. The actual cause is usually one or more of the other conditions listed. Like their fellow canines, the most common cause of death in aged Tibbies is probably end stage kidney disease.

Despite its lack of specificity, knowing that "old age" takes most Tibbies is nonetheless a useful fact. It confirms that Tibbies are long-lived and that their deaths are the end result of an expected decline in health, attributable to an array of conditions normally linked to aging. Chapter 9 describes the aging process in Tibbies.

With the exception of "birth defects" and "birth complications," which are covered in Chapter 13, the conditions on the above list are found in this section. "Kidney failure" is under *Urinary System Disorders,* "liver disease" is under *Digestive System Problems* and "spinal problems" are under *Skeletal Problems.* The others are self-evident.

Accidental Death and Injury

As the second leading cause of death, accidents deserve to be listed a significant health concern in this breed. Automobiles, entrapment, falls, poisoning, attacks by other dogs and heat are among the reported causes of accidental death or injury to Tibbies.

In the event of an accident, post the numbers of your veterinarian, emergency veterinary hospital and poison control center near your phone.

A Collar and Tag

During a fierce winter storm, Dealer and DeeDee, two Tibbies owned by the Richard Dahlen family (U.S.), escaped the backyard through a damaged gate. It wasn't until later, when Dealer returned, that the family realized DeeDee was missing. The family searched frantically—canvassing the neighborhood, running an ad in the paper and posting over five hundred flyers. Finally, a woman contacted Mrs. Dahlen; she explained that she had witnessed an accident in which a small, white dog was struck by a car and killed instantly. The dog's companion, the woman added, was another "Pekingese" who escaped injury and ran away. When Mrs. Dahlen tracked down the city employee who had removed the dog, he handed her the collar and tag he had cut from the body. Slowly turning over the little tag in her palm, she was already sure that it said, "DeeDee."

As you may suspect, being struck by a car is the most usual cause of accidental death. A few of these accidents involved Tibbies whose owners told me that their trustworthy Tibbies were allowed outside off-lead because "he never left the yard." However, the vast majority of these deaths involved Tibbies who had run away from home by climbing over, digging under or wiggling through fences. Others slipped through open doors or gates.

Another factor in accidental death is the tendency of independent-natured Tibbies to ignore calls of "Come" when frightened or in pursuit of some objective. I cannot understate the importance of not only escape-proofing your home, but also providing basic obedience training and continuing to reinforce the training throughout your Tibbie's life.

Heat-related deaths deserve a special mention. We are warned that short-muzzled breeds are intolerant of heat and that vigorously exercising such breeds, in hot weather, is dangerous. With their moderately short muzzles, Tibbies seem to suffer less from heat than do breeds with extremely short muzzles (such as Pugs). However, owners consistently report that their Tibbies "dislike" heat and sensibly balk at exerting themselves in it. Perhaps this canine common sense is why few owners report serious illness resulting from over-exertion in hot weather. On the other hand, a type of heat exposure, from which your Tibbie cannot protect himself, is entrapment in a hot car. Many Tibbies "go everywhere" with their owners and enjoy such outings but, even with the windows cracked, the temperature in a car can climb to a lethal level within minutes. Never leave your Tibbie in a car in warm weather; leave him at home.

Allergies *(see Skin Problems Due to Allergies)*

Anesthesia-Related Problems

Many owners of small breeds, especially those that are brachycephalic (short-muzzled), believe that their breeds may experience adverse reactions to anesthesia. Earlier literature on the Tibetan Spaniel has stated that our breed may be sensitive to anesthesia.

For most breeds, neither scientific evidence nor substantial clinical experience support a conclusion that anesthesia adversely affects *the breed as a whole.*

POISON CONTROL

Many poisons exist in and around the home, including cleaning substances, antifreeze, insecticides and many kinds of plants. Keep a list of poisonous plants posted along with the telephone numbers of your veterinarian and poison control centers.

The National Animal Poison Control Center (NAPCC), a non-profit service, is dedicated to animals. Numbers and fees charged as of this writing are:

1-800-548-2423 $30.00 per call, have credit card ready
1-900-680-0000 $20.00 first 5 minutes, $2.95 each additional minute

Your local poison control centers may also be able to provide helpful information in an emergency.

Similarly, the anecdotal evidence of anesthesia-related problems in our breed is inconclusive; the Tibetan Spaniel may have no greater incidence of these problems than other breeds. However, in any dog breed (and in humans!), certain *individuals* may react adversely to anesthesia. The dog's response may be an anaphylactic reaction or the result of an undetected underlying health problem. For example, a Tibbie with a liver disorder may succumb when anesthetized because the improperly functioning liver does not remove the anesthetic from the blood as a healthy liver would.

Tests performed before an anesthetic is administered help to identify underlying kidney and liver problems and thus reduce anesthesia-related risks. Improved anesthetics have also reduced risks. Certainly, no one should ever decide against spaying or neutering or other necessary medical procedures for fear of anesthetizing an otherwise healthy Tibbie. Discuss your concerns about anesthesia with your veterinarian.

Cancer

Tumors, growths made up of abnormal cells, may be either benign or malignant. A benign tumor does not spread and can usually be removed, but tumors that attack adjacent tissue or spread to other parts of the body are malignant. Cancer is the term applied to tumors classified as malignant. Removing malignant tumors sometimes cures the dog, but more extensive therapy including radiation and/or chemotherapy may be required to bring the cancer under control.

Tibbies, like other dogs, sometimes develop tumors, some of which are malignant. Most cancers are found in aged Tibbies, but the incidence of cancer in some Tibbie families and its relative absence from others suggests that some lines may be predisposed.

Mammary—Mammary gland cancer is the second leading type of cancer in all dogs, and female Tibbies are not exempt. The risk is minimal if you spay your female before her first heat cycle, but the risk increases with each heat cycle thereafter. Over one-fourth of unspayed female dogs and those spayed after their second heat cycle (such as those used in breeding programs), develop mammary gland tumors in their lifetime. Luckily, about half of canine mammary tumors are benign. Some of those that are malignant can be cured by mastectomy, but malignant mammary tumors often spread to other organs.

Most of this Tibbie's lower jaw was removed due to oral cancer. Many years later, she remains healthy and requires no special treatment. *Kris Gilmore photo*

It is important to check female Tibbies (especially the older ladies) monthly for lumps or swellings around the nipples. If you find any, seek treatment promptly. As in women, the possibility of a cure through removal of malignant tumors and other therapy depends on how early the cancer is caught.

Other—Tumors seen in other dogs are also found in Tibbies. Tumors reported in Tibbies include those of the lymph glands (lymphoma), spleen (hemangiosarcoma), mouth (usually squamous cell carcinomas and fibrosarcomas), skin (such as mast cell tumors) and bones (osteosarcoma).

Digestive System Problems

The usual problems with a Tibbie's digestive system involve gastritis or gastroenteritis (inflammation of the stomach and/or intestines), as discussed under *Gastrointestinal Problems* earlier in this chapter. Serious disorders of the pancreas and liver, two organs that help in the metabolism of food, are occasionally reported.

Diabetes—One function of the pancreas is to deliver insulin to the bloodstream. Insulin enables the body to process sugar. When the pancreas does not produce enough insulin, the resulting sugar buildup causes excessive thirst, with resulting increase in urination and in appetite. Paradoxically, weight loss often accompanies these signs. Diabetes is more likely to strike female dogs over five years old. Untreated, a diabetic's condition degenerates and results in death.

HEREDITARY CONDITIONS REPORTED IN THE TIBETAN SPANIEL

The overall incidence of hereditary conditions in the Tibetan Spaniel is believed to be low. However, individual families may experience higher incidence of certain conditions than the breed as a whole. To prevent the propagation of hereditary conditions in the Tibetan Spaniel, we must be aware of illnesses in which heredity plays or may play a role. Some conditions described in this book are known to be hereditary. Others are believed to be influenced by heredity in one way or another.

Since the population of the Tibetan Spaniel is small, little breed-specific veterinary literature exists. However, documentation for "small breeds" and for breeds thought to be related to the Tibetan Spaniel (such as the Lhasa Apso, Shih Tzu and Pekingese) is extensive. If veterinary literature indicates that heredity may be involved in conditions reported in other small breeds, especially the related breeds, it is prudent to conclude, absent evidence to the contrary, that the conditions may also be inherited in the Tibetan Spaniel.

These conditions include: **allergies, cancer (some types), distichiasis, entropion, hip dysplasia, congenital kidney disease (juvenile nephropathy), hernias (some), intervertebral disc disease (some cases), liver shunt (congenital portosystemic shunt), patellar luxation, progressive retinal atrophy**

If your veterinarian diagnoses diabetes, he or she will determine the correct insulin level for your Tibbie. You must then control the disease through diet and daily insulin injections. With proper treatment, a diabetic Tibbie may live many happy years. Cataracts *(see Eye Problems)* may be related to diabetes.

Pancreatitis—Whether pancreatitis is a prevalent problem in Tibbies is arguable. Vomiting, depression and loss of appetite are the signs of acute pancreatitis, and an accompanying fever indicates a grave prognosis. On the other hand, occasional bouts of soft stools or diarrhea, sometimes accompanied by vomiting, are more likely to be signs of digestive upsets such as gastritis or gastroenteritis. However, consult a veterinarian whenever any of these signs is present.

Treatment usually consists of withholding food and water, intravenous fluids to counteract dehydration and antibiotics. When food is resumed, a bland diet is given.

Pancreatic Exocrine Insufficiency (PEI)—Besides producing insulin, another function of the pancreas is to deliver digestive enzymes to the stomach. PEI occurs when the pancreas does not produce the enzymes needed to digest and absorb foods in the stomach and intestines. Although the dog eats well, he does not seem to utilize his food and produces large, soft, light-colored, oily stools.

To treat this condition, veterinarians generally prescribe pancreatic enzyme supplementation and recommend a low fat, moderate protein diet.

Living with PEI

One owner writes that it is a challenge to live with a Tibbie with PEI. During the first year and a half of her life, her beloved Tibbie was chronically and seriously ill, but several veterinarians were unable to diagnose the problem. Only after considerable expense and heartbreak, did the owner learn that her Tibbie suffered from PEI. Today, the condition has been brought under control with a special prescription diet and enzyme supplementation.

According to her owner, this Tibbie has an unfortunate fondness for "anything that creeps, crawls or flies." So, her owner must be vigilant in preventing her from capturing and gobbling up the insects that could cause her to become violently ill. The only treats she is permitted are the occasional salt-free/fat-free cracker, which she relishes, and tiny ice cubes. Occasionally, she is allowed one-half teaspoon of boiled, white rice. Once, in a moment of weakness, her owner decided to give her the pleasure of a dog bone. Despite repeated cleansing and cooking, the innocent-looking bone set off a terrible reaction from which the Tibbie needed several days to recover. Her owner vows never to repeat this mistake! This Tibbie is very lucky to have such a devoted owner.

Liver Shunt—Technically called congenital portosystemic shunt, liver shunt is a life-threatening condition in which a birth defect allows blood, containing the toxic byproducts of digestion, to bypass the liver's detoxifying function. When the toxins in the blood reach the brain, they cause diverse neurologic signs. A wide variety of other signs may also accompany liver shunt.

Liver shunts are thought to be inherited because they are diagnosed in pure-bred dogs more often than in mixed breeds. Some American Tibbie breeders have voiced concerns about propagation of liver shunt, but no cases are reported in other countries.

The signs of liver shunt usually appear in puppies but may not become evident until the dog is an adult. Neurologic signs include:

- restlessness or depression,
- sleepiness or mental dullness,
- pacing, circling, staggering or head pressing,
- seizures, and/or
- intolerance to anesthesia.

The many other possible signs of liver shunt include:

- excessive thirst and urination,
- diarrhea and/or vomiting,
- stunted growth, weight loss, failure to gain (in puppies),
- bladder stones, and/or
- blindness.

As you can see, many of these signs are "vague" because they may be signs of conditions other than liver shunt. Some may even pass unnoticed. For example, a sleepy-headed puppy that has a so-so appetite may have liver shunt, but other conditions also cause sleepiness and poor appetite. When a diagnosis of liver shunt is confirmed, signs that had previously been unheeded simply because they were "vague" are newly perceived as further evidence of the shunt. Hindsight is often 20/20.

To confirm a diagnosis of liver shunt, veterinarians use a battery of tests including blood tests, urinanalysis, radiography and ultrasound. Surgical correction of the shunt is the only cure, but the longer the condition is untreated, the less likely a surgical repair will be possible. Although a low protein diet, antibiotics and other medications reduce the toxins in the blood, these treatments cannot solve the problem.

Ear Problems

Ear Infections—Scratching at the ear, shaking the head, holding the ear down, inflammation of the external ear and smelly discharge are among the outward signs of ear infections. Although not as plagued by chronic ear infections as some other breeds, long hair and drop ears may predispose a Tibbie.

Possible causes of ear infections include bacteria, yeasts, mites, foreign objects or allergies. I believe that allergies are implicated in many ear infections in Tibbies. Working constantly at his itchy ears, the allergic Tibbie traumatizes them to the point where an opportunistic bacterial infection may develop *(see Skin Problems)*.

To prevent ear infections, keep the ears clean and dry. If an ear problem arises, your veterinarian identifies the source of the problem and treats with an appropriate medication. Do not use over-the-counter mite preparations; if mites are not the problem, you will make matters worse. If allergies are a factor, treatment of the underlying allergy is imperative.

Deafness—Although congenital deafness in one or both ears can occur in any dog breed, deafness in Tibbies usually results from the normal aging process.

Eye Problems

Eye-related problems currently generate the most concern among Tibbie owners and breeders worldwide. The Canine Eye Registry Foundation (CERF), an organization that synthesizes data from eye examinations of dogs in the U.S., reports that 21% of Tibetan Spaniels examined, from January 1991 through December 1994, had one or more eye problems.

Tearing—Epiphora, usually called tearing, is the most common eye problem reported by Tibbie owners. As explained earlier in this chapter, tears that are formed to lubricate the eye normally drain through the nasolacrimal duct at the inner corner of each eye into the nose. However, when tears spill onto the face, the overflow may form a displeasing dark brown tear stain on either side of the muzzle. Although a Tibbie's tearing may not be serious, it may indicate a potentially serious problem, such as a chronic irritation, that could eventually lead to blindness.

Consult your veterinarian whenever:

- your Tibbie's face is always wet, or
- he is uncomfortable, rubs or paws at his eyes or squints, or
- redness or swelling develops.

Among the underlying problems that your veterinarian may discover are:

- obstructed nasolacrimal duct (blockage causes tears to overflow the lids instead of flowing into nose),
- excess facial hairs at the inner corner of the eye (a naturally bulky lower lid pushes hair against eye or hair acts as a wick to draw tears onto the face),

- conjunctivitis (bacteria, viruses or air-borne substances, such as sprays or dust, irritate the eye),
- allergies *(see Fleas, Skin Problems elsewhere in this chapter),*
- entropion (defective eyelid rolls inward and irritates the eye)
- ectropion (defective eyelid rolls outward, exposing it to chronic irritation), and
- distichiasis (extra lashes on the upper, lower or both upper and lower lids may irritate the eye).

Distichiasis may be the most common of these eye problems. The condition was found in 11% of American Tibbies whose exams were reported to CERF (1991-1994) and in 31% of Danish Tibbies examined in 1994. However, note that many Tibbies with extra lashes experience little or no irritation.

Medication and/or surgery can correct most of the problems listed above.

Cherry Eye—Cherry eye is a red swelling at the inner corner of the eye that occurs when the tear gland, at the base of the third eyelid, enlarges and protrudes. No one really knows what causes cherry eye, but dust or pollens may be implicated. To remedy cherry eye, a veterinarian surgically repositions and anchors the gland. Once back in its proper place, the tear gland resumes its function. Removing the gland is not recommended because a condition called "dry eye" results from the lack of natural tears.

Eye Injury—The usual eye injury reported in Tibbies is corneal abrasion, which are scratches to the surface of the eye. Tibbies whose eyes protrude slightly are more likely to suffer these injuries. Corneal abrasions cause the eye to be painful and watery. The white of the eye may be red. The Tibbie often holds his eye closed or squints. He may paw at the eye or rub his face against the floor. Prevent your dog from further injuring his eye in this manner until you are able get veterinary help. Do not treat eye injuries yourself; using the wrong medication could make matters much worse.

Cataracts—Cataract is the term applied to a lens that is becoming (or has become) opaque. Since a cataract may develop slowly, an affected dog may nonetheless retain some vision for several years. Cataracts appear in dogs of any age but are more usual in dogs over eight years old. Just as with humans, cataract surgery successfully restores vision in a high percentage of cases.

Some cataracts are inherited while others result from conditions such as diabetes or injuries before or after birth. Retinal degeneration also contributes to cataract formation. In a study of nearly 1200 Swedish Tibbies, about 3% were found to have inheritable cataracts.

Do not confuse cataracts, which are white, with nuclear sclerosis, the typical pearly gray look in an older dog's eyes. Dogs with nuclear sclerosis can see, while those with a fully developed cataract are blind.

Optic Nerve Problems—In veterinary literature, the optic nerve problems reported for Tibetan Spaniels are coloboma of the optic disk and micropapilla.

A coloboma is a hole or pit in the optic disk, the place where the optic nerve joins the eyeball. It causes an impairment that may be described as "tunnel vision." Although present at birth, no evidence indicates that colobomas are inherited in the Tibetan Spaniel, and the condition is rare in this breed.

A micropapilla is a congenital condition where the optic disc is abnormally small, but otherwise fully functional. Repeated tests in Tibbies with micropapilla have not shown any vision impairment even as they have grown older. Optic nerve hypoplasia, a condition where the optic nerve is actually underdeveloped, causes vision loss but is very rare in the breed.

Microphthalmia—Microphthalmia is a condition where a puppy is born with an abnormally small eye. Besides its outward appearance, the inside of the eye may be deformed as well and, if so, the puppy may be blind at birth or suffer vision loss later on. Microphthalmia may be inherited. It is sometimes associated with hydrocephalus (see Chapter 13). Neither a Tibbie with the condition nor his parents should be allowed to reproduce.

Persistent Pupillary Membrane (PPM)— PPM is a congenital condition in which tiny strands of

---

The Board of the Tibetansk Spaniel Klubb wish to thank everybody who helps us spread the information about PRA, PRA carriers, and affected Tibetan Spaniels. We do believe that honesty is the only way to fight this tragic disease. We sincerely hope that, together with Tibetan Spaniel breeders/owners around the world, our struggle will be successful and our lovely breed will remain healthy.

Margaretha Hägglund, Secretary
Tibetansk Spaniel Klubb (Sweden)

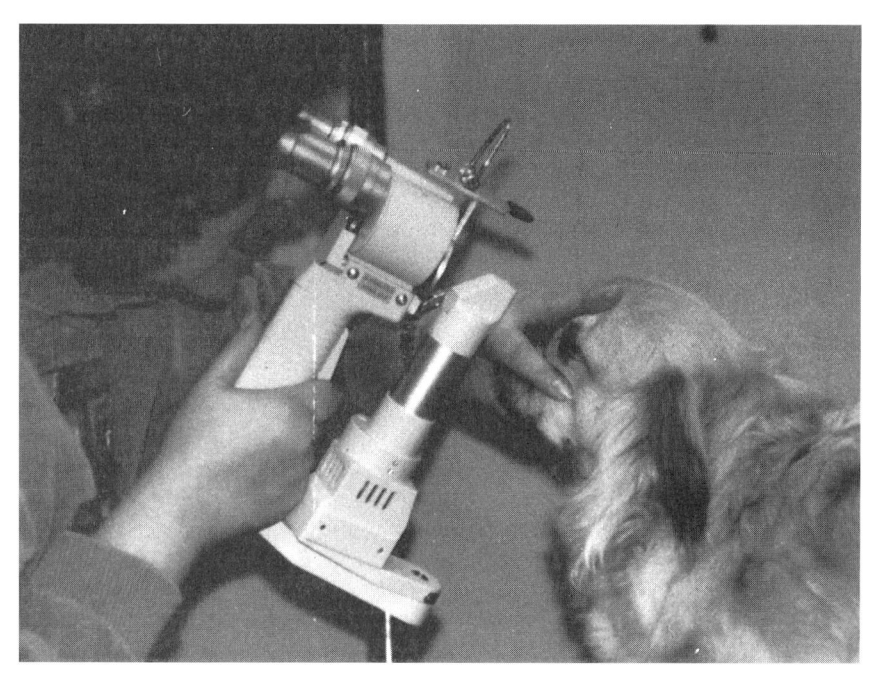

Nancy Bromberg, VMD, DACVO, MS, a veterinary ophthalmologist, examines a Tibbie's retina for signs of PRA. The test requires only a few minutes. *Chris Miccio photo*

tissue are left over from the eye's fetal development. PPM may form many patterns in the eye, but most cause no problems at all. However, where the PPM adheres to the cornea or lens (or both), vision is impaired. Although the defect may be identified in puppies as young as four to six weeks, there is no evidence to indicate that PPM in Tibbies is inherited.

Progressive Retinal Atrophy (PRA)—PRA is a serious condition in which the cells of the retina at the back of the eyeball gradually degenerate to the point where an affected dog becomes blind.

PRA is inherited. It affects both males and females. A dog that inherits the gene for the condition from both parents will develop PRA and become blind. A dog that inherits the gene for the condition from only one parent will not develop PRA and does not experience vision loss. Nonetheless, he or she is a "carrier" that may pass the PRA gene to his descendants. Neither a Tibbie that is actually affected with PRA nor a Tibbie that is a carrier should be allowed to reproduce.

To date, most cases of PRA in Tibbies have been diagnosed only after owners noticed vision impairment in adult Tibbies. One owner remembers noticing that her female Tibbie, then five years old, no longer wanted to go out after dark, a hesitancy that later proved to have been the first sign of PRA. In a study of 51 affected Tibbies in Norway and Sweden, PRA was diagnosed between two and one-half and seven years of age. All of these dogs became blind within a year of the first sign of vision loss.

An ophthalmoscopic examination and/or a more sophisticated test called electroretinography, conducted by a certified veterinary ophthalmologist, may reveal retinal changes in the retinas of Tibbies as young as one and one-half to two years old. Although these youngsters show no clinical signs of blindness, these changes may be the early signs of PRA. No test to detect whether a Tibbie is a carrier has been devised, but a recently developed genetic test to identify PRA carriers in Irish Setters gives us hope that researchers will be able to identify carriers in other breeds within the next few years.

Cases recently reported in Sweden, Norway, Finland, the U.K. and the U.S. have fueled concerns about PRA among Tibbie breeders worldwide. As of this writing, the number of confirmed PRA cases worldwide is fewer than 100. However, overall incidence of PRA in the world population of Tibbies is unknown

The Tibbie on the left has PRA and bilateral cataracts. The Tibbie on the right has normal eyes.

because testing is not universal. Some countries (such as Denmark) have been spared. The greatest incidence has been in Sweden, where test data on nearly 1,200 Tibetan Spaniels show 3.3% with PRA. Regardless of their country of birth, all Tibbies in the world outside the Himalayan region are probably descended, at least in part, from the stock with which the breed was established in the U.K. after the Second World War. Therefore, the "gene pool" is small, and all Tibbies are potentially at risk even if the gene that causes PRA has remained hidden for many years..

The names and pedigrees of Tibbies diagnosed with PRA are available from the Tibetank Spaniel Klubb (Sweden). The Tibetan Spaniel Association (U.K.) and Tibetan Spaniel Club of America (U.S.) also provide information on PRA. It is critically important to test all prospective parents for PRA before they are bred. As is the case with all genetic diseases, one or more carriers among a few widely used sires can strongly influence the incidence of the disease in a breed. A popular stud dog that is an undetected carrier may produce many descendants, many of whom are also carriers, before a mating with another carrier produces PRA-affected offspring and reveals that the sire carries the PRA gene. Concern about the influence of popular sires is a reason why the Finnish breed club asks breeders to limit the number of offspring a single sire may father in a year. Although a carrier dam may also transmit the gene to her descendants, she is less likely to produce the high number of offspring that a popular stud produces.

The first outward sign of PRA is loss of night vision. Gradual loss of the remaining vision in both eyes follows. Cataracts often develop along with PRA. Although there is no treatment for PRA, the condition is not life-threatening, and affected dogs do not suffer pain.

Living with Blind Tibbies

Remembering her reaction when she learned the devastating news that her lovely three-year-old Agnes had PRA, Inga Enstad (Sweden) writes, "I was shocked! I never dreamt of it! At such young age! ...I didn't suspect her lines at all." At first, Mrs. Enstad recalls, Agnes was "as happy as ever." She trailed after other dogs, who treated her the same as always, and she soon became adept at finding her way around the house and yard. So that Agnes could navigate freely, Mrs. Enstad was careful not to move furniture or other household objects, both indoors and outdoors. In her last year, Agnes began to move more slowly, her nose to the ground, like many elderly dogs. Succumbing to the heart disease of old age, she died peacefully in her sleep. She had been a good companion for many years, despite her blindness.

Mrs. Enstad's experience is shared by another owner, Mrs. Rita High (U.K.) whose Jonathan was twelve years old when she adopted him. Already blind for seven years, the old gentleman adapted quickly to his new home and was soon accompanying Mrs. High and her other Tibbies on visits to schools. There, to the delight of the schoolchildren, he demonstrated his ability to deftly move around and under furniture. Mrs. High recalls that Jonathan so impressed them that, to this day, the children, now grown up, inquire after his health. Jonathan died of old age in his twentieth year, having been a good companion to Mrs. High for eight years.

Heart Disease

Heart disease hinders the heart from efficiently circulating blood through the body. Most Tibbies suffering from heart disease are elderly, and heart disease in elderly dogs usually involves the heart values. Congenital defects or stenosis, a narrowing of blood vessels, account for most cases of heart disease in puppies. Reports from owners of young adult Tibbies that died from heart disease suggest that a serious infection earlier in life may have damaged the heart.

Even though some heart defects are present at birth, no evidence establishes that such defects are inherited in dogs. Nonetheless, no Tibbie with a known heart defect should be bred.

In evaluating the severity of a heart problem, a veterinarian considers:

- the dog's age, sex and breed,
- clinical signs (such as coughing, exercise intolerance),
- heart sounds (such as murmurs and arrhythmias),
- physical exam, and
- results of various tests (such as radiography, ultrasound and electrocardiogram).

Murmurs and Arrhythmias—A murmur is the sound made by blood when not flowing smoothly through the heart. Think of murmurs as a *sign* of a heart problem just as a fever is a *sign* of an infection. Although the murmur itself is not the problem, a murmur may indicate a disease (such as anemia) or a defect (such as a malfunctioning valve). Veterinarians are trained to differentiate the murmurs according to their sound and location.

Arrhythmia is an irregularity in the heartbeat. Like the murmur, it is not a disease but a sign of disease.

Valve Problems and Stenosis—When the heart valves allow blood to leak backwards, the dog suffers from valvular disease. Murmurs and other signs of diminished circulation warn of valve malfunction. Stenosis is a narrowing of blood vessels or tissue adjacent to the valves (outflow tract) that impedes efficient blood flow. Depending on the type of valve defect or location and extent of the stenosis, treatment with medication or surgery may be possible.

Heart Failure—Any type of heart disease can lead to congestive heart failure. When the heart can no longer compensate for the defect or disease, failure of one or both sides of the heart occurs. Although they vary according to the extent of heart disease, signs that owners may notice include coughing, inactivity and intolerance to exercise, labored breathing, barrel chest or pot belly, wasting and swollen limbs.

Treatment can prolong and sustain the quality of your Tibbie's life. Weight reduction, a low-salt diet, medications to reduce fluid buildup and to control the rhythm and force of the heart and moderate exercise are usually among your veterinarian's recommendations.

Kidney Problems *(see Urinary System Problems)*

Liver Problems *(see Digestive System Problems)*

Neurological Problems

Occasionally reported in young Tibbies, seizures result from interruption of normal electrical activity in the brain. Characterized by bizarre behavior such as falling down, paddling motions, foaming at the mouth, chewing or irrational barking, they often conclude with a period of unconsciousness followed by a return to normal behavior. Seizures may be caused by brain damage from poisonings, injuries, tumors, defects or diseases, such as liver shunt. Anxiety attacks and some heart problems may be easily mistaken for seizures. Seizures may be treatable once the veterinarian determines the underlying cause. For example, medication to control epilepsy is available.

Reproductive Disorders

Chapter 13 discusses diseases and disorders of the male and female reproductive systems as well as congenital defects and other health problems of newborns and young puppies.

Seizures *(see Neurological Problems)*

Skeletal Problems

Canine hip dysplasia, a condition dreaded by all dog lovers, has been reported in Tibbies but is extremely rare. Other skeletal problems that are seen more often include patellar luxation, arthritis and spinal problems.

Arthritis—Arthritis is the degeneration of a joint(s) that occurs when the smooth cartilage between the bones roughens and wears away, exposing the underlying bone. It is the most common skeletal problem reported in dogs. The natural "wear and tear" of aging is the usual cause, but arthritis may also result from injury or accompany other joint problems such as patellar luxation. Obesity contributes to the arthritic dog's discomfort.

The signs of pain, like those in aged people, include stiffness (more so when the dog gets up or with changes in weather) and limping. The hip, stifle (knee) and back seem to be the sites where arthritis most often attacks Tibbies. Since signs similar to those of arthritis may arise from prostatitis in male Tibbies, it is important to consult a veterinarian (see Chapter 13).

Correction of an underlying problem (such as patellar luxation) may relieve arthritic pain. Weight reduction, medication and moderate exercise are the usual recommendations. Warm, dry quarters and a soft bed also help.

Elbow Dysplasia—Elbow dysplasia due to ununited anconeal process results when the ulna (one of the bones in the foreleg) separates from the anconeal process (part of the ulna). The loose bone irritates and impairs the dog. Appearing in puppies, this type of elbow dysplasia is related to rapid growth. Heredity may also play a role.

The usual sign is lameness. The puppy may hold his elbow away from the body, but not all Tibbies who are "out at elbow" have elbow dysplasia! The severity varies; some dogs are slightly lame while others cannot bear weight at all. Arthritis may eventually develop in the defective joint. Radiography verifies elbow dysplasia, and surgical repair is the best treatment.

Patellar Luxation—Medial patellar luxation is a condition where the patella (kneecap) slips out of the groove in which it lies and moves to the inside of the leg. The purpose of the patella is to protect the stifle joint. Fairly common in all small breeds, patellar luxation also occurs in Tibbies. The physical attributes that predispose a small dog to this condition are inherited and present at birth. Most cases in Tibbies are mild (0 or I on a scale of 0-IV), and no outward signs of the condition are evident. Nonetheless, breeders should be aware of the problem. For example, Finnish breeders are warned that the sum of the patella test results of an otherwise healthy prospective sire and dam should not exceed 2 (e.g., I + I or 0 + II).

Intermittently holding up a leg is the main sign of patellar luxation in small dogs. Bowing in the rear legs and an altered gait may also be present. Over time, arthritis may develop in the affected joint. A veterinarian verifies patellar luxation by manipulating the joint. Radiography helps pinpoint the reason(s) for the slippage. Surgical repair is sometimes required.

Spinal Problems—A Tibbie owner remembers when her female Tibbie suddenly refused to jump onto the couch beside her. The Tibbie's back was hunched and she carried her head low. When her concerned owner tried to pick her up, the Tibbie cried out. A reluctance to climb steps or jump onto the bed may be the first sign of a back problem that you notice. Trembling or shaking indicates pain.

A Tibbie with these signs may have suffered a ruptured disc. Technically, this is called intervertebral disc disease. As in humans, a seemingly innocuous action that the Tibbie has performed many times before may result in trauma to the spine. Intervertebral disc disease occurs in all breeds, but veterinary literature lists long-backed breeds (such as Dachshunds) and breeds related to Tibbies (such as the Pekingese and Shih Tzu) as prone to ruptured discs.

Discs are cushions of cartilage filled with gel-like substance located between each vertebrae of the spine. A disc ruptures or "herniates" when the inner portion protrudes through a tear in the outer cartilage. Pain results from the pressure exerted on the spinal cord; other signs may include weakness, paralysis or loss of feeling. Swelling or hemorrhage in the surrounding tissue aggravates the condition.

Since signs similar to those of a ruptured disc may arise from an injury, osteoarthritis or, in male Tibbies, from prostatitis, it is important to get veterinary help. Treatment for ruptured disc depends on the severity of the herniation. Rest and medication to reduce inflammation is often all that is needed, but surgery may be required.

Hip Problems—Canine hip dysplasia and Legg-Calvé-Perthes disease are extremely rare hip problems in Tibbies. For example, only three out of nearly 1200 Swedish Tibbies tested were found to be dysplastic, and all were mild cases. Other countries report few or no cases. No data on Legg-Calvé-Perthes disease in Tibbies are available.

Hip dysplasia results from a deformed joint where the femur (thigh bone) and hip socket do not fit together properly. Its severity varies considerably, so that some dogs lead relatively normal lives while others are seriously impaired. Usually seen in large breeds, hip dysplasia is inherited. No dog with hip dysplasia should be allowed to reproduce. Signs may appear as early as four to nine months of age and may include limping, bunny hopping while running, difficulty when climbing and hip pain. Arthritis that develops in the deformed joint compounds the problem. Radiography confirms the diagnosis, and treatment includes weight control, moderation in exercise, pain relievers and, in some cases, surgery.

Legg-Calvé-Perthes disease is a degeneration of the femur. Signs appear as early as four months of age. It is more often seen in small breeds than large. The cause is unknown, but heredity may be involved. The outward signs are limping, hip pain and reduced range of motion. Radiography confirms the diagnosis, and surgery is required to treat the problem.

Skin Problems

Allergies are the chief cause of skin problems in Tibbies. Two other skin problems occasionally reported in Tibbies are pyoderma and demodectic mange. Dry skin *(see Itchy Tibbies earlier in this chapter)* and hormone imbalances *(see Thyroid Problems)* may also play a role in skin problems.

Allergies—An allergy is the over-reaction (hypersensitivity) of the body's own immune system to something your Tibbie touches (contact allergy), breathes in (inhalant allergy), eats (food allergy) or is bitten by (usually flea allergy). As in humans, it seems that allergies in dogs are on the upswing, and Tibbies are no exception. Although not generally life-threatening, the usual types of allergies found in Tibbies make them uncomfortable and often require life-long treatment.

The tendency to be hypersensitive to certain substances is inherited. Pairing two allergic Tibbies almost always produces allergic offspring. If only one parent is allergic, at least some of the puppies will probably develop allergies, too. Although allergy signs may appear under six months of age, your Tibbie may not show any signs until he is two or three years old or even older.

As in all other dogs, the leading allergic reaction reported in Tibbies is to flea saliva. Inhalant allergies to substances such as grass pollen, molds and housedust are thought to account for as much as ninety percent of canine allergies *other than* flea allergies. Consistent with this statistic, an allergic reaction to grass is the second leading allergy reported in U.S. Tibbies. It is interesting to note that a high incidence of inhalant allergy occurs in the Tibbie's relative breeds, the Lhasa Apso and Shih Tzu, and inhalant allergy may be similarly widespread among Tibbies. Although the incidence of food allergy in Tibbies is not known, between 10% and 20% of allergic reactions in all dogs are attributed to food allergy. A few Tibbie owners report occasional intolerance to certain foods, resulting in gastrointestinal upsets, but is not clear whether these are actual food allergies.

Unlike human allergies, the chief sign of canine allergies is itchiness. That is why allergies are listed here under *Skin Problems*. Allergic Tibbies lick, scratch or bite at their skin, rub their faces, and lick and/or chew their paws. Owner reports indicate that the ears seem particularly susceptible. However, the teary eyes and runny nose seen in allergic humans are more likely to be signs of an eye problem in a Tibbie *(see Eye Problems)*. Of course, a Tibbie may have both an allergy and eye problem.

Treatment of an allergy depends on its source. Unfortunately, it is impossible to determine which kind of allergy a Tibbie has based solely on these outward signs. In fact, Tibbies may suffer from more than one kind of allergy simultaneously. For example, licking and chewing the paws (which leaves a reddish brown stain on the Tibbie's gloves) is considered the classic sign of inhalant allergy. However, a Tibbie that chews his paws may also be allergic to some food ingredient in his diet. Treating this Tibbie only for the inhalant allergy may help but will not eliminate his itchiness.

Not all Tibbies that have fleas are allergic to fleas but eliminating them is a sensible first step in any case of itchiness. Flea prevention and control are discussed earlier in this chapter. To further relieve your Tibbie's discomfort, your veterinarian may prescribe medications including corticosteroids and/or antihistamines. Since prolonged corticosteroid therapy may cause serious side effects, you should view these injections or pills as a temporary, merciful expedient, not as a matter of routine. You must bring the real culprits, the fleas, under control.

Once fleas are ruled out, identifying the source of an allergy is difficult because there are so many possibilities. Seasonality is one indicator. Inhalant allergies are usually (but not always) seasonal, whereas food allergies are year-round. Another indicator is the response to corticosteroid treatment described above: inhalant allergies generally respond well, but food allergies respond little. Over a period of time, a methodical dietary trial can pinpoint a food ingredient to which the dog is allergic. On the other hand, a similar approach to identifying sources of inhalant allergy is not usually feasible because you can never completely eliminate your dog's exposure to the common allergens, such as grass pollen, that plague many Tibbies.

In his article in *Current Veterinary Dermatology*, Dr. John M. MacDonald comments that, because it "mimics" other canine allergies, food allergy may be overlooked as the source of a dog's itchiness. He continues, "Yet it is one of the easier diseases to control by means of avoidance. Ignoring food allergy...may either result in uncontrolled [itchiness] or require a high glucocorticoid dosage, posing a health risk. Evaluation for dietary hypersensitivity should be performed in all cases of intractable [year-round itchiness]." The key element in diagnosing a food allergy is a dietary trial. First, the dog is restricted to a hypoallergenic diet made up of food ingredients, with no additives, that he has *never* before eaten. For maximum effectiveness, studies indicate that this restricted diet must continue for six to ten weeks, during which the veterinarian periodically evaluates any improvement in the dog's condition. As the owner, your complete compliance is critical to success. After the restricted diet, re-introducing individual food ingredients to determine which provoke renewed itching confirms any food allergy present.

If inhalant allergy is suspected, veterinary dermatologists perform an intradermal sensitivity test (skin test), similar to that used in humans, to identify the offending substance(s). Immunotherapy, which consists of desensitizing injections formulated based on the outcome of skin testing, is the most effective treatment of inhalant allergies. Other than immunotherapy, treatment often includes a combination of topical therapy (e.g., hydrocortisone or oatmeal shampoos, sprays, etc.) and systemic therapy (e.g., corticosteroids, antihistamines, omega 3 and omega 6 fatty acids). Although corticosteroid therapy alleviates discomfort, some of the possible side effects are diabetes *(see Digestive System Problems)*, a drop in hormone levels and reduced resistance to infection. Use corticosteroids only under direction of your veterinarian. Instead of or in addition to corticosteroids, your veterinarian may suggest one of the many antihistamines available. However, you may need to experiment with several before finding one that is effective on your Tibbie. Unfortunately, many owners report that their Tibbies do not seem to respond to any antihistamine.

Pyoderma—A superficial pyoderma is a skin infection. As the most common skin infection in dogs, pyoderma is usually caused by staphylococcus bacteria and may be related to an underlying metabolic disorder, immune deficiency, hormonal imbalance or allergy. Pustules are the usual sign, and the severity of the infection varies. Veterinarians treat pyoderma with special medicated shampoos and antibiotics.

Hot Spots—Hot spots are red, moist painful sores accompanied by hair loss. Your dog aggravates the sore by scratching or biting at it. A vicious cycle develops: the more the dog scratches, the worse the sore becomes, the more the dog scratches, and so on. Large hot spots may develop on your Tibbie's neck or face, and the underlying cause is often an allergy.

To heal, a hot spot must dry up completely. For this reason, most hot spots need veterinary care. After shaving the area to expose the entire sore, the sore is scrubbed with betadine. An anti-inflammatory medication and possibly a topical salve are usually prescribed. At home, your Tibbie may have to wear an Elizabethan collar to prevent further scratching and biting at the wound. Do not bandage the sore; leaving it open to the air helps to dry it up.

Demodectic Mange—Demodectic mange is a disease caused by a mite that is present in the hair follicles of all dogs. The mites travel to newborn puppies as they nurse their mother. When a puppy's immune system fails to keep the mites in check, hair loss (usually on the face and forelegs) results.

Your veterinarian can confirm the diagnosis with a skin scraping. Medicated baths, medication to kill the mites and good nutrition should relieve the mild form called localized demodicosis. In the severe form called generalized demodicosis, the lesions spread and may become deeply infected. Although it may respond to a dip and/or new oral medications, the generalized form is difficult to eradicate and often recurs periodically throughout the dog's lifetime. Although the Tibetan Spaniel is *not* predisposed to generalized demodectic mange, no Tibbie with the generalized form should reproduce.

Thyroid Problems

Adult dogs of all breeds, male and female, may develop hypothyroidism, a condition in which the dog's thyroid gland does not produce enough thyroid hormone. Personality changes and lethargy, weight gain, craving for warmth, dry hair that sheds easily, and thickening and darkening of the skin are examples of outward signs that owners may notice.

A complete physical examination and a blood test confirm the diagnosis. Fortunately, treatment is available. A daily dose of thyroid medicine, which he will need for the rest of his life, improves the quality of life.

Urinary System Disorders

Although congenital kidney disease, a fatal disease of puppies and young adults, is the urinary system problem most often reported by owners of U.S. Tibbies, chronic kidney failure is probably the most prevalent kidney disease in Tibbies. Since owners may think that signs of chronic kidney failure in elderly dogs are the natural result of aging, they may attribute the deaths to "old age" rather than kidney disease. Among all dogs, chronic kidney failure accounts for more deaths than any other cause; the same is likely true of Tibetan Spaniels. Other diseases of the urinary system reported in Tibbies include bladder stones and cystitis.

Cystitis—An inflammation of the bladder, cystitis usually results from bacterial infection. Frequent urination of small amounts is the main sign of cystitis. In their distress, even well-trained dogs may urinate in the home. Both males and females are affected. Your veterinarian diagnoses cystitis by urinalysis, as well as clinical signs and history. Although antibiotics usually clear up the problem, prompt treatment is important to prevent the infection spreading to the kidneys. Chronic cases require more aggressive treatment and may even reveal bladder stones.

Stones—Stones, which usually form in the bladder, are composed of excessive amounts of minerals that crystallize in the urine. Bladder stones are common in dogs. The Pekingese, a breed thought to be related to Tibbies, seems prone to form stones.

Stones may remain unnoticed or cause an irritation such as cystitis (see above). In a few cases, stones wholly or partially prevent urination. If your Tibbie tries to urinate frequently but passes only a thin stream or dribbles, get veterinary help. Your dog needs immediate care if:

- the urine contains blood or has a strong ammonia odor, or
- he passes small stones, or
- he cannot urinate at all.

Treatment involves dissolving or, more usually, removing the stones. A special diet to prevent new stones from developing may also be necessary.

Congenital Kidney Disease—Congenital kidney disease is an umbrella term that applies to a number of kidney defects or diseases that are present at birth. Renal dysplasia (abnormal growth and structure) and hypoplasia (underdevelopment) in one or both kidneys are among the defects seen in cases of congenital kidney disease. For our purposes here, the term progressive (juvenile) nephropathy (kidney disease in puppies) is synonymous with congenital kidney disease.

Although it is the most prevalent form of kidney disease reported by U.S. Tibbie owners, the incidence of congenital kidney disease in the U.S. is not known. Data collected, since 1988, in Sweden show that 2.5% of 1,200 Tibbies died from progressive (juvenile) nephropathy. Countries with large Tibbie populations, such as Finland and the U.K., are concerned about congenital kidney disease and are trying to determine its incidence.

Along with documented cases of congenital kidney disease in related breeds (Lhasa Apso and Shih Tzu), data collected on Tibbies suggests that heredity plays a role in our breed. A healthy parent who is a "carrier" may pass the genetic basis for the disease to his descendants. The disease may remain hidden for many generations until, when two carriers are paired, it reappears. It should be noted, however, that other possible causes of these kidney-related deaths are being investigated in Norway.

Excessive thirst and frequent urination, early in a dog's life, are the first signs that an owner may notice. In addition to the signs of kidney disease evident from urinanalysis and other tests, weight loss and/or stunted growth may be evident. Dogs with congenital kidney disease usually suffer severe kidney failure (see next topic) between six months to two years of age. Treatment to prolong life is the same as for kidney failure.

Kidney Failure—Kidney (renal) failure is condition where the kidneys no longer produce urine properly. When wastes are not excreted in urine, they collect in the blood and tissues and cause uremia (uremic poisoning). If not controlled, uremia is fatal.

Acute kidney failure may develop suddenly due to certain infections (such as leptospirosis), poisoning (such as antifreeze) or shock. However, the more usual case is *chronic* kidney failure that is attributable to long term "wear and tear" on the kidneys. Inflammation (nephritis) contributes to deterioration of the kidneys. The inflammation is sometimes caused by congenital kidney disease (see above) but may also result from other causes such as insidious infections or obstructions in the urinary tract. With the exception of young dogs with congenital kidney disease, chronic kidney failure usually occurs in geriatric dogs.

Some U.S. Tibbie owners report cases of chronic interstitial nephritis. This term describes a characteristic appearance of tissue taken from the kidneys of a deceased dog or in biopsies from a living dog. It does not identify the underlying reasons for the dog's illness. However, for our purpose, it is reasonable to conclude that a dog whose kidneys showed chronic interstitial nephritis was (or is) suffering from chronic kidney failure.

Since a dog can still produce urine with as little as 25% of his kidney tissue functional, no signs of kidney failure appear until the kidney damage is extensive. Initial signs of kidney failure include excessive thirst and increased urine production, sometimes accompanied by housetraining accidents. Later, other signs—such as depression, loss of appetite, weight loss, dehydration, vomiting and/or diarrhea—warn of the onset of uremia.

Blood tests confirm the presence and extent of uremia. The veterinarian will recommend a course of treatment to help relieve the signs of kidney failure and prolong the dog's life. Treatment varies considerably based on the severity of the condition. To reduce the workload on the kidneys, a special diet that contains less protein, salt and phosphorous may be prescribed. Since the protein is a higher quality and more digestible, the Tibbie still gets the nutrition he needs. Kidney patients always need plenty of fresh water, too.

The Tibetan Spaniel

Chapter 12

Showing Tibetan Spaniels

Valerie Robinson (now of the U.S.) remembers crossing the border from Northern Ireland into the Republic of Ireland during the period of the "Troubles" in the 1970's, en route to show her Tibbies in the south. Asked if political differences ever troubled relationships between the dog fanciers of Ireland, Mrs. Robinson replies that there were always "plenty of politics" of the kind that always accompany human undertaking but not the kind with which heads of state concern themselves. "You know dog people!" she explains, "The love of dogs united us, no matter what happened elsewhere."

Mrs. Robinson's observation sums up the dedication with which serious exhibitors view the dog sport. Dogs are so inextricably woven in the fabric of their lives that schedules are arranged around show weekends, vehicles are purchased specifically to transport dogs and their paraphernalia, and budgets are strained to finance a show dog's career. As one exhibitor remarked, laughing, "Hurricanes may blow and earthquakes may rumble, but the dog show must go on."

THE DOG SPORT

People who participate in the dog sport come from all walks of life. Many, perhaps most, are breeders who show their dogs to advance their breeding programs and win prestige for their kennel names. That artists, scientists, social workers, veterinarians, physicians, educators, business people, photographers and writers are among those who show Tibbies once again attests to the universal appeal of our breed.

A national kennel organization regulates registration and competition of pure-bred dogs in each country. Besides their massive record-keeping functions, these governing bodies are also involved in other dog-related activities, such as promoting public awareness of dogs and advocating for dogs and their owners in the legislative arena.

The Fédération Cynologique Internationale (FCI), based in Belgium, is the dog sport's international governing body. Most national kennel organizations are FCI members, abide by FCI rules and conduct shows according to FCI procedures. However, some organizations follow their own show rules even though they are affiliated with the FCI; two of these are the Kennel Club (U.K.) and the American Kennel Club (AKC).

As the national kennel organization of the U.S, the AKC has registered between 12 and 15 million dogs. In 1991, over 10,000 AKC-approved competitions, including dog shows and obedience trials, took place in the U.S. Nearly 4,400 dogs competed at the largest of these shows in 1994. Over 4,000 dog clubs, including breed clubs and regional kennel clubs, are affiliated with the AKC. The Tibetan Spaniel Club of America (TSCA) is one of these.

Other organizations also sponsor competitive events in the U.S. For example, the United States Dog Agility Association conducts agility events, under different rules than AKC agility events. The United Kennel Club (UKC) and States Kennel Club (SKC) conduct dog shows and obedience trials and offer titles in both. The UKC is becoming increasingly popular with many competitors, especially those interested in obedience work. Patterning its events after the FCI, the SKC accepts all the FCI-recognized breeds, a far greater number than the AKC recognizes.

CONFORMATION COMPETITION

The competitive events open to the Tibetan Spaniel include conformation events (also called "breed"), obedience trials, agility trials, tracking tests and Junior Showmanship (Junior Handling). The vast majority of sporting Tibbies, however, compete in conformation events.

This is the type of event that most people picture when they think of a dog show. Designed to recognize and reward those Tibbies that most closely conform to the Breed Standard, conformation judging encourages the breeding of quality dogs. Although the dogs seem to be competing against each other, they are actually being judged against the elusive ideal spelled out in the Breed Standard (discussed later in this chapter).

Most Tibbies compete in hopes of winning a championship. Once this has been attained, some owners elect to continue showing their dogs in hopes of garnering additional Best of Breed wins. Group placements and, most prestigious of all, Best in Show wins are highly prized. While not commonplace, judges increasingly award Group placements to Tibbies, but few have achieved the honor of winning Best in Show at a show where all breeds are competing.

Dog Show Procedure American-Style

Dog show procedures vary from country to country. In some countries, a Tibbie may become a champion without ever meeting another Tibbie in the ring, but in the U.S. earning a championship depends on finding other Tibbies to defeat.

The procedure at an American All Breed show divides into four stages. The objective of each stage is to select the dogs that will advance to the next stage of competition. The stages are: selecting the Winners Dog and Bitch, selecting the Best of Breed, selecting the Group winners and selecting the Best in Show.

Each male Tibbie first competes in a class made up of other male Tibbies. The regular classes at All Breed shows are Puppy (dogs from six months up to twelve months old), Novice (dogs that have won no points and fewer than four first place ribbons in this and other adult classes), Bred-by-Exhibitor (dogs owned and handled by their breeder or a member his or her immediate family), American-bred (dogs conceived and born in the U.S.) and Open (any dog over six months old). Although the judge may award a first through fourth place in each class, fewer than four Tibbies compete in each class in many (if not most) U.S. shows. Next, the first-place dogs from each class gather in the ring, and the judge chooses one as Winners Dog. This Tibbie is awarded any championship points offered for males (discussed later). So that each class is represented, the second-place dog from the Winners Dog's class steps into the ring to join the remaining dogs that placed first in their classes. From these, the judge selects Reserve Winners Dog, the runner-up. The judge next repeats the foregoing procedure for the female Tibbies, starting with the classes and ending by selecting the Winners Bitch and Reserve Winners Bitch. The Winners Bitch receives any points offered for female Tibbies at this show.

To begin the Best of Breed stage, the Winners Dog and Bitch are joined in the ring by any champions (male and female) entered. American champions competing for Best of Breed are called "specials," and "to special" a champion means that the owner continues to compete for additional honors. After designating Best of Breed, the judge makes two further selections from this line-up. If the Best of Breed is a male, he or she awards the Best of Opposite Sex to a female. (A female may also be chosen Best of Breed and a male Best of Opposite Sex.) He or she also selects a Best of Winners from the Winners Dog and Winners Bitch. Of these selections, only the Best of Breed advances to the next stage, Group competition.

The Tibetan Spaniel is assigned to the Non-Sporting Group, one of seven American Groups. Facing the judge in the Non-Sporting ring are a wide variety of dissimilar companion breeds whose only common characteristic appears to be that they are not some other kind of breed, such as a Hound, Sporting dog or Terrier. The breeds joining the Tibbie in the Group ring include the Dalmatian, Bulldog, Standard Poodle, Lhasa Apso, Shar-Pei and Schipperke. The judge awards four placements in the Group.

Although each Best of Breed in the Group theoretically competes only against his or her own Standard and not against one another, only the top winner from each Group advances to compete with the winners of the other Groups for the honor of Best in Show.

Dog Show Procedures Around the World

It is possible to *roughly classify* the world's dog shows into those based on FCI rules and those based on other rules. At first glance, they seem very different from one another but, when the details are stripped away, all have a similar framework. Like the U.S. All Breed shows just described, both FCI and non-FCI shows focus on selecting one male and one female of each breed to receive credit toward championship and then selecting a Best of Breed that advances to compete for Group honors. Judging continues until a "top dog," the Best in Show, is selected. Beyond this framework, the shows differ in particulars such as the number and types of classes offered, whether championship credit takes the form of a certificate or points (or both!), ring procedure, number of placements awarded at each level of competition and so on.

U.K.—The number of classes varies from show to show, but more classes are usually offered at British Open and Championship shows than at American All Breed shows. Typical classes for Tibbies include Minor Puppy, Puppy, Junior, Novice, Post Graduate, Limit and Open. The first three classes are based on the puppy's age, while the Novice, Post Graduate and Limit classes restrict entry based on previous wins. The Open class is for all dogs eligible to enter the show.

On the way to choosing a Best of Breed, two significant differences between U.K. and American shows are the selection of a Best Puppy and the award of points toward the coveted Junior Warrant (J.W.) title (a special title awarded to dogs between 12 and 18 months old). Next, the Best of Breed Tibbie advances to compete in the Utility Group, one of the six U.K. Groups, with diverse breeds such as the Chow and Keeshond. Like the U.S. system, four placements are made in each Group, and the winner returns to the ring to vie for Best in Show. Unlike the U.S. system, a Reserve Best in Show is chosen, as well as a Best in Show.

Countries where the dog show procedure is based loosely on the U.K. system include Australia, New Zealand, Canada, South Africa and Ireland. However, each country's shows differ from British shows in many respects. For example, Australia, Canada and Ireland all have a form of point system, just as the U.S. does. In most of these countries, the Tibetan Spaniel is assigned to the Utility (sometimes called Non-Sporting) Group, but the Australian Tibbie competes in the Toy Group with breeds such as the Chihuahua, Pekingese, Italian Greyhound and Yorkshire Terrier. For a bit more detail about dog shows in these countries, see Chapter 5.

FCI—Where FCI rules apply, classes vary from country to country. Except for Norway, Sweden, Denmark (the Nordic countries) and Finland, classes include Puppy (nine to 15 months), Open (15 months and over) and Champion. In the Nordic countries, the classes include Junior (nine to 15 months), Youth (15 months to two years), Open (two years and over) and Champion; in Finland, champions compete in the Open class, but the remaining classes are the same as the Nordic countries.

Compared to other FCI countries, the Nordic countries and Finland accord greater significance to three other classes: Progeny (stud or dam with four offspring), Breeders (any four of a kennel's breeding)

Aust. Ch. Aztlon Kar-Zut-Ti, bred by Vivian Hartley (N.Z.), is owned by Michele Waterman. "Jamie," she says, "is a superb little showman...I feel totally unnecessary when I go in the ring with him. He knows what he is doing and off he goes!" *Animal Pics photo*

and Veteran (dogs over five years). As part of the grand finale at Nordic and Finnish shows, winners of the Tibbie Progeny and Breeders classes compete with the winners of these classes from other breeds, and placements are awarded to five of the breeds. Annual rankings of winning veterans are maintained alongside rankings of younger dogs, and a Best Veteran in Show is named in addition to the Best in Show.

In all FCI countries, the judge evaluates each dog, dictates a written critique to one of his or her stewards and assigns each dog a grade. In all but the Nordic countries and Finland, the grades are Excellent, Very Good, Good or Sufficient, while the corresponding grades in the northern countries are one, two, three and zero. From the dogs receiving a grade of Excellent or one, the judge may choose one of each sex to receive a certificate toward championship. He or she also chooses a Best of Breed and Best of Opposite Sex. Assigned to FCI Group 9 (Companion Breeds), the Tibetan Spaniel competes with breeds as diverse as the Chinese Crested, Maltese, Rhodesian Ridgeback and Toy Poodle for up to five Group placements. The judge also awards up to five placements in the Best in Show competition. The number of placements depends on the country.

Earning Championships

Like dog show procedures, championship requirements vary from country to country. Generally speaking, some countries have a "point system," while others have a "Challenge Certificate" (C.C.) system. Some have a combination!

U.S.—The American contender must win 15 points. At least six of these points must be from major wins—that is, wins worth three to five points. At least three judges must award the points, and a different judge must award each major win. The points go to the Winners Dog and Winners Bitch, the best Tibbies of each sex chosen from the classes. Any dog over six months old that meets these requirements becomes a champion.

The number of points assigned to a win (one to five) depends on how many Tibbies of each sex compete and where the show takes place. The AKC divides the U.S. into twelve geographic divisions and scales the point schedule for each division according to the number of Tibbies of each sex that competed in that division during the previous year. For example, to win a four-point major for your bitch at a 1995 show in Honolulu, Hawaii, at least five female Tibbies must compete. However, seven bitches are required to qualify for a four-point major in Chicago, Illinois.

Around the World—Like the U.S. championship just described, every other country's national kennel organization has its own scheme for awarding national championships.

The U.K. champion must win three C.C.'s from three different judges. Although he may begin competing at six months old, a Tibbie must win at least one of his C.C.'s after he is one year old. The C.C.'s go to the best Tibbie of each sex at Championship shows. Although the show procedure is otherwise the same, no C.C.'s are awarded at Open shows. The Kennel Club assigns a quota of C.C.'s to each breed, based on the breed's registration statistics; in 1994, the Tibetan Spaniel was allocated 31 pairs of C.C.'s.

Like the U.K., many other countries award *National* championships to dogs that receive a specific number of C.C.'s or, in FCI countries, C.A.C.'s. For example, a Swedish Tibbie that receives three C.A.C.'s under two judges wins his Swedish championship. However, like the U.S., other countries base championship on a point system. These include Canada, Australia and Ireland. For a bit more detail on each country's championship requirements, see Chapter 5.

In FCI countries, *International* championships are available in addition to National championships. For example, France's kennel organization, the Société Canine Centrale, is an FCI member. Therefore, two types of shows take place in France. At an "International show," exhibitors compete for a C.A.C.I.B. toward the title of International Champion de la Beauté (abbreviated Int. Ch. or INTCH), as well as a C.A.C. toward a French championship. However, only the C.A.C. is awarded at a "National show."

The International champion must win at least four C.A.C.I.B.'s in three countries (one of which is the country where the Tibbie is registered). Three or more judges must award the C.A.C.I.B.'s. The C.A.C.I.B. that qualifies a Tibbie for championship must be won at least one year after his first C.A.C.I.B., and the Tibbie must be at least 15 months old. The FCI awarded 67 International championships to Tibetan Spaniels between 1990 and 1994.

Multiple Championships—Exhibitors sometimes travel to other countries to capture multiple championships. This happens fairly often in European countries, other than the U.K. and Ireland. Due to quarantine laws enacted to prevent the spread of rabies, British and Irish Tibbies may travel between the U.K. and Ireland to compete but not to the continent and back.

In North America, multiple championships are becoming more popular, too. Exhibitors travel between

The Tibetan Spaniel Club of America assembles at their first national specialty show (1992). *Booth photo*

"Chief" (Am. Ch. Jo'Jevon Chief War Bonnet) awaits his turn in the ring with owner Rod Beckstead. Since Tibbies do not require elaborate grooming, this is a "classic" scene outside the Tibbie ring. *Wayne Ponton photo*

the U.S. and Mexico (where International championships are also available) and between the U.S. and Canada. Catering to exhibitors who fancy multiple titles, several travel firms now specialize in making arrangements for showing a dog in Bermuda, the Bahamas and Puerto Rico, as well as more far-flung destinations.

National titles are simply abbreviated Ch., but a Tibbie that holds multiple championships adds the countries where he won the title to the abbreviation. For example, GB, Ir. Ch. indicates that the Tibbie won championships in both the U.K. and Ireland. A Nordic champion (abbreviated Nord. Ch. or NORDUCH) has won the championships of Denmark, Sweden and Norway.

Prestigious Shows

Specialty shows sponsored by the breed club that represents the Tibetan Spaniel attract the largest gatherings of Tibbies. A win at any of these shows is a considered a choice prize.

In the U.S., about 150 Tibbies compete at the TSCA's annual National Specialty show. The day begins with a sweepstakes. A wonderful opportunity to view up-and-coming youngsters, the sweepstakes show- cases puppies from six to 18 months old, with prize money based on the number of puppies competing. Next, the Specialty show itself features several classes in addition to the regular classes seen at All Breed dog shows. These non-regular classes include 12-18 Month, Veteran, Brace, Stud Dog and Brood Bitch. In the Brace, a pair of similar-looking Tibbies go out with one handler. In the last two classes, the dog or bitch appears in the ring with up to three of his or her progeny. Following the selection of the Best of Breed, Best of Opposite Sex and Best Puppy, the judge also designates the Tibbies to be honored with Awards of Merit. Since the Specialty show usually coincides with a cluster or circuit of All Breed shows, the large number of Tibbies gathered for the Specialty have an opportunity to compete in several shows. Other activities on the agenda for Specialty weekend may include the club's annual business meeting, announcement of the Register of Merit (R.O.M.) certificates for champion-producing sires and dams, social and fund-raising activities, educational seminars and eye examination clinics. Finally, the Specialty gives breed enthusiasts from around the country a chance to meet and "talk Tibbie."

Like the TSCA's National Specialty, one or more all-Tibbie shows occur each year in most countries with substantial Tibbie populations. For example, the Tibetan Spaniel Association (U.K.) and four of the regional breed clubs each host an annual Championship show. To the north, Tiibetinspanielit ry, the Finnish breed club, hosts three specialty shows each year.

Besides the all-Tibbie shows, certain dog shows are considered especially prestigious. In the U.S., winning Best of Breed at shows such as the Westminster Kennel Club in New York or the International Kennel Club in Chicago ranks among the most memorable events in a show dog's career. The same is true of wins at prestigious shows such as Crufts in the U.K., the Royal shows in Australia or the Hund show in Sweden.

A win at certain prestigious shows also gives the winner the right to a special title. One of these is the World Dog Show, which is held in a different city each year. The best Tibbies of each sex earn the title World Winner (W.W.), followed by the year of their triumph. The best Tibbies of each sex from the Junior class (nine to 15 months) are named Junior World Winners (J.W.W.).

Some Pro's and Con's of Showing Tibbies

Many exhibitors consider Tibbies to be ideal show dogs. One reason that they are favored is that the exhibitor need only walk briskly, rather than run, in the ring. Also, Tibbies are small enough to be easily transported to and from shows. However, the most popular reason cited is that Tibbies are a "natural" breed that requires little pre-show grooming. "My greatest pleasure is to go to a show and to sit at ringside with my Tibbie curled in my lap watching the competition," says Becky Johnson (U.S.). Unlike profusely coated breeds that require elaborate grooming, Tibbies are not required to stand like statues for hours, right up to ring time, while they are brushed, trimmed, teased and primped. Exhibitors like Mrs. Johnson appreciate the Tibbie's "shake-and-show" coat.

With the possible exception of exhibitors in countries where Tibbies are numerous, most owners believe that championships, for quality Tibbies, are attainable at a reasonable cost (e.g., travel, fees). This contrasts markedly to wildly popular breeds where competition is fierce and costs prohibitive. For example, most American owners believe that the owner-handler is just as likely to succeed in the show ring as a professional handler. Unlike breeds where hiring a professional handler is considered *de rigueur*, American Tibbie rings are dominated by owners handling their own dogs.

On the other hand, in all but a few countries, it is sometimes difficult to gather enough Tibbies for a stiff competition, not to mention the all-important Tibbie chat among exhibitors. Tibbie owners in some places are so isolated that they must travel hundreds of miles or into other countries to find other Tibbies. For example, American exhibitors sometimes arrange to meet at a show so that there will be enough Tibbies entered to make it a "major" for the winner. Without this coordination, meeting the AKC requirement for two "majors" would be nearly impossible in some parts of the U.S.

Another possible "con" is the widely held belief that the Best of Breed Tibetan Spaniel does not have the same chance for success in Group or Best in Show competition as breeds that are more popular. Owners of other rare breeds share this view. While some Tibbie owners concede that the lack of placements may have been justified in the past, they assert that today's Tibetan Spaniel Best of Breed is as close to his own Standard as the other breeds in the Group ring are to theirs. Some owners blame the judges' lack of knowledge of, interest in or exposure to the breed, while others cite the judges' desire to choose from the breeds that faced the greatest number of competitors in reaching the Group ring. In fairness, Group placements appear to be on the rise.

Whatever else may be said about showing Tibbies, one thing is for sure—you never know what they are going to do! While many are natural-born show dogs, others choose to assert their indefatigable independence in the ring. They are as likely to execute a back flip or give the judge a smooch on the nose as to gait a perfect pattern. Fortunately, many judges appreciate the breed's impish personality and laugh right along with the spectators.

The Immovable Object

It was one of the biggest shows in the country. Crowds of exhibitors and spectators milled at ringside and blocked the aisles. Local media people worked the crowd. I was inexperienced and my Tibbie, Kissie, was scornful of her role as showgirl. The judge instructed me to gait "out and back," and pointed me toward the mat running diagonally across the ring. Halfway down the mat, at the center of the ring, Kissie balked, flipped onto her back and paddled all four paws in the air. A wave of laughter rose above the general din of the crowd. After waiting a few moments (eternity), I commanded her to stand up and tugged at her lead. She twinkled her eyes at me, a puckish grin on her lips, and paddled her paws again. I tugged; she waved to the crowd. The old saying about the irresistible force that meets the immovable object flashed through my addled brain. I tugged again and Kissie, having tortured me sufficiently, took mercy

Karen Chamberlain ills.

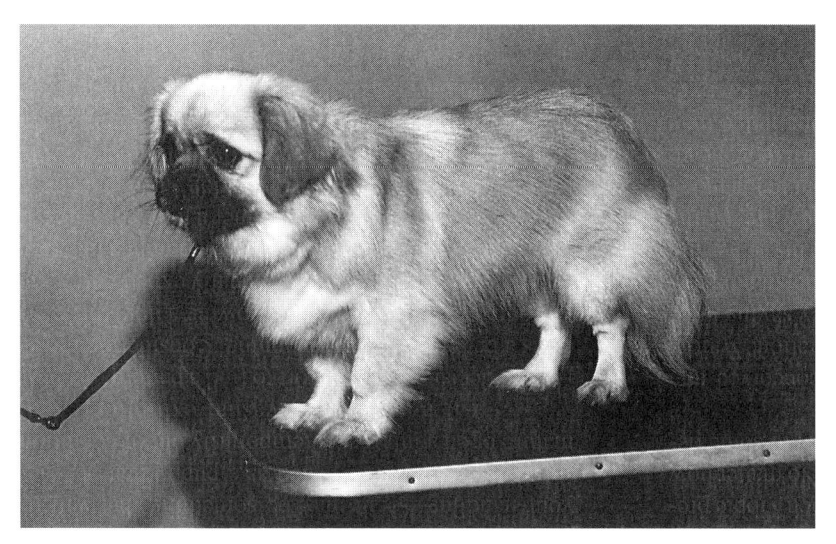

"Before"—"Gizmo," owned by Linda Cochran, has never been on a table. *Scott Chamberlain photo*

on me and flipped over onto her feet. After sprinting to the end of the mat, she balked again—just to reassert her independence. As I turned to face the judge waiting at the far end of the mat, I glanced up and noticed that he, too, was laughing heartily. Seeing that, I managed a smile but, all along the way back, my face flamed with embarrassment. When I later expressed my humiliation to a more experienced handler, she smiled and opined sagely, "Well, you just have to expect that with Tibbies. It's happened to all of us."

Since that mortifying moment, many similar stories have drifted my way, and it is somehow comforting to know that mine is not the only headstrong Tibbie.

Training for the Conformation Ring

Watching skilled handlers and experienced show dogs work together in the breed ring—their every movement choreographed and polished, with more than a touch of panache—makes showing dogs look simple. Trust me—it is not simple. Since it is beyond the scope of this book to teach ringcraft, my advice is to read at least one book about showing dogs, sign up for a conformation (or "handling") class, practice at a couple of "matches" or "fun shows" and attend several shows as a spectator before you ever tackle showing a Tibbie. In this way, you can learn about judging procedure, ring etiquette (yes, there is such a thing!), gaiting patterns, stacking and baiting. An experienced instructor can also give you tips on showing your dog to his best advantage. Remember that showing your Tibbie is a team effort; both of you need to do your part.

Start show training your Tibbie early, while he is a puppy, but make the training fun. Serious training will only teach the puppy that showing is an unpleasant chore rather than an exciting diversion. All of the techniques described in Chapter 10 apply to show training, as well as pet training.

Due to the multitudes of people and dogs found at shows, place emphasis on socializing your show puppy to all sorts of humans and canines. Accustom him to all kinds of distractions, noise and crowds. Find a conformation class where a few small breeds are intermixed with larger breeds. Your instructor can help you locate local "matches" or "fun shows" where you can practice in a setting that is realistic, but more relaxed than a real show (because no credit toward championship is awarded). Never "pressure" a puppy to perform like an adult.

To practice ringcraft, you need a sturdy table such as a grooming table (about waist high with a non-slip surface), mirror (full-length is best), show lead, bait and both indoor and outdoor spaces in which to move your Tibbie. It also helps to have an assistant who plays the part of the judge. Here are a few pointers for Tibbies:

- Teach your dog to respond to both verbal and visual cues that you give. When you want him to turn on his "show attitude"—that combination of alert posture, facial expression and spirited movement that makes him stand out in the crowd—cue him with a special command. Choose a word or phrase that you never say any other time. I use the rather unimaginative "Go Show!" Also, make sure that the Tibbie learns to associate the word only with things he loves—treats, praise, games and other rewards—no matter what the outcome of the contest!
- Similarly, put a show lead on your Tibbie only when you are practicing or at a show. This is another signal that it is time for him to turn on the charm.
- Place the Tibbie on a table and accustom him to allowing at least one, but preferably several, "pretend judges," both male and female, to examine him as a real judge does. Make sure that the table does not wobble.
- In some places, a judge examines the teeth by lifting the lips while, in other places, the exhibitor displays the teeth for the judge. Depending on the custom in your area, ask "pretend judges" to ex-

amine the teeth or practice showing the teeth yourself. Always give a chirpy command (such as "Teeth") and lots of praise for cooperation.

- Ideally, a Tibbie should stand still for the judge's examination—whether on the table or on the ground—without your rearranging his limbs. Until he acquires this skill, practice stacking your Tibbie in a natural stance that shows off his rectangular profile and angulation. Check his position in the mirror. Do not stretch out the rear legs; you may make a Tibbie with a good rear appear straight-stifled.

- Most judges consider a Tibbie's facial expression to be extremely important. Ask your "pretend judge" to give the Tibbie treats so that your dog learns to look at a judge expectantly and eagerly. The Tibbie should not glue his eyes to you (which he will if you are the only one who gives him treats). When your Tibbie is watching you, the judge is not able to see his expression, and his movement is not as positive and free as it would be if he were looking forward.

- When showing Tibbies in outdoor rings, exhibitors always hope that the grass has been well-mown or well-flattened before ring time because some Tibbies behave unpredictably in tall grass. Apparently, the grass brushing against the hair growing from their bellies tickles and causes them to hippity-hop or dance around the ring. At indoor shows, mats placed around the perimeter of the ring and on the diagonal provide exhibitors and Tibbies with a non-slip surface on which to move, and tape usually secures the edges where the mats meet. Sandy Lidster (U.S.) remembers showing a Tibbie who, on her way around the ring, hopped or leapt over each place where tape joined the mats. She even refused to pose nicely in front of the judge because he stood behind the taped junction of three mats. Fortunately, the understanding judge was amused by this typically Tibbie idiosyncracy. Since your judge may not be amused, practice gaiting patterns on a variety of surfaces, wet and dry, and with all types of distraction around you.

- Move your Tibbie on a loose lead. A tight lead spoils his overall outline, especially the flow of the neck, and alters his movement. It may also compel him to assert his independence by pulling away from you. Many judges complain about handlers "stringing up" their Tibbies on tight leads.

- To convince your Tibbie to move briskly and in the right direction, TALK to him cheerfully using your "happy voice" and tease him with bait. Avoid repetitive jerky corrections. Observe your Tibbie's movement in the mirror.

- When you return to the judge after gaiting a pattern, you must bring your Tibbie to a halt, in a perfectly stacked position, two or three feet in front of the judge and, at the same time, induce him to show the judge a lovely expression and keep his tail up. It sounds easy, but this is a complex lesson to teach. From your lofty perspective, it is often difficult to see where the Tibbie's paws come to a stop. Here again, observe your Tibbie's stance in the mirror and practice adjusting the position of the paws by tugging slightly on the lead, to the right or left. Praise him lavishly when he steps into the perfectly "square" stack. Soon, it will become second nature.

- Vary the bait. A Tibbie that loves pepperoni one week may turn up his nose at it the following week because he now prefers cheese, dried liver, a squeaky toy or a rabbit pelt. After he learns to respond to bait, teach your Tibbie to respond to your "baiting posture" in the absence of real bait. This is because some judges do not allow bait. However, reward him amply when you exit the ring.

- Vary the practice routine. Tibbies learn ring patterns quickly and, bored with repeating the same

"After"—To show "Gizmo" to his best advantage and to simplify the judge's examination, his handler stacks him in a natural position. *Scott Chamberlain photo*

ol' pattern, may try to cut the pattern short. Impatient to return to the judge (whom she always loved), one of my Tibbies disliked circling the ring; instead she pulled hard to take a short cut across the center of the ring. Offset "anticipation" by surprising the Tibbie with unexpected patterns and by varying your speed.

- A Tibbie is allowed to drop his tail while standing but must raise his tail while moving. However, if given a choice between two otherwise equal Tibbies, one standing with tail down and one with tail up, which would you choose? To encourage your Tibbie to keep his tail up at all times, practice a command for it (I use the rather unimaginative "Tail up!") and then reward him lavishly when he raises or wags his tail. Of course, you can always discreetly place your fingers at the base of the tail to hold it in place, but the natural stance is always more impressive. Note that puppies who chronically drop their tails often improve as they grow up and gain confidence.

Locating and Entering Shows

In the U.S., the AKC publishes schedules of upcoming dog shows, as well as obedience trials and other events, in the *Events Calendar*. A supplement to the monthly *American Kennel Gazette,* the *Calendar* also provides blank official entry forms, addresses of show superintendents and other useful information for those interested in showing dogs. You can also access the *Events Calendar* through the Internet at **http://www.akc.org/akc.**

On request, a show superintendent will send you a "premium list," a show announcement. The information in the premium list includes the name of the Tibetan Spaniel judge, directions to the show, nearby accommodations that accept dogs, and prizes offered. Official entry blanks for the show are enclosed. Once you enter a show handled by a given superintendent, he or she will automatically send you premium lists for future shows in your area.

The usual way to enter your Tibbie in a show is by completing an official entry form with basic information about yourself and your dog and mailing it to the show superintendent along with the required fee. The form must reach the superintendent by the "closing date" (usually three weeks before the show date) and before entries reach any numerical limit (always given in the premium list). Services that process entries by fax and computer network are also available.

To confirm your entry, the superintendent sends you an entry ticket. This should arrive no later than the Wednesday before a weekend show. The ticket shows an identification number for your Tibbie; this is the same number that appears on your armband and in the show catalog. Enclosed with the ticket is a "judging program." It shows how many Tibetan Spaniels are entered (including the number of dogs and bitches) and when, where and by whom they will be judged on the day of the show.

Preparing for the Show

You can make showing your Tibbie as simple or as complicated as you want. Generally speaking, you need less show-related paraphernalia for a Tibbie than for most other breeds, but what you pack depends on the distance to the show, whether you will stay overnight, how many dogs you are showing, the weather forecast and your personal preferences.

Exhibitors differ on the minimum essentials for showing a Tibbie. You will undoubtedly develop your own list but, no matter how carefully you plan, it is impossible to prepare for every contingency. I recall going to a National Specialty only to have the entire length of a seam down the front of my skirt rip out a few minutes before ring time. My clever husband came up with a solution and, to this day, I always carry, instead of a sewing kit, a roll of duct tape! (Duct tape can temporarily repair many things besides skirts.) Of course, the vendors at dog shows know what exhibitors need, too, and you can usually find someone who will sell you that critical item you left behind.

Keep your dog show kit ready to go, so that you can pack easily.

Paperwork—Remember the judging program and your entry ticket!

Care Supplies—Make your Tibbie as comfortable as possible while he is away from home. A crate for travel safety and stress-free rest is essential. For exercising, take his everyday collar and lead. Remember your poop scoop and a supply of bags.

Many exhibitors, particularly at summertime outdoor shows, bring a portable exercise pen. (Note that many indoor shows do not permit these pens inside the show building; refer to the judging program for any such restrictions.) To keep the dogs clean, they place a mat beneath the pen. A cover (such as a "space blanket" made of reflective material), draped over the pen and secured with squeeze clamps, gives a shady spot to rest. This is a nice way to let your Tibbies stretch out and stay cool. Since shady parking spots at a dog show are few and far between, you often see the same type of cover draped over the windshield and open windows of a vehicle to shade the interior.

Always carry water in a spill-free travel dish and, for quick cool-downs on hot days, a supply of ice in a cooler. If you will be away for more than a few hours, take a supply of dog food, too.

Having read the foregoing chapters, you know that it is important to keep your Tibbie interested and motivated. So, remember to bring his favorite toys and treats from home.

Last but not least, keep a first aid kit, for you and your dog, in your vehicle. You may never need it but, if you do, you will be glad to have it on hand.

Grooming Supplies—Try to do most of your grooming at home so that all you will need, at the show, is a brush and comb for last minute touch-up. Another useful item is a spray bottle to mist the coat. If the weather is inclement, have cloth and/or paper towels on hand to tidy up muddy paws; they are also useful for other little accidents that may transpire, such as messy trousers. If you plan to be away from home, take along shampoo supplies, extra towels and a blow dryer. Although a folding grooming table is not strictly necessary for a Tibbie, some owners bring one along, not only for grooming but also stacking practice.

Ring Needs—Remember your Tibbie's favorite show lead and bait. I sometimes tuck a tissue in my pocket to wipe away saliva or dry the nose.

Your Needs—It is the rare show, indoor or outdoor, that provides ringside seating, so bring your own folding chairs. Since Tibbies enjoy being as high as possible, many exhibitors sit comfortably at ringside with their dogs in their laps. Some Tibbies even have their own chairs, like the little kings and queens they are!

Although few exhibitors let a little drizzle dampen their spirits, pack rain gear in the event of a downpour. Nothing, but nothing, stops a dog show!

Although it is certainly possible to show your dog alone and people do so all the time, try to recruit an assistant. While this person lugs your "stuff" around, runs errands, takes photos and marks the catalog, you can concentrate on showing your Tibbie.

Grooming the Show Tibbie

Exhibitors accustomed to the perfectionistic grooming of other coated breeds may be puzzled by the emphasis on the natural coat of the Tibetan Spaniel. One Tibbie exhibitor still bristles when she recalls a handler, from another coated breed, smugly attributing her Tibbie's loss in the ring to "untidy" skirts and gloves. While a handler from another breed may be forgiven his or her ignorance, Tibbie exhibitors and judges should know better. Teasing and trimming Tibbies to make them look like elaborately styled breeds is contrary to the thrust of the Breed Standards, all of which promote the breed's natural qualities.

In grooming a Tibbie's coat, the emphasis should be on cleanliness and conditioning, not coiffure. Cherish the breed traits such as gloves and skirts. Be happy that Tibbies from Europe, North America or Australia would still be recognized on the streets of Lhasa. Take pride in the fact that your Tibbie can win on the merits of his structure, expression and movement, without the disguising contours of a scissored coat.

The only challenges of show Tibbie grooming are to stop the undercoat shedding out and to avoid damage to the fringes. In climates where days are long and hot, a Tibbie that spends time playing outside may shed his undercoat. Playful Tibbies also tug on each other's ears and tails, which tears the fringes. Shade and climate-controlled quarters are essential to the comfort of an undercoated show Tibbie. Keep a hawk's eye on your show Tibbies and try to break up tussles before the fringes are damaged.

Before a show, bathe your Tibbie and be sure to rinse thoroughly. Air dry (weather permitting) or blow dry if you prefer. I clip the hair from the *underside* of the paws and trim and file the nails at this time (see Chapter 9). To maintain the natural fullness to the mane and trousers or skirts, lift and mist them with warm water and leave them to dry. Just before ring time, brush out the coat gently. Smooth the hair on the face and comb through the ear fringes and gloves. *Voilà!*

Grooming Yourself

Customs vary but, generally speaking, exhibitors make an effort to appear well-groomed. Dressing nicely is a compliment to the sport, to the judge, to the spectators and to your Tibbie. For example, male exhibitors in the U.S. wear sport jackets (even on hot summer days) and female exhibitors generally wear a skirt, dress or nice pantsuit. (Speaking of which, you need hip-line pockets in which to stow bait, tissue, a comb or other items to take into the ring.)

Choose clothing that does not interfere with your movement. Make sure that you can kneel comfortably. If it would be a tragedy for your outfit to become soiled, select something else; I usually come home from a dog show with dirt on my knees and liver remnants in my pockets.

Always practice in your outfit. I once chose a very comfortable, flowing skirt with roomy pockets. To my dismay, the hem of the skirt swirled around my Tibbie's head, brushed her back and upset her movement as I walked alongside her.

Since the floors or grass in the ring may be slippery, make sure that your shoes give you good traction. Women should wear flat or low-heeled shoes.

Although there are many schools of thought on this subject, the general rule is to choose clothes that complement your Tibbie. Since the handler's clothing is the backdrop for the Tibbie, some handlers prefer a color that contrasts sharply with their Tibbies' coat color, while others opt for a milder contrast. However, all agree that your Tibbie should not blend into your clothes. For example, wearing a black outfit when showing a black-and-tan Tibbie would not be a good idea. Most handlers also agree that wearing flashy clothing is likely to detract from your Tibbie. Remember that it should be your Tibbie, not you, that grabs the judge's eye.

Above all, bring along the most essential element of your wardrobe—your smile.

Getting There

Have everything needed for your Tibbie's and your own comfort prepared in advance so that, on the day of the show, you have little to do other than enjoy the day with your Tibbie. A show should always be a fun outing for both of you.

If you are driving to the show site on the day of the show, allow plenty of time for the trip, especially when the weather is not cooperating. Although the judging program provides directions to the show, they may not be perfectly clear; allow time for backtracking, too. Plan to arrive about an hour before your scheduled ring time. This gives you time to scout the grounds, exercise your Tibbie, find the ring and check in with the ring steward.

At the Show

Whether it is a huge indoor show in a convention center or an outdoor show at a fairground, the show site may seem bewildering at first glance. Actually, there is a method to the madness. Superintendents usually set up the sites along similar lines. For example, at an outdoor show, head for the biggest tent; it is usually the one covering the central aisle between the breed rings. Some judging programs print a diagram of the show site's layout, but you will soon become accustomed to finding your way around.

Since Tibbie entries at most American All Breed shows are fairly small, the time you spend actually competing in the ring and waiting around before and after you compete is probably less than one-half hour! So, much of your time at a show is spent in other pursuits—eating, chatting, exercising your dog, shopping and grooming. Nonetheless, your Tibbie's comfort and safety should be your top priority. Never leave him unattended in an exercise pen or crate, and never leave him closed in a vehicle on a warm day.

Dressed for success! Sport jackets are standard attire for men. Here Am. Ch. Calamalca Cassidy, bred by Helen Almey (U.K.) and owned by Herb and Betty Rosen (U.S.) scores one of many ring victories. *Meyer photo*

To check in, find your ring and march up to the steward's table. Ask the steward, identified by his or her ribbon, for the armband for "Tibetan Spaniel" and give the number on your entry ticket. Place the armband on your left arm, securing it with a rubber band. (A bag of rubber bands hangs near the steward's table.) If you are showing more than one Tibbie, put on all their armbands, in the order you are showing them, with the armband for the first dog to go in the ring on top. This enables you to change bands quickly.

The club giving the show sells a catalog that lists all of the dogs entered. The entry for an exhibit includes the dog's birth date, parents, owner and breeder. The owners' names and addresses are also listed in a separate section. Space is provided for marking the winners, a good habit to form. Catalogs usually sell fast, so buy one early.

"When she's not in the mood, she won't show," an owner bemoans. Inconsistent show performance is perhaps the most frequent complaint from Tibbie exhibitors. Inconsistency may be attributable to "moodiness," but it may also result from lack of exercise, motivation or experience. It may also mirror the exhibitor's own mood.

Since every Tibbie has a unique personality, it is difficult to give hard-and-fast advice on showing the Tibetan Spaniel. Saying "Let's go show!" is all that is required to motivate some Tibbies, while inspiring others is more of a challenge. Generally, a little exercise and fun shortly before ring time can either instill spirit in a sleepy or disinterested Tibbie or, conversely, settle down an overexuberant or anxious Tibbie. Of course, treats are a prime motivator for most. Another approach for relaxing an inexperienced Tibbie is massage. For example, gently but thoroughly rub the ear leathers between your fingers, top to tip. Or, lift and caress the upper lips, inside and out, with your fingertips. Make sure you give your Tibbie a chance to "go" before he "goes" in the ring.

Relax and be happy. Remember that your emotion travels down the lead. If you dislike showing, your Tibbie will hate it, too. If you are jittery, he will be nervous, too. If you are excited and upbeat, he will be ready to show off for the judge.

At Ringside

Normally, you should bring your Tibbie to ringside no later than fifteen minutes before you expect to go in the ring. Since the number of Tibbies entered in a given show is usually small, several breeds are usually scheduled at the same ring time as the Tibbies, but the breeds are always judged in the order they are listed under the ring time. Experienced exhibitors learn to estimate when to appear at the ring entrance. For example, suppose your ring time is 9:00. The judging program shows 25 Poodles and 15 Dalmatians ahead of the Tibetan Spaniels. If you arrive at ringside at 8:45, you will wait a long, long time for your turn in the ring—which is fine, if you can keep your Tibbie "up" for all that time. On the other hand, if the only entry ahead of the Tibetan Spaniels is one French Bulldog and three Schipperkes, you should arrive at 8:45. Do not shave it too close! Dogs scheduled before your breed may drop out, and some judges work faster than others. Even if you have checked in earlier, the judge will *not* wait for you once the steward calls out your number.

While you wait your turn, use your time wisely. Check out the ring for hazards, such as slippery spots or unlevel ground. Note which gaiting pattern the judge requests and any other subtle clues that may help you better handle your Tibbie.

Another word of warning. Do not allow the people or larger dogs crowding the ring entrances to overwhelm your Tibbie. Put him on the ground only as you enter the ring and scoop him up when you exit.

In the Ring

Basic American ring procedure is fairly simple. Unless you are the only Tibbie in your class (as sometimes happens), you and your Tibbie first line up with the other Tibbies. The judge may ask you to line up in "catalog order"—that is, the exhibitors' armbands are in numerical sequence—especially when the class is large. After he or she looks at the entries briefly, the judge asks the class to move around the ring, and the first Tibbie in line is placed on the table. If you are the only Tibbie in your class, the judge may skip the first step and motion you to place your Tibbie directly on the table as you enter the ring.

After examining the Tibbie on the table, the judge directs the exhibitor to move the Tibbie in a particular gaiting pattern, such as a "triangle" or a simple "out and back." Returning to the judge, the exhibitor brings the Tibbie to a halt two to three feet in front of the judge, and the Tibbie does his or her best to show the judge a nice expression. The judge then repeats this procedure with each remaining Tibbie in the class—examination on the table followed by gaiting a pattern. After he or she has examined all the Tibbies, the judge next asks the whole class to move around the ring again. He or she may change the sequence of the Tibbies at this time, a precursor of the selections. As you move around the ring for the last time, watch the judge closely and hope that you are the first he or she points to.

The procedure I have just described may vary somewhat with the size of the class (such as the very large classes seen at a Specialty) or with the judge's preferences. A similar procedure is repeated at each level of competition. Just listen to what the judge tells you to do. If you do not understand, apologize and ask the judge to repeat his or her directions.

Ken Talbot poses his Aust. Ch. Toreana Ti-Kho in the show ring. This impressive homebred was the top-winning Tibbie in Australia for many years.

Everything that you have just read is "procedure," rather than "strategy," and "strategy" is a distinct, more complex subject. Procedure without strategy is just "going through the motions"! For example, what should you do if the ground is unlevel at your place in line? What should you do if the handler ahead of you charges away before you are ready to move your Tibbie? What if the dog in line ahead of you moves too quickly or slowly? These and hundreds of other practical handling questions arise in the ring, and it is beyond the scope of this book to cover them all. However, a good instructor will address them in a conformation class. You should also read some of the many books about showing dogs. These include *Dog Showing,* by Connie Vanacore, and *The Road to Westminster* and *Breeding and Showing Purebred Dogs,* by Robert B. and Toni C. Freeman.

Always remember to praise your Tibbie whether or not he wins the ribbon. There is nothing more offensive than a grim-faced exhibitor stomping out of the ring with a sad little Tibbie in tow.

The Judge's Perspective

Besides you and your Tibbie, there is someone else busy in the ring—the judge. As an exhibitor, your job is to present your Tibbie in a way that makes it easy for the judge to note his good qualities. The judge's job is to compare each Tibbie to the Breed Standard and determine which one most closely conforms to the ideal it describes.

Libby the Tibbie

Every Tibbie knows little tricks. As a puppy, Libby (Windom Sierra's Miss Liberty) spontaneously sat back on her haunches, held up her forelegs and circled her forepaws as though turning a prayer wheel. Capitalizing on Libby's natural gesture, owner Jacki Scarborough (U.S.) taught her to respond to "Libby, say your prayers!" by doing her charming trick.

Libby was never a consistent showgirl. She sometimes shuffled around the ring, her tail at half mast, and otherwise displayed her indifference. Besides innumerable Reserve ribbons, Jacki and Libby collected 17 points but no major wins.

After winning yet another Reserve placement, Jacki approached the judge to collect her ribbon. Beside her, Libby halted and, for no apparent reason, decided to "say her prayers." As the judge handed the ribbon to Jacki, she glanced down at Libby, busily gesturing, and remarked dryly, "Honey, it's too late to pray now!"

Wherever a judge's opinion is rendered, whether in a court of law, an Olympic stadium or at a dog show, someone usually disagrees. Faced with a selection of Tibbies, each with varying degrees of conformity and nonconformity to the Standard, any decision the judge makes may be controversial.

The apparent simplicity of the Tibetan Spaniel is deceptive. Miss Bridget Croucher (U.K.), a breeder judge, points out that Tibbies are difficult to judge even though they possess fewer "oddities" and less coat than other breeds in the Utility Group. Most judges agree that variations in size and type present a challenge in judging Tibbies.

The judge is in a better position than those at ringside or other exhibitors to examine a Tibbie's mouth and view his movement. It is the judge's hands that gauge the angulation of the bones and test the texture of the coat. The judge must evaluate the whole dog, pondering his strengths as well his weaknesses, in comparison to an image of perfection, the likes of which has not been born—all in a couple of minutes!

Judges' Education

To do his or her job effectively, the judge must be conversant with the Breed Standard (discussed later), the foundation of breed knowledge. Exhibitors are understandably frustrated when a judge's decision appears to run counter to the Standard. For example, one Tibbie owner complained about disqualification of a white Tibbie (the Standard allows all colors). Another criticized an award to a 27-pound Tibbie (the Standard prescribes a top weight of 15 pounds). In light of such incidents, it is not surprising that exhibitors occasionally perceive a lack interest in or knowledge of the Tibetan Spaniel.

Each governing organization has its own rules for accrediting judges. Since the stringency of the requirements varies, it is in the best interest of the club that represents the Tibetan Spaniel to undertake a program of judges' education. Most Tibetan Spaniel breed clubs in the world consider judges' education a priority.

Among the possible components of a judges' education program are:

- Illustrated Breed Standards (discussed later)
   As a supplement to the Breed Standard, the pictures give concrete images of the ideal Tibbie as well as commonly observed faults.
- videotapes
   Another step toward realism, a videotape portrays movement and helps the judge better visualize what he or she will later see in the ring.

- seminars

    A seminar provides judges with "hands on" experience in examining Tibbies and feedback from breed experts.

One example of a judges' education program is that of the U.K.'s Tibetan Spaniel Association (TSA). As the Kennel Club puts greater emphasis on judges' education in accrediting those who will award C.C.'s, the TSA expects the need for and emphasis on judges' education to increase. The TSA's program consists of two seminars per year. Featured topics include a talk on the Breed Standard, discussion of the Tibetan Spaniel Breed Video (produced by the AKC), a discussion of conformation lead by a veterinarian and a presentation of Rachel Page Elliott's video, *Dogsteps*. The course concludes with an optional examination.

Breeders, exhibitors and judges all benefit from breed club educational programs. During a seminar presented by the Tibetan Spaniel Club of America (TSCA), breed experts pointed out that Tibbie's tail may droop while he is standing. Since a drooping tail would be severely penalized in most breeds with upright tails, Mrs. Charlotte Patterson (U.S.), who attended the seminar, was glad that the TSCA's breed experts highlighted this point and comments that educational programs should always emphasize the "real" as well as the "ideal."

Understanding the Judge's Decision

In a perfect world, each exhibitor could be confident that his or her Tibbie would receive a knowledgeable, objective appraisal under every judge. Ideally, the overall pattern of each judge's choices would indicate a consistent, correct interpretation of the Breed Standard and a balanced evaluation of each Tibbie presented. In reality, judges are people, too. No matter how hard he or she tries, a judge's decision is, to some degree, subjective.

The Standard, although well conceived and written, is nonetheless open to interpretation. Wait! I am not criticizing the Standard! I am only saying what every writer knows—that a reader's understanding of the written word is always influenced by his or her life experience and preferences—no matter how precise the wording! For example, the relative weight that a judge places on the various points of the Standard (e.g., head, movement) is particularly subjective. One judge may accord greater significance to the head than to movement, while another favors movement over head. A Tibbie with an excellent head and so-so movement could win under the first judge but probably not the second. Although the language of the Standard attempts to make such evaluations less subjective, judging will never be a precise science.

Another factor at play in the judge's decision is his or her previous exposure to the breed. In most countries, Tibbies are fairly rare and even a judge who has qualified to judge the breed, under the rules of the kennel organization, may have actually seen few of them. This is why owners flock to enter their Tibbies under a respected "breeder judge."

You may occasionally encounter a judge who, for whatever reason, does not award your Tibbie a placement although other judges regularly place him. It is possible that the judge in question is not very knowledgeable about the breed, but it is also possible that he or she strongly favors a particular feature that your Tibbie lacks or cannot forgive a particular fault that he does possess. Most exhibitors give a judge a couple of chances, but don't be a glutton for punishment. If he or she clearly does not care for your Tibbie, your recourse is not to enter under that judge.

If assorted judges consistently leave your Tibbie out of the placements, you must consider the possibility that he has not turned out to be show quality or that you are not showing him to his best advantage. In many countries, a judge's critiques are routinely available to everyone. For example, the Finnish breed club, Tiibetinspanieli ry, publishes the critiques in the club magazine. These detailed evaluations are constructive tools for breeders and exhibitors alike. However, in countries where judges do not prepare critiques (such as the U.S.), their reasoning remains a mystery, and you may decide to ask for the opinions of other exhibitors and breeders. Choose the people you consult thoughtfully; some second opinions are more informed and impartial than others. Remember that the problem may be something that you can correct—such as a flaw in your handling—or it may be something that will resolve itself over time—such as a puppy that needs to mature or an adult that is temporarily out of condition.

All but the most casual exhibitors study judges' decisions in an effort to find a pattern that indicates a better prospect of winning. Considering the effort and expense involved in showing a dog, this competitive strategy is also economically expedient. Some show people have eyes like hawks and minds like steel traps; they remember every winner a judge has picked, where and when it happened, the dog's age and condition at the time, his pedigree and which other dogs he beat, as well as what they had for dinner that night. Well, I can only sit back and marvel at them. Most of us have to come up with a way to jog our memories. Although marked show catalogs come in handy, researching a judge by riffling through a stack of catalogs can be cumbersome. Instead, you need a system where you can quickly retrieve facts about a given judge. Try a notebook, a note card file or a computer file. Besides summarizing the judge's awards, jot down your observations about his or her methods and apparent preferences (e.g., "chooses smallish Tibbies," "likes well-trained dogs"). Your exhibitor friends may share their experiences with the judge; note their tips, too. For a far-reaching study of American judges' awards, serious competitors review the results of all American dog shows in *AKC Awards*.

Advice from Judges

Judges who see many Tibbies in the course of their assignments agree that the quality of the Tibetan Spaniel seen today has improved over those seen a decade or more ago. For example, Mrs. Rita Beale (U.K.), breeder judge, notes that round, "Peke-like" eyes are less in evidence today. Although Tibbies still vary in type, the type of today's competitors is generally more consistent than that of earlier generations.

Most judges agree that today's Tibbies have the desired "ape-like" expression. Mr. Richard Tang (U.S.) elaborates: "The sweet expression comes from the movement of the ears, the foreface, the twinkling of dark brown oval eyes and the cute muzzle." To achieve that, he advises us to pay close attention to the shape of the skull, ear set, eye shape and color, and correct length and type of muzzle. All of the judges urge us to preserve the charming and unique "scowl."

We are asked to resist the temptation to breed over-coated Tibbies. The judges remind us that moderate length coats of silky texture are our goal. A judge should see a "rectangle of light" under the Tibbie—*without* trimming!

Although most judges agree that mouths have improved, they note that bites that are too undershot still occur. Many recommend that we try harder to eliminate misaligned and missing teeth. This is a thorny point with European judges, who are considered especially rigorous in evaluating the mouth. On the other hand, breeder judges advise against sacrificing the Tibbie's characteristic depth of chin, a crucial element of the "ape-like" expression, for the sake of perfect dentition.

Among other improvements Tibbie judges would like to see are: better balance (neither too long nor too low to the ground), smaller size, less bow in the forelegs (no Queen Anne or fiddle fronts), more level toplines and better tail sets. Many judges urge us not to neglect movement, which is the ultimate test of the Tibbie's construction; Mr. Paul Stanton (Sweden) asks us to pay particular attention to "drive" in the hindquarters. Judges in the U.K., Ireland and Australia caution us not to allow the catfoot to slip in amongst the harefeet.

Mr. John J. Lyons (U.S.) advises, "Guard temperament with your life," and continues, "There is nothing more disappointing than a [Tibbie] with a sour attitude, or who trembles when put on the table for examination. The owner is to blame for this in most cases, not the dog." He asks us to remember the image of the miniature lion: "The lion's mane and bold attitude is most attractive in this breed."

Judges remind us to handle Tibbies gently and to avoid over-handling. "Show your Tibbie, not yourself!" remarks one judge. Among the diverse breeds in the Group ring, encouraging animation can help the Tibetan Spaniel stand out in the crowd.

Let me close by saying that many judges appreciate and admire our spritely little Tibbies and wish us well in our efforts. In sharing his thoughts on our "wonderful breed," Mr. Lyons writes, "Tibetan Spaniels have many outstanding qualities. First and foremost, they love their owners and are as one with them. This is not surprising given their Buddhist background... Secondly, they are a fun breed, almost clownish in nature. They often make me laugh in the middle of judging them. Thirdly, they are a spirited breed, both in movement and in attitude. They are...*multum in parvo*, or a big dog in a small package."

BREED STANDARDS

The Breed Standard is a short narrative describing the ideal Tibetan Spaniel. It clearly differentiates the breed from every other breed and describes each of the breed's traits in a way that discriminates quality from lack of quality. It serves as a blueprint for breeders and a guideline for judges.

The breed club representing the Tibetan Spaniel in each country writes the Standard, which is then

---

I do realize that most exhibitors [of Tibetan Spaniels] are owner-handlers and wish to compliment [them] for their sportsmanship. They seem to really love and enjoy their dogs. So far, most are free from the affliction, 'Winning is not everything; it is the only thing.' I hope breeders and exhibitors will continue to have this attitude because both they and the dogs will be the real winners.

Mrs. Carolyn Herbel (U.S.)

approved by the country's national kennel organization. Any changes in the Standard must originate with the breed club. When the organization is an FCI member, the Standard is submitted for FCI approval. Any changes in an FCI-approved Standard must be submitted by the country where the Standard originated.

In addition to the Breed Standard, some breed clubs have developed an Illustrated Standard to further explain and clarify the Breed Standard. Since a picture is worth a thousand words, the Illustrated Standard is a essential tool for breeders, exhibitors and judges.

Beyond these documents, any published or oral commentary on the conformation of the Tibetan Spaniel, no matter how useful it may be, is unofficial and non-binding on breeders, exhibitors and judges.

The American Breed Standard

The Standard written by the TSA and approved by the Kennel Club (UK) is the basis for the standards for the Tibetan Spaniel approved for use in other countries. Most are virtually identical to the Kennel Club Standard, save only the language. The American Standard, reprinted here, differs significantly in only one point; whereas the current UK Standard requires a body "slightly longer from withers to root of tail than height at withers," the American Standard retains the older requirement for a body "slightly longer from the point of shoulder to root of tail than the height at withers."

The Official Standard for the Tibetan Spaniel

General Appearance—Should be small, active and alert. The outline should give a well-balanced appearance, slightly longer in body than the height at withers.

Fault: Coarseness of type.

Head—Small in proportion to body and proudly carried, giving an impression of quality. Masculine in dogs but free from coarseness. Stop slight, but defined. Medium length of muzzle, blunt with cushioning, free from wrinkle. The chin should show some depth and width. Black nose preferred.

Faults: Broad, flat muzzle; accentuated stop; pointed, weak or wrinkled muzzle; long, plain down face, without stop; mean expression; liver or putty colored pigmentation.

Skull—slightly domed, moderate width and length.

Fault: Very domed or flat wide skull.

Eyes—Dark brown in color, oval in shape, bright and expressive, of medium size set fairly well apart for forward looking, giving an apelike expression. Eye rims black.

Faults: Large full eyes; light eyes.

Ears—Medium size, pendant, well feathered in the adult and set fairly high. They may have slight lift from the skull, but should not fly. Large, heavy, low-set ears are not typical.

Mouth—Ideally slightly undershot, the upper incisors fitting neatly inside and touching the lower incisors. Teeth should be evenly placed and the lower jaw wide between the canine tusks. Full dentition desired. A level mouth is permissible, providing there is sufficient width and depth of chin to preserve the blunt appearance of the muzzle. Teeth must not show when mouth is closed.

Faults: Overshot mouth; protruding tongue.

Neck and Body—Neck moderately short, strong and well set on. Covered with a mane or "shawl" of longer hair which is more pronounced in dogs than bitches.

Body slightly longer from the point of shoulder to root of tail than the height at withers, well ribbed with good depth, level back. Tail set high, richly plumed and carried in a gay curl over the back when moving. Should not be penalized for dropped tail when standing.

Forequarters—The bones of the forelegs slightly bowed but firm at shoulder. Moderate bone. Shoulder well placed.

Faults: Very bowed or loose front.

Feet—Harefooted, small and neat with feathering between toes often extending beyond the feet. White markings allowed.

Faults: Cat feet.

Hindquarters—Well made and strong, hocks well let down and straight when viewed from behind. Stifle well developed, showing moderate angulation.

Faults: Straight stifle, cow hocks.

Coat—Double coat, silky in texture, smooth on face and front of legs, of moderate length on body, but lying rather flat. Ears and back of forelegs nicely feathered, tail and buttocks well furnished with longer hair. Should not be overcoated and bitches tend to carry less coat and mane than dogs.

Color—All colors, and mixture of colors allowed.

Gait—Quick moving, straight, free, positive.

Size—Weight 9-15 pounds being ideal. Height about 10 inches.

Temperament—Gay and assertive, highly intelligent, aloof with strangers.

Fault: Nervousness.

Presentation—In the show ring it is essential the Tibetan Spaniel be presented in an unaltered condition with the coat lying naturally with no teasing, parting or stylizing of the hair. Specimens where the coat has been altered by trimming, clipping, or by arti-

ficial means shall be so severely penalized as to be effectively eliminated from competition. Dogs with such a long coat that there is no rectangle of daylight showing beneath, or so profuse that it obstructs the natural outline, are to be severely penalized. Whiskers are not to be removed. Hair growing between the pads on the underside of the feet may be trimmed for safety and cleanliness. Dewclaws may be removed.

Approved May 10, 1983
Reprinted with permission of the Tibetan Spaniel Club of America and the American Kennel Club.

Goals of the Standard

Given enough time and stock, dog breeders could construct a dog of just about any type. If you doubt that, picture a Toy Poodle, a Bulldog and a German Shepherd in your mind. These breeds and all others are members of the same species and descendants of common ancestors. They are living proof that the physical appearance of dogs can be altered. In fact, the appearance of many breeds has been altered so much, sometimes in the interest of "improving" the breed but often just to suit the whims of fashion, that it is sometimes difficult to identify a dog's breed in old paintings or photos.

The Tibetan Spaniel's appearance could be similarly transformed. For example, he could be bred larger or smaller, his muzzle made shorter or longer or his coat longer and thicker. To prevent this happening, one of Standard's goals is to preserve the historical Tibetan appearance of our breed. In defining this appearance, the committee that convened to write the first British Standard (1934) were much influenced by the precedent of the Standard of the Indian Kennel Club, where Tibbies had been shown since the early years of the century, as well as by the Tibbies then in Britain.

What exactly did the historical Tibetan Spaniel that we are trying to preserve look like? Support can be found in the scanty photographic record from the early 20th century for other types of Tibetan Spaniel besides the type reflected in today's Standard. If you study the photos that appear in Chapter 3 of this book, in Miss Mayhew's *The Tibetan Spaniel* and Mrs. Wynyard's *Dogs of Tibet and the History of the Tibetan Spaniel,* you can readily see differences in traits such as size, proportion, ear carriage and shape and length of muzzle. In fact, any debate over a single, "true" Tibetan Spaniel type is rather specious; although they were clearly related to one another, several types of Tibetan Spaniels lived in Tibet. Thus, the first British Standard effectively selected which traits of the indigenous types were to be favored, and its successors have followed suit.

Like any Breed Standard, another goal of the Tibetan Spaniel Standard is to differentiate our breed from all others. Revised three times since 1934, all of the British Tibetan Spaniel Standards and, as a result, the Standards of other countries, have consistently penalized traits such as the "broad flat face" so as to clearly distinguish the Pekingese from the Tibetan Spaniel.

Another goal of the Breed Standard is to reward the elegant understatement and natural dignity that characterizes the Tibetan Spaniel and to denounce any suggestion of exaggerated features. Each British Standard has continued to clarify and reinforce this moderate ideal. It should be mentioned that changing a Standard, while not impossible, must be undertaken judiciously.

One of the perks of writing a book is that one can occasionally slip in a personal opinion or two. I heartily support the goals of the Standard, and I adamantly agree that the Tibetan Spaniel should never be arbitrarily reconstructed to please some transitory notion of beauty. However, I believe that a bit of variety in the appearance of today Tibbies, just as the Tibbies of old Tibet varied in appearance, enriches the breed and is infinitely preferable to a breed in which every dog is virtually a clone of the next. While many may disagree with this view, I see this variety as simply another expression of the marvelous individualism of each Tibetan Spaniel.

Understanding the Breed Standard

A Breed Standard can be a bewildering and confusing document for a novice. It assumes that the reader has a basic knowledge of canine anatomy and often uses specialized terms unknown to the novice. I can remember, as a newcomer, looking up words such as "stifle" and "undershot" and puzzling over phrases such as "hocks well let down" or "shoulder well placed."

Fortunately, Illustrated Breed Standards help newcomers visualize the ideal Tibbie. For example, the Tibetan Spaniel Club of America has published an excellent Illustrated Standard that makes the words used in the Breed Standard come alive. Studying the Illustrated Standard is a must for anyone planning to show, breed or judge Tibetan Spaniels.

When I first became involved in Tibbies, I remember wondering why some of the points in the Standard were there—why should the eyes be oval instead of round or the paws harefeet instead of catfeet? I eventually came to realize that we should not view the Standard in isolation. Each of the points is there for a reason that reaches into the breed's past. When the points are fused with knowledge of his homeland and the role the Tibbie played in Tibetan life, you can gain a fuller

THE EVOLUTION OF A STANDARD

This table highlights and contrasts *some* key points in successive versions of the British Standard. The changes refined and clarified the earlier Standard. Note the manner in which moderation is further emphasized in each iteration.

	1934	1959	1975	1986
Weight	5-14 lbs.	dogs 10-16 lbs. bitches 9-15 lbs.	9-15 lbs.	9-15 lbs.
Height	—	dogs up to 11" bitches up to 9 1/2"	about 10"	10"
Body Proportion	longer from point of shoulder to point of buttocks than height at withers	longer from point of shoulder to point of buttocks than height at shoulder	slightly longer from point of shoulder to root of tail than height at withers	slightly longer from withers to root of tail than height at withers
Head	medium size, skull slightly domed	medium or small size in proportion to body, skull slightly domed	small in proportion to body, proudly carried, masculine in dogs, skull slightly domed, moderate width and length, slight but defined stop	small in proportion to body, carried proudly, masculine in dogs, skull slightly domed, moderate width and length, slight but defined stop
Muzzle	strong cushioned, of medium length	fairly short and blunt	medium length, blunt with cushioning, free from wrinkle, chin should show some depth and width	medium length, blunt with cushioning, free from wrinkle, chin should show some depth and width
Mouth	level (otherwise slightly undershot preferred)	slightly undershot preferred, teeth should not show when mouth closed	ideally slightly undershot with upper incisors fitting neatly inside and touching the lower incisors, teeth evenly placed and lower jaw wide between canine tusks, full dentition, level mouth permitted if sufficient width and depth of chin to preserve blunt appearance, teeth should not show	slightly undershot, teeth evenly placed and lower jaw wide between the canine teeth, full dentition desirable, teeth and tongue not showing when mouth closed
Nose	black	black but brown/liver permitted	black preferred	black preferred
Eyes	brown, medium size	dark brown, bright and expressive, fairly wide apart, not full or prominent	dark brown, oval, bright and expressive, medium size, fairly wide apart but forward looking giving an ape-like expression, black rims	dark brown, oval, bright and expressive, medium size, fairly wide apart but forward looking, black rims
Gait	—	—	quick moving, straight, free, positive	quick moving, straight, free, positive

Faults

large, prominent eyes, domed forehead, accentuated stop, broad flat face

large full eye, broad flat face, very domed head, accentuated stop, pointed muzzle

large full eyes, broad flat muzzle, very domed or flat wide skull, accentuated stop, pointed/weak/wrinkled muzzle, overshot, long plain down face without stop, straight stifle, cow hocks, nervous, cat feet, coarseness of type, mean expression, liver/putty pigmentation, light eyes, protruding tongue

any departure from the points in the standard—in proportion to the degree of departure from the ideal

(Left) Aztlon Seng-Kyi, bred by Vivian Hartley, was chosen Best of Breed at the 1994 National Dog Show, New Zealand's most prestigious show.

(Right) Aus. Ch. Braeduke La-La-Babu, bred by Ann Wynyard (U.K.), was imported by Michele Waterman, of Victoria, in 1989.

(Left) Int., Nor., Sw. Ch. Bibacc's Winnie the Pooh, bred and owned by Sune and Ann Rosén, was Winner of the Year at the prestigious Hund-94 show.

(Right) This proud looking Tibbie is Beauandel Zac, bred by Michael Fenwick (Australia)

and richer understanding of why it is important for the Tibetan Spaniel to have the qualities that the Standard requires. Let's look at some of these individual points. (Descriptive words from the Standard are italicized.)

General—As a watchdog and bed dog, *small, active and alert* were essential ingredients of the ideal Tibbie of old Tibet.

Temperament—As befits the family pet and bed dog, the Tibbie is *gay*. As befits a dog that was expected to take care of himself around the monastery compound, he is *assertive and highly intelligent*. And, as befits a watchdog, he is initially suspicious and *aloof with strangers*.

Neck and Body—The *moderately short, strong neck, well set on,* contributes to a dog's stability, a useful quality for a Tibbie scampering over ground strewn with rocky debris or climbing to the rooftops. The *mane* around the neck, a vulnerable area, helped to protect the Tibbie from the elements and other animals, such as the other free-ranging dogs of the monastery compound.

The *well-balanced body, slightly longer* than its height at the withers, is constructed to enable the rectangular-shaped Tibbie to cover more ground than a box-shaped dog, a useful quality when hunting mice or other vermin.

A *well ribbed body* with *good depth* (from withers to breast bone) gives the Tibbie the greatest heart and lung capacity—essential for the dog to take in enough oxygen in the thin Tibetan air—and, at the same time, allows the Tibbie to move efficiently because the size of the chest cavity does not interfere with the movement of the shoulders and forelegs.

Forequarters—The *well placed* shoulder ("well laid" in the U.K.) is a point routinely found in the Standard of most breeds. The structure of the shoulder greatly influences the dog's movement. Not only does it dictate the "reach" of the forelegs but also impacts the efficiency of the "drive" of the hindlegs. As remarked by McDowell Lyon, author of the classic text *The Dog in Action,* "You cannot put drive behind unless the front can take care of it without having a disorganized mechanism...."

Hindquarters—Similarly, the *well developed* stifle with *moderate angulation* and *strong* hindquarters are points found in most Standards. These features allow the Tibbie to climb, spring and jump—activities in which he often engaged in old Tibet as he went about the business of being a watchdog and vermin-catcher. His *well let down* hocks provide stability and endurance, important when he traveled with his master on caravans or pilgrimages.

When the Tibbie settled down to rest, the *richly plumed* tail curled over the sensitive nose to protect it from the extremely cold weather and wind on the roof of the world.

Feet—The harefoot is one of the traits most perfectly adapted for the Tibbie's life in Tibet. Thanks to its longish, gripping toes, the harefoot gives him superior traction and dexterity, useful for both climbing, maneuvering over rocky, uneven ground and manipulating objects. Like the harefeet of the coursing breeds, the area of the Tibbie's pads that comes into contact with the ground is greater than that of a catfoot, and this contributes to his speed. The *feathering between the toes* acts like snowshoes on snow and ice, allowing the Tibbie to stay atop the surface rather than sink in, and also protects the pads from cold and rough ground.

Gait—As busy and inquisitive beings with things to do and places to go, Tibbies need to be *quick moving*. They should have a smooth stride that is *straight, free and positive*. Given the thin air in Tibet, the more efficiently the dog's body operated, the less effort he or she needed to expend in the oxygen-poor air. It should be noted that such a gait is not possible unless the forequarters and hindquarters are built correctly; good structure equals good gait.

Head—We come now to the most distinctive feature of the breed. Being *relatively small in proportion* to the body not only fosters an elegant appearance but also helps Tibbies avoid the high rate of Caesarian deliveries seen in small breeds where heads are large in proportion to the body. Bitches that could not freewhelp in old Tibet surely would have died.

In addition to differentiating the Tibbie from the Pekingese, the *medium length of muzzle, blunt with cushioning, free from wrinkle* and the *depth and width* of the chin are elements of the Tibbie's monkey-like face, giving it an appealing, babyish quality. Moreover, an overly short muzzle impedes breathing, which would be a very undesireable characteristic in a dog that must breathe the thin Tibetan air.

Eyes—In his traditional role as watchdog, sitting atop walls and roofs and squinting into the winds, *oval eyes* were a distinct advantage because they do not protrude and can close down to slits. Being *set fairly well apart for forward looking* contributed not only to the Tibbie's appealing appearance but also improved his ability to spot oncoming intruders. Large, round, protuberant eyes seen in some small breeds are more subject to injury and irritation.

Ears—Since all native Tibetan breeds have *pendant* (drop) ears, it seems probable that the leather protected the delicate parts of their ears from the elements. Meanwhile, the charming *lift from the skull* enhanced the ever-alert Tibbie's superb hearing.

Coat—By trapping air between the short, thick undercoat and long outercoat, the Tibbie's *double coat* provided maximum protection from the weather extremes on the "roof of the world." Like the double-paned windows that insulate a house, the double coat helped to insulate the Tibbie from the winter wind and cold and to protect his skin from the fierce sun. The *silky* outcoat, that is *smooth on the face,* only *moderate in length* and *rather flat,* set the Tibbie apart from the other small Tibetan breeds (Lhasa Apso and Tibetan Terrier). A silky-textured bed dog was pleasant to the touch.

There is a persistent temptation to create a more glamorous Tibbie—whether by breeding for more coat or through elaborate grooming. The Standard expressly prohibits the overcoated Tibbie. It also prohibits *teasing, parting or stylizing and trimming or clipping.* Turning the Tibbie into an overcoated or overgroomed breed not only breaks with a tradition stretching back over centuries but is wholly inconsistent with the breed's distinctly non-frivolous character. While this is the only reason that most people need to preserve the natural, non-artificial look of the Tibetan Spaniel, a few are still motivated by the misguided idea that lengthening or styling the coat equates to "improving" it. While it is certainly appropriate to consider the coat when selecting breeding stock, the soundness and genetic health of an individual or of the breed could be inadvertently or deliberately sacrificed in favor of cultivating an eye-catching coat. Unfortunately, an extravagant coat would also undermine one of the main attractions of the breed, not only for breeders and exhibitors but also for pet owners. Abandoning the easy-care coat would necessitate more grooming, which translates into more time and expense for all Tibbie owners. It would also discourage owner-handling in the show ring. Mrs. Phyllis Kohler (U.S.), a breeder judge, succinctly sums it up, "I do not want to see our breed become another 'coated' breed just to WIN. The problems too much coat will bring into the breed, to me, far out-weigh the prestige of a few show wins. Those judges [who] are truly knowledgeable...will also appreciate them in competition without coat dragging the floor."

Size—At nine through 15 pounds and about ten inches at the shoulder, the Tibetan Spaniel is a small, but not toy, dog. Although the Tibetans favored small Tibbies, we should not permit the Tibbie to become smaller. A millennia or more ago, the Tibetan Spaniel was bred down to its present-day size by taking advantage of naturally occurring mutations that cause dwarfing. The technical term is achondroplasia. Dwarfing (miniaturization) inevitably leads to genetic side-effects, some of which are "faults" listed in the Standard and some of which are health problems. One notable consequence is a loss of proportion of the body parts. For example, a protuberant eye may be the result of the eyeball not "reducing" at the same rate as the skull, thus causing it to protrude. Long-bodied, very short-legged Tibbies are similarly out-of-proportion. Excessively bowed forelegs are likewise a possible result of miniaturization. Some congenital defects, such as cleft palate and umbilical hernias, are linked with brachycephalic (short-muzzled) breeds and believed to be the result of dwarfing. (See Chapter 13.)

In essence, the Tibetan Spaniel is a moderately dwarfed breed in which desireable traits, such as his size and moderate muzzle, are preserved while undesireable traits, such as overall loss of proportion and exaggerated features, are minimized. At his current size, we can control the consequences of miniaturization, but any further dwarfing of the Tibetan Spaniel would be unwise.

Now, shift your focus from the individual points of the Standard to the Standard as a "whole." After all, you have a whole Tibbie, not just the "parts" of one. This brings to mind the old story about the blind men who were asked to describe an elephant; since each touched only one part of the animal (e.g., its trunk, its leg, its tail and so on), none could accurately describe the whole animal. Don't fall into this trap; you must evaluate each of your Tibbie's "parts" in relation to his "whole."

Consider, for example, the head. All the variables that go into its makeup—including the shape of skull, set and shape of eyes, set and shape of ears and the muzzle and its component parts—make the head a complex feature. When analyzing the overall quality of the head, it is easy to be confused by so many variables and even deceived by optical illusion. For example, a skull that is slightly domed, as the Standard requires, may appear to be flat if the ears are set too high. Evaluate not only each individual component but also its relationship to all of the others.

Structurally speaking, to make a dog very fast, you must sacrifice endurance. Conversely, to give a dog immense endurance, you sacrifice speed. The Tibetan Spaniel Standard endeavors to strike a balance. For example, some points are designed to give the Tibbie speed (e.g., the harefoot), while others give him endurance (e.g., hocks well let down). The Tibetan Spaniel should be a swift, sturdy dog that also has stamina and stability. The versatility of our breed, which I have repeatedly praised throughout this book, is the direct result of this balanced approach to his structure.

It is beyond the scope of this book to fully explore the rationale underlying the points in the Standard that pertain to canine musculo-skeletal structure, such as the angulation of the shoulder and stifle. However, understanding these structural points is essential to applying the Tibetan Spaniel Standard in choosing your show and breeding prospects. Your bookshelf should include texts on dog conformation, such as the invaluable *The New Dogsteps* by Rachel Page Elliott. Her *Dogsteps* is also available on video.

SELECTING THE SHOW PUPPY

Few of us are beautiful or handsome enough to become movie stars. Even if we were physically qualified, most of us would lack the talent, stamina and chutzpa to compete successfully for high-paying parts. Not every Tibbie is cut out to be a show dog either. Even if he has the physical qualifications, he may simply prefer to be your pet and confine his showing off to your living room.

Selecting a Tibbie puppy with show potential is no simple task. It requires a good working knowledge of the Standard and canine structure, an understanding of Tibbie growth and development, a sharp eye, time, patience and a little luck.

When to Pick Your "Pick"

Imagine, if you can, how you would go about deciding if a two-year-old child should become a movie star later in life. Choosing a show Tibbie is a similar problem because you usually select your future champion when he is only a puppy.

The ideal age to choose your puppy is between eight and twelve weeks old. Although he has a puffy puppy coat and his proportions are still those of a baby, he looks more like a miniature adult at this age than at any other time until he actually grows up. Soon, he will enter adolescence, a stage that lasts many months, sometimes over a year. Breeders call this stage by its revealing nickname—"the uglies." By the time he is in "the uglies," it is too late to pick your "pick."

Even at eight to twelve weeks, it is not possible to predict with perfect certainty how well any puppy will turn out. This is perhaps more true of the Tibetan Spaniel than many other breeds because Tibbies mature slowly. Muzzles lengthen, wobbly legs strengthen, personalities evolve and so on. At best, you can form only an overall impression of the puppy's potential.

Evaluating Puppies Informally and Formally

The primary qualifications for any puppy, show or pet, are good health and good temperament. Chapter 7 discusses how to assess these qualities. However, a show puppy must also conform as closely as possible to the Breed Standard.

Experienced breeders and exhibitors quickly inform any novice that, for purposes of competing in the breed ring, the perfect Tibbie has never been born. Rarely is one outstanding youngster the clear "pick" of the litter. You often find yourself weighing the relative strengths and weaknesses of two or three puppies—and wishing that Puppy A with the nice head had Puppy B's attitude and Puppy C's tail set. Every breeder can tell a "horror story" about the puppy placed in a pet home that turned out to be the most beautiful specimen of the breed that he or she has ever seen. Although the breeder is happy that the Tibbie is in a good home, he or she nonetheless regrets losing the chance to show and breed a Tibbie that could have made a great contribution to the breed.

You can learn much about your puppies by observing them informally as their bodies grow and their personalities develop. Since it is immense fun to watch Tibbie puppies learning to walk, run, chase toys, tussle and talk, mentally cataloging their virtues and faults is a pleasant task.

If you are a novice, you will be desperate for a second opinion about your puppies. Even experienced breeders solicit the opinions of other breeders. However, choose carefully which people you ask. Instead of asking only for their "pick," ask for their analysis of the prospects so that you can better understand their reasoning. Although most Tibbie breeders will give you an honest appraisal, you should think

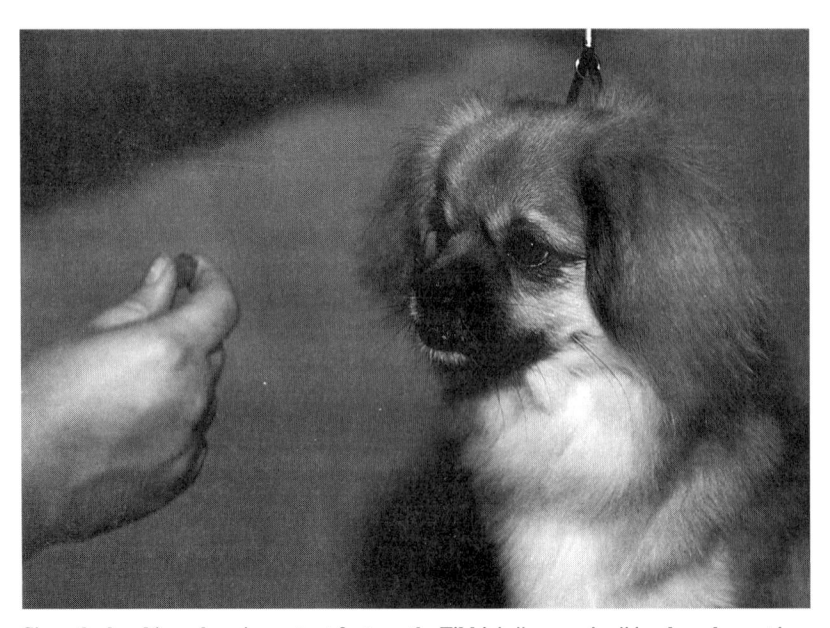

Since the head is such an important feature, the Tibbie's "expression" is a key element in a judge's decision. Exhibitors use bait to elicit expression. *Scott Chamberlain photo*

about factors that may influence their views. Since families of Tibbies tend to mature in different ways and at different rates, advice from a breeder whose experience is limited to other lines may be less helpful than advice from a breeder who is familiar with your line. Similarly, some breeders may be able to see virtue only in their own dogs or those from the same bloodlines; a breeder who is "kennel blind" may not be able to give an unbiased opinion, pro or con, on your puppies. Sadly, it is conceivable that a breeder whose opinion you have solicited may see your request as an opportunity to eliminate competition. By all means, consider second opinions but, as the old saying goes, take them with a grain of salt.

When buying a puppy as a show prospect, the breeder's opinion about the puppy's potential is, of course, important. Be sure that you understand the basis for his or her opinion, and ask the breeder to go over each point with you carefully. However, make sure that the sale agreement specifies a remedy if the puppy does not grow up as expected.

Soon it is time for a formal evaluation where you observe the puppies closely while they stand and move. Recruit an assistant or two. You also need some special treat or toy to distract or attract each puppy, a table on which to pose the puppies and an area free of distractions. If you work indoors, clear an area at least ten feet long so that you can watch the puppy as he moves in various directions. Outdoors, work on a driveway or other paved surface or on a well-mowed, level grassy patch. Work with one puppy at a time.

After many hours of keen informal and formal observation of your puppies and study of the Standard, you are in the best position to choose your "pick" puppy. In the final analysis, put aside the opinions of others and rely on your own informed judgment.

Evaluating While Standing

Place the puppy in a natural stance that approximates a "stack." Try to distract him so that he will stand still for a few moments, which is about all you can expect from a wiggly Tibbie puppy. It will be easier on you if the puppy stands on a table.

1. Examine the head from the front and side. Look for a slightly domed head, ears that are set fairly high so that they lift slightly and then fall to frame the face charmingly, the almond-shaped eye and a nicely cushioned and shaped muzzle of moderate length. Make

Will this youngster become a champion? *Scott Chamberlain photo*

sure the eye rims, nose and lips are black.

The muzzle usually continues to grow beyond eight to twelve weeks.

2. Gently lift the lips to check the bite. The required bite is undershot; optimally, the upper incisors fit neatly inside the lower incisors. The young puppy's pretty little teeth are almost always perfectly aligned, but most breeders agree that the puppy's mouth offers little clue to the alignment of his adult teeth. Nor do the parents' mouths necessarily foretell the adult alignment of the puppy's teeth. However, a puppy whose parents both have slightly undershot jaws and nicely aligned adult teeth has a greater probability of having a nice mouth as an adult, too.

A young puppy's level or slightly overshot bite may become slightly undershot because the lower jaw continues to grow for a longer time than the upper jaw. An undershot bite in a baby puppy may become too pronounced in the adult. Perfectly aligned baby teeth may give way to adult teeth that are (or later become) misaligned. This may be partly due to the lack of support for the teeth in the undershot jaw. The degree of misalignment varies. In some Tibbies, the lower incisors are slightly gapped but otherwise symmetrically positioned in the jaw, while others are crooked and jumbled ("higgledy-piggledy"). For example, when he was a puppy, my Bear's six lower incisors were perfectly aligned between his canines. As an adult, four of his incisors, a pair on either side, are set slightly behind his two middle incisors, a slight gap separating them, but each pair is symmetrical with the other. Although both of his parents have properly undershot jaws, Bear may have inherited his tooth alignment from one of his parents; the other parent has perfectly aligned teeth. Two of Bear's littermates have always had nice alignments; the other started out with a perfect alignment but now has become higgledy-piggledy!

3. Now look at the puppy from the front, side and back. Form an overall impression of the shape of the body and how the head and tail set on the body. Analyze the puppy's balance and proportions.

Evaluate the profile from the side. Look for a body that is slightly longer than tall, but not too long! The topline should be level. The tail should be set high, before the little rump starts curving downward, and should curl over the back. At the other end, the neck should be long enough so that the head does not seem to be fused to the shoulders and, at the same time, it should not appear to be a stalk on which the head swivels. Note the curve of the stifle and the distance from table to hock.

From the front and from behind, look for paws that point forward and legs that are spaced moderately apart, neither close nor wide. The forelegs should be slightly bowed (not a fiddle shape), and the rear legs should be straight.

As the chest broadens, forepaws that "turn out" slightly (that is, turn away from the body) may come to point forward, but this may not happen until the dog fills out at two or more years of age. A pronounced "east-west," where the paws turn sharply to the left and right when the dog stands naturally, is not likely to improve with age.

4. Now lay hands on the puppy. Standing in front of him, run your hands down the front legs. They should bow slightly. Feel the shoulder assembly and make sure the blade lays back moderately, rather than running straight up from the forearm to the withers. Test whether the elbows lay nicely against the side or stick out. Move behind the puppy and run your hands over the hips and down the leg to the stifle. Look for moderately angulated, not straight, stifles. Make sure the puppy has harefeet.

Check for two testicles in the scrotum of male puppies by gently sliding your fingers back and forth between the rear legs.

5. Predicting coat quality is nigh on impossible. Puppy coats are usually short and thick, soft and plush. The fringes on the ears and paws are absent, the tail is not plumed, the trousers are sparse or non-existent, and the shawl or mane is missing. Long hairs protruding from the undercoat give some puppies the appearance of a woolly caterpillar. Any puppy coat, whether plush or silky and thin, may become a satisfactory adult coat. Insofar as coat is concerned, base your prediction on the parents' coats.

Evaluating While Moving

Now get down on the floor, *all the way down,* so that you and the puppy are at eye level. Have your assistant move him at a trot (a medium-paced gait somewhere between a casual saunter and a mad dash), coaxing him along with tidbits of cheese or another treat.

1. Watch his legs as the puppy moves toward you. Even though those little forelegs are bowed, look for strides that are straight with no circling motion to the side as the puppy brings each forepaw forward. Nor should he seem to lumber or sway from side to side. As he places his forepaws, draw a line in your imagination between the points where the paw on each side falls. The parallel lines should be straight and spaced moderately apart, neither too close nor too wide. Note that the faster the puppy trots, the closer together his forelegs naturally move, but his forepaws should not "cross over."

Movement that is slightly wide may narrow (although it may also widen). A front that is slightly "loose" may tighten as the puppy's muscles become stronger. A very wide, loose front may improve but probably not enough to merit consideration as show quality.

2. Now watch the puppy as he moves away from you. Again, look for straight legs and a stable action, no wobbling or bowing in the rear legs. As he places his rear paws on the floor, each should fall along a straight line and lines should be moderately spaced apart. As the legs swing back, you should be able to see the pads of his rear paws.

The distance between the rear paws often narrows as the puppy grows up. So, if his movement is close, it will probably get closer. A slightly "weak behind" (that is one in which the hocks seem to bow out) may improve with exercise, preferably moving up and downhill at a gentle jog. On the other hand, a puppy with severely weak hindquarters (that is, legs that are sharply bowed or appear to be unstable) or cow hocks (that is, legs where the hocks are very close together and paws further apart) is not a show puppy. Note that females tend to move a bit closer in the rear than males. If you cannot see the rear pads, the puppy does not have good "drive."

3. Now have your assistant move the puppy across your line of sight so that you can view the side movement and topline. Look for the forward stretch of the forelegs that indicates good "reach." In the hindquarters, look for a full range of motion of the rear legs—that is, he brings each leg well forward under his body and then drops the paw, pushes off and extends the leg well behind him. This is the action that indicates good "drive."

Showing Tibetan Spaniels

Karen Chamberlain ills.

201

The topline from the withers back to the tail should be level, sloping neither toward the front (like a dip at the withers) nor toward the back. Motion should look smooth and brisk, even in a puppy, but not jerky or labored.

Evaluating the Show Personality

Besides evaluating the physical attributes called for in the Breed Standard, you must also consider the puppy's personality. All Tibbie puppies, whether show or pet, should have a good temperament, but there is a further intangible quality that makes a superior show Tibbie. Call it "attitude."

The ideal show attitude is partly the product of breeding, partly of socialization and partly of handling. Some Tibbies hate showing, some tolerate it, and some glory in it. Michele Waterman (Australia) describes her Aust. Ch. Aztlon Kar-Zut-Ti as a "superb little showman," adding, "I'm quite sure he could go in the ring and do it all by himself. I feel totally unnecessary when I go in the ring with him. He knows what he is doing and off he goes."

A Tibbie with a naturally good attitude toward showing can be spoilt by too little training, rough handling or poor socialization. On the other hand, activities to build confidence, gentle training and skillful handling can improve a Tibbie with a so-so attitude. While there may be marvelous handlers who can bring around a Tibbie who detests showing—the ones who balk, scream or cringe—perhaps these puppies are best suited to be pampered pets.

You can somewhat assess show aptitude in a Tibbie puppy by temperament testing, by observing the puppy's interaction with littermates and with people and by playing show games with him. However, his reactions in the friendly places he knows may differ from his reactions on the show grounds or in the ring. The best way to assess show aptitude is to observe his performance in puppy or conformation (handling) classes and practice matches.

In 1994, AKC/UKC Ch. Windom-Imperial It's My Parti, ROM, bred by Janet Kozatek and owned by Jacqueline Scarborough, became the first Tibbie to be awarded a championship by the United Kennel Club, Inc. *Photos Today photo*

Molding Attitudes

One of my Tibbies became oh-so serious the instant he entered the ring. He did precisely as I required without the slightest protest. He assumed the stack position flawlessly and remained completely motionless and emotionless. He disdained my offers of bait. His expression of hauteur was the epitome of "aloofness" mentioned in the Breed Standard. I think that most judges appreciated the ease with which they could examine him, and some admired his regal attitude.

By contrast, his slightly less obedient litter sister had a certain joie de vivre that appealed to judges. As the judge walked along the line of hopefuls, I could always count on her to cock her head expectantly and smile at the judge. Whether gaiting or waiting, the mischievous twinkle in her eye and her joyful expression enticed smiles from all but the most solemn judges. She was the very image of the "gay and assertive" Tibbie named in the Standard.

What accounts for the difference in these siblings' attitudes toward showing? Certainly, in-born traits might account for some of it. However, I truly believe that these dogs' attitudes differed in large part because I viewed them differently and, consequently, trained them in subtly different ways. The female was my favorite, and her classes were fun for us both. Although I loved him dearly, my approach to training the male was more businesslike and a bit sterner.

Any experienced exhibitor will tell you that the handler's emotions—whether anxiety or confidence, exasperation or serenity—travel down the lead to the dog. This could not be more true than in showing the intelligent and sensitive Tibetan Spaniel. It isn't just your Tibbie's attitude that counts; it's yours, too.

Accent on the Positive

Sometimes you hear people say, "No matter which one you pick, it won't turn out to be what you want. They change so much." There is a grain of truth in that; Tibbie puppies do change substantially. But rather than harbor a fatalistic attitude, listen to the experiences of breeders who have watched many Tibbie puppies grow up.

While you should evaluate your puppy critically and acknowledge his faults, it is more important to focus on his positive points rather than negative points. Be strength-oriented, not fault-oriented. If you doubt the quality of the puppy you choose, he will know it and it will show. So, above all, choose a puppy that you will be proud to take in the ring.

OBEDIENCE, AGILITY, JUNIOR SHOWMANSHIP AND TRACKING

Although most competitive Tibbies are shown in conformation, a few Tibbies and their stalwart owners venture into the obedience, agility and junior handling rings while a few others are breaking into tracking competition.

Obedient Tibbies

In obedience trials, the Tibbie and his handler, working as a team, complete a series of exercises on which they are scored. Basic exercises include, for example, the "Heel on Leash," "Long Sit," and "Long Down." During the "Long Down" exercise, the dog must obey commands, such as "Down/Stay," when his handler walks away from him, and "Come," when his handler calls him from a distance. More advanced obedience work includes various types of retrieves and jumps, scent discrimination tasks (selecting an article with his handler's scent) and signal exercises (no verbal commands).

In the U.S., dogs working toward the Companion Dog (C.D.) title compete in the Novice class. They must win qualifying scores, out of a maximum 200 points, in three trials. Competition for advanced obedience titles takes place in the Open and Utility classes where the exercises are both more difficult and more rigorously scored. The advanced titles are Companion Dog Excellent (C.D.X.), Utility Dog (U.D.) and the highly prestigious Obedience Trial Champion (O.T.Ch.). A few Tibbies have won the C.D.X. title, and others are working toward it. To the best of my knowledge, only one or two have competed at the U.D. level.

Although Tibbies are not known for their obedience aptitude, a clever, moderately independent Tibbie, coupled with a creative trainer, can achieve success. Since most Tibbies are very clever indeed, the trainer's creativity in managing the Tibbie's independent nature is most important. The chief drawback appears to be that long periods, without praise or fun of any kind, tax the Tibbie's tolerance for being obedient.

Oh, How Cute!

Working in the obedience ring, Sandy Lidster (U.S.) and Petey (Am. Ch. Phylmarko Par-Ti-Bu) successfully completed the "Heel-on-Lead" and "Figure-Eight." During the next exercise, the "Heel Free," during which the dog is supposed to "Heel" off-lead, Petey decided he was bored and he veered away from Mrs. Lidster. After flipping three times, he came to rest in the center of the ring, his chin on his paws. To the great amusement of the judge, Petey watched (inwardly chuckling, no doubt) as Mrs. Lidster dutifully finished the pattern around the ring, sans Tibbie, to the accompaniment of a chorus of "Oh, how cute!" among the spectators at ringside.

Many owners competing in obedience discover that a Tibbie's priorities differ from those of his handler.

Taking a Break

Having attained an American obedience title as well as her Canadian championship and obedience titles, Mimi (Can. Ch. Timothy's Penchenga Mimosa, Can/Am C.D.) was obviously an accomplished Tibbie. But it wasn't always smooth sailing, recalls her owner,

In 1977, TSCA Ch. Westerly Lotus of Amroth, C.D., owned by Gwen Wexler and later by Don Roy, was the first American Tibbie to win an obedience title. *Jerry Reinlieb photo*

Barbara McConnell (Canada). Mimi's first match was in July. It was a balmy day, and the grass in the ring was soft and sweet-smelling. When Ms. McConnell gave her the "Sit/Stay" command and walked away, Mimi remained still—for a while. Then she oozed onto her side and then rolled onto her back where she remained, baking her belly, until the dog next to her "broke" his "Stay" (by strolling over to his owner). She flipped back over and resumed her "Sit."

At another match, Mimi was well on her way to qualifying when she decided that she had done enough that day. She rose from her "Stay" and sauntered over to the ring exit. To prevent her leaving, the steward picked Mimi up and held her in her lap until the exercise concluded. The next day, Mimi again broke her "Stay" but, this time, she marched straight to the steward and asked for a lift up and a cuddle.

If you are interested in obedience competition, *Competitive Obedience Training for the Small Dog,* by Barbara Cecil and Gerianne Darnell, is highly recommended. All of the training tips discussed in Chapter 10 apply, too. Above all, you need persistence and a sense of humor.

Third Time's a Charm?

The first time he went into the ring, Danny (Am. Ch. Bet'R Standing Ovation, C.D.) earned the first of the three legs needed to win his obedience title. The second time he went into the ring, Danny successfully completed the second leg. At this point, Rod Beckstead (U.S.), his owner and handler, began to think that either a) Danny was the smartest dog in the world, or b) Rod was the smartest trainer in the world, or c) the obedience sport is not as difficult as he previously thought.

Danny must have sensed Mr. Beckstead's smugness because, in typically Tibbie fashion, he decided to miss his third leg in the next trial...and the next...and the next...and so on...until, on his 19th outing, Danny reasoned that his owner had learned his lesson and took pity on him. Breezing through the exercises without a hitch, Danny won his Companion Dog (C.D.) title.

"Madam" (Am. Ch. Ambrier's Chairman of D Board C.D.X.), bred by Mallory Driskill and owned by Diana Rutherford (U.S.), is one of a few Tibbies to have won an advanced obedience title.

Agile Tibbies

The objective in agility competition is for the Tibbie to successfully complete an obstacle course in the shortest possible time. Although the dog is off-lead, his handler runs along and guides him through the course. The Tibbie must demonstrate skills such as jumping, crawling and climbing as he negotiates obstacles including the A-frame, see saw, tunnels and hurdles.

Under AKC rules, dogs working toward the Novice Agility (N.A.) title must win qualifying scores, out of a maximum 100 points, in three trials and under two different judges. In classes for advanced agility titles, a few new obstacles are added (e.g., weave poles), but the principal differences are a greater number of obstacles, less time (per obstacle) to complete the course and more stringent judging. The advanced titles are Open Agility (O.A.), Agility Excellent (A.X.) and the Master Agility Excellent (M.X.). As of this writing, no Tibbie has yet attained an advanced title, but a few are working toward it.

It bears mentioning that there are several differences between competitions sponsored by the U.S. Dog Agility Association (USDAA) and the AKC. For example, USDAA course times are faster and jumps higher than in AKC trials. However, USDAA trials also include "games events" and classes for veterans. The USDAA offers these titles: Agility Dog (A.D.), Advanced Agility Dog (A.A.D.) and Master Agility Dog (M.A.D.).

Agility is a wonderful sport that both Tibbies and owners enjoy. It is great fun for spectators, too. Barbara Berg (U.S.) comments that her dogs like to engage in typically Tibbie play while on the course. After gamely dashing through the collapsed tunnel (a long fabric tube), they wiggle around at the end and then leap out for dramatic effect. "You can almost hear them say, 'Look at me!'" she says. Another darts to the top of the A-frame and then pauses to survey his kingdom, another typically Tibbie posture.

Tibbie Lecture

Handling advice comes from many sources—your friends, your spouse, a judge and, if you are showing a Tibbie, from the Tibbie herself. For many months, Karen Chamberlain prepared her Tibbie, Pippin (Am. Ch. Jemari Joyous Pippin), to compete for the new AKC Novice Agility (N.A.) title.

One obstacle on the novice course is the "pause table." According to the new rules for this competition, the judge specifies at the outset of the course whether the dog is to "Sit/Stay" or "Down/Stay" while on the table, where the dog must hold the position for five seconds before going on. However, before AKC promulgated this new rule, only "Down/Stays" were allowed and Mrs. Chamberlain had carefully trained Pippin to promptly drop down on the table. In the weeks before the AKC competition, she worked intensively to teach Pippin the newly permitted "Sit/Stay."

Pippin easily completed two of three required legs for the N.A. title—each with a "Sit/Stay" on the table. On the day of the final leg, the judge called for a "Down/Stay" on the table. When they reached the table, Pippin hopped up and Mrs. Chamberlain gave her the "Down/Stay" command. Pippin looked at her owner quizzically and decided to argue. She moofed (muffled woof) and squealed her opinion that a "Sit/Stay" was the required command here. Only after twenty seconds had elapsed did Mrs. Chamberlain win the argument. Pippin, disgruntled, consented to "Down/Stay" for the required five seconds, then resumed and completed the course flawlessly. Unfortunately, the precious seconds lost in lecturing her owner cost her the final leg for the title.

When, on the following day, Pippin promptly dropped to the "Down/Stay" on the pause table, a collective sigh of relief rose from the spectators. She streaked through the remainder of the course and easily won her third leg to become the first Tibetan Spaniel to be awarded the N.A. title.

In 1994, Am. Ch. Jemari Joyous Pippin, N.A., bred by Richard and M.C. Jeffery and owned by Karen Chamberlain, became the first Tibbie awarded the Novice Agility title. *Scott Chamberlain photo*

"Whimsi" (Am. Ch. Nittni's Whimsical Creation, N.A.), bred and owned by Scott and Karen Chamberlain, easily clears the rainbow jump. An A-frame and tunnel, other agility obstacles, appear in the background. *Scott Chamberlain photo*

Junior Showmanship (Handling)

A competitive event in which children handle dogs, Junior Showmanship is conducted in the same manner as competition in the breed ring. The difference is that the judge evaluates each child's handling skill rather than his or her dog's qualities. Many children around the world present Tibbies in Junior Showmanship competition.

In the U.S., children from ages ten through seventeen, who have an AKC-issued number, are eligible to compete. Those who are ten through thirteen years old compete in the Junior class, while the Senior class is made up of fourteen through seventeen-year-olds. To enter in the Open class, a Junior or Senior must have previously won three first-places, with competition present, in the Novice class. Until he or she wins these three first-places, the child competes as a Novice.

Junior Showmanship also has it prestigious competitions, where a win becomes the highlight of a child's junior handling career. Children who have each won eight first-places in an Open class vie for top honors at the Westminster Kennel Club show in New York. Across the Atlantic, a World Junior Championship competition is held in conjunction with Crufts, the U.K.'s most prestigious show.

Besides learning to handle a show dog in the ring, the child takes responsibility for training, grooming, exercising and caring for the dog. Learning to present oneself and one's Tibbie under pressure is a useful skill. Even if the child later loses interest in the Junior Showmanship program, the composure and discipline he or she has learned carry over into other walks of life. Junior Showmanship should instill confidence and teach the child how to win and lose gracefully.

Rachel London shows Tibbies in conformation and junior handling. Here she handles Am. Ch. Bet'R Mighty Mickey at El Ray, bred by Betty Rosen and owned by her Mom, Bonnie London (U.S.). *Earl Graham photo*

Tracking Tibbies

American Tibbies are eligible to compete for tracking titles under AKC rules. Three owners and their tracking Tibbies are Annette Kittleson and Tumble (Am. Ch. Santera Spitnimage Tumblweed, T.D.), Barbara Berg and Tailor (Am. Ch. Aki Shima's Tailor Made) and Martha Rosner and Lita (Tibroke Nirvana, C.G.C.). These owners agree that tracking work builds a bond between owner and dog and is great fun for both.

During a tracking test, the dog follows a scent trail (laid by a stranger) to find one or more scent articles along and at the end of the track. The track for a T.D. title runs between 440 and 500 yards and includes three to five turns (where the scent trail changes direction). The dog's objective is one article at the end. For the Tracking Dog Excellent (T.D.X.) title, the

In 1995, Santera Spitnimage Tumbleweed T.D., bred by Sandra Novocin and owned by Annette Kittleson, became the first Tibbie awarded the Tracking Dog title. *Toni Osojnicki photo*

Followed by his owner, "Tailor" (Am. Ch. Aki Shima's Tailor Made) moves through a field on the trail of a glove, lifting his head for the photographer. He is wearing a tracking harness.

dog must successfully negotiate a longer scent trail, with more turns, at least two obstacles (e.g., a fence) and a diversionary "cross-track." Four articles are on the T.D.X.-level track. Two more AKC titles recently became available: Variable Surface Tracking (V.S.T.), for dogs that can work on surfaces other than vegetation (e.g., concrete, gravel, sand), and Champion Tracker (C.T.), for dogs that have won all three tracking titles. As of this writing, only one American Tibbie has won a T.D., but several are working toward their titles.

Barbara Berg, who has conducted tracking tests for many years, advises owners that Tibbies instinctively know how to track; the trick, she says, is for the trainer to trust the dog to do the job. Ms. Kittleson, whose Tumble was the first Tibbie to win a tracking title (perhaps the only one in the world), concurs and adds that you must be confident in your Tibbie's ability.

During training, all of these owners use food to motivate and vary the training routine to sustain the Tibbie's attention. For example, Ms. Kittleson planned practice turns that included curves and 45° turns as well as right angles. She also sprinkled the trail with multiple scent articles to pique Tumble's interest.

Although Tibbies work enthusiastically in cold weather, their eagerness may flag when summer rolls in. To keep a tracking Tibbie cool in hot weather, Ms. Rosner advises, soak him down to the skin. He will be dry by the end of the course. But do not spray-mist, warns Mrs. Berg; the insulating effect of the droplets on the Tibbie's thick coat heats him up even more!

Mrs. Berg laughs that Tailor glues his nose to the earth and sniffs so hard that she sometimes thinks he will suck the dirt up his nose. He tracks quickly, plowing unimpeded through the undergrowth, and, when he finds the article, he tosses it in the air and rolls around on it. Tumble also has an amusing, typically Tibbie way of "indicating" his article. He stops, sits down, looks back over his shoulder. The disdainful expression on his face says, "If you want it, come and get it." Only when Ms. Kittleson teases him with, "What do you have?" does he grab the article and race back to show off his prize.

Clearly, these Tibbies and their owners love tracking. Is this a sport your outdoorsy Tibbie would enjoy, too?

One More Title

Having read this chapter, perhaps you are thinking how thrilling it would be to show your Tibbie. Are you dreaming of winning a title in a blaze of glory, your Tibbie dancing at your side? Are you imagining your living room walls festooned with show photos, certificates and ribbons? Can you hear the crowd cheering?

Perhaps you are also thinking, wisely, that showing a Tibbie in any of the events that I have just described is probably even more complicated than I made it sound. You are right! For most of us, showing dogs turns out to be more difficult and expensive and much less glamorous than we first imagined. And yet, that first shiny ribbon followed by that first major win followed by that first Best of Breed rosette relentlessly suck you in.

If you are not yet sure whether you are ready to become involved in showing, let me offer another suggestion. As your Tibbie's first title, why not aim for Canine Good Citizen (C.G.C.)? This AKC-administered program, along with others like it around the world, promotes responsible dog ownership. By passing a test to certify that he is well-behaved at home, in public and around other dogs, your C.G.C. Tibbie joins the ranks of dogs of all breeds and mixed breeds that can reverse the tide of anti-dog sentiment in the world. Chapter 10 explains more about this worthwhile program. Check it out, and *good luck!*

The Tibetan Spaniel

Karen Chamberlain ills.

Chapter 13

Breeding Tibetan Spaniels

The Tibetan Spaniel breeder is first and foremost a manager. His or her job is to *actively, intelligently and ethically manage* the process of:

- bringing puppies into the world, and
- placing each puppy with a responsible owner in a loving home.

To bring puppies into the world, the breeder's job includes selecting and caring for breeding stock, assisting mating and whelping, and supervising the early physical and social development of the puppies. Placing the puppies entails screening and selecting buyers and then educating the new owner about the puppy's care.

The ethical breeder makes a lifelong commitment to each and every puppy that he or she causes to be born. In concert with other breeders, he or she assumes responsibility for preserving the Tibetan Spaniel in the beautiful, natural and healthy form which has been entrusted to us.

Not an enterprise to be undertaken casually, breeding Tibetan Spaniels is demanding, time-consuming and expensive. It is often rewarding but sometimes heartbreaking, exhilarating but frustrating, invigorating but exhausting—in short, an emotional roller coaster. Even a person who loves and is dedicated to the breed may not be cut out to be a breeder.

Each breeder brings to the table opinions that he or she has formed, based on his or her own experience and knowledge. Breeders who have endured more than their share of problems naturally express opinions that differ from those of breeders whose experiences have been by-and-large positive. Although there is seldom a consensus, this chapter endeavors to find a balance among these viewpoints. One point on which every breeder agrees: breeding Tibetan Spaniels is an inexact science that requires hands-on experience and a lifetime of learning.

A QUESTION OF ETHICS

The prevailing public perception of a breeder is someone who breeds dogs and sells puppies to make money, not someone who responsibly brings beautiful, healthy puppies into the world and finds them good homes. Publicity about the unethical and inhumane practices of people engaged in dog breeding, in the U.S. and elsewhere, has aroused a groundswell of adverse public opinion and damaged the reputations of all breeders. Added to this, some organizations have sought to lay responsibility for the millions of pure-bred and mixed breed dogs destroyed in American shelters every year at the doorstep of breeders. Although the extent to which breeders of pure-bred dogs are responsible for these sad statistics is debatable, ethical breeders abhor them as much as, probably more, than the public at large.

While it is not within the scope of this book to explore all of the emotionally charged issues swirling in this debate, neither is it possible to carry on any reasoned discussion of breeding without touching on the subject of ethics. Concerned breeders in nearly every country where Tibetan Spaniels are bred cite ethics, the rules of conduct to which breeders should conform, as an issue critical to the future of our breed.

The Decision to Become a Breeder

From the moment you decide not to spay or neuter a Tibbie, that dog's life and health is put at risk. The idea that having a litter is beneficial to the health of the bitch is a myth. The truth is that an intact Tibbie is subject to a host of reproductive diseases and disorders— such as prostate problems in males and uterine infections and breast cancer in females—not to mention the risks posed to the female by pregnancy, whelping and lactation.

Given these facts, it is utterly incomprehensible to me why anyone would casually decide to breed a beloved pet. In fact, any decision about breeding that is made without careful thought and planning is foolhardy. Let's examine some of the misconceptions that lead people into breeding:

- *I can make money.*
  If there is any breed of dog that you can breed ethically and responsibly and make a profit (which I doubt), it certainly is not the Tibetan Spaniel. This breed has a low reproductive rate—that is, fewer puppies per dam—and Tibbies are difficult to sell in most countries.
- *It will be fun to compete in dog shows.*
  If your motive is competition, you can buy a show puppy and compete without the hassle of breeding.
- *It is educational for the kids to see puppies born.*
  While it is true that children who are taught respect and responsibility for animals turn out to be better people, bringing a litter of defenseless puppies into the world for their amusement sets an appalling example of lack of respect and irresponsibility toward animals. Think about how traumatic it would be for children to see the death of the puppies or their dam, should something go wrong.

The only valid reason to become a breeder is a profound desire to preserve and protect the Tibetan Spaniel.

Responsibilities of the Ethical Breeder

An ethical breeder:

- strives to preserve the natural, sweet-tempered qualities of the breed,
- works actively and cooperatively to preserve the health of the breed,
- makes a lifelong commitment to each puppy created through his or her efforts,
- screens and educates buyers,
- makes truthful representations about his or her dogs, and
- nurtures the upcoming generation of breeders.

An ethical breeder makes a lifelong commitment to each puppy created as a result of his or her efforts. This litter of six-week-old puppies was bred by the author. Kris Gilmore photo

An organization that represents the Tibetan Spaniel exists in most countries where Tibbies are bred, and most of them promulgate a Code of Ethics. Member breeders pledge to abide by the Code's provisions. Although specific provisions vary from club to club, the Codes typically:

- require equal consideration of factors such as type, temperament and health in breeding,
- specify the age for first and last breeding of a bitch, along with a maximum number and recommended frequency of litters,
- require health screening for genetic diseases,
- specify a minimum age for puppy sales,
- prohibit sales to certain buyers such as retailers (pet shops) and laboratories,
- stipulate the documents (such as, registration forms, sales agreement and pedigree) that are to be furnished to buyers, and
- direct the breeder to:
    - explain how to feed and care for a Tibbie,
    - be truthful about the show potential of a Tibbie, and
    - require buyers to spay or neuter pet quality Tibbies.

An ethical breeder not only complies with, but probably exceeds, the requirements of the Code of Ethics to which he or she subscribes. However, most of the Codes depend on the breeder's voluntary compliance. Few have any "teeth"—a means of enforcing provisions and disciplining breeders who fail to follow the rules.

Fostering Ethical Practices

At any point in time, there must be a new generation of breeders in training to carry on the work of preserving the breed. It is incumbent on experienced breeders to educate novice breeders, fostering in them an ethical foundation as well as imparting the practical know-how they need. An apprenticeship to an ethical and experienced breeder is likely to produce an ethical and knowledgeable breeder of the future.

Historically, the Tibetan Spaniel's lack of popularity coupled with its low reproductive rate has worked to discourage breeders who depend on big litters and easy sales to yield a profit. However, it is probably inevitable that the breed will become more widely known and favored. Virtually every breed that has become popular has faced the same dilemma: along with the greater demand for puppies comes an influx of new breeders—some of whom are the ethical breeders of the future, while others are opportunists looking to make money. Indiscriminate breeding and inhumane treatment soon begin to destroy the reputation, beauty, temperament and health of the breed. Relying solely on passive factors, such as the Tibetan Spaniel's low birth rate, to control the dangerous force of popularity is shortsighted.

Breeders must act singly and collectively as advocates for the breed. It is each breeder's obligation to assure that no Tibetan Spaniel is ever placed where he or his offspring will come to harm. Each breeder must actively and thoroughly screen buyers and refuse to sell to any person whose motives or methods are questionable.

Although promulgating a Code of Ethics is a praiseworthy first step, it is the responsibility of every club that represents the Tibetan Spaniel to open further dialogue on the subject of ethics. Means by which to encourage ethical practices as well as means by which to censure unethical practices should be explored.

For example, nearly every breed club in the world is concerned about breeders voluntarily testing breeding stock for genetically transmitted disease. In light of the fact that propagating a genetic disorder may destroy a line (and possibly others) and the breeder's future in breeding, determining whether a perceived problem is rooted in fact or rumor is essential. Some of the questions the club may consider include: To what extent is voluntary compliance ineffective and why? Could a program of incentives increase the rate of voluntary testing or is a mandatory program necessary?

What can be done to educate breeders outside the club? One key step is to create a climate of open communication and cooperation, in which breeders who voice concerns or reveal problems in their own lines are heard compassionately rather than denounced or ostracized. If cost or unavailability of testing proves to be an impediment, sponsoring a series of clinics where tests may be obtained at reduced cost and in convenient locations (such as a show site) may be part of the answer. If lack of education is a factor, distributing reliable facts in club publications and sponsoring seminars is far preferable to faulty information passed haphazardly by word of mouth. And setting aside club funds to support worthwhile research speaks volumes about the club's commitment to the future health of the breed.

> *Through his imagination, he brought the mountain to him, but meanwhile the place where he sat crumbled away.*
> — Tibetan proverb

SELECTING BREEDING STOCK

All Tibetan Spaniels in the West are the descendants of five dogs with which the breed was resurrected in the U.K. after the Second World War and a few other Tibbies introduced in the late 1960's and early 1970's (see Chapter 3). Due to this small gene pool, selecting breeding pairs of Tibetan Spaniels is not easy.

Those early Tibbies varied in appearance and some, we have discovered, apparently carried defective genes. This is hardly surprising because dogs as a species, like humans and other animals, have genetic health problems. To increase the population, the early Tibbies were in-bred and line-bred, which "brought out" traits that were hidden in their genotype and "doubled up" not only on desirable traits but undesirable ones as well.

Breeders have worked diligently to produce dogs which conform closely to the Breed Standard. Recently, concerns about the Tibetan Spaniel's genetic health have become a focus of ethical breeders worldwide. If you will forgive the metaphor, we are fighting a battle on two fronts—strengthening the desirable traits of the breed in terms of appearance, movement, and temperament and, at the same time, eliminating inherited health problems. Every pair you select is a skirmish in the battle. You will win some and lose some, but you must always keep victory for the breed in sight.

Great Expectations

The thrust in Tibbie breeding ought to be to create an balance of traits that, overall, range from acceptable to superb. Focusing a breeding program on a

A pleasing head is a consideration of many breeders. This is GB Ch. Kensing Currant Bun, owned by Jane Lilley (U.K.) *Diane Pearce photo*

single trait (such as the "typey" head or the pretty coat color) and effectively excluding other traits from consideration may produce an array of unfortunate byproducts. Observers generally agree that Tibbies born in the last twenty years have been more consistent in type. For example, traits such as too-short muzzles or too-undershot jaws appear less often than before. At the same time, any efforts to create an exaggerated style of Tibbie have not taken root.

Do not expect instant improvement in one generation. Since most traits are the product of multiple genes and other influences, such as modifiers, it may take more than one generation to stabilize a desirable trait. Although recent ancestors are more influential on the current generation than distant relatives, traits not seen for generations may suddenly crop up in a Tibbie litter. This is one of the challenges of breeding.

To add to the frustration of breeders, it often appears that a desirable quality is in some manner linked to less desirable traits. For example, breeders have observed that many Tibbies with extraordinarily beautiful heads possess poorly aligned teeth. Is it possible that some of the genes that contribute to the lovely head are linked to others that prescribe poor dentition? Or, is the poor dentition coincidental to the search for the perfect head in a breed that is often judged more by its head than any other feature?

Line-Breeding Vs. Out-Crossing

Line-breeding is breeding two dogs that are closely related to a common ancestor. The classic formula for line-breeding is "Let the sire of the sire be the grandsire of the dam on her dam's side." *Inbreeding*, which may be viewed as an extreme form of line-breeding, is breeding very close relatives, such as parent to pup or brother to sister. *Out-crossing* is breeding dogs that are unrelated or not related within several generations.

Experts consider judicious line-breeding to be the best form of breeding. The technical term for a dog's complete genetic makeup is *genotype*. In his genotype, a line-bred puppy possesses more homozygous pairs of genes than an out-crossed puppy. In other words, fewer recessive genes are hidden by dominant genes. That means that a breeder can more easily predict which observable characteristics (such as physical appearance) a line-bred litter will inherit. The technical term for these inherited characteristics is *phenotype*.

Although line-breeding may "double up" or "bring out" a common ancestor's desirable characteristics in the progeny, the flip side is that it may also bring out undesirable characteristics of the common ancestor. These undesirable qualities may or may *not* be apparent in the ancestor's phenotype. Since no dog is perfect and all possess weaknesses as well as strengths, the breeder hopes that line-bred puppies will inherit the common ancestor's good features but not his poor ones. For example, suppose a breeder wants to perpetuate the exquisite head of a male grandfather, but the breeder is also aware that the revered forebear's forelegs were too bowed. If his descendants (the intended parents of the puppies) show their ancestor's quality head but acquired better leg structure from other relatives, the breeder may sensibly elect to gamble that the puppies will inherit the lovely head but not the too-bowed forelegs. Note that I use the verb "gamble"; there are no guarantees.

Another risk is that line-breeding may bring out a recessive trait of the common ancestor, a trait that was passed to both of the puppy's parents but that has remained hidden in their genotypes. In the example above, the puppies may indeed inherit the ancestor's lovely head, but they may also inherit a gene(s) for low tail set from him even if his tail set was perfect. Even when experienced breeders practice intelligent line-breeding, an undesirable trait may lurk unseen for many generations and then reappear. Many recent cases of progressive retinal atrophy (PRA) in Tibetan Spaniels are the result of line-breeding that doubled-up on the recessive gene for PRA.

Some Tibbie breeders out-cross every breeding. They rely on a study of phenotype and previous offspring to select pairs that outwardly complement one another and to avoid pairings that may pass on an obvious, undesirable trait. Proponents argue that out-crossed litters are not only as good as line-bred litters but at less risk for undesirable recessive traits inherited from the common ancestor(s).

In his genotype, a puppy that is the product of an out-cross usually possesses a greater number of heterozygous combinations of genes—in other words, more recessive genes hidden by dominant genes. Therefore, the phenotypes of out-crossed litters are less predictable than those of line-bred litters, because out-crossing hides recessive traits, be they good or bad. Proponents of line-breeding usually agree that the first out-crossed generation may look good, but add that persistent out-crossing introduces more variables with each generation. The more generations that are out-crossed, the longer it takes to sort out, recapture and perpetuate desired traits.

When considering which type of breeding best benefits Tibetan Spaniels, proponents of line-breeding argue that tight line-breeding or even the occasional in-breeding quickly reveals both the weaknesses and strengths of a line. Analysis of breeding patterns enables a breeder to identify the carriers of previously hidden traits and then to eliminate (breed out) the undesirable traits while preserving the desirable ones. An equally good argument can be made that, because all Tibbies in the West descend from a very small number of dogs, it is impossible to eliminate all undesirable traits from the gene pool. Trying to excise all carriers of these traits from breeding programs would be tantamount to "throwing the baby out with the bath water." Most experienced Tibbie breeders interviewed agree that a breeder practicing very tight line-breeding or in-breeding is playing with fire unless he or she is experienced and carefully plans and executes the breeding for a specific reason.

In view of these views, pragmatic breeders compromise. Most line-breed for two to three generations, then out-cross a generation and then resume line-breeding. They hope that the out-cross will not only introduce a desirable characteristic(s) but will also dilute the effect of any obvious or hidden undesirable traits. Meanwhile, they pray that the good traits they have perpetuated through line-breeding are not lost in the genetic soup. This appears to be a sensible approach to the situation.

Getting Started in Breeding Tibbies

In *The Tibetan Spaniel,* Phyllis Mayhew remarked, "The starting of a serious breeding and showing kennel should be looked upon as an absorbing hobby." True words. Being a good Tibbie breeder requires more than love of the breed. You must be intelligent, open-minded, patient and willing to persevere in the face of disappointment. So, if you are a person who requires swift gratification, breeding Tibbies is not an occupation for you. You must also have ample free time and financial resources that you are willing to dedicate to showing and breeding. So, if you need to recoup your expenses from the sale of puppies or stud service, breeding Tibbies is not an occupation for you. You also need adequate space, inside and outside your home, outfitted to provide your Tibbies with the shelter and exercise they need. So, if you are unable to modify your lifestyle and living quarters to meet the needs of your dogs, breeding Tibbies is not an occupation for you.

First, study the Breed Standard. The Standard guides you in selecting your foundation stock (the Tibbies with which you will begin your own line) and also describes the objective of your own breeding program. Next, study all available literature on the breed, such as yearbooks published by breed clubs, in order to familiarize yourself with the principal bloodlines. Meanwhile, haunt shows to observe living representatives of various lines and get to know their breeders. Study the show results.

Thoroughly investigate the health history of any line that you may incorporate into your program. Study texts on canine reproduction, genetics, and inherited diseases and disorders with particular attention to material pertaining to small dogs. Obtain up-to-date PRA registers and all other available health data from the breed club in your country and/or from Tibetansk

The selection of good foundation stock is important. Dan., Ger. Ch. Sommerlyst's Assam Tes-La, bred by Ragnhild Poulsen and owned by Gitte Primdal Poulsen, is Denmark's top Tibbie bitch for 1994.

Spaniel Klubb (Sweden), Tibetan Spaniel Association (U.K.) or Tibetan Spaniel Club of America.

One key to success (and a minimum of heartbreak) is to choose as a mentor an experienced, ethical Tibbie breeder whom you can trust to help you select your foundation stock and on whom you can rely to provide guidance. Be selective in choosing your mentor. Look behind the impressive record and get to know the person. He or she must be willing to share his or her hard-won knowledge and believe in nurturing a novice breeder. Even if you are experienced in another breed, a mentor from this breed is an invaluable resource.

Establishing a Solid Foundation

Many people just starting out are eager to "create" a new line that they view as distinctly theirs. As tempting as this may sound, it is more important that your first litters are a strong, healthy foundation on which to build your future. With your mentor's advice, line-breed your first litter.

Having selected the lines with which you plan to work, choose one or two foundation bitches of excellent quality. The age at which to buy a brood bitch is debatable. The show and breeding potential of young puppies, even those from line-bred championship lines, is less predictable than the obvious assets of a partially grown or grown bitch, and the wait for the first litter from a puppy bitch is two or more years. Nonetheless, many people advise that watching your own bitch puppies develop is the best way to learn their strengths and weaknesses. Also, obtaining a high quality older brood bitch may require convincing her breeder to part with a bitch that he or she is cultivating for his or her own program. Carefully examine an older bitch that her owner readily relinquishes.

Keep the best puppies you produce. They are the future of your program and the underpinning of your reputation. Although many breeders give the stud's owner a puppy in lieu of cash, pay the stud fee rather than watch the stud dog's owner walk away with the pick of your litter!

Planning Your Future

A breeding program requires a plan. Although it will undoubtedly change over time, your plan serves as a realistic point of departure. A long-range plan, outlining your program's objectives for the next five or ten years, is as important as the short-range plan for your next litter.

Consider your finances, time and facilities. As I have repeatedly stated, Tibbies thrive only when raised as part of the family. Most Tibbie breeders maintain only a few brood bitches because keeping a greater number in a home setting becomes increasingly difficult. Ann Wynyard, renowned British breeder, recommends maintaining a stud dog only after you have six or more bitches. Further, most small breeders keep only one stud dog at a time due to the logistical difficulties of housing more than one. Most breeders also find themselves housing several "pet" Tibbies, such as retired breeding stock and unplaced or re-homed adults.

Realistically appraise the current and future costs for all of these dogs—puppies, adults and seniors. Purchase price is only the beginning. Consider routine expenses for high quality food, supplies, fees (e.g., stud, registration, licenses), show costs (e.g., entry fees, travel), and preventative veterinary care. Factor in unforeseen costs such as emergency veterinary services (e.g., Caesarian sections, accidents). In evaluating housing needs, consider how to separate stud dogs from other stud dogs and from the bitches in season, both indoors and outdoors.

Considerations in Selecting Pairs

Selecting a pair of Tibbies is a tough decision. The objectives of your decision-making process are to:

- forecast the outcome of a potential pairing, and
- determine whether each prospective parent is healthy and fit for breeding.

Consider the age, type, soundness, temperament and reproductive history of each prospective parent. Comparing the phenotype of each to the Breed Standard is useful, but you must also thoroughly investigate and analyze the candidates' pedigrees. Determine which type of breeding produced the prospective sire and dam. Gather any available information about the pair's antecedents, including photos, in an effort to form an impression of the genotype that may underlie the pair you are considering. Their current health as well as health history of their lines is a key consideration.

When forecasting breeding potential, experienced breeders advise that it is more important to look at any progeny the prospective parents have produced than the titles and ribbons they have accumulated. Since pairing an unproven dog with a maiden bitch is not recommended, at least one of the pair should have offspring walking around; studying the earlier litters may be revealing. If the female has produced a litter, ask about her earlier performance as a dam.

Contrary to popular misconception, the sire and dam contribute equally to the genotype of each individual pup—50% from each parent. However, a popu-

Since Tibbies thrive only when they are members of the family, most breeders consider temperament an integral part of any breeding program. Dennis and Kelsey, children of Peter and Joel DeCloux, pose with their friend "Freddie."

lar stud normally contributes a greater proportion of genes to his breed since he is bred more often and produces more offspring than a bitch.

A puppy's phenotype is governed by the dominance of the genes he receives from his parents. As a simplistic example, a dominant gene(s) for ear set determines where his ears are placed on the skull; it is irrelevant which parent contributed the dominant gene(s).

The ideal outcome of a pairing is to produce pups that reflect the best qualities of both parents. No matter how high their individual quality, not every dog "nicks" with every bitch. What breeder can honestly claim that he or she has never wished that a puppy had inherited some trait of his mother's instead of his father's or vice versa?

The owner of stud dog should be as choosy about accepting a bitch as the owner of the bitch is about selecting a stud dog—perhaps even more so since the stud's influence on the breed is potentially greater than that of any of his partners. Aside from the simple humanity of wanting every Tibbie pup born to be loved and well-cared-for, a stud dog's owner should be confident that the bitch's owner will raise the pups in a manner that reflects credit on the dog's reputation as a sire and his owner's reputation as a breeder.

Millions of words of advice have been written about collecting and organizing the data you need to make informed, coherent breeding decisions. The general idea is to list the desirable traits (e.g., no PRA, no allergies, good patellas, fine head, good tail set, good coat) and less desirable traits (e.g., short on leg, ear set too high, thin bone) of each prospective sire and dam *and* to identify where in his or her pedigree you believe each trait originated. Although it is beyond the scope of this book to explore these techniques in further detail, it may be helpful to formulate a "worst case scenario" and a contrasting "best case scenario" as part of your analysis. Imagine a puppy with all the worst traits of both parents and decide whether he would nonetheless be healthy, good-tempered representative of the breed that you could proudly place in a pet home. Then imagine a puppy with all the best traits of both parents and decide whether he would truly advance your breeding program in the direction you desire.

Correcting Faults of Conformation

The perfect Tibbie has yet to be born. If we follow the conventional wisdom that doubling up a trait, whether it is desirable or faulty, preserves and passes on the trait, then it follows that we may eliminate or dilute a faulty trait by breeding to an opposing trait. Given that descriptive words such as "readily" are subjective, some faults are more readily overcome than others—perhaps because those that resist correction involve more complex genetic factors. If you cannot correct a faulty trait, it makes sense to avoid using a Tibbie possessing that trait in your breeding program.

Unfortunately, even the most experienced breeders disagree about which specific Tibetan Spaniel traits resist correction and which do not! For example, some Tibbie breeders believe that weak pigment is "easy" to strengthen, while others rate it as "difficult." Good pigment appears as black eye rims, nose, lips and dark pads. Poorer pigment appears as less intense color, liver, and/or pinkish patches in these areas. A blue "window" (spot) in the iris of the eye or a wholly blue iris is also evidence of pigment loss. Pigment loss occurs in most colors but is usually noticed in particolors. Strong pigment is indisputably a desirable trait in Tibbies, but is poor pigment readily improved or does it resist correction? Many breeders experienced with Tibbie particolors maintain that they can quickly improve pigment by introducing a strongly pigmented dog into the line, and, as a further precaution, many recommend introducing a strongly pigmented dog every two or three generations.

Since the ideal Tibetan Spaniel described in the Breed Standard has never been born, all breeding stock is imperfect to some degree. Most breeders have in mind a short list of traits, some of which they insist all prospective parents must possess and others of which effectively eliminate a dog or bitch from consideration as a parent. Past experience with trying to improve certain traits influences this list but the desired or detested

> **BREEDING REMINDERS**
>
> - Find a breeder-mentor to advise you.
> - Investigate the genotype of prospective parents (through pedigree and progeny) as well as their phenotype.
> - Consider both strengths and weaknesses and identify the origins of each.
> - Double-up on traits you want to preserve but be careful not to simultaneously double-up on faults.
> - Do not focus on appearance to the exclusion of temperament, soundness, movement and health.
> - Start with the best possible bitches, choose the best possible stud and keep your best puppy.
> - Practice thoughtful line-breeding with an outcross every two or three generations.
> - Avoid in-breeding or tight line-breeding unless you are experienced and have a specific objective.

traits may also be a matter of personal preference. For example, a long-time breeder told me bluntly, "I don't care how beautiful the rest of the dog is, I would never breed a Tibbie with a snipy muzzle." She admits that her opinion is not based on the probability that a Tibbie with a snipy muzzle (who may be otherwise an exquisite specimen), when mated to a Tibbie with a perfectly proportioned and cushioned muzzle, usually produces a certain percentage of puppies with ideal muzzles. Instead her intense dislike of snipy muzzles has influenced her decision to never produce even a single pet quality puppy with a snipy muzzle! Another breeder refuses to consider an otherwise lovely but poorly pigmented Tibbie although strong pigment is attainable. It is natural to have such prejudices, and all breeders have them. However, remember that you are breeding whole puppies, not parts of puppies.

Since they do not believe that these traits can be "readily" improved, a consensus of Tibbie breeders sampled advise against using in your breeding program a Tibbie that possesses any of these faults:

- poor temperament,
- unsound structure,
- poor movement,
- lack of balance (e.g., too tall, too long, too square),
- very short legs or heavily bowed forelegs, and
- overshot or very undershot.

For example, straight stifles, which contribute to poor structure and movement, appear to dominate correctly angulated stifles. Therefore, avoid breeding a Tibbie with straight stifles.

Note the faults that are absent from the above list. Most breeders sampled, for example, concurred that a poor coat would not eliminate an otherwise top notch Tibbie from consideration because coat can be "readily" improved.

Healthy Thoughts

Inheritable diseases and disorders that afflict Tibetan Spaniels are rare. However, as a breed becomes more popular and numerous, the incidence of inherited illness usually increases. Since the future health of the Tibetan Spaniel as a breed is in the hands of its breeders, it is incumbent on each breeder to avoid inherited health problems by choosing only Tibbies with no known problems and to "breed out" any problems that appear.

The difficulty in "breeding out" health problems is that it is sometimes unclear whether a condition is inherited and, if so, the way in which it is inherited. Some conditions are simple autosomal recessives. PRA is thought to be one of these. That means a single gene carries the information that eventually causes the dog's retina to degenerate and that the dog must inherit a "PRA gene" from both parents in order to develop the condition. A dog that inherits the gene from only one parent does not develop the condition, but he is nonetheless a carrier that may transmit the "PRA gene" to offspring. When the mode of inheritance of a genetic condition is unknown, the smart decision is to avoid using a dog with the condition in your breeding program. Unfortunately, some inherited conditions, such as allergies, may not become apparent until the Tibbie has already produced offspring.

Chapter 11 discusses the health of our breed at length. In my opinion, you should not breed a Tibbie who carries genes for any of these genetic conditions:

- PRA,
- congenital kidney disease,
- portosystemic (liver) shunt.

Unlike PRA, congenital kidney disease and liver shunt are life-threatening.

You should also pay special attention to three other conditions thought to be influenced by heredity. Although they are not life-threatening, these conditions may cause long-term discomfort.

- Distichiasis (extra eyelashes), probably the most common inherited condition in Tibbies, may cause chronic irritation of the eye.
- Allergies may be largely responsible for persistent itchiness reported by owners all over the world.
- Patellar luxation (slippage of the kneecap), prevalent in small dogs, may cause lameness and discomfort.

The above lists are not meant to imply that you should ignore other conditions. For example, no male Tibbie with an undescended (or undeveloped) testicle should be bred. More on that later in this chapter.

Take advantage of any available tests devised to detect genetic conditions. Countries that have initiated prevention programs should serve as models for other countries, and breeders of all countries should share information in a systematic and cooperative manner. None of us is immune from these problems.

Colorful Thoughts

An intriguing aspect of Tibbie breeding is the color and marking variations of offspring. Sables range from bright golds to strawberry blonds, particolors pop up in many litters, and black-and-tans and tricolors are now considered more pleasing. Stunning "true" reds (like an Irish Setter) and solid blacks are both rare and treasured. Since the earliest breedings, Western breeders have been fascinated by the seeming randomness of color distributions in their litters and, to preserve this charming variety, Standards of all countries permit all colors and color combinations in Tibbies.

In 1911, Mrs. McLaren Morrison, the most prolific early writer on the Tibetan Spaniel and its avid devotee for a half century, wrote: "The coloured Tibet Spaniel was until quite recently a very rara avis amongst dogs.... I imported two perfect coloured females..., a cream and a fine red brindle. The family of the former and a black sire was truly extraordinary—one cream, one black, one deep chocolate-brown, and one orange! The brindle had two males; one was my noted first-prize winner Marpo, the other (same colour) died in puppyhood. Now, curiously enough, the cream daughter of the cream mother had two black puppies, thus throwing back to her black sire. The sire of the puppies was black. The orange female (sire orange) gave me two males as her latest litter, a biscuit colour and a light brown." The author continues, "A pure black female and pure black sire produced a brown and white puppy; in this case I cannot trace any colour in the mother's pedigree, which I know far back, but the sire being imported probably accounts for it. It is rare to have Tibets with very much white, but the black sire (whose dam is deep black-brown, the female above spoken of) gave me a white female with a little tan, her mother being dark. The light shade of biscuit is one I particularly admire in Tibets.... I think that the colours here are so beautiful and manifold that to all colour-breeders the breed should offer particular interests. The shades are really lovely. The little dogs themselves, apart from the colour question, are hardy, most fascinating, intelligent, and attractive, and whether coloured, or black with white, or all black, are, apart from the immense antiquity of the breed (cultivated and preserved in the monasteries of Tibet from times unknown), delightful companions, who need only to be once known to establish a firm hold in this country."

Even while striving to preserve strong pigment, most breeders decline to otherwise influence color inheritance, preferring to focus on other inherited traits. While no one should breed exclusively for color to the possible detriment of soundness, health or other traits, color is nonetheless an interesting factor in the genetic soup.

This all-particolor litter was a great thrill for Becky Johnson (U.S.), the owner of the dam, Ch. Tiara's Double Bubble of Tabu.

If you are interested in working with color, study all available information about color inheritance. *The Inheritance of Coat Color in Dogs* by Clarence Little is the classic text. Although it is silent about the Tibetan Spaniel because (thankfully) the breed did not figure in the scientist's breeding tests, his discussion of the Pekingese is apropos. Next, seek the advice of breeders who have worked with color inheritance or are knowledgeable about pedigrees that carry the color genes you want.

Sable with all its shades and variations of markings is the most common "color" in Tibbies. Regardless of their shade, all sable Tibbies possess black tips or fringes to a greater or lesser degree. Technically, this marking pattern, rather than the color over the rest of the body, is what differentiates the sable. The pitfall in breeding sables is to avoid dilution of pigment by maintaining strong color and sabling.

One of the most appealing color/marking variations is the particolor. Since there is a potential for pigment loss in particolors, breed them carefully. Several breeders, experienced with particolors, advise that a predominantly dark-faced parti has stronger pigment than a predominantly white-faced parti. When planning to show or breed a parti, those of us who fancy partis (myself included) should select a puppy whose head is dominated by darker-colored patches, preferably covering the ears and surrounding the eyes. Although all partis are born with pink noses and eye rims that later darken, the chosen puppy should have the black nose, eye rims and lips that denote strong pigment. Avoid blue-eyed partis or partis with blue spots in the iris. Although the inheritance of the markings is unpredictable, strive for a symmetrical appearance of the head. Symmetry of the markings on the rest of the body is unimportant.

Other appealing color/marking combinations are the black-and-tan and its tricolor variation (a black-and-tan with white markings) and the black (with or without white markings). The black-and-tan combination is a recessive trait that, theoretically, may spring from any color of parent provided that both parents carry the trait hidden in their genotype.

Moonstruck

Glory Be (GB Ch. Kensing Glory Be) and Peach (GB Ch. Kensing Peach) were due to whelp a week apart, which seemed a sensible kind of arrangement but, as a breed, Tibetan Spaniels seldom do what you expect. Glory Be held her breath until the last possible moment and started the night she was due, producing five, two of which were gold and three—to my astonishment—were black!

Glory Be and her puppies were clean, cosy and contented so, very tired, I was just about to go to bed at 2 AM when Peach came into the kitchen panting and shivering. She thought having puppies would be a good idea! Neither of us had any sleep and the following day she started pushing hard and screaming with pain. Fortunately she was young and strong. Somehow she managed to produce a HUGE black bitch that weighed 9 ounces. Another three normal-sized puppies followed, two of whom were black!

Out of nine live puppies born to these two bitches, five were black! No one would believe me. Glory Be and Peach were gold, as were the sires, with only golds and partis behind them all for generations—certainly no blacks! What was the explanation? No one has, so far, been able to improve on my theory that it must have been something to do with the moon!

Contributed by Jane Lilley (U.K.)

CARING FOR BREEDING STOCK

Actively managing a breeding program includes caring for breeding stock in a way that improves the chances that pairs will produce the kind of puppies that you want. You must consider housing, nutrition and ongoing health care.

Housing Needs

Optimal accommodations for a Tibbie family include:

- separate outdoor runs for dogs and bitches, each surrounded by a four to six foot fence,
- outside exercise area,
- indoor areas in which you can separate females in season from intact males for a period of a month,
- an area in which to keep females visiting your stud dog (if any), and
- an area in which to locate dams and their pups.

Also consider how you would house dogs that become ill.

Although a few breeders report that their Tibbie males tolerate one another, most report tension and fighting between intact males. Conflict is inevitable when females in season reside in the same household as the males.

Never underestimate the male and female Tibbies' resourcefulness in reaching one another when the female is receptive to mating. Male Tibbies, ten inches tall, have been known to scale a six-foot chain link fence, up one side and down the other, to reach the lady on the other side. Many breeders recommend covered runs to deter a climbing male from reaching the object of his desire. Similarly, construct fencing in a manner that thwarts tunneling. Chapter 9 discusses fencing tips.

A household with females in season can be nerve-wracking for us humans. Since some males whine and keen continuously, keep females in season as far away from them as possible. For ease of care, areas where you keep females in season, mothers with their pups, and geriatric Tibbies should be easy to clean.

Nutrition and Conditioning Needs

Chapter 9 recommends feeding premium dog foods that contain high *quality* (highly digestible), not quantity, protein. When fed an excellent diet, most Tibbies need no vitamin/mineral supplementation. This dietary recommendation also applies to breeding stock. Feeding poor quality food has been associated with lower conception rates in bitches. The nutritional requirements for pregnant and lactating bitches, which are far greater than those for bitches that are not pregnant, are covered later in this chapter.

It is also important to maintain both brood bitch and stud dog at an ideal weight and in peak condition. Obesity and lack of fitness are implicated in cases of difficult labor, but pregnancy is not the time to shape up your brood bitch.

Preventative Health Care

The recommendations for preventative health care in Chapter 11 apply to breeding stock as well as household pets. Additional considerations are related to the reproductive organs and the timing of the female reproductive cycle.

Preventative health care for breeding stock must be an ongoing effort, not a last-minute rush. Since you should avoid giving a brood bitch most drugs, dewormers, and flea and tick preparations during pregnancy, assure that she is parasite-free (internal and external) before she becomes pregnant. Similarly, keep her immunizations up-to-date. If her vaccinations will be due while she is pregnant, have her vaccinated before she comes in season. This assures that the puppies will receive maximum immunity from her. Any "modified live virus" vaccine should be administered at least 30 days before she is due to come in season.

Routine physical examinations should identify any abnormalities or infections of the reproductive structures as well as heart problems, hypothyroidism or other conditions that may impact on reproductive health. Specific examinations to detect hereditary problems in Tibbies (described in Chapter 11), including progressive retinal atrophy (PRA) and patellar luxation, are critical to your breeding program. Have your Tibbies examined for PRA annually. Maintain records of all health care received and note in these records other pertinent dates such as the onset of and duration of each bitch's seasons.

Always be alert for signs of health problems. For example, any sign of difficulty while urinating or defecating or of abnormal urine or discharges in your stud dog may indicate a problem that could imperil his life as well as compromise his ability to produce pups. (Note that a small amount of whitish or yellowish discharge from the penis is normal in adult intact males.) Similarly, watch your brood bitches closely for signs of reproductive illness, such as vaginal discharge.

Since Tibbies are low to the ground, inspect their genitals after romps outside. It is not uncommon for burrs or other irritants to lodge in the prepuce or elsewhere in the male or female genitals. Do not allow any contact between the genitals and chemicals, such as the cleaning products used on flooring or flea products applied to the coat. Always rinse thoroughly after baths.

Unless your veterinarian is treating your Tibbie for an infection, never routinely give antibiotics to breeding stock. These doses can kill the "good" bacteria that keep the "bad" bacteria in check. Misused in this manner, antibiotics can be dangerous drugs with side-effects that may endanger the Tibbie and offspring.

Reproductive Problems (Not Associated with Breeding, Pregnancy or Whelping)

Vaginitis and occasional cases of pyometra are reported in female U.S. Tibbies. Brucellosis, although not reported, is a devastating infection against which all dog owners must guard.

Brucellosis—An insidious infection, the bacteria that causes brucellosis is found in semen, vaginal discharges, aborted fetal tissue and urine of affected dogs. It may cause infertility, abortion, newborn death, inflammation and abnormalities of the reproductive organs, or problems in the lymph system. It affects both males and females. There may be no outward signs in infected dogs, or signs may be as subtle as a mild case of scrotal irritation.

Brucellosis is persistent, highly infectious and difficult to eradicate. Testing the blood of all breeding stock for brucellosis is an essential precaution. Since brucellosis is transmitted sexually, a diagnosis of brucellosis effectively ends the breeding career of all infected dogs.

Pyometra—A life-threatening bacterial infection of the uterus, pyometra usually occurs during the two months after a female's season. Although it is more common among older, maiden bitches of all breeds and mixed breeds, it may occur in any unspayed female. Pyometra is sometimes associated with drugs that delay heat cycles and estrogen-based mismating shots. The outward signs vary from slight lethargy to severe generalized illness. Although you may notice a discharge from the vulva, none may be evident if the cervix is closed or the bitch grooms herself well. Untreated, she deteriorates rapidly. The traditional treatment for pyometra is ovariohysterectomy (spaying) and a course of antibiotics. In less severe cases, it may be possible to preserve the uterus with a recently developed drug, Prostaglandin $F2_{alpha}$, that causes the cervix to dilate and the uterus to contract and expel its contents. As promising as it is, this drug should be used only under veterinary guidance because its side-effects may be life-threatening.

Vaginitis—An inflammation, vaginitis affects females of all ages, whether spayed or not. The usual signs are discharge and genital licking. Puppy (juvenile) vaginitis occurs in a puppy under one year old and usually clears up as she reaches puberty. Depending on the cause of the vaginitis, antibiotics are the usual treatment.

MATING

Having selected the intended breeding pair, evaluate their fitness. If you have attended to their ongoing needs and preventative health care, this evaluation should be pro forma. If another breeder is involved, complete all of the breeding arrangements well in advance. When all is ready, sit back and wait for the young lady to come into season.

Checkups

Have your brood bitch examined by a veterinarian about two weeks before her season is due. During this visit, request tests for brucellosis and intestinal parasites. If she is a maiden, ask the veterinarian to check for a vaginal stricture or other impediment to mating.

Before his first service, ask the veterinarian to examine the male's external genitals and prostate. Ideally, males would undergo brucellosis testing before each service; as a practical matter, however, popular stud dogs are not tested before each breeding but should be tested once or twice a year.

Visiting a Stud Dog

If using another breeder's stud dog, negotiate all the details in advance. At a minimum, the issues to be ironed out include the payment and when it is due, which choice of pup (if any) the stud dog owner will have and whether the stud will provide another service if the bitch does not conceive. There may be other considerations as well. For example, you may wish to spell out whether you are entitled to another service from the stud if the bitch delivers only a single viable pup or if all of her puppies die. Although some deals are concluded informally, it is always a good idea to draw up and sign a stud dog contract.

The bitch always goes to the dog. Since two to three breedings (one every other day) are recommended, she is in the care of the stud dog's owner for a week or more. Being left at someone else's home sometimes causes her stress, especially if she is not accustomed to being away from home. Since it is important for her to be relaxed, consider visiting the stud's home before she comes in season and/or bringing her there a few days early. The "settling-in" time may help her accept the male when she is ready to be bred.

To further assure that your bitch is happy while at the stud dog's home, inform the stud's owner about her diet (provide the food if necessary) and idiosyncracies. Take her toys and bed from home.

The bitch should be taken to the male's home for breeding. Fin. Ch. Toyway Ah-Matti, bred by Jouko Leiviskä and owned by his breeder and A.M. Arjas, is a top-producing sire.

Coming In Season

Most Codes of Ethics specify the earliest age at which a Tibbie female should be bred and state that she should be at least in her second season. The idea behind these limits is that the female should be both physically and mentally mature before we ask her to raise puppies. If she is still a puppy herself, she is less likely to be a good mother. Since Tibbies mature slowly and each at a different rate, use your common sense. Most breeders wait until the bitch is at least two years old.

Further, most guidelines forbid breeding "back to back"—in other words, every estrus—but require that you wait until a season has passed before breeding again. The idea behind this limit is that recovery from the physical and mental stress of pregnancy and lactation is often lengthy, sometimes as much as a year.

The reproductive cycles of Tibbie females vary considerably. Unlike female dogs that come into season every six months, Tibbie females come into season once a year on average. However, the range may be as little as seven or eight months or up to fifteen to eighteen months. (There is some indication that the frequency of seasons in Tibbies has increased over the last twenty years.) Once a female's pattern is established, you may reasonably expect her to go in season "on time," give or take a month.

Females living together in the same household tend to cycle together. One will come into season, a week or two later another comes in, and a week or two later another comes in. Although the influence of one female on another can result in a houseful of busy Tibbie puppies and an exhausted breeder, it may also work to your advantage if you are trying to induce a female to come into season. Providing her with towels or bedding scented by any other female in season may trigger her season as well.

Since the interval between estruses may be somewhat unpredictable, keep a sharp eye on your females. The approach of estrus (proestrus) is marked by the swelling of the vulva followed by the onset of a bloody discharge and further enlargement of the vulva. The swelling may commence several days before any discharge appears. You may notice that she suddenly sits down and/or appears uncomfortable, possibly due to the sensation of swelling. During walks, you may also notice that she urinates small amounts in several places to advertise her availability much in the same way males mark their territories. All of these physical and behavioral changes signal impending estrus.

Be aware that Tibbie females usually keep themselves clean. She may be well into proestrus before you realize that she is coming into season!

Ready for Breeding

Most books say that a bitch is ready to be bred 10-14 days after the onset of discharge. Some Tibbies are ready as early as two to six days and others as late as 21-25 days! Even assuming that you know the actual day when the discharge began (which you may not), counting days is not a reliable way to predict ovulation in Tibbies.

Instead, the method employed by most successful breeders is to watch carefully for an array of physical changes that indicate receptivity to the male. When these changes lead you to believe that her ovulation is imminent, a microscopic examination of a vaginal smear confirms her readiness. Alternatively, successive vaginal smears, commencing when you notice the first signs and every one to two days thereafter track the progression of vaginal changes that indicate approaching ovulation. A relatively new blood test used to pinpoint ovulation is the serum progesterone concentration.

As her fertile period draws near, the swollen vulva appears to tilt upward slightly and becomes softer. The color of the discharge changes from predominantly red to yellow (usually called straw-color). The tail deviates to one side, also called "flagging," and the spine curves laterally. A vaginal smear taken at the time these signs appear contains cornified squamous epithelial cells, the signature of the onset of estrus. The closer estrus is, the higher the proportion of cornified cells. During the third to fifth days of estrus, receptivity to the male peaks. This is called the "standing heat" because the female permits the male to mount.

Courtship

Each morning, the intact males of a household greet the ladies of the household with an investigation as to their sexual status. During this sniffing, you may notice that a male's lips move rapidly. He is moving saliva that has come in contact with the bitch's delectable sexual scents (pheromones) into his vomeronasal organ, a sensory organ located in his palate. This action stimulates sexual pleasure and arousal. Since her pheromones advertize the female's status, do not bathe her while she is in season.

Most Tibbie males go off their feed and lose weight while any of the females in the household are in season. Some drive themselves (and you) crazy with whining and keening. He struggles to reach *Her*—scratching at closed doors and gates, clamoring over barriers or tunneling under fences. He sniffs you up and down when you come from *Her* presence. While he is certainly pitiful as well as annoying, another sort of male is sneakier. Being more worldly and wily, this male bides his time. Seemingly aware that he risks separation if he openly declares his interest, he remains quiet until he senses that *She* is ready.

A courtship ritual spurs the secretion of male and female hormones needed for intercourse and conception. Besides making the pair attractive to one another, these hormones ultimately contribute to litter size by increasing the rate of ovulation and conception. Most male Tibbies engage in a form of courtship ritual. Joan Child (U.S.) remembers that Am. Ch. Truk-Ku Apollo "wined and dined" his ladies. When suppertime came, he proudly pushed his food to his intended. Others lavishly lick the lady's ears, inside and out, nibbling away her fringes and smiling "like idiots." Others dance circles around the lady, play-bowing and romping with her.

Since these rituals stimulate the female's interest, allow them, but keep the happy couple in a confined area and under your supervision during foreplay.

Consummation

Mate a pair two to three times with a day between each breeding. Leaving them together unattended is courting disaster because one or both could be hurt. For example, if the female turns and snaps at the male, she can spoil his career as a stud dog. If she tries to sit while they are tied, both could be injured. Supervise the consummation so that none of these accidents occurs.

The mating should take place on a stable, non-slip surface in a confined area. Optimally, two people should be present to assist the pair.

Tape back or catch up the female's trousers in a rubber band so that the vulva is fully exposed. You may wish to lubricate the vulva and vagina by applying a sterile lubricant with a gloved finger.

If the male has long hair growing from his belly, it may be helpful to place an elasticized band of cloth, roughly six inches in width, around his middle ahead of his penis. This keeps the hair out of the way of penetration and enables the people assisting to see better.

Assistant #1 is in charge of the female's forequarters. Grasping her firmly, he or she holds the bitch's head or collar and speaks soothingly to her. Assistant #2 steadies her hindquarters and directs the male as he mounts. Gently holding the vulva, assistant #2 guides the vulva until the male's penis fully penetrates the vagina. Since Tibbies are well-coated, the assistants may not be able to see precisely when he penetrates fully, but the strength and speed of his thrusts increase noticeably.

When the male stops thrusting and rests atop the female, hold him there for at least two minutes. Assistant #1 should continue to hold the bitch's head so that she cannot turn or move forward and may also place a hand beneath the bitch to prevent from her sitting. Meanwhile, at his or her station at the hindquarters, assistant #2 holds the male's head so that he cannot dismount. Assistant #2 may also need to anchor the hindlegs of the pair until the tie is secure.

When the assistants are confident that the pair are tied, they allow the male to dismount and turn around, helping him lift his leg over (if necessary), so that the pair are standing tail to tail. Since the male continues to ejaculate for several minutes during the tie, it is important to continue to hold the pair so that neither is injured should the female decide that she no longer likes the dog or one of them tries to sit.

After the stud withdraws, continue to hold up the female. Do not allow her to sit for several minutes or urinate for one-half hour. After a short period, the male's penis should completely retract into its sheath. Cleanse his sheath.

When It's Over, It's Over

You can be sure that a bitch's season is over when:

- 28 days from the onset of discharge have passed, and
- there is no further discharge, and
- the vulva returns to normal.

Reproductive Problems of the Female Related to Breeding

Female reproductive disorders related to mating, reported by U.S. breeders, include irregular heat cycles, failure to conceive and refusal to mate. Due to their native ingenuity, mismating has been known to occur.

Irregular Heat Cycle—Of all the possible causes of irregular cycles or failure to cycle, the most likely is thyroid insufficiency. Typically, hypothyroidism causes a prolonged anestrus (that is, absence of a heat cycle), prolonged proestrus with only mild signs and failure to ovulate. Irregular heat cycles due to hypothyroidism may be hereditary. Treatment is thyroid hormone replacement.

Other possible causes of failure to cycle or irregular cycles include poor nutrition, genetic abnormalities and ovarian disease or deformity. A female's seasons become irregular as she ages.

Mismating—When you believe a mismating has occurred, a veterinarian can confirm pregnancy by ultrasound as early as 21 days after the accidental breeding. Beginning at 30 days, the fetuses may be palpated. If she is pregnant, the pregnancy may be terminated with Prostaglandin F2$_{alpha}$ injections. Due to possible side-effects (some of which are serious and permanent), never use an estrogen-based "mismating shot."

Refusal to Accept—Most Tibbie bitches are flirtatious and undiscriminating when offered a mate. Assuming that her season is normal, the time is right and she is relaxed, the bitch should be receptive. Trying to breed a female at the wrong time is the main cause of refusal to accept. As described above, you may need to be more careful in pinpointing her estrus by relying on a combination of observed signs and behavior, microscopic analysis of vaginal smears and serum progesterone concentrations.

Other possible causes of refusal are an anatomic barrier, such as a vaginal stricture (see next topic), or a problem that hinders the male's performance, such as prostatic inflammation or a spinal condition.

Some Tibbie females are simply choosy about their mates. If you have ruled out other causes, such as those listed above, male preference is probably a factor in her refusal to accept the male selected for her. Artificial insemination (AI) is an option.

Vaginal Stricture—A barrier that impedes penetration, a female may be born with a vaginal stricture or acquire it later (e.g., by trauma or infection). Although somewhat common in dogs, few strictures are reported in Tibbies. Surgical correction may be possible. It is not known whether this condition is inherited.

Failure to Conceive—Failure to conceive may be attributable to either the male or female. Male infertility is discussed later in this section. The female may fail to conceive because:

- mistimed insemination does not coincide with ovulation, or
- ovulation does not occur, or
- the female has a hypothyroid condition.

Less usual causes include uterine infection (e.g., brucellosis) and lack of sufficient hormone to sustain pregnancy. Stress may also be involved.

Conception may fail even when the outward signs of estrus (swollen vulva, discharge and attractiveness to males) are present. A complete fertility workup may pinpoint the underlying problem. If there appears to be no condition that would impede conception, assume mistiming and take greater care to properly time breedings during the female's next season.

Reproductive Problems of the Male Related to Mating

Among male Tibbies, breeders report lack of interest (low libido) and genital infection as problems related to mating. Less frequent problems include prostatitis, abnormal testicles and impotence. Infertility due to sperm-related problems is rarely reported. A physical examination, semen analysis and other tests (e.g., thyroid function) help assess mating problems in a male.

Infertility—For purposes of this discussion, infertility in the male refers to failure to produce normal sperm in adequate quantities. Among the many reasons for male infertility are congenital abnormalities, (e.g., cryptorchidism), infections, tumors, immune system problems and defective sperm. It has also been suggested that excessive heat or cold and drugs or toxins (e.g., environmental chemicals) may account for some cases of infertility.

Low Libido and Impotence—The causes of low libido (lack of interest) and impotence (inability to mate) may be psychological or non-psychological. Pain (e.g., due to prostatitis, spinal problems), hypothyroidism and congenital defects are the usual non-psychological causes. Hypothyroidism is treatable and, depending on its underlying cause, pain may be relieved.

Psychological factors are thought to be the chief cause. According to experienced breeders, males not used at stud before they are three or four years old may be ineffective. Similarly, a bad experience during an earlier breeding, such as a snappish female, may make the male fearful of a rendezvous. It is also possible that repeated punishment for sexual behavior may also "turn off" the male.

Prostate Problems—Common in all breeds and mixed breeds, prostate problems occur in 80% of dogs over five years old. The usual problem is benign prostatic hypertrophy/hyperplasia (BPH), a condition in which the prostate enlarges and cysts may develop. Dogs with BPH often suffer from prostatitis, an inflammation of the prostate gland. The signs of prostatitis and BPH are the same: pain, abnormal gait or stance, fever, depression, loss of appetite or blood in the urine. The swelling of the prostate may obstruct the rectum as well as the urethra, impeding both defecation and urination. Owners sometimes mistake prostatitis for arthritis or a spinal problem.

Untreated, prostate infections may lead to chronic urinary tract infections which may then spread to the kidneys. Since such infections can result in death, early detection is important. Treatments include antibiotics and neutering.

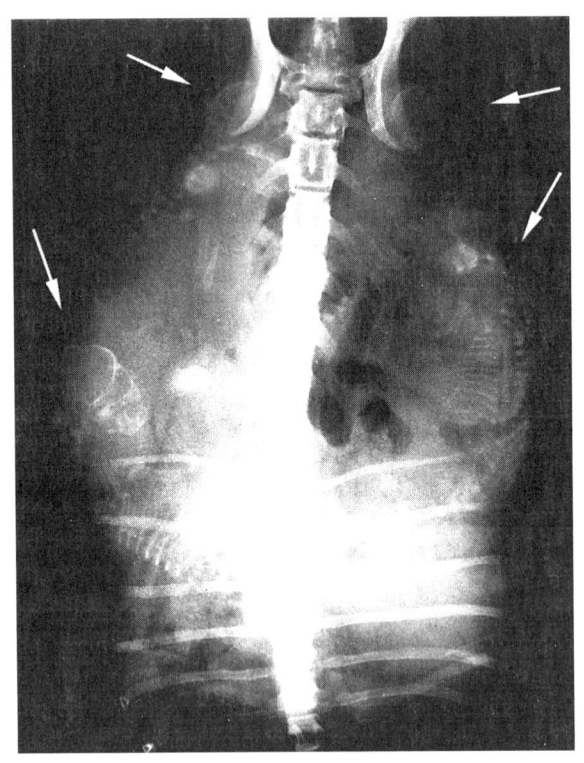

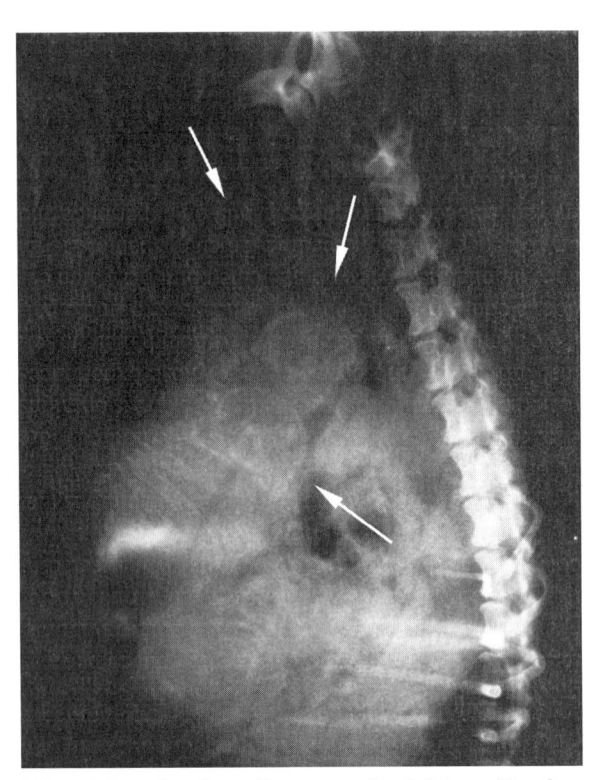

These radiographs were made on Day 65 of this Tibbie's pregnancy. She delivered three days later. Can you see the skeletons of her four puppies? Note that they are in position for head-first presentations. *Reproduction by Kris Gilmore*

Paraphimosis—A condition where the penis cannot be withdrawn into the prepuce, paraphimosis usually occurs because long hairs tangle around and constrict the penis. Treat this condition as an emergency. Without immediate treatment, irreversible tissue damage may occur as a result of the penis drying out. Treatment includes relieving the underlying cause, cold packs, lubricants, and medication to reduce swelling.

Testicles, Problems of—Cryptorchidism, the failure of one or both testicles to descend from the abdominal cavity into the scrotum of a male puppy, is the most common cause of infertility in male dogs. Since this condition is thought to be genetic and is associated with a high incidence of testicular tumor, neutering is recommended for cryptorchid dogs. They should not be allowed to reproduce.

PRE-NATAL CARE AND WHELPING

As a breed, Tibetan Spaniels are known for uneventful pregnancy and easy whelping. In comparison to many other small breeds, some of which cannot deliver puppies naturally, this is undoubtedly true. Many Tibbie breeders enjoy telling stories about the bitch that whelped a litter all alone, without any help from humankind, and the pups turned out just fine.

Remember that it is your job as a breeder to actively manage the pregnancy and whelping just as you planned and carried out the breeding. Do not be lured into passive complacency about the impending event. Many Tibbie pregnancies and births are problem-free, but some are not. Among the highlights of my own first litter, for example, were a dual presentation (simultaneous birth of two puppies—one 8-oz. and the other 4-oz.) followed by a large puppy that was "dry" and breech and required resuscitation when finally delivered.

Before undertaking to whelp puppies on your own, arrange to witness or assist in a whelping. Your mentor-breeder can help. Always have an assistant on call: two pairs of hands are better than one, especially if something goes wrong. Be prepared for an emergency: know how to get veterinary help quickly, regardless of the day of the week or the time of day.

Physical Changes During Pregnancy

Tibbies usually deliver at 62-63 days counting from the date of the first mating. However, the length of the pregnancy may vary because estrus itself varies in length, two or three matings take place during estrus and canine sperm are viable for several days after mating.

Since little fetal growth occurs in the first month of canine pregnancy, you cannot determine the success of the breeding until three to four weeks into the pregnancy. Ultrasound and palpation are the usual ways of detecting developing puppies. Although an ultrasound may detect tiny sacs as early as 21 days, the embryos are clearer and the heartbeat visible at 25 days. Puppies may be palpated beginning at 30 days, but once the uterus fills with fluid, it is more difficult to feel them. After their bones calcify 42 days into the pregnancy, the puppies appear on a radiograph.

Since Tibbies carry their pups "high" (that is, under their ribs), you may not notice any physical changes in the mother-to-be until the last two to three weeks of pregnancy. At this point, her weight increases, abdomen enlarges and nipples swell. In the final days of pregnancy, you may be able to express milky fluid from the nipples.

Feeding During Pregnancy

Continue feeding the mother-to-be a premium adult maintenance dog food during the first four weeks of pregnancy. After that, the increased rate of fetal development demands greater nourishment. During the fifth week of pregnancy, transition gradually from adult maintenance to a premium dog food that states it is formulated for growth and lactation (puppy food). Gradually increase her food intake so that, by the end of her pregnancy, she is consuming about 25% more than at the start of her pregnancy. Since her abdomen is filling with puppies and she feels uncomfortable eating large meals, divide her daily intake into smaller, more frequent meals around the sixth week. For example, if she usually eats one meal per day, increase to two or three. Although you want her to eat more, do not allow a pregnant Tibbie to gain too much weight since it may contribute to difficult labor.

Virtually every authority agrees that you should not give pregnant bitches any kind of calcium supplement. Although it seems that supplementing calcium would prepare her for nursing, an excess actually "turns off" her body's natural way of producing calcium and deposits the excess calcium in her tissues. In other words, giving her calcium during pregnancy increases the likelihood that she will suffer calcium deficiency when her body later tries to make milk for her puppies. Supplementing her with other minerals and vitamins (such as iodine, vitamins A and D) could also lead to dangerous excesses.

When the developing pups are growing rapidly during the two to three weeks before they are due, a pregnant Tibbie often "goes off" her food. To coax her to eat as much as possible, mix something delectable with her dog food. Veal baby food does the trick for my girls.

Other Precautions

Although heartworm preventative is not harmful, most drugs are "off limits" for pregnant bitches. For example, aspirin, corticosteroids and some antibiotics may harm developing puppies. Avoid flea preparations, and use dewormers only under veterinary supervision. Check with your veterinarian before giving your bitch anything except good food and fresh water.

Moderate exercise is good for your Tibbie, but avoid strenuous running and jumping. Do not allow her to become overheated.

Preparing for the Big Event

The first order of business is to set up the whelping box, the nest in which the mother-to-be delivers and raises her pups for the first few weeks. Each breeder has his or her own idea of the ideal whelping box. Some purchase a commercially manufactured box or use a travel kennel; others rely on the home-made variety.

The minimum requirements for a whelping box are:

- either disposable or easily cleaned (no wood),
- roomy enough for warm and cool areas,
- sides high enough to afford privacy,
- opening through which the dam can exit but the pups cannot, and
- removable top for easy access during whelping and later observation of pups.

Many breeders construct a disposable whelping box from a fairly large, sturdy, clean cardboard box. Cut off the top and, at one end, cut out a section of the cardboard leaving a barrier low enough for the dam to step over but high enough to keep the pups in. (Later, you can cut down the barrier to allow the pups to exit.) Towels draped over the top contain the heat and create a cozy "den."

Whether or not to supply the puppies with a source of heat other than their dam and siblings is controversial. Some insist that an artificial heat source is essential to avoid the risk of chilled puppies, while others insist that a supplemental source is not only unnecessary but may overheat the puppies. The only point upon which everyone seems to agree is that young puppies cannot regulate their own body temperature. I am uneasy about relying solely on the dam's good mothering and on ambient temperature that may fluctuate (especially during the winter). So, I prefer to minimize the risks of hypothermia (chilling) and hyperthermia

MILESTONES OF PREGNANCY

DAY*	WHAT HAPPENS
24	possible mild morning sickness
25 on	pups detectable by ultrasound
30 on	pups detectable by palpation
35-42	transition to puppy food and gradually increase intake to 15% more than normal
42 on	pups detectable by radiography
43-49	weight increases, abdomen expands, nipples enlarge, increase food intake to about 20% more than normal and divide into smaller, more frequent meals
50-56	increase food intake to about 25% more than normal, nipples produce milky fluid, introduce whelping box, assemble equipment, test heat source
56	begin taking rectal temperature once per day
62-63	due date

*Time frames are approximate.

(overheating) by providing a gradient of heat in the whelping box. In this way, the dam has a spot where she can rest comfortably away from the heat source and yet remain with her pups. Similarly, the pups can crawl or be moved between the warmer and cooler areas.

If you elect to supplement heat, you must decide on a safe, reliable continuous heat source. Although the use of heating pads is also controversial, many breeders use a small size heating pad placed inside the box, leaving part of the space unheated. *If you choose to heat with a pad, use only a heating pad made for dogs.* This is constructed of a hard material so that the Tibbie cannot chew through it and liquid cannot reach the electrical components. The cord is also covered. Other possible heat sources include a heat lamp, small space (room) heater, or hot water bottle. Each has drawbacks: a lamp with a bright bulb may harm sensitive, newly opened eyes; a space heater may tip over; hot water sources must be frequently rewarmed.

At least a week before the pups are due, test the heat source. Newborns need 85° F. Since a heat source may take a while to reach the proper temperature, preheat it as soon as the dam's rectal temperature drops indicating that whelping is imminent.

Arrange a spot for the whelping box in your bedroom. Choose a quiet, warm and draft-free location. Although the delivery may take place elsewhere, the dam and her newborns should live where you can keep an eye on them day and night during the first few weeks.

Before and during the whelping, cover the bottom of the whelping box with newspaper. The dam will instinctively shred the paper to make a nest. When the birth is over, discard the soiled newspaper and move the box to your bedroom. If you decide to use a heating pad, place the preheated pad at one end of the box, leaving the other half unheated. *To prevent burns to their tender skin, never allow puppies to rest directly on a heating pad.* Cover the entire bottom of the box with a layer of fresh newspaper or other absorbent material and cover this with a layer of thick, white toweling. White towels enable you to monitor the color of discharges and feces. A thermometer placed on the toweling allows you to monitor the temperature of the surface on which the pups rest.

Besides the whelping box, set up an "incubator" for temporarily housing the newborns during the whelping. Again, this need not be a fancy affair. I use a small disinfected aquarium in which I place a heat source *covered with toweling.* I place a thermometer atop the towels and drape another towel over the top to contain the heat. The incubator goes in a warm, draft-free location well away from the dam. Preheat it to 85° F as soon as the dam's rectal temperature drops.

Next, assemble and clean the remaining equipment. Disinfect, launder and set aside plenty of white towels. Since Tibbie pups are so small, have a supply of handtowels for drying the whelps as well as a supply of larger towels for lining and covering the whelping box.

One Week to Go

With only a week to go until the due date, be extra vigilant. This is not the time to let the mother-to-be wander around the yard and disappear under the porch for hours!

Introduce her to the whelping box. Encourage her to scratch at the newspaper. Chances are she will not be very interested until labor nears, but it is important to let your wishes be known.

Consider a final veterinary checkup about one week before her due date. A radiograph shows you how many pups she is expecting. Knowing the number may help the whelping run more smoothly, and you will know when she is finished!

At least a week before her due date, begin taking her temperature once a day, preferably in the morning. As the date draws closer, take it twice a day. A dog's normal temperature ranges from 100°-102.5° F. A drop of one to two degrees below her normal means that the birth should take place within 18-24 hours. For example, birth is imminent when the mother-to-be's temperature drops to 99° F.

Trim her trousers and clip the hair around the vulva so that it does not interfere with whelping. Also trim the long hair around the nipples.

Whelping

Let's talk first about the everything-goes-perfectly whelping. After that, I'll discuss some of the what-can-go-wrongs that Tibbie breeders have reported.

Coinciding with temperature drop, the mother-to-be displays other signs of impending labor. She becomes uneasy and restless and scratches at the newspaper in her whelping box. Food no longer interests her. She begins to pant. A look of anxiety may appear on her face.

Let her go out to relieve herself but do not let her wander off by herself. Meanwhile, call in your assistant and put your veterinarian on alert.

A slight calm usually precedes labor. You may or may not see the early contractions but you can feel a wave-like movement by placing your hand on her flank. As a normal labor progresses, the interval between contractions decreases and their strength increases. When the contractions become strong, she hunches her body and grunts. The first puppy usually arrives between one-half to two hours after labor begins but should be delivered no longer than an hour after the strong contractions start. Subsequent pups usually arrive at intervals of ten minutes to one hour but should be delivered no more than an hour after the strong contractions resume.

A puppy may be born head-first or breech. The first part of a breech puppy to emerge is his hindlegs or rump. Breech presentations are so common in dogs (one source reported 65% in Tibbies) that they are considered as normal as head-first births.

When encased in the amniotic sac, the puppy cannot breathe. Some breeders allow the dam to remove the sac, but removing it yourself is less risky. Since the pup should breathe within 30 seconds of delivery, swiftly break open and strip away the sac, starting at the head. Even if he breathes spontaneously when the sac is removed, a puppy requires physical stimulation to assist breathing and blood circulation. Before cutting the cord, envelope the wet puppy in a towel and tilt his head downward (to help fluid drain out his mouth and nose). Rub him briskly. His mother usually tries to help with vigorous licking. Meanwhile, the next contraction or two usually expels the placenta (afterbirth) to which the pup is still attached by the umbilical cord.

> **WHELPING EQUIPMENT CHECKLIST**
>
> Betadine
> Blunt-tip scissors
> Bulb (ear) syringe
> Dopram
> Heat source for whelping box
> Heat source or hot water bottle for incubator
> Incubator (homemade)
> Lubricant (sterile such as K-Y Jelly™)
> Newspaper or other absorbent material
> Scale (gram)
> Surgical gloves
> Thermometer (room)
> Thermometer (rectal)
> Thread or dental floss (optional)
> Towels (white, disinfected)
> Towelettes (pre-moistened) for cleaning babies
> Whelping box

It is important to be sure that the puppy's airways are clear so that he does not accumulate fluid in his lungs. Squeeze a bulb syringe ever so slightly to create a tiny amount of suction and gently apply the syringe to clear the mouth and each nostril. *Too much suction will collapse the lungs!* If the puppy is not breathing well, place a drop of Dopram, available from your veterinarian, under his tongue to stimulate deep respiration.

When the pup is breathing well, take a moment to cut the umbilical cord. This is another point on which breeders differ; some permit the dam to sever the cord with her teeth while others cut the cord. Because Tibbies are undershot, their inefficient tugging at the cord may induce or worsen an umbilical hernia. Cutting the cord yourself is less risky. Starting at a point about three inches from the body, clasp the cord between the thumb and forefinger of each hand. Slide the thumb and forefinger closest to the puppy toward his body, squeezing the cord so that the blood within it is forced into the body. Tying the cord before you cut it is not usually necessary in this breed, but, if you elect to do so, loop dental floss around the cord and tie a knot about one inch from the body. Cut the cord about one and one-half inches from the body using sterile scissors. If the placenta has not arrived, hang on to the end of the cord that is still attached to the placenta within the mother's body; it is usually expelled momentarily. Always dip the stump of the cord into Betadine to prevent infection.

Now listen to the pup's chest (either with an ear against the chest or stethoscope). If his breathing still does not sound free and easy and his lungs clear, cradle him in both hands, facing you, with his back resting in your palms. Clasp his body firmly and support his head and neck with your fingers. Lifting him above your head, swing the puppy in a smooth downward arc and stop abruptly when his head is pointing straight down. One or two swings should clear the lungs. Never attempt this method of clearing the airways until your mentor-breeder or veterinarian demonstrates how to do it properly. Make sure that you have a good grip on the puppy (that he cannot slip from the towel) and that there are no obstacles in the way of your swing.

Once his breathing is clear and easy, resume drying the pup. So that she can get acquainted, place him next to his mother and introduce him to a nipple. Although starting him nursing is sometimes tedious, keep at it until the pup latches on with a strong suck. This first meal of colostrum is very important because it transmits his mother's antibodies to the puppy. It also helps to bring on labor for the next puppy.

When contractions resume, distract the dam momentarily while your assistant whisks away the previous puppy to the incubator waiting out of the dam's sight and hearing. Do this as sneakily as possible so as not to upset the dam. Dry, warm and nourished, each puppy rests in the preheated incubator (85° F) until all of his littermates have arrived.

The dam should deliver one placenta per puppy. Most breeders simply remove the placentas. It is not necessary that she consumes them and, if she does, she may throw them up.

Michael's Bet

Seven-year-old Michael has a Tibbie, as well as a cat and a mixed breed dog at his own house. But, when he visits Grandma's house, his favorite playmate is Sylvie, one of her Tibbies. Once, while visiting Grandma, Michael disappeared into the family room to play with Sylvie. Reappearing at his grandmother's side only a few minutes later, "Grandma, how come Sylvie is so fat?" he asked sternly. His grandmother replied, "Sylvie isn't fat, Michael. She's going to have puppies in a few days." "How many?" countered Michael. "Well, we don't know yet," his grandmother answered. Since guessing games are a family custom, Michael asked whether he could guess the number of puppies. His grandmother agreed and, after much weighty pondering, Michael decided on "4." Michael's "4" along with the guesses of other family members were duly recorded on the fridge door, and Michael returned to play with Sylvie.

A couple of hours later, Michael reappeared at his grandmother's side. "Can I change my guess?" he asked. "Sure" his grandmother said, "What number do you want?" "8," Michael replied firmly. "How did you come up with '8'?" asked his grandmother, thinking that eight would be a very large Tibbie litter. "Because," Michael said emphatically, rolling his eyes in disbelief that his grandmother did not already know why, "Sylvie has eight ninnies! Eight ninnies means eight puppies!"

When Michael arrived at Grandma's house later that week, Sylvie was in labor and had delivered four pups. Wanting to help her, Michael seated himself beside her in the whelping box. As sometimes happens, Sylvie did not want to be helped by anyone—no one, that is, except Michael. Though she growled at everyone else, she accepted Michael's presence gratefully, laying her head in his lap and allowing him to pick up her nurselings. As the next puppy made its appearance, Michael watched until he saw his grandmother approach with the scissors to cut the cord. Clapping his hands over his eyes, he announced, "You're on your own now! I cannot even watch!"

By the way, Michael's guess won the game. Sylvie delivered eight lovely puppies. (Michael is the grandson of U.S. breeder Sandra Lidster.)

Problems Related to Pregnancy and Whelping

Everything described above assumes that all proceeds normally and swiftly. However, a number of signs may indicate that something is amiss. For example, a dark green or bloody discharge *after* the first puppy is normal but a similar discharge *before* the first puppy indicates that the placenta is no longer supplying the puppy with oxygen. The latter is an emergency situation.

It is not within the scope of this book to describe all possible problems that may occur in a canine pregnancy nor to provide procedures for every contin-

SIGNS OF LABOR TROUBLE

- temperature drops 1° to 2° F below normal but no puppies within 18-24 hours,
- black, dark green or bloody fluid *before* the first puppy,
- first puppy does not arrive within three or four hours after labor begins or within an hour after strong contractions begin,
- labor does not resume within two to three hours after previous puppy's delivery,
- subsequent puppy does not arrive within two hours after labor resumes or within an hour after *strong* contractions resume,
- rupture of amniotic sac (water bag, balloon, bubble) marked by passage of yellow fluid but no puppy within thirty minutes,
- labor stops,
- large amounts of blood,
- restlessness or anxiety,
- fatigue.

gency. Your bookshelf should include texts on canine obstetrics and pediatrics. However, here are a few of the problems reported by Tibbie breeders.

Breech Presentation Without Sac ("Dry")—A puppy's amniotic sac is supposed to cushion and speed his way down the birth canal, but it may rupture before he is delivered. Although the puppy may still be wet, birth without a sac is called a "dry" birth. Breech presentations are often dry.

Dry, breech presentations may entail a different approach to delivery. When his placenta pulls away from the uterine wall, the puppy no longer receives oxygen from his mother. By the time his head finally emerges, the dry puppy is often oxygen-deprived. For whatever reason the delay occurs, a delay in delivering the puppy may also endanger the puppies in line behind him. Time is of the essence.

Start by lubricating the vulva and pushing the lips to expose as much of the puppy as possible. Stand the dam up and place your hand beneath her abdomen to lift her pelvis. This straightens the birth canal and may help speed the puppy on his way out. If most of the puppy's hindlegs are still inside, insert a gloved, lubricated finger into the vagina and hook it around one or both legs at the stifle. You are then in a position to add gentle traction when the next contraction pushes. Similarly, when the legs are out, you can grasp the skin of the back with a towel and assist the next contraction.

Dystocia (Difficult Labor)—Dystocia is an umbrella term for prolonged labor that may result from many different causes. The amount of labor that is considered reasonable before the first and between subsequent puppies depends on what source you consult. The guidelines given here are conservative. Consider them, but also use your common sense. If your Tibbie is screaming in pain or obviously coming to the end of her rope, get veterinary help whether or not these time periods have elapsed. Also consider how long it will take to get veterinary help, and do not allow her to become exhausted before help is available.

Treat these signs of dystocia as an emergency:

- over 70 days elapse (counting from first breeding),
- failure to whelp within 18-24 hours after her temperature drops below normal,
- first puppy does not arrive within three to four hours after labor begins or within an hour after strong contractions begin,
- labor does not resume within two to three hours after previous puppy's delivery,
- a subsequent puppy does not arrive within two hours after labor resumes or within an hour after strong contractions resume,
- obvious pain or exhaustion,
- vaginal bleeding, or
- signs of shock (e.g., pale mucous membranes, cool to the touch, lethargy) or other illness (e.g., fever, vomiting).

The main cause of dystocia is uterine inertia, the failure of the uterus to contract strongly enough to deliver a puppy. The two types of uterine inertia are primary and secondary.

Secondary uterine inertia involves an obstruction. For example, after a protracted struggle to deliver a large puppy, the dam's uterus stops working. Examples of obstructions are a large puppy in a small birth canal, inadequate dilation of the cervix or a malpresentation. The treatment is to deliver the puppies by Caesarian section.

Primary uterine inertia has a variety of causes.

- The uterus of a dam carrying a small litter may be insufficiently stimulated to contract.
- The uterus of a dam carrying a large litter may be too stretched to contract.
- Stress or anxiety in first-time dams may suppress contractions.
- Deficiencies that may prevent contractions include:
    - hypocalcemia (low blood calcium),
    - hypoglycemia (low blood sugar).
- Infections may also curb contractions.

The treatment for uterine inertia depends on the underlying cause. To identify the cause, a veterinarian takes the Tibbie's temperature, performs a vaginal examination, radiographs her abdomen to determine the number and status of the puppies, and tests the blood for hypoglycemia. Depending on the cause, possible treatments include administration of oxytocin (a pituitary hormone that stimulates contractions), injections of dextrose or Caesarian section.

Some breeders keep a supply of oxytocin on hand and administer injections, called "Pit shots" (referring to a specific brand of oxytocin), on their own. Oxytocin can be very dangerous if given inappropriately. For example, if the underlying problem is an obstruction, stimulating stronger contractions may rupture the uterus. Oxytocin may also cause severe pain to the dam and halt fetal blood supply. Use oxytocin only under direction of a veterinarian.

When she is suffering from dystocia, failing to seek help in a timely manner can cause severe problems for the Tibbie and her puppies. These problems can be far worse than the stress of a Caesarian section. The longer you wait, the riskier the surgery is. This is why you should alert your veterinarian to the impending birth and why you should always have a contingency plan.

Some breeders worry about a dam's acceptance of puppies delivered by Caesarian section. Although this concern is not borne out by the anecdotal evidence I collected, it is certainly important for the puppies to nurse on their own. One tip is to smear a bit of placenta on the dam's mouth and the puppies to give her the scent of a natural whelping.

A Classic Case of Primary Uterine Inertia

When I took Ciana's temperature on Sunday morning, it had dropped to 98° F overnight. With the exception of a lack of appetite for the last two weeks, her pregnancy had been uneventful. "Today's the day!" I called out to Chris as I reviewed all my preparations for the four Tibbie puppies that we knew were waiting to be born.

Ciana paced and panted all day. She tried to hide under our bed and shredded the newspaper in her whelping box. Twelve hours passed with no sign of contractions. Tomorrow is a holiday, I fretted as I went to bed, and the vet's office will be closed.

When Monday morning arrived, both Ciana and I were exhausted. She had panted and I had watched all night. Twenty-four hours had passed since her temperature dropped. Now it was back up to 98.8° F, a sign that her hypothalamus had reset. Still no contractions. She watched me, her worried gaze speaking volumes.

At noon, I reached my veterinarian at home, and he agreed that the puppies must be delivered as soon as possible. An hour later (the longest I've ever waited), Dr. Thumel met Chris and I at his office. Ciana's cervix is fully dilated, Dr. Thumel explained when he had completed his examination, and so the risk of infection is present. He first tried administering oxytocin. The panic in Ciana's eyes subsided, and she waited calmly. She surely sensed my own relief that she was now in the care of a trusted veterinarian.

As we waited for the oxytocin to take effect, Dr. Reitzloff, another member of the practice, and the assistants arrived, their holiday celebrations also interrupted. The oxytocin proved ineffective.

A half an hour later, Dr. Reitzloff and an assistant backed through the swinging door from the surgery, each carrying in outstretched hands a newborn wrapped in toweling. They passed the puppies to us and returned to the surgery. Chris and I held them up for examination—two boys—and we began to dry them. Dr. Reitzloff and the assistant backed out of the surgery with two more puppies—a boy and, at last, a girl—and joined us in briskly rubbing puppies. All four were sables and weighed about six ounces each. All cried lustily. In the midst of grinning and cuddling, I glanced again and again through the surgery window, still worried about Ciana.

Twenty minutes later, Chris struggled to clamp each puppy to a nipple. Though groggy and shivering from the effects of the anesthesia, Ciana willingly gave her puppies their first taste of colostrum. They were soon sucking noisily. All was well.

Fetal Death—The two kinds of fetal death are resorption, which usually occurs in the first four to five weeks of pregnancy, and abortion, which occurs during the remainder of the pregnancy. There are usually no signs of resorption; the puppies that were developing in the uterus simply disappear. A discharge may signal an abortion later in pregnancy. Although one or more fetuses may die, it may be possible for others to survive.

The usual causes of fetal death are infections (such as brucellosis), defective fetuses, abnormal uterus, inadequate progesterone and drug use (especially corticosteroids). To avoid fetal death, test for brucellosis before breeding, keep pregnant bitches away from other dogs (including dog shows) and avoid drugs that contain corticosteroids. Note that many popular ear and eye medications contain corticosteroids.

Not Breathing—Vigorous rubbing usually stimulates a newborn to breathe. However, when delivery is prolonged and the newborn has been deprived of oxygen, further measures may be required. Speed is essential.

1. Assure that the airways and lungs are clear by swinging the puppy. Clasp him firmly with both hands around his middle, his face toward you. Support his head and neck with your fingers. Make sure that he cannot slip from your hands and that the path of your swing is clear. Lift the puppy above your head and swing him down in a smooth arc. Stop abruptly when his head is pointing straight down.

2. Squeeze the chest side to side and front to back.

3. If the puppy is still not breathing, give artificial respiration. Place your mouth over the newborn's nose and mouth and blow a puppy-sized puff of air into his lungs. Overdoing it can rupture his lungs; blow just enough that his chest rises. Repeat three or four times.

4. If the puppy is still not breathing, continue to alternate artificial respiration with stimulation of the body and manipulation of the chest. Keep this up as long as you can feel a heartbeat.

The Blue Puppy

It had been a difficult delivery. When two little legs appeared at the vulva, we knew that the puppy was coming breech and "dry." When the next contraction pushed out his rump, we knew that the puppy was a large male. The next contraction produced no progress. The puppy was stuck.

Standing the bitch up and supporting her pelvis, Chris quickly added more lubrication to the vulva. Working on the theory that the head may be malpositioned in the birth canal, Chris grasped the skin over the puppy's rump and rotated him slightly, one way and then the other in an effort to dislodge the head. As the next contraction pushed at the puppy, Chris added steady traction by pulling on the skin of the back. The puppy was delivered. Since he was a particolor, it was obvious that he was starved for oxygen. He was blue all over and limp.

Chris quickly began to rub the puppy briskly. After a moment, he applied the bulb syringe to mouth and nostrils and then resumed rubbing. The puppy was still limp. When swinging him produced no response, Chris despondently laid the blue puppy on the table.

After thinking for a moment, Chris picked up the puppy and, cradling him in one big hand, bent his head over him. Covering the puppy's tiny mouth and nostrils with his own, he breathed into the puppy's lungs. He squeezed the little chest and breathed into the puppy's lungs again. Again and again, he alternated chest massage with respirations. Since I had eyes only for the puppy in his hand and did not think to look up at the clock, I do not know how long Chris worked over the puppy. Life came into him not with a rush of breath but slowly, almost imperceptibly. It was only after his body turned from blue to pink that we realized that our Patches (now Am. Ch. Patchouli Panda of Alan-Li) had been well and truly born at last.

Litter Size

Tibbie litters are usually small. Although a recent survey of U.S. breeders yielded an average litter size of 3.8, litters of five or six are common. A litter of ten healthy pups is the largest reported to me, but litters of one or two puppies from first-time dams are not unusual.

Shavarin's Azaleea, bred by Tiina Pentinmäki (Finland), with her first litter.

The average weight of a newborn ranges from about six to seven ounces. The largest reported to me was a single pup of 14 ounces that did not survive. Weight at birth does not seem to correlate to adult weight. A 4-ounce puppy of my own required no special care (other than assuring that he was not nudged away from the nipple by his larger siblings) and developed normally into a average-sized Tibbie.

The Big Deal

Becky Johnson (U.S.) vividly remembers her Lama's (Am. Ch. Deetree Lama of Tiara) first litter. When the puppy appeared, Mrs. Johnson's heart sank. The two little paws told her that the puppy was breech and "dry." Quickly grasping the legs, she tried to hold on as the contraction subsided but Lama yelped and startled her into letting go. The paws disappeared.

Ten minutes later, Lama began another contraction and once more the puppy's paws appeared. Certain that the puppy was already dead, Mrs. Johnson was determined that Lama's remaining pups would have a chance to live. Although she acknowledges that she was "rough" in her desperate struggle to deliver him, the breech puppy was born in perfect condition—not even blue. Mrs. Johnson was dumbfounded when the little creature, only moments after birth, tried to stand. Driven by instinct, the puppy struggled again and, by sheer force of will, stood on his wobbly legs. A frown on her face, Lama regarded the puppy skeptically from afar. He circled blindly, half crawling and half toddling, each circle bringing him closer and closer to Lama. When he touched her at last, Lama's body curled reflexively around him and, in that moment, she became a mother.

As it turned out, this precocious puppy was Lama's whole litter—an only puppy that weighed nine oz. Perhaps puppies who fight to come into the world are naturally endowed with extra big egos, and Lama's puppy was no exception. He forges through life, a mischievous glint in his eye, utterly confident that he is adored by everyone he meets. It is fitting that Mrs. Johnson named him "Big Deal" (Tiara's Big Deal), Dealer for short. Dealer lives with the Richard Dahlen family.

Before going on to newborn care, here is one more story about a whelping—this one slightly unusual—with a happy ending.

The Carpet Queen

After the fourth puppy in her litter was born, Glory (GB Ch. Kensing Glory Be) settled down to sleep. Since I could feel no other puppies, I concluded that Glory had finished whelping. Later, when I asked if she wanted to visit the garden, Glory agreed. Carrying her through the darkened drawing room, I recall knocking something off a low chair as we passed, but I did not pause.

Glory walked about in the garden, sniffing the air and gazing at the moon until I reminded her about her babies indoors. Back inside we went and, by the grace of God, I turned on the light to check what I thought had fallen off the chair. Unbelievably, a puppy, still in her sac and complete with afterbirth, was lying there on the carpet. Glory had no idea she'd produced a puppy at the time nor did her owner! My veterinary surgeon would not believe me either until he saw the mark on the carpet the next day.

Although somewhat small, the puppy was strong and well. Perhaps understandably, Glory took no interest in her. Fortunately, Peach (GB Ch. Kensing Peach), who pupped the next day, happily fostered the rather obviously named "Carpet Queen."

Contributed by Jane Lilley (U.K.)

CARING FOR MOTHERS AND PUPPIES

Helping a Tibbie dam raise a litter of healthy puppies is profoundly rewarding, but it is also a great responsibility. You must assure that each puppy your breeding program conceives has the best possible chance to be born and grow up healthy. As a cherished member of your family, the welfare of the dam is also a top priority. Despite your best efforts, nightmares do sometimes come true. But then there are also times when everything turns out all right...

Against All Odds

Bertha (GB Ch. Kensing Bertha Bear) is the sort of dog that is always on the wrong side of any closed door. She seldom haunts the kitchen with the other dogs. Instead, she materializes in the larder when the door has been shut, or she mysteriously appears in the bedroom. Is it because she is black and slips through the doors unnoticed? Or, is it because she is so strong and determined? All I know is that it is easier to give in to her because, if I try to shut her out, she slips in anyway.

Bertha was not a pretty puppy and never did much in the ring as a youngster. Although I took her to the Bath Championship Show simply for companionship, Bertha sparkled like a firecracker and went on to win the C.C. What a great day! I am not very emotional by nature, but I cried—perhaps with shock as I never thought of her as a big winner.... Tibetan Spaniels are expert at proving you wrong.

Bertha and I mutually decided it would be a good idea if she had puppies. She very much enjoyed the marrying part but was horrified by the result. Needless to add, she decided the puppies were to be born on my bed but when she started pushing in earnest I removed her downstairs to a cosy whelping bed—Madam didn't approve of this at all and stopped pushing. She won, of course, so after an hour we went back to my bed with towels and sheets of plastic underneath. The moment she was in situ, all systems turned to go again and she produced two male puppies with little trouble.

She loathed them! These two inconveniences interfered with her life and I had to remain with her constantly for the first 24 hours making sure she didn't swing them round, drop them behind the pillows or carry them round the bedroom. She calmed down after a few days but she never liked them although she fed them and washed them. They shone like fat chestnuts and never cried as they were permanently full, but their mother refused to stay with them. Fortunately, their kind Aunt Beano proved to be an excellent babysitter and gave them the love they lacked. One became GB Ch. Kensing Berkeley, the top-winning Tibetan Spaniel of 1992.

I swore never to mate Bertha again but three years later she insisted and again enjoyed her marriage to the same dog as before. She is nothing if not faithful, but I held my breath with dread at the outcome.

Eight weeks went by most peacefully and she was obviously in whelp, not hugely but quite comfortably. It all seemed too good to be true until a combination of ridiculous "if only" mistakes occurred that can happen however careful you think you are: four doors were left open (that never are); the same with the front gate and, idiotically, I had parked the car too far into the garage to allow easy access to the freezer from the kitchen. I nipped out of the front door into the garage to fetch something for supper—a recipe for disaster.

In-whelp bitches seem to be particularly protective and Bertha was no exception. She heard a Cairn walking past and, as in a horrible nightmare, flew like a black arrow out of the front gate directly into the path of an oncoming car, which knocked her over and onto the other side of the road. The elderly driver, who was not going fast, was most concerned and upset as was the owner of the Cairn.

By some miracle she seem-ed unhurt although she was screaming with fear and extremely shocked. I thought she would probably lose the puppies but could still feel a slight foetal movement five days later. She then started washing herself frantically and an ominous green discharge appeared....

Bertha and her daughter Golly.

On the night she was due, she became quieter and quieter. Since I have had two nasty experiences of primary [uterine] inertia, this quietness was frightening. Came the dawn and she looked thoroughly miserable but perked up a little when she started having contractions, which I could just feel but not actually see. After an hour, even these stopped so I rushed her to my veterinary surgeon. My clever vet suggested that we x-ray her just in case she had the complication of one large dead puppy. Mere minutes later all was revealed on the screen—not one but three puppies. We hoped that she would whelp naturally within a few hours with the help of oxytocin. I prayed.

In accordance with her wishes during her first whelping, Bertha was firmly established on my bed and, like a miracle, strong contractions started within half an hour of our arriving home. Two dead puppies arrived but I knew from the x-ray that there was a third to come. I prayed again and, a whole long hour and many strong contractions later, almost unbelievably a pair of obviously live hind legs appeared. After much encouragement and mutual straining, the miracle of all miracles arrived—a strong, vigorous black bitch! More of my tears of relief and delight soaked into Bertha's black head than I ever would have believed possible.

Quite contrary to her first litter, Bertha adored this stout miniature of herself and seldom left her for over six weeks. Good Golly—what else could she be *called?—was perhaps exceptionally fat since she was eating for three and so was rather backward as a young puppy. She rose unsteadily to her feet at four weeks and plopped fatly down again until six weeks when she insisted on trying to stagger about although her legs went all over the place. She finally walked properly at seven weeks and was only fully weaned, I am embarrassed to say, at thirteen weeks. We and her mother dote upon her and she is extremely spoilt—our miraculous black Golly. We never cease to be grateful for her existence, against all odds, and that she and her mother are very much alive and well....*

Now two black shadows slip through apparently closed doors instead of one.

Contributed by Jane Lilley (U.K.)

The green discharge that Bertha passed shortly before giving birth marked the separation of a placenta(s) and therefore the death of one or more of her puppies. That she delivered a healthy, full-term puppy in spite of the accident was, as Mrs. Lilley writes, against all odds.

Bringing Up a Litter

The breeder's objective is to improve the odds by actively managing the upbringing of a litter. You must:

- provide optimal conditions for growth and social development, and
- monitor the pups and their mother frequently.

Environmental factors (e.g., temperature), disease prevention and nutrition of the mother and puppies are all within your control.

Environmental Temperature

Since a puppy cannot regulate its own body temperature until he is a month old, environmental temperature is a critical aspect of managing a litter. Many puppies are lost to hypothermia (chilling) or hyperthermia (overheating) (discussed later in this section). Failure to maintain optimal temperature may bring on an array of problems including dehydration, hypoglycemia and seizures. All of these conditions are discussed later in this chapter.

Assure that the mother provides warmth and that the puppies remain huddled in a normal manner. Control the ambient temperature of the room and eliminate drafts. Provide a supplemental heat source if the above measures are inadequate.

During the first week of life, maintain a temperature of about 85° F in the whelping box. During the 2nd and 3rd week, lower the temperature to 80° F. During the 4th and subsequent weeks, gradually lower the temperature to 70°-75° F. Maintain humidity of 55%-65%. When the puppies are about a month old and able to regulate their body temperature, you may move them from the whelping box to a puppy pen (discussed later).

If the puppies do not huddle, these suggested temperatures may be too high. If you suspect illness, raise the temperature by 5° F.

Feeding During Lactation

While she is nursing a litter, a Tibbie mother requires up to three times more calories. That is because her body needs up to 300% more energy to maintain her own weight and state of health as well as to make milk for her puppies. Her dietary requirements peak when the puppies are three to four weeks old.

Continue to feed the dam a premium dog food formulated for growth and reproduction until the pups are weaned. Increase her intake to three times the amount she ate before she became pregnant, divided into three or four meals per day. Also, provide plenty of fresh water at all times. Feeding the dam in the vicinity of the whelping box (so that the puppies observe their mother eating) may help in weaning. For information on the dam's diet while you are weaning the puppies, see the discussion of weaning.

Generally speaking, supplementation during lactation is not necessary if the dam is fed a premium food. However, a medical problem may require dietary measures to support the dam or puppies.

Maintaining the Whelping Box

Although an attentive dam keeps her nest and puppies as clean as possible, help her out by changing the bedding at least once each day. The best bedding is white toweling atop a layer of absorbent material. The towels prevent contact between the heating pad and the puppies' tender skin, a cause of hyperthermia. Never use bedding materials that puppies may inhale or swallow.

Assure that the puppies' bodies, including the anal area, are kept clean. Pre-moistened commercial baby wipes or a soft cloth (such as gauze) moistened with warm water are handy for this purpose.

Disease-Related Precautions

Take precautions to prevent disease introduced from outside. Do not allow visitors other than the family for the first couple of weeks. Since parvovirus can be carried in on shoes, do not allow anyone access to the puppies without removing outdoor shoes. (This includes you and your family as well as other visitors.) In fact, I do not allow anyone to enter the house with their outdoor shoes on. Further, no one should handle the puppies without first washing the hands.

Monitoring Newborns

To effectively monitor mother and puppies during the first few weeks of life, most breeders keep the whelping box in their bedrooms where they can hear any sounds of distress as well as visually check on the litter.

Make sure that each pup is nursing strongly and receiving adequate nourishment. Be on guard that no pup is rejected or neglected by his dam or deprived by the competition of larger or stronger littermates. The strongest indicator of adequate nourishment and status of puppy health is daily weight gain. Weigh each pup daily and record the weights. Use a gram scale because it is more precise. Watch for signs that the puppies are achieving developmental milestones.

Happy, healthy puppies rarely cry; when they do, it does not last very long. Always check on puppies that cry. It may be a simple, easily solved problem such as a puppy wedged behind his dam where he cannot nurse or one frustrated by his inability to climb over rumple in the towel. On the other hand, crying could be a sign of a serious, maybe life-threatening, problem such hunger, cold or illness.

Sleeping Tibbie puppies tend to rest in a myriad of positions—on their backs, sides or abdomens. However, do not allow a newborn puppy to rest on his abdomen for prolonged periods. Place him on his side or back. *(See Flat Puppy Syndrome)*

Monitoring the Dam

Look for signs that the dam is adequately nourished and that she does not suffer from any postpartum illness. Observe how much she eats, check her breasts daily and assure that her discharges are normal. If she had a Caesarian section, taking her temperature and cleaning the incision are also necessary. Observe her behavior toward her litter.

Handling Puppies

Even at a tender age, healthy Tibbie pups are surprisingly mobile. A newborn puppy propels himself by pulling with the forelegs and pushing with the hindlegs, his nose guiding him toward his mother. The toweling in the whelping box gives him good footing. Clip the sharp tips of the puppies' nails so that they do

---

PUPPY MILESTONES

TIME FRAME*	WHAT HAPPENS
2-3 days	umbilical stump drops off
4 days	flexor (fetal) position changes to relaxed position
4-6 days	reflexes that control blood pressure and shivering develop
7-10 days	birth weight doubles
10-16 days	eyes and ears open, ear leathers drop
15-16 days	stand
15-21 days	tails go up, walk
21 days	control elimination, first bark
4 weeks	able to maintain body temperature, first worming
4-6 weeks	baby teeth come in
5-7 weeks	weaning
6-8 weeks	first immunizations, testicles can be felt**
16-20 weeks	half adult weight

*Time frames are approximate.
**Testicles may descend from birth up to six months, but they are sometimes difficult to feel in tiny puppies.

not become entangled in the toweling or injure the dam's breasts as they nurse.

A newborn puppy's physical and social development is enhanced by frequent handling. Caress and cuddle them gently. Note whether the puppy's responses and body temperature appear to be normal.

Give older puppies plenty of opportunity to play with you and their littermates. Introduce chew toys, fuzzy toys and other forms of stimulation. When they are immunized, begin socialization by exposing them to many different sights and sounds, including people of all shapes and sizes. Assure that all these experiences are positive. (See Chapter 10.)

Isolating the Mother and Pups

If other Tibbies live in the house, keep them away from the mother and pups. Although some Tibbie mothers are quite tolerant of other Tibbies, this is not always the case. When Bambi, owned by Debra Bennett (U.S.), delivered her first litter, an older and more experienced bitch in the house decided that Bambi was not sufficiently attentive to her puppies. A quarrel ensued when the older bitch tried to get into the nest and nurse the pups. Thereafter, Mrs. Bennett took care to keep the bitches apart. However, once Bambi's pups were gone, the two bitches again became fast friends!

Some breeders report that the sires and other household males are interested in and tolerant of the puppies, while others report that males have little interest in or, worse, are intolerant of boisterous youngsters. The male's level of interest/tolerance may depend on his ancestry. One of my males, Shen, simply adores babies of all kinds. When he hears a puppy squeaking, chick peeping or kitten mewing, he clamors to reach them so that he can stand watch over them—a very endearing scene.

Maintaining a Diary

Record weights, medications given, physical and behavioral observations, attainment of developmental milestones and anything else which may prove helpful in a daily diary. These diaries are not only useful for monitoring the day-to-day progress of each puppy in a litter, but also for comparing current and past litters. In the event of an illness, they are also handy for providing accurate information to your veterinarian.

Normal Newborns

A normal, well-hydrated newborn Tibbie has a moist nose and mouth. The skin over his shoulders springs back into place when you pinch it up into a "tent" with your thumb and forefinger. Pinkish gums and paws tell you that he is well-oxygenated, and plumpness says that he is well-nourished. He feels warm and wiggly in your hand. His coat is short, smooth and sleek. The eyes and ears are closed, and the ear leathers point up instead of flopping over. The tail is carried down instead of up in a curl.

The healthy puppy's strongest instincts are to suckle vigorously and to "root" (as a means of finding his mother and siblings). Almost from birth, he is able to stretch, roll and crawl. He yawns and squeaks but rarely cries. He promptly falls asleep between meals.

Newborns need to nurse frequently. Since he processes fluids at twice the rate of an adult, a newborn is very susceptible to rapid dehydration if he takes in too little milk or he loses too much fluid, as in a case of diarrhea. Furthermore, newborns cannot eliminate without stimulation.

Puppies should gain weight every day at rate equal to one to one and one-half grams per pound of expected adult weight. That translates to 12 to 23 grams per day, based on adult Tibbie weights of 12 to 15 pounds. Each puppy should double his birth weight between seven and ten days old.

Newborns are unable to regulate their own body temperature until they are about one month old. The newborn's body temperature is 94° F and rises to 99° F by the end of the first week. After the first month, the puppy's temperature reaches the adult norm of 100°-102.5° F. The reflexes that control blood pressure, blood flow and shivering do not develop until the fourth to sixth day. Similarly, the heart rate and respirations of a newborn gradually increase until they reach adult rates.

A future sable is born a dark chestnut brown, sometimes almost black, with black nose and eye rims. Since he lightens as he grows, it is impossible to predict his adult shade based on his color at birth. A particolor is born with a pink nose and eye rims, which should soon turn black, and patches of color that will probably lighten.

Normal Dams

For 12-24 hours after a natural delivery, a Tibbie dam passes a dark greenish discharge. During the next two to three weeks, the discharge is reddish. After a Caesarian section, the dam may pass a bright red discharge for several hours followed by the usual dark greenish discharge. Normal breasts are slightly warm, full and soft.

Most Tibbie mothers feed their nurselings faithfully. Soon after their first meal, the dam should lick the puppies to stimulate elimination. If she does not, let her watch as you massage a puppy with a cotton ball moistened with warm water until he defecates and urinates. Offer her the remaining puppies to lick and make sure they all eliminate. The dam also cleans up the nest.

Initially, the dam stays with her puppies more or less constantly. She is reluctant to leave the whelping box, even to tend to her own needs. She keeps an eye on them whenever she takes a break.

While the foregoing description is by-and-large true, a first-time Tibbie mother may not be as dedicated as an experienced dam. Although they perform their maternal duties, some appear uninterested in their puppies. A few neglect to feed and/or clean their offspring without reminders from you. Even if they take excellent care of their puppies, many (perhaps most) first-time Tibbie mothers show signs of anxiety. An inexperienced dam may seem unsure how to handle her puppies or become upset by their normal noises and movement. Although some dams are protective and allow no one near their pups, no cases of maternal aggression toward puppies were reported to me.

A Tale of Two Mothers

When she delivered her first litter, Kissie's programming required her to nurse and clean up after her whelps. She performed these duties efficiently but without enthusiasm or affection. And so, when her pups were five weeks old, she declared success and marched off without a second thought or glance back. From that day forward, she never expressed the slightest interest in her offspring.

As her mother before her, Kissie's daughter Ciana performed her maternal duties but, unlike Kissie, Ciana was a selfless paragon of motherhood. As the weeks passed, her unstinting care of her babies, the constant nursing and ceaseless fussing, took their toll. A veritable martyr, she grew painfully thin. Her coat, formerly rich and glowing, became lusterless and thin. Worried, I began to remove Ciana from the nest for several hours and offered the five-week-old pups weaning formula. Ciana would have none of it. Crying and whining incessantly, she escaped from the dog room by wiggling under a gate and made her way to the puppy pen where she clawed frantically at the ex-pen while the equally vocal pups shrieked for her.

My soft-hearted husband occasionally gave in to Ciana's pleas and allowed her to nurse. But this concession, though well-meant, only stimulated her to let down more milk and prolonged the ordeal. At eight weeks, she was still nursing. At ten weeks, the pups were eating dry puppy food on their own, but she still fought to nurse them. Their sharp puppy teeth raised welts on her belly and left her nipples black and blue.

A normal bitch keeps a close watch over her pups, as does Fin. Ch. Chu-Shun Lejja owned by Tiina Pentinmäki (Finland).

As I write this, her pups are twelve weeks old, and Ciana still exhibits a mother's concern for their well-being. Whenever they enter the room, she rushes to sniff, nuzzle and lick them. Ears alert for any sound of distress, she hovers nearby or watches over them from her perch on the sofa back. Whenever a guest scoops one up for a bit of socialization, she dances anxiously around the interloper's feet until the pup is safely returned to the floor. She would still nurse if she could, but, lacking milk, she occasionally regurgitates a meal for them.

Recalling her utter contentment and eyes shining with pride as her nurselings cuddled to her, is it any wonder that we call her our little "Madonna of Tibbies"?

Veterinary Care

Take the new mother and her puppies to the veterinarian within 24 hours of the birth. This trip requires logistical planning so that the puppies remain with their mother, warm and secure. In cold weather, bring along a hot water bottle as a supplemental heat source.

During this examination, the veterinarian observes the new mother's discharge, checks her breasts,

PUPPY DIARY

Thursday (Day 17) — Two of the four puppies are wobbling around on all fours, and one tries to escape the whelping box. Although their eyes appear well-focused, they do not seem to hear well.

Friday (Day 18) — Spotting Mom outside the whelping box, the pups begin to jostle and whimper for a feeding. Suddenly, I hear a little woof, not a puppy squeal but a definite bark, issue forth from one of the puppies. They walked a bit more today—more like staggering than walking. I took them out of the whelping box and they toddled purposefully toward their mother for a meal. One promptly pee'd on the carpet. Little tails are coming up, and little ears flop down more than they stand up. Yawns and stretches and long naps are the order of the day. They sleep on their tummies or side or, more often, on their backs. So dear.

Saturday (Day 26) — The puppies' frequent spurts of activity all day, in such sharp contrast with their activity level yesterday, leads me to believe that a quantum leap in their development occurred overnight. They launch themselves at one another, bowling their playmates over and wrestling while trilling and squealing. Chomping one another is great fun. I noticed one male place a dominant "paw" on the head of another to subdue him.

Tuesday (Day 29) — Today is deworming day. The veterinarian ooh'ed and aah'ed over each puppy. "No extra charge," she laughed. After their doses of dewormer, each puppy passed several disgusting masses of white worms. I hear Ciana nursing them in the night. They sound like little piglets.

Wednesday (Day 30) — Perfectly aligned, pearly white puppy teeth are very much in evidence, and they have begun to chew on the toweling and sides of the whelping box. Although they show little or no interest in the soft weaning food, they gnaw on the dry kibble in Ciana's dish. Practicing running is fun, but the foreparts and hindparts are not well-coordinated. They plunge into a run, and when the hindlegs tangle with the forelegs, they stumble, tumble, recover and carry on. When confined to their puppy pen, they are very keen on escaping. They drape their forelegs over the lowest barrier, where their mother enters and exits, and struggle and struggle to lift themselves up and over. No one has made the escape yet, but they soon will.

(Above) Tamashing Dumra Changku ("Wolfje"), bred by Thea Heltzel and owned by Cobi Greve (Netherlands).

Curiosity is a sign of the Tibetan Spaniel's intelligence as this Nittni puppy, bred by Scott and Karen Chamberlain, demonstrates. *Scott Chamberlain ills.*

Saturday (Day 33)	*The puppies seem to be more interested in my presence. They lift their forepaws in greeting when I approach and, for the first time today, one struck a play pose. Coordination improves each day, and two stood to box with one another in typical Tibbie manner. They ate their weaning food with gusto but still prefer to crunch on the puppy kibble. Ciana is pitiful looking. Her coat has thinned due to hormonal changes, and her breasts appear to be irritated by their shark-like teeth and nails.*
Monday (Day 49)	*I began crate training today. They napped for two hours in their crate and promptly "did their business" upon emerging.*
Thursday (Day 52)	*Ciana is still desperate to nurse her puppies. She sits atop the sofa, watching them, and dashes over to feed them the moment that I take them out. They are chewing fiends. No shoe, shoelace or toe is safe. Pencils become mulch and newspapers are shredded. It really takes two people to watch them when all four are out.*
Tuesday (Day 57)	*I have named them all tentatively now—Cubby, Socky, Bobby, and the female Sassy. Having received their second series of immunizations last night, today will be their first day outside, a momentous occasion for us all. I lower each to the ground. They tremble, but three soon take a few tentative steps, stretching their necks to their full length and sniffing the new world around them. One puppy, however, remains glued where I had put him down, imploring me with his eyes. Cubby delivers the first stool. I crow and praise him, which encourages Bobby to follow suite. Sassy, much more hesitant, tiptoes onto the gravel and likewise performs. Turning my attention to Socky, I kneel on the gravel and hold out my arms encouraging him to "Come" in the happy voice. He gingerly places one paw onto the gravel for which he receives my profuse praise. A second paw touches the gravel. More praise. He's on his way. A few minutes later, I turn my attention away from the other puppies playing to see that Socky, like his littermates before him, has defecated on the gravel after which he gives a miniature demonstration of scratching and gravel-kicking worthy of an grown male.*
Saturday (Day 68)	*The first of our puppies goes to his new home today. We are subdued. Which puppy is best for this home? We have struggled with the decision. Since the puppy testing indicates that Socky is so highly trainable, we choose him. I am confident about my choice, but parting with a puppy is agony for me. When the new owner and her daughter arrive, I introduce them to Socky. When, after only a moment or two, he settles contentedly into the little girl's lap, I smile in my heart. Tibbies always know.*

The charm of a Tibbie puppy is exemplified by Braeduke Miu, owned by Primoz Peer (Slovenia).

Emma Miccio, daughter of Michael and Teresa Miccio, with "Baron." *Chris Miccio photo*

takes her temperature and looks for other signs of problems. An injection of oxytocin assures that no puppies, placentas or fragments that could cause an infection remain in the uterus and helps the uterus return to normal size as quickly as possible. If she had a Caesarian section, her stitches are removed when the puppies are ten days old.

The veterinarian also evaluates each puppy's state of development and nourishment. He or she listens to the heart and lungs, assures that the puppy is well-hydrated and well-oxygenated, checks the umbilical stump and examines the puppy for obvious congenital defects, such as hernias and cleft palates. Dewclaws may be removed when the puppies are two or three days old. During a followup visit when the pups are a month old, the veterinarian assesses the puppies' progress and deworms them.

When they are six to eight weeks old, the pups receive their first vaccination. This is the age at which the immunity they received from their mother begins to wear off and they may be at risk, so it is important not to delay! Although immunization schedules vary, the pups will probably require three or four sets of vaccinations, the last when they are about sixteen weeks old. For information about vaccinations, see Chapter 11.

Before placing them in new homes, each puppy should receive a complete physical examination by a veterinarian. At this age, congenital defects such as heart murmur, undescended testicles and hernias are identifiable.

Puppy Pen

If you are able to maintain an environmental temperature of at least 70° F, discontinue use of the supplemental heat source when the puppies are about four weeks old. This coincides with a healthy, well-developed puppy's ability to regulate his body temperature without outside help. You may wish to change from the whelping box arrangement to a puppy pen setup so that the puppies, who are now able to walk, have more room to exercise.

The minimum requirements for a puppy pen are:

- a "den" for sleeping,
- room to play,
- a place to eat and drink, and
- good footing.

As with the whelping box, each breeder has a different idea of the perfect puppy pen. You may try several arrangements until you hit on the one that works best for you.

My own puppy pen is made up of a wire crate (the "den") that exits to an "ex-pen" (collapsible, portable metal pen) with which I can adjust the size and shape of the play area. Make sure that the puppies cannot poke their heads through the bars in any pen you use.

The floor should be a material that provides good footing so that the puppies can practice walking and running without harm to growing bone and fragile joint structures. I do not recommend placing the puppy pen on a carpeted area. Since it is difficult to clean all traces of odor from carpet, padding and subfloor, the puppies may learn to eliminate on carpet (not to mention the annoyance of constantly cleaning it up). Instead, find an easily cleaned or machine washable material such as a *textured* vinyl mat or area rug to place under the puppy pen. Similarly, when you let them out of the puppy pen to play, make sure they have good footing.

Since I set up my puppy pen before training the puppies to "do their business" outside, I teach them to "go" on newspaper temporarily. Most Tibbie puppies learn quickly; it seems to be almost instinctual with them. Place several thicknesses of newspaper at the end or in the corner of the puppy pen furthest from the "den." Praise them, but not too much, because you will soon want them to learn to "go" outside *(see Crate Training)*.

A trio of Tibbie puppies play outside. *Scott Chamberlain photo*

Weaning

While trying to wean a litter of her puppies, Joan Child (U.S.) remembers that their mother, Bes (Am. Ch. Bim's Secunda Bes), was so frantic that she fought to get in the whelping box and, failing that, tried to feed her puppies by regurgitating her dinner. Regurgitation is not uncommon among Tibbie mothers. Long-time breeders are often heard to say that Tibbie mothers are "feral," especially when, like Bes, they are not far removed from their Tibetan origins. In regurgitating partially digested food for their pups, these Tibbie mothers behave much as a mother wolf does.

Every Tibbie breeder surveyed concurs that weaning at three weeks (sometimes mentioned in dog books) is much too early for Tibbies. Beyond that, there is little agreement. Some complain that weaning is difficult while others swear that it is easy. They also differ on when and how the weaning is accomplished. Some advocate starting to wean at about four to five weeks; others prefer eight or nine weeks. My advice is to offer weaning formula when the puppies first show interest in their mother's food. This may be as early as four to five weeks while their teeth are erupting. Place the weaning formula right in the whelping box or puppy pen. After watching their mother eat it, clever little Tibbie puppies soon get the idea and begin to lap.

Although some puppies begin to crunch (or at least gnaw) dry food straight away, most prefer a semi-liquid weaning formula. Every breeder has a favorite recipe. A simple recipe is to mix a *premium* canned puppy food or *premium* ground dry puppy food with puppy milk replacer (either canned liquid or reconstituted from powdered form). Another recipe calls for equal parts of baby rice cereal, premium dry puppy food ground in the blender, and ground boiled chicken moistened with evaporated milk or puppy milk replacer. Many favor adding cottage cheese for texture and flavor. Whatever the formula, mix it to the consistency of slightly thick soup so that the puppies can lap it and warm it up as you would for a baby.

Wean puppies gradually. Abrupt, forced weaning can result in malnourished puppies and a dam with mastitis (galactostasis). If you decide to wean the puppies at your pace, it may take as little as a week. If you allow the dam to proceed at her own pace, she may take much longer—several weeks in fact. There are pro's and con's to both methods. Although letting the dam take charge may be kinder to the pups, it is a drain on her. Further, the absence of a feeding "schedule" impedes crate training.

To wean the puppies, remove the dam from her puppies (out of sight and hearing) for a few hours— between four to eight hours depending on how quickly you want to wean them. Since the dam has been busy with her puppies for over a month, now is a good time to take her for a long walk, play with her or groom her. Meanwhile, place the weaning formula in a low saucer or similar dish made of chew-resistant material, and press each puppy's mouth (not nose!) into the formula so that a little gets on the tongue. After they have eaten some formula (and probably rolled in or walked through it as well), bring their mother back to them. Allow her to finish up the weaning formula and nurse her puppies. As you increase the duration of the separations and the puppies increase the amount of formula they eat, decrease the number of times you allow the dam to nurse each day. When all of the puppies are consistently lapping up the weaning formula, gradually transition to a less sloppy form that requires chewing as well as lapping. Eventually, transition to dry puppy food soaked in or moistened with water and then to regular dry puppy food.

While you wean the puppies, you also transition the mother to her pre-pregnancy diet. As she nurses less, reduce the amount of food and the number of meals you give her each day. When she is no longer nursing, gradually revert to a premium food formulated for adult maintenance.

A Head Start

A breeder whose Tibbie puppy has only one or two accidents (or none!) after going to a new home not only enhances his or her own reputation as a breeder but also the reputation of the Tibetan Spaniel breed. Giving young puppies a head start on crate training is easy and surely one of the nicest things a breeder can do for the future owners of his or her Tibbies.

Start crate training at a point that coincides with placing the puppies on scheduled feedings during weaning. Depending on when you start weaning, this may be anywhere from about five to seven weeks old. First, feed the puppies and wait for them to eliminate. Then, leave them in their closed crate for a couple of hours. Covering the crate may help them to settle down for a nap. When you release them, see to it that they "go." Praise them profusely for doing their business.

It is not safe for unvaccinated puppies to set paw anywhere where they may come in contact with canine diseases. For example, canine parvovirus, which can be carried on the soles of shoes, is almost always deadly to puppies before they are immunized against it. Consequently, most breeders are rightfully cautious about allowing puppies that have not been vaccinated to go anywhere that strange dogs, animals or people may have passed. Although it is preferable to train puppies to "go" outdoors from the very beginning, do so only if there is a completely safe location. Otherwise, train them to "go" on newspaper in the puppy pen until they are immunized; then remove the paper and re-train them to eliminate outdoors. Chapter 10 explains more about crate training.

Signs of Possible Health Problems in Mothers

Abnormal Discharges—Some discharges following delivery are normal, but abnormal discharges may indicate serious illnesses such as metritis.

NORMAL
- greenish discharge (not malodorous) for 24 hours after delivery of last puppy
- brownish-red or sero-sanguinous discharge (not malodorous) during four to six weeks after a natural delivery
- bright red discharge for several hours after a Caesarian section

ABNORMAL
- dark green discharge that persists 48-72 hours or more after last puppy's delivery
- brownish-red or sero-sanguinous discharge that lasts over four to six weeks
- any malodorous discharge
- bright red discharge that lasts more than a few hours after a Caesarian section

Eclampsia—Also called milk fever, postpartum hypocalcemia or puerperal tetany, eclampsia is the failure of the body's calcium regulatory mechanism that causes low levels of calcium in the blood. In simple terms, the dam's diet and bones cannot replace the calcium lost in the milk she produces for her puppies. It may occur shortly after birth, but is more usual when the puppies reach three to four weeks old because this is the peak of lactation. Although some small breeds are predisposed to eclampsia, especially when a large litter is delivered, it has been suggested that some Tibbie families may be more susceptible than others. Eclampsia may also be the result of misguided attempts to supplement calcium during pregnancy or of inadequate diet during lactation.

The signs are varied and include high fever (sometimes over 105° F), restlessness, anxiety, rapid breathing, panting, salivating, whining, stretched or pinched look to the face, pacing, stiff-legged gait, seizures and tremors.

Eclampsia is a life-threatening emergency. Get veterinary help. Treatment includes rapid cooling and intravenous calcium. Relapse is possible, and several treatments may be required.

Mastitis (Galactostasis)—An inflammation of the breast in which the breast becomes caked with milk (inside, not outside) as a result of too much milk and/or too little nursing. Galactostasis is one of two forms of mastitis.

Affected breasts are swollen, painful, feverish and hard to the touch. Galactostasis may be caused by weaning too abruptly or by underusing breasts. (Puppies sometimes favor the lower breasts and ignore the others.) To avoid this type of mastitis, assure that all breasts are nursed equally and wean the puppies gradually. Treatment for galactostasis includes massage and warm compresses and, when possible, expressing the milk. Baby aspirin dosed at 5-10 mg./lb. helps to relieve discomfort and reduce inflammation.

Mastitis (Septic)—An infection, septic mastitis is usually caused by bacteria entering the breast through a scratch or puncture inflicted by the puppies. The dam is at greatest risk during the first week after the birth.

Like galactostasis, the affected breasts become swollen and painful; unlike galactostasis, the breasts turn reddish-blue and the milk becomes bloody, yellowish and/or stringy. Moreover, the dam may show signs of severe illness (e.g., appetite loss, restlessness, fever) and neglect her puppies. Measures to prevent septic mastitis include trimming the pups' nails and cleaning the nest. Treatment includes oral antibiotics, massage and warm compresses. Since the milk may contain bacteria, your veterinarian may recommend that temporary bottle-feeding. If that is not feasible, watch the puppies carefully for signs of illness.

Uterine Infection (Metritis)—A bacterial infection that occurs usually in the first week after birth, metritis is not reported significantly among Tibbie mothers. The usual cause is retained placenta, puppies or fragments thereof. Difficult or prolonged labor is also implicated.

Signs include depression, fever, smelly brownish or reddish-brown discharge and neglect of puppies. This is a severe illness that may cause shock, dehydration, toxemia and death. Intravenous fluids, antibiotics, Prostaglandin $F2_{alpha}$ and, if necessary, ovariohysterectomy are the usual treatments.

Health Problems in Newborns and Young Puppies

Illness and death of puppies is certainly a heartbreaking aspect of breeding. Puppy mortality among all dogs is between 10% and 30% from birth to weaning, and three-quarters of these deaths occur in the first two weeks of life. A recent survey of U.S. breeders reported 9% mortality of Tibbie puppies.

It is important to necropsy all dead puppies to determine the cause of death. Otherwise, we will never know with certainty what killed them and whether we can prevent such deaths in future puppies.

Like puppies of other breeds, Tibbies may suffer from congenital defects, parasites and bacterial and viral diseases. The chance of any of these problems occurring is reduced by selecting healthy parents and providing the mother with good prenatal care. Good management practices, such as those discussed earlier in this section, also reduce mortality and illness in newborn puppies.

In all breeds combined, congenital defects cause few puppy deaths. Some defects are very serious, but others either have no effect on the puppy's well-being or impair him minimally. Signs of possible trouble in puppies are:

- continuous crying or restlessness,
- inability to nurse or leakage of milk from nose,
- separation from dam or littermates,
- resting in flexor (fetal) position beyond three days of age,
- regurgitation,
- bruising or poor color of the skin,
- dehydration,
- any discharge,
- lethargy,
- signs of infection (e.g., fever).

Unless the puppy is already overheated *(see Hyperthermia)*, sick puppies usually benefit from raising the temperature of his environment by 5° F until you are able to get veterinary help.

Cleft Palate—A hole in the roof of the mouth, the cleft palate is an opening between the mouth and the nasal passages. Severity varies; the defect may be obvious when you look inside the mouth, or the first sign may be milk dripping from the nose. A puppy with a cleft palate may develop pneumonia caused by inhaling milk. Surgical repair of a cleft palate is sometimes possible.

Although it may occur in any breed, cleft palate is associated with other brachycephalic (short-faced) breeds such as the Pekingese and Bulldog. It may be hereditary in the Tibetan Spaniel, and you should consider this fact in breeding Tibbies whose lines have produced puppies with cleft palate. Chapter 11 discusses the elongated soft palate, another palate-related disorder of brachycephalic breeds.

Dehydration—Too little intake or loss of fluid, often resulting from diarrhea or ineffective nursing, is a life-threatening condition for puppies. The main signs of dehydration in a small puppy are dry gums and nose and yellow (concentrated) urine. "Tenting" of the skin, weakness and crying are also indicators. To check whether a puppy's skin "tents," pinch a fold of loose skin at the top of the shoulder blades between your thumb and forefinger and lift it up and away from the body. Then let go and watch what happens. If the skin remains "tented" or slides down slowly instead of springing back into place, the puppy is dehydrated.

Diarrhea is a common cause of dehydration. Dehydrated puppies are usually hypothermic and/or hypoglycemic, too. This is a life-threatening condition; get veterinary help. Treatment includes warming the puppy and restoring fluid levels with subcutaneous injections of warm sterile fluid. Until veterinary help is available, keep the puppy warm and give drops of fluid on the tongue, taking care that the puppy does not inhale the liquid. Water may help, but an electrolyte solution made for babies is preferable. To counteract possible hypoglycemia, smear a drop of warmed corn syrup on the gum.

Diarrhea—A condition characterized by frequent loose stools, diarrhea in puppies often results from overfeeding, parasites or hypothermia. Other causes are excess solid or fat in the diet, toxins or parvovirus. Mild diarrhea in nursing puppies may also result from normal hormonal changes in their mother. It bears mentioning that a normal puppy stool resulting from an all-milk diet is soft but "formed" in contrast to the "loose" stool of diarrhea.

Because they process fluids so rapidly, puppies with diarrhea are susceptible to rapid dehydration and hypoglycemia. Prolonged diarrhea is life-threatening. Get veterinary help, and remember to take a fecal sample. Besides identifying and treating the underlying problem, treatment involves the same measures as for dehydration and hypoglycemia. Until veterinary help is available, keep the puppy warm, give drops of fluid on the tongue and smear a drop of warmed corn syrup on the gums.

Fading Puppy Syndrome—A term applied to the condition of a puppy that seems to be healthy at birth but then fails to gain weight, weakens and stops nursing. Why puppies fade is not known; the syndrome may be the result of a combination of factors such as underdevelopment of the fetus (physiological immaturity), birth defects, hypothermia, dehydration, nutrient deficiency and so on.

This is an emergency. Get veterinary help. Treatment focuses on stabilizing the puppy using the same measures described for the various signs of the condition such as dehydration, hypothermia and hypoglycemia (all discussed in this section). Oxygen therapy may also be needed. Following this treatment, a liquid nutritional supplement may help build the strength of a fading puppy.

Flat Puppy Syndrome—A condition in which the chest appears flat, an affected puppy is also called a "swimmer." Flattening of the rib cage may progress to the point where breathing is impaired by lack of room for the lungs to expand normally. An overweight puppy may be more prone to this condition. A lone puppy may also be more susceptible because he lacks physical interaction with littermates and because he, too, is often overweight. Heredity may play a role.

To help prevent flattening, keep puppies on nonslippery surfaces where they are able to stand and walk more easily. It has been suggested that "rolling" a puppy side to side once or twice a day may help, too. If the puppy's chest appears to be flattening, taping the forelegs together, in a natural position, prevents the puppy from resting on his stomach and helps him stand.

Hernia (Umbilical)—A weak spot in the muscles of the abdominal wall, an umbilical (navel) hernia occurs at the site where the umbilical cord attached to the puppy. It looks like a bulge under the skin. A common occurrence in brachycephalic breeds, umbilical hernias are likewise seen in many Tibbie puppies.

Most umbilical hernias in Tibbies are small. Some of these small hernias close spontaneously by the time the puppy is about six months old, but one that does not close on its own is easily repaired surgically. The repair usually takes place when the puppy is spayed or neutered. Allow a puppy with a small umbilical hernia to exercise normally. Do not bind the hernia in an effort to "cure" it. Have large umbilical hernias repaired immediately. When in doubt whether repair is needed, consult your veterinarian.

Hernia (Inguinal)—Another type of hernia, the inguinal affects the groin. It is rare in Tibbies but more serious. Surgical repair is the only treatment.

Heterochromia—A discoloration of the iris, some Tibbies are born with heterochromia. The iris may be a wholly different color than dark brown, or a brown iris may contain one or more spots of another color. The other color is often blue or white but may also be a lighter shade of brown. Heterochromia is related to pigment loss, and particolors are affected more often than other Tibbies.

Although undesirable from the showing/breeding point of view, heterochromia is not painful and does not impair vision. However, if a change in iris color occurs at any time after birth, consult a veterinarian.

Hydrocephalus—A condition in which fluid collects in the brain, hydrocephalus causes enlargement or exaggerated doming of the head. Other signs include lack of alertness, impaired vision and seizures. Part of the brain may be underdeveloped (cerebellar hypoplasia). Eye problems associated with hydrocephalus include microphthalmia and cataracts (see Chapter 11).

Medications and surgery to relieve the buildup of fluid are possible treatments. Sadly, the prognosis is poor, and affected dogs may be mentally impaired.

Hypoglycemia—Lack of adequate glucose (sugar) in the blood is called hypoglycemia. Unless they nurse frequently, puppies are susceptible because of their high energy needs. Another cause is diarrhea. A hypoglycemic puppy may also be hypothermic and dehydrated. Hypoglycemia is confirmed by testing a drop of blood (from a toenail) using a glucometer. A normal reading is 80 to 120.

As an emergency measure, smear drops of warmed corn syrup on the puppy's gums to raise the level of glucose in the blood, but do not overdo it. Get veterinary help.

Hypothermia or Hyperthermia—Chilling or overheating are deadly problems for puppies under one month old, especially during the first week or two, because they cannot regulate their body temperature.

Hypothermia (chilling) is usually caused by lengthy separation of a puppy from its dam or littermates and/or failure of the backup heat source. A puppy that is flaccid and cool to the touch is hypothermic. Chilled puppies are often dehydrated, hypoglycemic, weak and anorectic, too. You must warm the puppy *gradually*. Do not use a heating pad. Instead, place the puppy against your body under your clothing to warm him while you prepare an "incubator" (such as my aquarium) warmed by heat sources such as a hot water bottle or towels warmed in the dryer. To counteract hypoglycemia and dehydration, smear a drop of warmed corn syrup on the gums and give him drops of water or electrolyte solution. Until his rectal temperature rises to at least 95° F, do not feed milk replacer or formula because the digestive system does not function while he is chilled. Watch over him. Turn him frequently and gently massage the skin to stimulate circulation. Get veterinary help as soon as possible.

Placing or allowing a puppy to rest directly on a heating pad is the usual cause of hyperthermia (overheating). The pad may also cause severe burns. If you choose to use a heating pad, cover it with toweling and monitor the surface temperature closely. To avoid hyperthermia, always give puppies a choice of temperature in the whelping box so that a puppy can crawl to a cooler area if he is too warm. Signs of hyperthermia include prolonged crying, bright red mucous membranes and separation from littermates. You must reduce the puppy's body temperature to 103° F within ten minutes. Rinse the puppy with cool water. Towel dry him and take his temperature. Repeat until the temperature returns to normal. Take care not to chill the

What every breeder hopes for—a loving home for his puppies. Mary Rose Tobin, daughter of Maureen Reisinger, cuddles "Toby."

puppy! When you return the puppy to the whelping box, continue to watch him closely. If any skin problems develop, the puppy may have a thermal burn; get veterinary help quickly.

Megaesophagus—Also called dilatation of the esophagus, megaesophagus is an enlargement of the tube that transports food from the mouth to the stomach. First noticed about the time of weaning, a puppy with a congenital megaesophagus regurgitates (not vomits) his food and, as a consequence, is small and weak. Pneumonia as a result of inhaling food is a common complication. It is unknown whether this defect is influenced by heredity.

Treatment consists of a diet that helps the puppy keep his food down. Eating small, frequent meals in an upright position (rather than bending the head down) seems to help, too. A surgical repair may be possible. Breeding a Tibbie with a megaesophagus is not recommended.

Parasites—Intestinal worms are common in all puppies—even when the mother was properly and regularly dewormed before she became pregnant. That is because worms encysted in the dam's tissues are "activated" by her hormones. The first deworming takes place at about four weeks of age. More information on parasites appears in Chapter 11.

Seizures—Convulsions in puppies between four and five weeks of age may be related to problems such as hypoglycemia or hyperthermia. Seizures may also result from numerous diseases and defects, such as liver disease, hydrocephalus or canine distemper. If you observe a puppy having a seizure, immediately smear warmed corn syrup on the gums. If you are sure that the puppy is not hyperthermic, warm him up. Get veterinary help. Further information about seizures appears in Chapter 11.

PLACING PUPPIES

After giving each puppy a good start in life, an ethical breeder's job is to place each puppy in a good home and to educate the new owners about caring for him.

Screening Guidelines

Beginning with the first phone call, an ethical breeder screens a potential buyer to determine if he or she will provide a good home. Many breeders comment that they rely on a "gut feeling" in deciding whether to place a puppy, but I suspect that this "feeling" is the result of knowing which questions to ask and long experience in sizing up people.

Screening varies depending on whether the potential buyer is seeking a Tibbie as pet, show prospect or breeding prospect. A good icebreaker is to ask the potential pet buyer why he or she is interested in a Tibetan Spaniel. His or her answer usually tells you how much the buyer knows about dogs in general, as well as Tibbies specifically. Be sure to ask questions in a tactful, courteous and friendly manner that reflects credit on the reputation of the Tibetan Spaniel and its breeders. Since many people may not realize that buying a Tibbie is like applying for a job, it may help to explain forthrightly that you must ask questions to make sure that the Tibbie goes to the best possible home. Other important facts to learn include:

- family (e.g., number and ages of children),
- other pets,
- residence (e.g., urban/rural, house/apartment), and
- lifestyle (e.g., adults work away from home, interests)

The answers to these questions help you form an impression of the buyer's suitability and gather information about the buyer's plans for taking care of the Tibbie. Situations such as those below require additional probing.

- When none of the adults has previously owned a dog, try to ascertain how knowledgeable they are and their interest in learning about dogs.
- When all of the adults work, determine what arrangements will be made to care for the puppy during the day.

- In a household with a small child(ren), consider whether the children understand how to treat a puppy.
- In a home without a fenced yard, find out how the puppy will be exercised.

It is a good policy to insist on a face-to-face interview with the prospective buyer before you decide to place the puppy. A meeting enables you to observe how the family interacts with dogs. Although a meeting may not be possible in all situations (especially in large countries where distances are prohibitive), try to arrange a meeting with the buyer at least once rather than ship a puppy to an unseen person.

Many buyers expect to view the litter and then choose a puppy. Since this is not usually possible, explain that it is in the buyer's best interest, as well as the Tibbie's, for you to make the match based on your experience and knowledge of each puppy's personality and activity level.

If you are selling a show/breeding prospect, the extent of the screening depends on whether the buyer is an established exhibitor/breeder or a novice. Determine the prospective buyer's previous experience in showing or breeding, if any. Ask why he or she is interested in showing/breeding Tibbies. Ask about his or her plans for the future and about his or her philosophy of breeding. Don't stop there! Visit his or her premises and observe existing breeding stock. Evaluate whether the buyer has the financial resources to carry on a serious showing/breeding program.

Avoid these buyers:

- someone giving the Tibbie as a surprise gift,
- people who have no knowledge of dogs and seem unwilling or unable to learn,
- people who seem intolerant of boisterousness,
- a parent who indicates that a child will be solely responsible for caring for the Tibbie,
- a buyer interested in making money.

Taking Care of Paperwork

Provide your buyer with a sales agreement, five-generation pedigree, registration form and health records. Explain the contents and purpose of each document.

The agreement that you and the buyer sign should:

- identify the Tibbie (e.g., registration number, tattoo, parents' names and registration numbers),
- spell out the terms of the agreement (e.g., purchase price, terms of payment, terms of ownership or co-ownership),

You owe it to your Tibbie puppies to take time and care to find just the right home for them. Lucas Meyer, son of Martha Rosner, holds his friend "Lita."

- explain your return policy (e.g., refund, replacement),
- provide a health guarantee and related stipulations (e.g., representations as to the health of the Tibbie, requirement for veterinary exam),
- state whether the Tibbie is a pet or show prospect,
- require spaying/neutering of Tibbies sold as pets, and
- require the buyer to give you first refusal in the event that he or she cannot keep the Tibbie for any reason and at any time.

Let me call your attention to two of these provisions. The first concerns spaying/neutering. Point out the requirement for neutering and spaying pet Tibbies and explain the grim facts: the fact that unneutered/unspayed Tibbies are at greater risk for dying from accidents, the fact that unneutered males eventually develop undesirable behaviors such as marking, the fact that unneutered/unspayed Tibbies are likely to develop diseases/disorders of the reproductive system such as prostate problems and breast cancer. Next, emphasize that your commitment to each puppy you produce is a lifelong one, that you will always be available for their questions and that you will always re-home a Tibbie that the buyer is unable to keep. Explain that you will inform the buyer of your whereabouts and that he or she need only notify you if the Tibbie needs re-homing.

If you are selling a show/breeding prospect, the sales agreement should cover additional concerns such as future breedings and replacing the puppy if he does not grow up to be show quality.

Each country's national kennel organization has varying registration rules, procedures and forms. Some provide for different types of registration for dogs that may be bred and those that are considered pets. Regardless of whether you are selling a pet or show prospect, it is important to register your litters and to provide the buyers with forms to transfer ownership and register each puppy. Explain how to complete the forms and any time limits that apply.

As an example, let's look at a routine registration procedure in the U.S. To register an American-born litter, submit an application to the AKC accompanied by the required fee and signed by both the dam's and stud's owners. Do this shortly after the litter is born. In return, the AKC supplies an individual registration application (blue form) for each puppy. When placing a puppy, partially complete the blue form by filling in the puppy's sex and color, buyer's name and address and the date of transfer. All owners of the litter must sign the form, which is then given to the buyer. To register his or her Tibbie, the buyer then completes the blue form by selecting the puppy's name and sending the form, with the required fee, to the AKC. The AKC returns a registration certificate listing the dog's official name, registration number, breed, birth date, names and registration numbers of his parents, the breeder and the owner of record. If you elect to use AKC's limited registration procedure to prevent registration of the offspring of a pet-quality puppy, you must apply for a limited registration certificate and, when placing the puppy, use this certificate to transfer ownership. The AKC requires breeders to keep records identifying and reporting the disposition of each puppy.

Finally, the health record you provide should show the date(s) of:

- each type of immunization,
- deworming, and
- physical exams.

Preparing Buyers to Collect Their Tibbie

Recommend that the buyer purchase certain essential supplies before he or she picks up the Tibbie. These essentials include:

- wire crate,
- collar and lead,
- travel crate, and
- ceramic or metal food dishes.

Give some guidance on what to buy, such as the size and type of crate and the size and type of collar and lead. Recommend that your buyer pick up the Tibbie

Hannah Schrauben loves to visit with "Cricket," owned by her aunt, Kelly Ruehle.

when he or she has a few days off from work (at least a weekend) to spend with the puppy. Do not allow a buyer to pick up a puppy on a holiday.

Educating Buyers

Most Codes of Ethics require that breeders instruct buyers about the feeding and care of a Tibbie. The more you explain, the more likely both buyer and Tibbie will be satisfied and happy. If the buyer is taking home a puppy, explain how puppies behave, their daily needs and routines, and how they grow and develop. When placing an older Tibbie, go over the Tibbie's likes and dislikes (e.g., favorite toys, going for rides).

Here are the items on my "puppy list":

- *handling*
  Show the buyer how to pick up and carry a puppy.
- *housetraining by the crate method*
  Describe this method of housetraining thoroughly and explain how you have started training. Strongly discourage leaving the puppy in his crate for over four hours.
- *putting the puppy on a feeding/exercising/sleeping schedule*
  Explain that dogs like "routines," and that a "routine" is important to the effectiveness of housetraining. Describe the puppy's current schedule and recommend that the buyer initially stay on the same schedule.

Timothy Gard, son of breeder Judy Gard (Barrajy), and several of the family Tibbies.

- *feeding*
  Recommend high quality premium food. Provide samples and explain how to transition the diet.
- *exercising*
  Show how to walk on lead without jerking or dragging. Discuss toys. Point out that a "tired puppy is a good (and happy) puppy."
- *puppy-proofing*
  Explain how to make the buyer's home safe for a puppy, including securing electrical wires out of reach, chew-proofing, removing plants and preventing escapes.
- *caring for health*
  Usually discussed while going over the health record, cover not only what health care you have provided, but upcoming needs such as heartworm preventative, next set of immunizations and additional vaccines (such as Lyme or bordatella) that you recommend. If the puppy has an umbilical hernia, explain closure and repair. Emphasize the importance of spaying/neutering a pet Tibbie.
- *training*
  Have a serious discussion about training Tibbies along the lines covered by Chapter 10. Explain that Tibbies require positive, not punishment-oriented, training methods, and that no one should ever hit the Tibbie. Recommend a good training book. Show the buyer some basic puppy-training techniques such as giving commands, rewarding and praising (e.g., food and "happy voice"), saying "No" and distracting from unwanted behaviors such as barking or chewing, and giving a scruff shake for life-and-death infractions.

This Is What It's All About

Rita Beale (U.K.), long time Tibbie breeder and judge, also coordinates Tibbie rescue in northern England. Mrs. Beale remarks, "I am very careful to vet people before they get a dog—this goes for the puppies I sell, too. If more breeders took care where their puppies went, there would be less dogs to re-house. [And] I never rush to re-house dogs immediately unless I know I have a good home waiting. Perhaps I have been fortunate, but I usually find that the right person comes along within a week or two and in the meantime [I have] a chance to assess the dog. I certainly never go out looking for homes—people have to really want a Tibetan Spaniel!" Becky Johnson (U.S.) echoes Mrs. Beale's viewpoint, "There is a right home for every Tibbie. It might be mine or it might be someone else's, but the perfect home will come along. I'm never in a hurry. I'm prepared to keep them."

You have only to look at the happy faces of Tibbies and their families and you know these ladies give good advice.

Karen Chamberlain ills.

The Tibetan Spaniel

For More Information

Visit www.tibbies.net for up-to-date Tibbie information and links to websites around the world.

Selected Bibliography

BOOKS

Aslett, Don. *Pet Clean-up Made Easy*. Cincinnati: Writer's Digest Books, 1988.

Batchelor, Stephen. *The Tibet Guide*. London: Wisdom Publications, 1987.

Bridges, Constance. *Thin Air*. New York: Brewer and Warren Inc., 1930.

C—, Major. *Indian Notes about Dogs: Their Diseases and Treatment*, 6th ed. Location unknown: Thacker, Spink and Coe, 1896.

Carlson DVM, Delbert G., and James M. Giffin, MD. *Dog Owner's Home Veterinary Handbook*. New York: Howell Book House, Inc.1980.

Cecil, Barbara, and Gerianne Darnell. *Competitive Obedience Training for the Small Dog*. Council Bluffs IA: T9E Publishing, 1994.

Colflesh, Linda. *Making Friends*. New York: Howell Book House, 1990.

Compton, Herbert, ed. *The Twentieth Century Dog*. London: Grant Richards, 1904.

Elliott, Rachel Page. *The New Dogsteps*. New York: Howell Book House, 1983.

Ettinger DVM, Stephen J., and Edward C. Feldman DVM. *Textbook of Veterinary Internal Medicine*.Philadelphia: W.B. Saunders Co, 1995.

Freeman, Robert B. and Toni C. Freeman. *The Road to Westminster*. White Hall VA: Betterway Publications,

———. *Breeding and Showing Purebred Dogs*. White Hall VA: Betterway Publications, Inc., 1992.

Gelder, Stuart and Roma. *The Timely Rain*. London: Hutchinson & Co., 1964.

Griffin DVM, Craig E., Kenneth W. Kwochka DVM, and John M. McDonald DVM. "Food Allergy." In *Current Veterinary Dermatology*. New York: Mosby Year Book.

Hutchinson, Walter, ed. *Hutchinson's Popular and Illustrated Dog Encyclopedia*. 3 vols. London: Hutchinson & Co. Ltd., 1934-5.

Kerr MD, Blake. *Sky Burial*. Chicago: The Noble Press, Inc., 1993.

Kirk DVM, Robert W., ed. *Current Veterinary Therapy*. Philadephia: W.B. Saunders Co., 1989.

Lewis DVM, PhD, Lon D, and others. *Small Animal Clinical Nutrition III*, 3rd edition. Topeka KS: Mark Morris Associates, 1987.

Little ScD, Clarence C. *The Inheritance of Coat Color in Dogs*, 9th printing. New York: Howell Book House, 1988.

Mayhew, Phyllis M. *The Tibetan Spaniel*. Published privately, 1971.

Patt, David. *A Strange Liberation*. Ithaca NY: Snow Lion Publications, 1992.

Peiffer, Jr. DVM, PhD, ACVO, Robert L. *Small Animal Ophthalmology: A Problem-Oriented Approach*. Philadelphia: W.B. Saunders Co 1989

Rohrer, Ann and Cathy Flamholtz. *The Tibetan Mastiff: Legendary Guardian of the Himalayas*. Centreville, AL: OTR Publications, 1989.

Rubin VMD, M.Med.Sci. (Ophth.), Lionel F. *Inherited Eye Diseases in Purebred Dogs*. Baltimore: Williams and Wilkins, 1989.

Secord, William. *Dog Painting 1840-1940*. Woodbridge: Antique Collector's Club, 1992.

Slatter, Douglas H. *Textbook of Small Animal Surgery*. Philadelphia: W. B. Saunders Company, 1985.

Tellington-Jones, Linda and Robyn Hood. *TTouch TTips for Dogs and Puppies*. La Quinta CA: Thane Marketing International,1994.

Tibetan Spaniel Club of America. *Illustrated Breed Standard*. Published privately, 1993.

———. *Tibetan Spaniels in America Handbook 1984-1986*. Published privately, 1987.

———. *Tibetan Spaniels in America Handbook 1988*. Published privately, 1989.

———. *Tibetan Spaniels in America Handbook 1990*. Published privately, 1991.

———. *Tibetan Spaniels in America Handbook 1992*. Published privately, 1993.

Turner, J. Sidney, ed. *The Kennel Encyclopedia*, Vol. 2. London: Sir W.C. Leng & Co., 1908.

Vanacore, Connie. *Dog Showing: An Owner's Guide*. New York: Howell Book House, 1990.

Volhard, Jack and Wendy Volhard. *The Canine Good Citizen*. New York: Howell Book House, 1994.

Wakefield, Sir Edward. *Past Imperative: My Life in India 1927-1947*. London: Chatto & Windus, 1966.

Wynyard, Ann Lindsay. *Dogs of Tibet and the History of the Tibetan Spaniel*. Leicester: Book World Rugby, 1982.

———. *Dog Directory Guide to Owning a Tibetan Spaniel*. The Dog Directory, 1980.

Younghusband, Sir Francis. *Everest the Challenge*. New York: Thomas Nelson and Sons, 1936.

PERIODICALS

Ackerman DVM, Lowell. "Allergic Skin Diseases." *Pure-Bred Dogs/American Kennel Gazette* (September 1990): 94-101.

Bailey, Hon. Mrs. Eric. "Notes on Tibetan Dogs." *Kennel Gazette* (August 1934).

———. "Dogs from the Roof of the World." *American Kennel Gazette* (March 1, 1937): 5-8.

Bjerkås DVM, DSc, E. and Narfström, DVM, PhD, K. "Progressive Retinal Atrophy in the Tibetan Spaniel in Norway and Sweden." *The Veterinary Record* (April 9, 1994): 377-379.

Blevins, Donna Caton. "Straight from the Dog's Mouth," *Dog World* (November 1994): 22-25.

Connor DVM, Toodie. "Yes, There are Tibetan Terriers inTibet!" *Tibetan Breeds International Magazine*, no. 4 (1993): 6-8.

Danpure, Christopher J. and others. "Enzymological Characterization of a Putative Canine Analogue of Primary Hypoaxaluria Type 1." *Biochemicia et Biophysica Acta*, 1096 (1991): 134-138.

David, Herm. "Three Women Who Dared, Persevered...and Won!" *Dog World* (July 1983), 14-16, 53.

Donoghue VMD, Susan. "Gastrointestinal Disorders." *Pure-Bred Dogs/American Kennel Gazette* (November 1993): 18-19.

——. "Feeding the Brood Bitch." *Pure-Bred Dogs/American Kennel Gazette* (February 1994): 20-21.

——. "On the Label." *AKC Gazette* (March 1995): 22-23.

Evans PhD, Howard E. "Anatomy of the Male Reproductive System." *Pure-Bred Dogs/American Kennel Gazette* (February1993): 42-45.

Freshman DVM, MS, Joni L. "In Sickness and in Health." *Pure-Bred Dogs/American Kennel Gazette* (February 1993): 47-54.

——. "Diseases Particular to Bitches." *Pure-Bred Dogs/American Kennel Gazette* (February 1994): 56-61.

Graves DVM, Thomas K. "Crimes of the Heart." *Pure-Bred Dogs/American Kennel Gazette* (September 1993): 68-72.

——. "Keeping Your Brood Bitch Healthy and Happy." *Pure-Bred Dogs/American Kennel Gazette (February 1994): 44-49*.

——. "Portosystemic Shunts." *AKC Gazette* (January 1995): 58-61.

Hally, Will. "The Non-Controversial Tibetans." *Our Dogs* (22 June 1934).

Hayes, Mrs. Geoffrey. "The Many Breeds of Mysterious Tibet." *Our Dogs* (June 3, 1932).

Hayes, Margaret. "Four Breeds of Dogs are in Far-Off Tibet." *American Kennel Gazette* (February 1, 1933): 14-15.

Hoppe, A. and others. "Progressive Nephropathy Due to Renal Dysplasia," *Journal of Small Animal Practice*, 31 (1990): 83-91.

Hutchison DVM, Robert V. "Improving the Odds." *AKC Gazette* (August 1995): 48-49.

Jansen, J.H. and Arnesen, K. "Oxalate Nephrophathy in a Tibetan Spaniel Litter. A Probable Case of Primary Hyperoxaluria." *Journal of Comparative Pathology* 103 (1990): 79-84.

Jones, Arthur Frederick. "A Tale of Two Slippers That Made a Kennel." *American Kennel Gazette* (September 1, 1937): 15-19, 127.

Knapp PhD, Gail. "Creating a Genetic Profile for Your Stud." *Pure-Bred Dogs/American Kennel Gazette* (February 1993): 74-80.

Korzenik, Andrea. "The Tibetan Spaniel." *Pure-Bred Dogs/American Kennel Gazette* (September 1983): 45-48, 121.

Lilley, Jane. "The Tibetan Spaniel." *Dogs Monthly* (April 1987): 30-42.

Masthoff, Shiela. "Leading a Dog's Life on the Roof of the World." Pure-*Bred Dogs/American Kennel Gazette* (August 1978), 32-39.

McLaren Morrison, Hon. Mrs. "The Coloured Tibet Spaniel." *The Kennel* (1911): 159.

Miccio, Susan. "American Tibetan Spaniels Shine in Therapy Work." *Tibetan Breeds International Magazine*, no. 4 (1993): 8-9.

Pepper, Jeffery. "Stud Dog Management." *Pure-Bred Dogs/American Kennel Gazette* (February 1993): 61-66.

Reif, Jane. "Owning a Great Brood Bitch." *Pure-Bred Dogs/American Kennel Gazette* (February 1994): 16.

Roy, Don. "Tibetan Spaniels: Farewell, Leo Kearns." *Pure-Bred Dogs/American Kennel Gazette* (February 1988), 136-137.

Ruslander DVM, David. "Controlling Cancer in Dogs." *Pure-Bred Dogs/American Kennel Gazette* (April 1994): 58-62.

Schadlich, Janet Story and Abbott, Beverly. "Whelping the Small Breeds." *Pure-Bred Dogs/American Kennel Gazette* (May 1992): 52-57.

Shaw, Fran Pennock. "Living with Geriatric Dogs." *Dog World* (January 1995), 20-22.

Shojai, Amy D. "Beating Cancer." *Dog World* (January 1995): 24-26.

Taylor-Ide, Daniel. "Meet the Rare Mountain Dog of Tibet." *Dog World* (November 1993): 20-21, 23.

Tomlinson, June. "Showing the Tibetan Spaniel." *New Zealand Kennel Gazette* (Supplement 1) (September 1993): 11-12.

Vargo, Stephanie. "Tibetan Tribute." *Pure-Bred Dogs/American Kennel Gazette* (July 1992): 70-75.

White C.I.E., John C. "Some Interesting Breeds of Dogs." *The Kennel* (February 1911): 525-529.

Wilford DVM, Christine. "Big Dogs, Bad Hearts." *Pure-Bred Dogs/American Kennel Gazette* (October 1994): 55-59.

——. "Vaccines Revisited." *Pure-Bred Dogs/American Kennel Gazette* (January 1994): 62-67.

Williams, Nadine. "Champion Companion Top Dog." *The (Adelaide, South Australia) Advertiser*, 9 May 1992.

OTHER SOURCES

Dogsteps. Produced by Dr. Mark Elliott. Directed by Elvin Carrini. 65 min. Rachel Page Ellicott, 1988. Videocassette.

Kaufman, Geraldine McCall. "The Critical Neonate." Paper presented at the annual meeting of The Society for Theriogenology with the cooperation of The American College of Theriogenologists, Gainesville FL, September 1988.

Olson DVM, PhD, Patricia N. "Periparturient Diseases of the Bitch." Paper presented at the annual meeting of The Society for Theriogenology with the cooperation of The American College of Theriogenologists, Gainesville FL, September 1988.

Riis DVM, MS, DACVO, Ronald C. Lecture on eye problems of the Tibetan Spaniel presented at a meeting of the Tibetan Spaniel Club of America. Tape recording by author. Syracuse NY, 9 April 1993.

The Tibetan Spaniel. Produced by Edna K. Horn. Directed by Jessica Goodyear. 17 min. American Kennel Club, 1988. Videocassette.

Tibet: The End of Time. Produced by Joel Westbrook. 48 min. Time-Life Video and Television, 1995. Videocassette.

Tibetan Spaniel Club of America Newsletters, 1983-1995. TSCA Archives, c/o Don Roy, Whitefield NH.

Index

Accidents 156, 164 *see also Poisons*
Adoption 99, 124
Agility 57, 138, 204
Aging 124, 163
Allergies 157, 160, 161, 166, 172, 217
Anal sacs 159
Anesthesia 163, 164
Antibiotics 219, 225
Arrhythmia 170
Arthritis 126, 171
Artificial respiration 231
Autopsy 243

Bait 184
Barking 19, 147, 150
Bathing 119
Behavior problems 147
Bladder stones 174
Blue puppy 231
Bones 106, 117
Bordetella 157
Breathing problems 161, 171, 231
Breech birth 227, 229
Breed Standard 42, 48, 60, 191, 194
Breeders 96, 209
Breeding 209, 211, 212, 216
Brood bitch 181, 211, 221, 236
Brucellosis 219
Brushing 118
Buddha Mark 11

Caesarian section 230, 235, 240, 242
Calcium 225, 230, 242
Cancer 157, 163, 165, 166
CERF 100, 167
Canine Good Citizen (CGC) 92, 142, 207
Cataracts 124, 168, 244
C.C. 48, 180
Championships 179
Cherry eye 168
Chewing 106, 149
Children 23, 95, 138, 206, 210
Chilling 234, 244
Classes (show) 178, 181, 203, 204, 206
Cleaning up 98, 135
Cleft palate 197, 243
Climbing 22, 218
Clubs 49, 52, 61
Coat 10, 113, 186, 192, 196, 200
Coloboma 168
Colors 11, 40, 192, 217, 236

Colostrum 228
Come (command) 140
Confidence 131, 134, 137
Congenital disorders 166, 237, 243
Congenital kidney disease 174
Co-ownership 101, 246
Coprophagy 153
Corneal abrasions 168
Coronavirus 157
Corrections 132, 143
Crate training 105, 134, 241, 247
Crying 235, 243
Cryptorchidism 224
Cushioning 13, 192
Cystitis 174

Death 127, 163, 230, 243
Dehydration 243
Dental care 120, 126, 159 *see also Mouth*
Dewclaws 193, 240
Diabetes 117, 165
Diarrhea 160, 243
Digestive system problems 160, 165
Discharges (whelping) 242
Distemper 157, 245
Distichiasis 166, 168, 217
Dominance 15, 147
Down (command) 140
Drive 196, 200
Dry eye 168
Dystocia 229

Ears 13, 118, 121, 167, 192, 196
Eclampsia 242
Elbow dysplasia 171
Elongated soft palate 162
Emergencies 156
Entropion 166, 168
Epilepsy 171
Epiphora 162, 167
Escaping 19, 151, 164
Ethics 96-98, 210
Euthanasia 127
Exercise 111, 122, 125, 158, 219, 247
Expression 184
Eyes 13, 121, 167, 192, 196 *see also Progressive Retinal Atrophy (PRA), Cataracts*

Fading puppy 243
Fatty acids 116, 173
FCI 177, 179, 180
Fears 114, 137, 148, 153
Feeding 110, 114, 125, 158, 219, 225, 234, 241, 248

Fetal death 219, 230
Fighting 152, 158, 218
Flat puppy syndrome 244
Fleas 121, 159, 172, 219
Forequarters 192, 196, 200

Gaiting 184, 188, 192, 196
Galactostasis 242
Games 17, 87, 111, 133, 141, 144, 146, 150
Genotype 212
Gloves 11, 119
Grooming 118, 125, 158, 186
Groups 178, 179, 182
Growing up 10, 12, 113, 199

Hand signals 134, 203
Handling 108, 139, 183, 206, 235, 247
Harefoot 13, 192, 196
Head 13, 192, 196
Health 50, 60, 101, 155, 219, 248
Heart disease 126, 163, 170, 219
Heartworm 158
Heat 122, 164, 234, 244
Heat cycle 114, 157, 221, 222
Heel (command) 140, 142
Hereditary problems 166, 216, 219
Hernia 197, 216, 244
Herniated disc 172
Heterochromia 244
Hindquarters 192, 196, 200
Hip dysplasia 166, 172
Hot spot 174
Housetraining 105, 134, 241, 247
Hydrocephalus 244, 245
Hyperthermia 122, 164, 234, 244
Hypocalcemia 230, 242
Hypoglycemia 230, 244
Hypothermia 234, 244
Hypothyroidism

Identification 98, 102, 109
Importation 44, 49
Inbreeding 45, 212, 216
Incubator 226
Indcpendence 19, 95, 132
Infertility 219, 223
Intelligence 17, 95, 132
Intervertebral disc disease 166, 172
Intuitiveness 22
Itchiness 119, 161 *see also Skin problems*

Judging 50, 60, 188-191
Jumping up 151
Junior Showmanship 206

Kennel cough 157
Kidney disease 50, 68, 77, 126, 163, 166, 174, 216

Labor 227, 229
Lead 106, 139, 183, 184
Legg-Calvé-Perthes disease 172
Level mouth 13, 192, 194
Line-breeding 212
Litter size 231
Liver disease 126, 163, 166, 216, 245
Longevity 123, 155, 163
Lyme disease 157, 162

Male behavior 15, 152, 157
Mammary glands 157, 165
Mane 10, 192, 196
Mange 174
Marking (urination) 114, 152, 157
Markings 12, 113
Mask 12
Mastitis 242
Mating 220
Mats 118
Megaesophagus 245
Metritis 242
Micropapilla 168
Microphthalmia 168, 244
Mismating 223
Motion sickness 161
Motivation 131, 144
Mounting 114, 158
Mouth 13, 113, 159, 183, 192, 199, 216
Movement 13, 192, 196, 200, 216
Murmurs 170
Muzzle 13, 113, 192, 196, 199

Nails 120, 235
Neurological problems 171
Neutering 98, 151, 152, 157, 210, 246
Nuclear sclerosis 168
Nursing 228, 235, 236, 242, 243

Obedience 57, 140, 203
Obesity 117, 125
Optic nerve problems 168
Out-crossing 212
Ovulation 221
Oxytocin 230, 240

Pancreatic disease 165-166
Paper training 137, 240, 241
"Papers" 99
Parasites 161, 162, 245

Particolor 12, 215, 217
Parvovirus 157, 234, 241
Patellar luxation 68, 166, 171, 217, 219
Paws 119 *see also Harefoot*
Pedigree 99, 246
Persistent pupillary membrane (PPM) 168
Personality 14, 100, 132, 192, 196, 202, 216
Pet quality 13, 99
Pet therapy 90
Phenotype 212
Pigmentation 192, 215, 217
"Pit" shot *see Oxytocin*
Placenta 228
Placing puppies 245
Plant-eating 150, 161
Poisons 108, 123, 141, 164
Praise 134 *see also Rewards*
Pregnancy 224-227
Progressive retinal atrophy (PRA) 50, 60, 68, 70, 77, 81, 166, 169, 212, 216, 219
Proportion 192, 196, 200, 216
Prostate disease 158, 172, 223
Punishment 132
Puppies 99, 105, 113, 134, 198, 235, 242
Puppy mills 57, 96, 210
Puppy-proofing 108, 148, 248
Pyoderma 173
Pyometra 220

Quarantines 72, 180

Rabies 157
Rawhide toys 106
Registration 56, 64, 99, 246
Reproductive health 219, 222, 229, 230, 242
Rescue 50, 59, 102
Resorption 230
Reverse scissors bite 13
Reverse sneezing 161
Rewards 131, 144
Running away *see Escaping*

Safety 108, 131, 139, 149, 155
Sale agreement 249
Scowl 14
Screening prospective owners 245
Scruff shake 149
Seizures 171, 245
Sensitivity 22, 133
Shawl 10, 192
Shedding 96, 118
Show quality 13, 101, 198
Showing dogs 177
Sit (command) 140, 143

Size 10, 192, 197
Skeletal problems 171
Skin problems 172
Snoring/snorting 161
Socialization 137, 183, 236
Spaying 98, 151, 157, 165, 210, 246
Spinal problems 163, 166, 172, 223
Stacking 184
Stay (command) 140
Stenosis 171
Steroids 173, 225
Stifle 192, 216
Stool-eating 153
Stop (head) 192
Street avoidance training 139
Stud dog 181, 214, 220
Swimmer 244

Tail 13, 185, 192, 200
Talking 19
Tearing 162, 167
Teething 106, 113, 149
Temperament *see Personality*
Temperature 157, 226, 234, 236, 243
Testicles 200, 224
Therapy dogs 90
Thunderstorms 153
Thyroid problems 174, 219, 222, 223
Tibetan names 109
Ticks 121, 157, 162, 219
Topline 200, 202
Toys 18, 106, 235
Tracking 57, 206
Training 131, 164, 183, 248
Traveling 86, 105, 122, 139
Tumors 165

Umbilical cord 227
Umbilical hernia 197, 216, 244
Undershot 13, 192, 194
Urination 114, 135, 152, 157
Urinary system disorders 174
Uterine inertia 229

Vaccinations 110, 156, 219, 240
Vaginal problems 220, 223
Vitamin/mineral supplements 110, 116
Vomiting 160

Watchdog 23, 148, 150
Weaning 241
Weight 10, 117, 125, 192
Weight (puppies) 232, 235, 236, 243
Whelping 163, 227, 229
Worms 158, 161, 219, 245